P9-DDJ-315

Saving the Constitution from the Courts

SAVING THE CONSTITUTION FROM THE COURTS

By William Gangi

University of Oklahoma Press : Norman and London

Library of Congress Cataloging-in-Publication Data

Gangi, William.
Saving the Constitution from the courts / by William Gangi.
p. cm.
Includes index.
ISBN 0-8061-2732-5 (acid-free paper)
1. United States—Constitutional law—Interpretation and construction. 2. Political questions and judicial power—United States. 3. Separation of powers—United States. 4. Judge-made law—United States. I. Title.
KF4552.G36 1995
342.73'02—dc20
[347.3022] 94-43089
CIP

Text design by Cathy Carney Imboden.

The paper in this book meets the guidelines for permanence and durability of the Committee on Production Guidelines for Book Longevity of the Council on Library Resources, Inc.∞

1 2 3 4 5 6 7 8 9 10

To Mom, who always supported and had great faith and confidence in me. She named me William, which she told me meant resolute. *That I am. I miss her.*

To Dad, who shaped the attitudes that still guide me: that there are more good than bad people, that all people are just that, and if you don't have the cash you can't afford it. The last one has been tough. Luckily, Dad is still with me. He continues to teach me how to be a man.

Contents

Acknowledgments

This book has had several predecessors that did not see the light of day. The project began over a decade ago with a proposal to study the exclusionary rule and was funded by the Earhart Foundation. My research, however, soon lead me in other directions; it now comes back together in this volume. So I would like to express my appreciation to the Earhart Foundation, particularly Antony Sullivan, for his support—and patience.

Although they remain anonymous, several critics of earlier drafts also deserve my thanks: their comments prompted me to reexamine *The Federalist Papers,* which has proved so rewarding for me as a scholar and teacher.

Over the years, I also had the pleasure of corresponding with several scholars; notably, George W. Carey, of Georgetown University, and H. Jefferson Powell, of Duke University School of Law. Both gave freely of their time and intellect. I am especially grateful to Raoul Berger, who never ceased to encourage me and tell me to "cut, cut, cut." It is difficult to go against the grain, to stand fast in defense of the Constitution, when most other scholars are swept up in the contemporary zeitgeist. Over the past fifty years, on several occasions Raoul Berger stood fast and so deserves the gratitude of a generation of scholars and the nation.

Blessed are those to whom writing comes easily: I am not one of them. This book has been a struggle and I needed all the help I could get. Some were kind enough to read single chapters (Vincent Braccia and Joseph Cascio); other brave souls read entire drafts (Peter Williams), sometimes more than once (Kristan Fexas). And thank you, again, Kristan Fexas and Elvira Barisano, for your help with conforming to the standards of the Uniform System of Citations. I cannot thank them enough. They are all busy people and all contributed to the final product. Several others, in addition to reading various drafts, deserve special mention because of their specific contributions. Edward McGowan, Jr., an MA/JD student at St. John's University, Queens, New York, prompted me to take seriously the idea of my "journey" and the niceties of *A Uniform System of Citation.* John B. Greg, of the Department of Speech, Communication Science and Theatre, at St. John's University, Queens, New York, helped me to focus on the art of persuasion. I was lucky to have his input. He has been a friend for more than twenty years, and for as long we have not thought alike politically. It mattered not at all. My now retired colleague Henry Paolucci not only is a master of the English language but has a breadth of knowledge that enriched the manuscript in many ways. He has been very patient and supportive, trying to teach me the English language after a progressivist elementary education had failed. My reeducation is just beginning. I also would like to thank the staff at the University of Oklahoma Press, particularly Kimberly Wiar, acquisitions editor, and Sarah Nestor, managing editor, as well as copy editor Dennis Marshall, for their expertise in making the manuscript clearer, more precise, and more readable.

But most of all I owe a great deal to my wife, Patricia, who not only had to endure my preoccupation but who is a far better writer than I. She contributed her editorial skills and for this I am especially grateful. Twenty years ago, she dragged me on a "marriage encounter" weekend, and almost every day for the next three years we wrote love letters to one another on nearly every conceivable topic—letters that required me to get in touch with my feelings, not thoughts. The Introduction explains how that fact has shaped the manuscript. Periodically, but not often enough, we write love letters to each other when we find ourselves paying too much attention to our individual projects and drifting apart—as creative people often will. The marriage encounter experience shaped our relationship, permitting me to experience intimacy and, through Pat's love, God's love. I would not have had the strength to dissent from others in my profession without her loving support.

Finally, my appreciation goes to the *Harvard Journal of Law and Public Policy,* for permission to reprint excerpts from an article, "Coerced Confessions and the Supreme Court: Fulminante v. Arizona in Perspective," that I recently published in their journal, vol. 16 (June 1993):493–528, contained in chapter 7.

Having completed this manuscript, I hope to take some time off—at least from writing. Reading trashy books at my summer home or at a beach sounds just about right. And I think I owe Pat some love letters.

WILLIAM GANGI

Sag Harbor, New York

Introduction

We have . . . reached the point as a Nation where we must take action to save the Constitution from the Court and the Court from itself. We must find a way to take an appeal from the Supreme Court to the Constitution itself. We want a Supreme Court which will do justice under the Constitution—not over it. In our Courts we want a government of laws and not of men.[1]

Many scholars today contend that the Supreme Court of the United States should decide important public policy questions. I reject that view for the same reason Americans repudiated it during the New Deal: Most judicial decisions today rest on no greater authority than what a majority of justices think is good public policy—which I contend amounts to no authority at all. Hence, the title for this book, *Saving the Constitution from the Courts.*

But more about this later. Here I wish only to acquaint the reader with three of this book's main themes: the people's right to self-government; the obligation of all citizens and elected officials to remain faithful to the clearly discernible intentions of the framers; and the United States Supreme Court's obligation to interpret the Constitution.

I will begin with my first contention, that the most important right secured for the people of the United States by the American Revolution was the right of self-government, which is another way of saying, the people's right to decide what public policies are conducive to the public good and the right to define the content of individual rights. When a group of people recognize themselves as "a people," by definition they share a set of common beliefs. Then an opportunity must exist for those people to win political independence and in so doing it must not only overpower its oppressors but it must also overcome those who do not share its vision.

Put another way, our forefathers decided to commit treason. They understood perfectly well that they had to risk their "Lives . . . Fortunes and . . . sacred Honor."[2] Blood would be shed and loved ones lost. They

1. President Roosevelt's radio address on the proposed Court-packing plan in 1937. Franklin D. Roosevelt, *Fireside Chat* (March 9, 1937), in Melvin I. Urofsky, Documents of American Constitutional & Legal History, Vol. II, 183 (1989).

2. Declaration of Independence (1776), in Basic Documents in American History 31 (Robert B. Morris, ed., 1956). As U.S. history demonstrates so well, even after independence is won other confrontations may occur in the process of defining our truth as a people. *See* the Public Broadcasting Service's highly acclaimed program "The Civil War," available at many public and university libraries.

also understood that, more frequently than not, such sacrifices proved to be in vain. However glorious military victories are, they cannot assure political independence and self-government. Most revolutions end in the substitution of one tyrant for another. Obviously then, securing the right to self-government requires luck as well as military prowess: the right people, the right leadership, the right circumstances—all at the right time. In 1776 and 1787, we were lucky.

Since the American Revolution and the adoption of the Constitution, many generations of Americans have fought and died to defend and preserve our political independence and the right to self-government. Judges today are thwarting the American people in their defense of that birthright. Pick up any day's newspaper. Leaf through its pages and scan the headlines. Almost certainly, you will find that somewhere a judge is instructing legislators about what to do and how to do it. The lecturing of the public reflected in the headlines is often about important matters such as whether burning the U.S. flag is "protected" by the First Amendment; or to what extent a woman has a right to "control" her own body; or by what standards police searches or interrogations may be conducted; or if a convicted felon may or may not be executed. The impression gained by reading the headlines is accurate: judges more often than not do have the last word on issues that most concern the public. The more one explores the subject, the more one realizes that legislatures today often operate at the sufferance and direction of judges.

Second, I contend that all citizens owe allegiance to the framers' clearly discernible intentions. Should some poor soul in good mental health bequeath his entire fortune to his pet cat, even today his lawyers and the courts would work diligently (barring some technicality in the will) to see that such an intention was scrupulously honored. But many of the finest legal minds in the United States champion the view that the Constitution lacks any fixed meaning and that the framers' intentions may be legitimately ignored *even if they are clearly discernible.* That view is incompatible with our forefathers' understanding of the Constitution.

The first reading assignment given to students in my constitutional law class is from Plato's *Republic:* the cave analogy.[3] In my version of that

3. The Collected Dialogues of Plato, Republic: Book 7 (514–519) (E. Hamilton ed.), 747–751 (1961). There, readers may recall, an elite teaches the inhabitants the nature of reality by projecting shadows of real objects from the rear of the cave onto the front wall. The Cave inhabitants are forced to face the wall, and therefore never see the objects themselves. One inhabitant escapes the cave into the light of day, where at first he is blinded and confused. Nothing looks familiar to him. But then he begins to see objects clearly—as they are—instead of only the shadows of objects, as those that had been cast on the wall of the cave. Excited, he returns to the cave, but once seated his ability to identify those shadows has deteriorated. He becomes confused, disoriented, and subject to ridicule. When he speaks to his companions about the real objects (those he

analogy, the Supreme Court justices stand at the rear of the cave, casting shadows upon the front wall. Seated in the first few rows, viewing the projected shadows, are a number of constitutional scholars. Behind them are members of the intelligentsia (other lawyers, political scientists, and educators). In successive rows are seated elected officials, then media representatives, and common citizens who fill the remainder of the rows. All the seated are prisoners, with chains about their necks, their heads fixed to view the shadows.

Each October, when the Court starts its new term, the justices begin another round of shadow-casting upon our national political life. Before long, media representatives speak knowledgeably of new rights or rights dashed, while the intelligentsia and constitutional scholars (so called) explain how the newly designed shadows portend a deepening of or a retreat from the Cave's commitment to, for instance, greater personal liberty and social justice. In this manner do citizens eventually learn from those more expert that the new shadows are full of wonders or dangerous consequences.

Americans today are surrounded by shadows and shadow makers and many constitutional experts champion imagination as the profession's most prized tool. These scholars advocate that courts abandon past constitutional definitions in favor of reading the Constitution in open-ended fashion. They work diligently to recast public policy questions into legal issues so that courts, rather than legislators, decide them. They thus pretend to address constitutional issues expertly, as if they had a set of distinct tools, when in fact they bring nothing more to public deliberation than a legalistic restatement of their own biases.

I dissent. I maintain that preoccupation with the framers' understanding of its provisions should mark the beginning of every constitutional inquiry. Not only is that approach essential to the idea of a written constitution, it is also consistent both with the framers' expectations of how the Constitution would be interpreted and the earliest legal precedents.

Fidelity to the framers' intentions is the price Americans must accept for being able to govern themselves as they please *when those intentions do not exist or cannot be clearly discerned.* When properly understood, such a submission does not, as some suggest, hamstring the people's ability to deal with changing circumstances. The opposite is true. Acknowledging fidelity to the framers' intentions is ultimately liberating, for it leaves majorities free to address, change, and change again by simple majority vote vast areas of public policy making that the framers

---

witnessed when he was in the light), they are not interested. His companions prefer what they know and have invested considerable energy in mastering: the shadows. After all, what does the returnee offer? He cannot even see things correctly anymore!

did not constitutionalize. Hence, unless we have abandoned our faith in democratic self-government and are ready to say so or are willing to allow the Constitution to be trivialized, many public policy choices imposed on the American people since the 1950s (and perhaps earlier) must be deconstitutionalized, once again becoming matters of legislative discretion. When the framers' judgments are no longer consistent with current sensibilities, citizens ought to repudiate them.

The framers understood that each generation must be able to decide its own destiny and, in the amendment processes, they wisely included procedures for doing so. Use of those procedures is the only legitimate way the people may substitute their judgment for those of their forefathers, or substitute a judicial oligarchy for the Republic established by the Constitution. The American people owe at least that much to those who shed their blood for independence, for Union, and against tyranny.

Third, I contend that the United States Supreme Court's duty to interpret the Constitution is circumscribed by the Court's obligation to discern, submit to, and apply the clearly discernible intentions of the framers. My views on this issue are set forth throughout the book, especially in chapter 5, but in this introduction I will say this much: While judicial review is a legitimate power, those who ratified the Constitution understood it to be a limited one. Its legitimate exercise is dependent upon imposing the will of the Constitution's ratifiers, not upon a judge's sense of wisdom or morals. The framers did not understand the power of interpretation (or that of judicial review) as authorizing either the expansion of restrictions contained in the Constitution or the creation of new rights. They understood that a judiciary so empowered would repudiate the republican character of the government that they had created.

Throughout this book, then, readers will find me unabashedly contending that many contemporary judicial decisions lack legitimacy. Once readers learn to cut through the legal and philosophical jargon, they will understand why I take the position I do. They may also recognize that many legislators, even, today are misinformed, because those legislators believe that the judiciary is the very soul of our political system. That belief is historically insupportable; it is inconsistent with the American heritage.

For more than a decade, I have struggled with the issue of how best to challenge an enormous body of literature that already has shaped the attitudes of several generations.[4] Theories of constitutional interpretation in recent years have become virtually a cottage industry, whole systems being

4. Attitudes are a powerful tool of communication and conformity. Please refer to appendix A for more expansive comments.

developed by eminent philosophers and legal scholars. In the end, in this book I decided not to undertake point-by-point refutations of such theories (although an effort is made to refer the reader to those who do), because I found that, as with the mythical Hydra, many more heads appeared for each one cut off. I feared being overwhelmed by the effort. Such point-by-point refutations inevitably bore most readers to death, and rightly so. I promise this much: by the time you finish this book you should be more aware of how judges mask their imposition of personal views behind the rubric of enforcing constitutional law, and you will have been exposed to every significant argument that challenges the ideas I hold dear.[5] After that, you alone must decide.

Some miscellaneous matters remain. Some readers may find that the first two chapters present too narrow a focus: the views of a few prominent framers as they were expressed in *The Federalist Papers.* Or they may judge that those chapters lack the breadth of, for example, Gordon Wood's classic work.[6] They are right. But two questions seemed particularly pressing to me: What role did the framers and ratifiers of the Constitution envision the judiciary playing? And why should the beliefs of those who framed and ratified the Constitution still be important to us today? Those are the questions I chose to pursue.

At this juncture I will also make a few observations on my use of *The Federalist Papers.* Most scholars acknowledge the importance of these eighty-five "papers"—essays published in newspapers of the time and written by Alexander Hamilton, James Madison, and John Jay, defending the proposed constitution.[7] There is nothing particularly controversial about turning to them better to understand the objectives sought by the

5. The reader nevertheless must remain vigilant. Deeply entrenched attitudes make it possible that the significance of some arguments might well escape my attention. As discussed in appendix A, that is a problem integral to understanding the nature of attitudes.

6. GORDON WOOD, CREATION OF THE AMERICAN REPUBLIC (1967). *See also,* 44 WM. & MARY QUARTERLY 549 (1987) (evaluations of Wood's book twenty years after publication). Let me add an aside. Scholars who take panoramic views of the American founding are to be admired. They have the ability, if I may use an analogy, to construct a gigantic spreadsheet, wherein every single relevant motivation (political, social, economic, psychological, and so on) and every possible contribution (religious, women, minorities) have a cell; different scholars have differently constructed spreadsheets, and there is always room to add a few more cells. Then, they argue among themselves, using the academic equivalent of "Query By Example," whether this person, idea, or whatever, was really more important than past scholars imagined. At the keyboard, the recalculate command is entered, the numbers change instantly, and when the screen is refreshed a new school of thought is born. It is a wonderful, exciting, and intellectually stimulating endeavor.

7. JAMES MADISON, ALEXANDER HAMILTON, AND JOHN JAY, THE FEDERALIST PAPERS. ARLINGTON HOUSE [hereinafter FEDERALIST]. These authors are described in John P. Diggins, *Between Bailyn and Beard: The Perspectives of Gordon Wood,* 44 WM. & MARY QUARTERLY 563, 566 (1987), as, with the exception of Lincoln, "the last statesmen to tell the truth about the human condition, not to extol the people but to remind them of their imperfect nature."

framers, or for how the framers interpreted various portions of the Constitution, or to learn how the proposed governmental structures would or should work, or what the framers thought of opposition arguments.[8] However, I use *The Federalist Papers* far more extensively than have other scholars recently. They are used, often solely, not only with reference to the subjects mentioned above but also in order to convey the timelessness of particular contributions. Accordingly, the present tense is employed where the past tense might be more grammatically correct.

One more deviation from the mores of contemporary scholars' use of *The Federalist Papers:* I rarely identify whether any quotation from the *Papers* is attributed to James Madison, Alexander Hamilton, or John Jay. Scholars for some time now have identified a passage and then provided inconsistent or supposedly more revealing quotations on the same subject from that same author—words that were expressed elsewhere or at another time. They miss the point. Individual authorship never was claimed; instead, the three authors used a common pseudonym—Publius—and so will I. The *Papers* were intended to convey the shared belief that, for a variety of reasons, ratification of the proposed constitution was in the overall public interest.[9] Subsequent public policy disputes pushed James Madison and Alexander Hamilton into different camps, where each defended particular aspects of the original consensus, but neither of them ever abandoned the belief that, for better or worse, the American people had secured by the Constitution a republic in which the people enjoyed the right to govern themselves.[10]

Another matter: This book has taken far too long to write and the time taken has shaped it in at least two unanticipated ways. To detail the first of these, I will tell a story of my own development. Several years ago, delivering a paper on communication techniques, I concluded that, armed with greater self-awareness, students of public administration could improve their managerial skills.[11] It was suggested to me that perhaps my ap-

8. Wood however describes the arguments made by Publius as "disingenuous." Wood, *supra* note 6, at 562. Indeed, in a more recent article he describes critical comments on *Creation* as "resembl[ing] nothing more than one of the *Federalist Papers.*" *See* Gordon Wood, *Ideology and the Origins of Liberal America,* 44 Wm. & Mary Quarterly 628, 632 (1987). *But see* John P. Diggins, *supra* note 7, at 565–566, and Pauline Maier, *A Pearl in a Gnarled Shell: Gordon S. Wood's the Creation of the American Republic Reconsidered,* 44 Wm. & Mary Quarterly 583 (1987) (Wood's scholarship remains too dependent upon progressivist attitudes).

9. *See* John M. Murrin, *Gordon S. Wood and the Search for Liberal America,* 44 Wm. & Mary Quarterly 597, 598 (1987) ("The Constitution had to be ratified by popular convention, not state legislatures.").

10. Federalist, *supra* note 7, at xii–xiii.

11. Appendix A contains a modified version of that paper. Attitudinal disposition is an integral

proach might prove useful in constitutional law, too, helping constitutional law students to explore their ideas, attitudes, and feelings about such topics as majority rule, judicial power, and individual rights. I did not much like the suggestion. My attitudes at that time clearly dictated that constitutional law was an objective discipline of principles—of hierarchy, logic, and precedent. Put another way, I had not paid enough attention to my own lecture. In this book, that reluctance is reconsidered and, while much of the book is written in the third person (the voice associated in nonfiction writing with greater objectivity), when I reflect on my own experience as a scholar and human being I will use the more familiar first person singular. That voice permits a dialogue with the reader beyond the intellectual one of most of the text.[12]

The second unanticipated development may perhaps be introduced analogously by way of Charles Beard. Many readers of course are aware of Beard's work—his probing attack on the late eighteenth-century deification of the framers—and his enormous impact on subsequent scholarship.[13] He alleged, among other things, that economic self-interest motivated the framers' and ratifiers' support of the proposed constitution.[14] Today, Critical Legal Studies adherents provide a more contemporary manifestation of such views,[15] while other scholars today reevaluate the role of women, racial minorities, and other influences on colonial history, the American Revolution, life under the Articles of Confederation, and adoption of the Constitution.[16] What I did not anticipate in early drafts of this book is that I eventually would suggest that a few more logs be tossed on the fire: I call these logs attitudes (see appendix A), which I have already mentioned, and the matter of temperament (see appendix B).[17]

---

part of the scholarly process: the subject ranges from what issues intrigue scholars to the unfortunate inability of some to recognize the pertinence of contrary evidence. These issues are also related to matters of personality type and temperament, to be discussed shortly.

12. *See* Carolyn Ellis and Michael G. Flaherty, Investigating Subjectivity: Research on Lived Experience (1992).

13. Charles Beard, An Economic Interpretation of the Constitution of the United States (1913). *But see, e.g.,* Robert E. Brown, Charles Beard and the Constitution (1956) (Beard's thesis lacks support).

14. George W. Carey, In Defense of the Constitution 1–15 (1989) (review of literature paralleling and including Beard).

15. James G. Wilson, *The Most Sacred Text: The Supreme Court's Use of The Federalist Papers,* 66 B. Y. U. L. Rev. 65, 103–105, 126–127 (1985) (some parallels between Beard and the Critical Legal Studies movement).

16. *Generally, see* Symposium, 44 Wm. & Mary Quarterly (1987).

17. It may be advisable for the reader to examine both appendices prior to continuing. *See* David Kiersey and Marilyn Bates, Please Understand Me [hereinafter Please] (1984). For an excellent primer, *see* Larry Hubbell, *Engendering Interest and Encouraging Self-development In Lower Division Public Administration Courses,* 13th National Conference on Teaching Public Administration 121 (February 15–17, 1990).

An inquiry into temperament opens up intriguing speculations: What personality types were the authors of *The Federalist Papers*? Did they bring with them collectively a broad range of intuitive and sensible talents? Was James Madison an ISTJ?[18] Were both Madison and Hamilton (and the Federalist party generally) dominated by thinkers rather than feelers (judgers rather than perceivers)? Was Hamilton's broad vision of America's future economy intuitive, whereas his archrival Thomas Jefferson remained more inclined toward the sensible?[19]

There are other, equally intriguing, issues: What would a greater awareness of such personality preferences reveal about scholarship? Do researchers select topics subconsciously based on their intuitive or sensible preferences?[20] Do feelers place greater weight than do thinkers on considerations such as sincerity?[21] Do judgers need less evidence than perceivers before finding evidence compelling?[22] And what about judicial appointments: should candidates be tested so as to ascertain their "type"? Should the Supreme Court be dominated by any particular type? Would a mixture be best? Would intuitives or sensibles, feelers or thinkers, judgers or perceivers make better judges? Indeed, could the Judiciary Committee that examined Robert H. Bork have been dominated by feelers, more inclined to measure principles by their impact on individuals rather than, in Bork's own view, applying more "objective" principles?[23]

Given the above considerations, should scholars today reveal their own attitudes and personality prefer-

18. Please see appendix B for a more thorough discussion. The four-letter acronym stands for Introvert, Sensible, Thinker, and Judger.

19. A description of Jefferson is given in Davidson and Lytle: "Jefferson possessed a . . . passion for precision and quantification. . . . For years [he] kept detailed notes indicating when the first dogwood blossomed, when the first whippoorwill was heard, when the first fireflies appeared, when the first asparagus came to table, when the first peaches were ripe, when the first shad arrived" JAMES W. DAVIDSON AND MARK H. LYTLE, AFTER THE FACT: THE ART OF HISTORICAL DETECTION 77 (1982).

20. Peter Onuf comments that "the primary disagreement is over the proper subject and objects of interpretation" Peter Onuf, *Forum—Reflections on the Founding: Constitutional Historiography in Bicentennial Perspective,* 46 WM. & MARY QUARTERLY 341, 365 (1989).

21. Is that why Gary Wills concludes that an attempt to divine sincerity leads to things like the confusion of legislators' motives, with legislative intent"? Gary Wills, *Talking Ourselves Out of a Fight,* 44 WM. & MARY QUARTERLY 623, 626 (1987).

22. Experts have concluded that SJ types are "natural historians" (PLEASE, *supra* note 17, at 44) and therefore may be particularly attracted toward that profession. Simultaneously, Peter Onuf informs us that historians "tend to discount and disregard texts," maintaining that they are more interested in exploring what the authors of such texts disclosed "unintentionally" than what might be discerned of their intent. ONUF, *supra* note 20, at 365.

23. Robert H. Bork describes the judge's task as making a "choice between a cold impersonal logic, on the one hand, and, on the other, morality and compassion," adding, "This has always been the song of the tempters." ROBERT H. BORK, THE TEMPTING OF AMERICA: THE POLITICAL SEDUCTION OF THE LAW 2 (1989).

ences (I am an ENTJ), since there seems to be a natural tendency to be persuaded only by considerations that confirm our preferences? But is not that true about attitudes generally? Conspiratorial types tend to find conspiracies; power seekers to find power; and the public-spirited, public-spiritedness. That is not a startling or new insight—or at least not for those trained in the classics or by their modern counterparts.[24] While such considerations occasionally will be mentioned in both the text and footnotes, neither will be done very frequently: doing so would prove burdensome and repetitious to the reader. For now it is enough that the questions are set out and examples of possible application are mentioned.[25]

I have strong feelings about the subject matter of this book and I assume the reader does, too. That is as it should be, since the subject matter is the nature of the United States' governing principles. Have you ever read an article or book or heard a television commentator make a point whose untruth was so patently obvious to you that you had an almost irresistible urge to close that paper or book and toss either aside, or shut off the television, or leave the room? That still happens to me. Over the years, as I discuss in appendices A and B, I have learned to understand better the dynamics at play in those instances and have tried to use that understanding to enhance my scholarship, rather than allow the challenge of dearly held attitudes either to damage or destroy it (others will point out where I still fall short!).

I have learned that when an embraced truth is challenged and subconsciously I judge my defense of it inadequate, frustration increases exponentially.[26] In other instances, when what is being read or said may ring truer than at the moment I care to admit, I find anger, annoyance, and/or exasperation suddenly joined by feelings of uncertainty, confusion, or doubt. I now recognize that the frustration builds because of my own, not-fully-acknowledged doubts about that particular belief, a belief to which I have nevertheless clung.

24. Ralph Ketchem, *Publius: Sustaining the Republican Principle,* 44 Wm. & Mary Quarterly 576, 578 (1987). For more contemporary exponents of the classics, *see* Eric Voegelin, Order and History: Plato and Aristotle, Vol. 3 (1957) and Leo Strauss, Natural Right and History (1952).

25. In all candor, a repeated application of the principles would be burdensome and distracting to the author! So-called Intuitive types like myself tend to be satisfied once principles are identified and judged applicable—leaving what they consider "detail" (i.e., identifying each and every possible application) to the sensible type more inclined to such matters. *See infra,* appendix B.

26. I do not simply mean, as the textual discussion implies, that one cannot address an inanimate object. The frustration also includes judgments of inadequacy: being confronted with a more knowledgeable or more articulate opponent. *See* appendix A. As also noted subsequently in the text, I have since learned that different personality types handle that situation quite differently. But I, for one, have had many a fierce debate with a newspaper or television screen!

Deep in my subconscious I am asking: What will take its place? Letting go of old truths and embracing new ones is often frightening, never easy.

So I am comfortable with the fact that at times this book may well infuriate the reader. After all, in the course of researching and writing it—often frustrated and confused, chastised, or intimidated—I enjoyed many a long walk! So stuff this book into the darkest recesses of your night table, or under the litter of your desk, or periodically toss it across the room; but if this book only infuriates you, and does not bore you, please hear me out. While I may challenge your views on judicial power, I believe you will find that the challenge is a thoughtful one and, in the end—despite what may be subconscious fears—one that ultimately does not at all challenge your public policy preferences. Rather, it seeks to enable all citizens (whatever their views) to debate and attempt to resolve their differences without illegitimate judicial interference.

That brings me to the matter of my expectations. The primary purpose of this book is to persuade readers interested in public affairs that their most precious right as Americans is that of self-government; that this right is being eroded by the judiciary; and that only they can reclaim it. For the more politically minded reader, my expectations run higher. Liberals and conservatives both must abandon illegitimate judicial power, whether they are in or out of power; both must stop the unseemly scurrying to the courts that is evident every time a public policy battle is lost. Doing so increasingly endangers constitutionalism and republicanism because it encourages and adds an air of legitimacy to judicial usurpations. My expectations, however, run highest for constitutional scholars. They are asked to weigh the evidence and to do the most difficult thing of all: to separate their constitutional expertise from their personal beliefs.

A word also about footnotes, the professional tools of the scholar: Just as my automobile mechanic uses all sorts of whatchamacallit tools to fix my car, fellow professionals—but not the average reader—find footnotes to be important. Hence, most of the footnotes are addressed to scholars, the people who are more wary of the power of rhetoric; more inclined to dig deeper. More often than not, most readers can safely ignore the footnotes. Since they are placed where they belong—at the bottom of the page—a glance should suffice to determine whether they can be profitably explored. The Contents and Index should also help the reader to pursue related topics.

This book is divided into five parts. Part 1 (The American Political Tradition) consists of three chapters, exploring the colonial experience, the framers' constitutional design, and early cases decided by the Supreme Court. Part 2 (The Decline of Self-Government) consists of a single chapter that explores post–Civil War developments and details contemporary assumptions about judicial power. Part 3 (The Road Divides) and Part 4 (Stopping for Directions) also have only one chapter each, exploring—respectively—constitutional interpretation and contemporary assumptions. In Part 5 (Returning to Self-Government), the author examines the interpretivist credo and details his preferences for the route ahead.

Saving the Constitution from the Courts

PART I.

THE AMERICAN POLITICAL TRADITION

CHAPTER ONE

Self-Government and the Failure of the Articles of Confederation

That the people have an original right to establish, for their future government, such principles as, in their opinion, shall most conduce to their own happiness, is the basis on which the whole American fabric has been erected. The exercise of this original right is a very great exertion; nor can it, nor ought it, to be frequently repeated. The principles, therefore, so established, are deemed fundamental: and as the authority from which they proceed is supreme, and can seldom act, they are designed to be permanent.[1]

For more than a decade I have been on a kind of journey, inquiring into the framers' understanding of judicial power. All journeys can be said to have a beginning, a middle, and an end and the first three chapters recount the beginning of my journey. Like many travelers eager to arrive at their destination, however, some readers may grow impatient with my approach, but I believe this journey must begin with an understanding of why the delegates at Philadelphia believed a new constitution was necessary and for what purposes the national government was created—the subject of the first chapter. Chapter 2 begins with the framers' understanding of the different types of government; only after that is the subject of judicial power explored. Chapter 3 briefly confirms that some of the theoretical principles discussed in chapter 2 received concrete historical application in six cases decided by the Supreme Court, beginning with *Marbury v. Madison* (1803) and ending with *Dred Scott v. Sandford* (1856).

THE OFFICIAL LITERATURE AND ITS INCONSISTENCIES

Most American students are taught that their political tradition is one of liberty and equality. The lesson often goes something like this: Our tradition begins with the Declaration of

1. Marbury v. Madison, 1 Cranch 97, 175 (1803).

Independence; in the Declaration of Independence one finds the great truths that prompted the Revolution—the desire for liberty and equality; once independence was won by force of arms, these great truths were eventually embedded in the Constitution, defended in *The Federalist Papers,* and forever secured in the Bill of Rights.[2] Does this sound familiar?[3]

It is also likely that American students are taught that their political tradition is an evolving one. This aspect of our alleged tradition goes something like this: agonizingly slow, the U.S. tradition is unique because over the years the framers' idea of equality has enlarged and new liberties are constantly created while older ones are expanded. One constant theme in the tradition has been to break down barriers to class stratification, whether economic, political, or social.

Unfortunately, much of what American students are taught is inconsistent with certain facts, or it distorts or omits those facts. For now, I will concentrate on the supposed consistency between the Declaration of Independence, the Constitution, and the Bill of Rights.[4] George W. Carey and Willmore Kendall identify five such inconsistencies. First, and perhaps the most glaring of the facts often omitted, is that at the Philadelphia convention the framers refused to include a bill of rights in the Constitution and it was ratified without one.[5] That omission was defended on the grounds that, among other things, a declaration of rights was appropriate only against a king and, since the people were to be sovereign under the proposed constitution, against whom would such rights be asserted?[6]

Second, whereas the Declaration of Independence had made several allusions to the people's dependence upon God,[7] the Constitution, with one

2. Willmore Kendall and George Carey, The Basic Symbols of the American Political Tradition 10 (1970) [hereinafter basic]. George C. Carey and Willmore Kendall have aptly labeled the most common set of beliefs described in the text as the "official literature."

3. *See e.g.* a leading American college textbook by James M. Burns, *et al.,* Government by the People, 15th ed. 117 (1993) ["In this one sentence the Declaration affirmed the precious rights of equality and liberty"].

4. I acknowledge that proponents of the official literature also view the Fourteenth Amendment as a key development in the evolution of the American tradition, not so much for any immediate changes it made but more for the potential of its language. *See infra,* chapter 4, text accompanying notes 2–30.

5. *See* Basic, *supra* note 2, at 11–12. Sherry notes: "The House . . . viewed the Bill of Rights mainly as a public relations device: the Representatives themselves recognized that enumeration of rights made little or no difference to the legal efficacy of such rights, but wanted the people to be . . . 'secure in the peaceable enjoyment of [their] privilege[s].'" [Suzanna Sherry, *The Founders' Unwritten Constitution,* 54 U. Chi. L. Rev. 1127, 1166 (1987)].

6. James Madison, Alexander Hamilton, and John Jay, The Federalist Papers [hereinafter Federalist]. no. 84, at 513. This matter will be explored in subsequent chapters.

7. Declaration of Independence (1776), in Basic Documents in American History 27–31 (Robert B. Morris, ed. 1956) ["Nature's God," "Creator," "Supreme Judge of the World," and "divine Providence"].

curious exception (requiring that no religious oath be used as a condition of holding office) is hauntingly silent about religion.[8] Should we conclude that the ratifiers of the Constitution were less pious than those who supported the Declaration?[9]

Third, the Declaration stirringly proclaims "that all men are created equal, that they are endowed by their Creator with certain unalienable Rights, that among these, are Life, Liberty, and the pursuit of Happiness."[10] But after independence was won (five years after the Declaration was written), what became of these "unalienable Rights"? Would it not be odd to fight a war in the name of unalienable rights and after victory promptly to forget about them? Why did these colonialists, who had such a fondness for writing things down, not do so after independence was secured? Should one conjecture that the "unalienable Rights" mentioned in the Declaration would eventually be the same ones added in the Bill of Rights? It is odder still that at the Philadelphia convention, as mentioned above, the Framers specifically opposed their inclusion.[11]

Fourth, (and perhaps most unpleasantly) the postrevolutionary behavior flies in the face of the Declaration's description that "all men are created equal." Indeed, the Constitution itself tolerated slavery[12] and not until 1868, with the ratification of the Fourteenth Amendment, is there any reference to equality in the text of the Constitution. Even then, the amendment's language provides only that no person should be denied "the equal protection of the laws."[13]

Lastly, while American students are frequently taught that our forefathers rebelled because they had been denied the rights of Englishmen

8. U.S. Const., art. 6, sec. 3 ("but no religious Test shall ever be required as a Qualification to any Office or public Trust under the United States"). Although it is commonly believed today that antifederalists were unqualified supporters of liberties, that is untrue. Indeed, scholars such as Pauline Maier contend that their objections to the proposed constitution did not center on the absence of a Bill of Rights. *See* Cecilia Keyon, *Men of Little Faith: The Anti-Federalists on the Nature of Representative Government,* 12 Wm. & Mary Quarterly 3 (1955). For example, some antifederalists were specifically displeased with the noted provision that prohibited any religious test. They characterized that provision as "'dangerous and impolitic' and tantamount to an 'invitation for Jews and pagans of every kind to come among us.'" James H. Hutson, *The Drafting of the Bill of Rights: Madison's 'Nauseous Project' Reexamined,* 3 Benchmark 309, 310 (1987).

9. Basic, *supra* note 2, at 12.

10. Declaration of Independence, *supra* note 7, at 27.

11. Basic, *supra* note 2, at 12–13. The matter is given further attention in chapter 2. *See infra,* chapter 2, text accompanying notes 98–114.

12. U.S. Const., art. 1, sec. 3 ("three fifths of all other Persons"), sec. 9 (regulating slave trade), and art. 4, sec. 3 (authorizing return of fugitive slaves).

13. U.S. Const., amend. 14, sec. 1 ("nor deny to any person within its jurisdiction the equal protection of the laws"). The qualification in the text refers to the simple fact that the protection afforded by the amendment did not mean that all persons had to be treated equally (e.g., women), or that legislatures could not distinguish between groups (e.g., convicted felons). *See* Herta Meyer,

(e.g., taxation without representation), it is difficult to prove that all British citizens enjoyed the rights that were allegedly denied the colonists and it is hard to explain what happened to those rights after the rebellion.[14] To expand on this: Had the American Revolution been fought to secure the rights of Englishmen, one should have little trouble identifying what these rights were and recounting how our forefathers sought better to secure them against violation. Is it not particularly curious that after the American swords were sheathed no effort was made to write down these rights?[15] Besides, when speaking about the rights of Englishmen, are we referring to the rights that eventually would be enumerated in the Bill of Rights? If so, the same inconsistency exists here as it did with respect to unalienable rights, noted above: Why did the framers knowingly, specifically, and successfully oppose their inclusion in the constitution?

Regardless of the form that the American alleged tradition of liberty and equality takes, this "official literature" remains unconvincing. For one thing it begins too abruptly (with the 1776 Declaration). Surely something must have happened during the nearly one hundred and fifty years of colonial history (between the founding of the first colony and the declaration of independence) that inspired our forefathers to risk being hanged for treason? Why is it that, when a piece of official literature is critically examined, far too often what is emphasized is only how Bill of Rights provisions have been interpreted by the Supreme Court over the past forty or so years? Why—instead of explaining what those provisions meant to those who ratified them? Those who framed and ratified the 1787 Constitution did not focus on individual rights; they concerned themselves with the one "'indubitable, inalienable, and indefeasible right'" to emerge from the one hundred and fifty years of colonial history: *the right of the American people to govern themselves.*[16]

THE HISTORY AND MEANING OF THE FOURTEENTH AMENDMENT 150–157, AT 156 (1977) ("The fourteenth amendment nowhere prevents the states from passing unequal laws.")

14. My suspicion is that in several instances the rights enjoyed by the colonists in fact exceeded those of the British, and the sum of such differences was partially responsible for Americans seeing themselves as a different people. *See* William Gangi, *The Sixth Amendment: Judicial Power and the People's Right to Govern Themselves,* 66 WASH. U.L.Q.71,75 n.15(1988).

15. Peter Onuf, *Forum—Reflections on the Founding: Constitutional Historiography in Bicentennial Perspective,* 46 WM. & MARY QUARTERLY 341 (1989). "By the time of the Constitutional Convention, the written constitution was a familiar genre." *Id.,* at 367. Chief Justice Marshall observed that in order "that those limits may not be mistaken or forgotten, the constitution is written." Marbury v. Madison, *supra* note 1, at 97.

16. BASIC, *supra* note 2, at 67 (quoting the Virginia Declaration of Rights). As Gordon Wood puts it: it "was conceivable to protect the common law liberties of the people against their rulers, but hardly against the people themselves." GORDON WOOD, THE CREATION OF THE AMERICAN REPUBLIC 1776–1787 63 (1969).

THE AMERICAN POLITICAL TRADITION: SELF-GOVERNMENT

After ten years of inquiry, I am convinced that our forefathers viewed constitutionalism and individual rights in a way very different from the way we do today.[17] I share Carey and Kendall's conclusion that for Americans the most important right secured by the Revolution was the right of self-government. That right was far more important to Americans than any particular right or even the sum of such rights.[18] It explains why Americans could initially forego a Bill of Rights and then turn around and add one.[19]

The American tradition of self-government is older than, but certainly not inconsistent with, the Declaration of Independence. Examine, for example, the Massachusetts' Body of Liberties (1641), where many of the rights specified often seem familiar enough (e.g., guaranteeing due process of law and prohibiting involuntary servitude). But read carefully, something seems amiss and certainly incompatible with what American students are taught today. To take a specific example: Buried within the statement of each right announced in the Massachusetts' Body of Liberties is what some today might call an escape clause. It permits the general court (the name by which the Massachusetts legislature was known) to make exceptions.[20] For example:

> No mans life shall be taken away, no mans honour or good name shall be stayned, no mans person shall be arrested, restrayned, banished, dismembered, nor any wayes punished, no man shall be deprived of his wife or children, no mans goods of estaite shall be taken away from him, nor any way indammaged under colour of law or Countenance of Authoritie, unlesse it be by vertue or equitie of some expresse law of the Country waranting the same, established by a generall Court and sufficiently published, or in case of the defect of a law in any partecular case by the word of God. And in Capitall cases, or in cases concerning dismembring or banishment according to that word to be judged by the Generall Court.[21]

And then there is my favorite: "No man shall be forced by Torture to confesse any Crime against himselfe nor any other unlesse it be done in some Capitall case, where he is first fullie convicted by cleare and suf-

17. *See* Christopher Wolfe, *A Theory of U.S. Constitutional History,* 43 J. OF POL. 292, 296–297 (1981).

18. BASIC, *supra* note 2, at 59–60.

19. *See infra,* chapter 2, text accompanying notes 115–134.

20. BASIC, *supra* note 2, at 52. *See also* Raoul Berger, *Ely's "Theory of Judicial Review,"* 42 OHIO ST. L.J. 87, 124 (1981).

21. BASIC DOCUMENTS IN AMERICAN HISTORY 12 (ROBERT B. MORRIS, ed., 1956).

ficient evidence to be guilty, After which if the cause be of that nature, That it is very apparent there be other conspiratours, or confederates with him, Then he may be tortured, yet not with such Tortures as be Barbarous and inhumane."[22] What outrage such a statement of purely procedural rights would evoke today from an organization such as the American Civil Liberties Union!

For now, however, I want only to press two points upon the reader. First, the citizens of Massachusetts both demanded and were satisfied with the Body of Liberties. Second, that document indicates the political tradition preceding the Declaration of Independence—a tradition that illustrates that, while individual liberties were cherished, those liberties were preceded by a far superior right—that of self-government. The right of self-government encompasses the right of a political community to create and define individual liberties. To put this in concise form, the American Revolution secured totally what the citizens of Massachusetts in 1641 only partially enjoyed—republican rule: the right of the people to hold accountable those elected to make public policy decisions, including those pertaining to individual rights.[23]

The rights contained in the Massachusetts Body of Liberties were promulgated in procedural terms because, for several reasons, the good citizens of that colony believed that a substantive statement of rights—rights that not even a legislature could broach, under any circumstances—was imprudent, if not futile. They were students of both history and experience and these taught that few, if any, governmental actions might be absolutely prohibited without diminishing the people's capacity to defend their existence and independence. Attempts to do so either were naive (i.e., indicating an ignorance of history or an unwillingness to accept political realities) or dishonest (i.e., knowingly ignoring the fact that, if certain circumstances arose, those prohibitions would be ignored). In either case, adding imprudent declarations would undermine other written prohibitions.[24] Additionally, and not unrelated to the first reason, absolute substantive prohibitions could inhibit

22. *Id.*, at 13–14. Nothing in the original understanding of the Bill of Rights precludes such a legislative provision.

23. "The American Revolution was not a social revolution. It did not alter the domestic condition or capacity of persons within the colonies, nor was it designed to disturb the domestic relations existing among them. It was a political revolution, by which thirteen dependent colonies became thirteen independent States." Dred Scott v. Sandford, 60 U.S. (19 How.) 393, 502 (1856) [Campbell, J., concurring].

24. For a more systematic discussion, *see infra*, chapter 2, text accompanying notes 3–10. Kendall and Carey ask: "Do you talk first about the individual and the rights that he ought to have, ought to enjoy, or do you talk first about some other things, and most particularly one other thing, namely: the general good?" Basic, *supra* note 2, at 59.

the society's ability to adapt to changing circumstances. Lastly, and most important, absolute substantive prohibitions were considered unnecessary because, in a republic, elected representatives served at the people's pleasure.

Hence, after the American Revolution, state legislatures emerged as the primary public policy makers, and the citizens of each state depended on an informed electorate to protect them from abuses. Legislators were the people's servants.[25] They were given considerable discretion to formulate public policy because a vigilant people did not fear extending policy making discretion.[26]

This postrevolutionary self-government also created new dangers. State legislative assemblies soon possessed awesome power. They were answerable to no one except the people and at times were capable of quite obnoxious behavior.[27] (Perhaps I can draw a modern-day analogy by citing the increase in ethnic conflict after the collapse of the Soviet Union.) Publius made a key distinction in this regard.[28] After the Revolution, the right to self-government meant that no other political authority (i.e., the British Crown) existed above the citizens of each state. But that did not mean that the citizens of each state viewed elected representatives or themselves—either individually or collectively—as free to do whatever they wished. Instead, Americans commonly believed in a higher law of divine ori-

25. Kendall and Carey identify "deliberation" as one of the most important symbols to emerge from that period of history. *See* BASIC *supra,* note 2, at 37. But the character of that deliberation evidently separated the federalists from the antifederalists. In *The Essential Antifederalist,* Allen and Lloyd note: "Theoretically, Antifederalists conceived of representation as a device to facilitate the direct expression of the will of the people. Federalists regarded representation as a device to facilitate deliberation. Antifederalists, on the other hand, conceived of the deliberation prerequisite to sound governing as primarily social; that is, taking place within the body of the people." WILLIAM B. ALLEN AND GORDON LLOYD, THE ESSENTIAL ANTIFEDERALIST 138 (1985) [hereinafter cited as ANTIFEDERALIST].

26. Wolfe observes:

> While modern Americans assume that the chief defense of constitutional rights is judicial power, the traditional view, e.g., during the Founding, was quite different. The primary vindicator of rights was thought to be an "aroused popular conscience" acting through elections—judicial enforcement was thought of as a less frequent and more secondary enforcement. This view is true of Hamilton, who argued against a Bill of Rights in the *Federalist* on the grounds that security of rights "must altogether depend on public opinion," and of Jefferson, who (in a letter denying judicial supremacy) stated that he knew "no safe depository of the ultimate powers of the society but the people themselves . . . this is the true corrective of abuses of Constitutional power."

Wolfe, *supra* note 17, at 296.

27. For example, Publius, speaking of events in Pennsylvania, notes that the legislature violated the requirement "that all bills of a public nature shall be previously printed." FEDERALIST, *supra* note 6, at 312. Publius also extensively quotes Jefferson's observation on the growing power of the legislature in Virginia. *Id.,* at 310–311.

28. "You must first enable the government to control the governed; and in the next place oblige it to control itself" FEDERALIST, no. 51, *supra* note 6, at 322.

gin and in Massachusetts, for example, its legislators specifically considered themselves bound "to do that which [was] humane, civil and Christian."[29] Citizens would ultimately decide at the polls if the judgments of elected representatives' reflected their views, priorities, and concerns.[30] That is no less true today. Elected representatives have with them a set of principles based on religious faith, patriotic fervor, or philosophical belief. Or no such beliefs! To this day, every substantive deliberation in state and federal legislatures includes at least indirectly the tradition of a higher law. But nothing in the Constitution prohibits the American people from abandoning even the most cherished beliefs of their forefathers.

TYPES OF GOVERNMENT AND THEIR DEFECTS

Not all colonialists were comfortable with the idea of republican government. Many shared the belief that monarchies and aristocracies offered far better long-term prospects for securing peace and prosperity than did democracies or most republics.[31] Hence, delegates to the Philadelphia convention approached placing governmental power in the hands of the people very cautiously. They were familiar, as we shall see shortly, with past "pure democracies" and many republics, and they were not terribly impressed with either.[32] But the beliefs held by these delegates were far more complex than a simple choice between, on the one hand, democracies and most republics and, on the other, monarchies and aristocracies. One issue concerned the proper size of states. Pure democracies, where all citizens participated directly in decision making, had obvious limits. Only so many people could meet in one place at one time and so such democracies had to be "confined to a small spot."[33]

Small republics, however, had an equally poor track record for providing efficient, stable governments capable of preserving themselves and citizen liberty.[34] They were frequently

29. Basic, *supra* note 2, at 71.
30. *Id.*, at 71–72. As Kendall and Carey point out, by the time of the Virginia Declaration of Rights (1776) that state's citizens considered philosophy (as well as religion) to be pertinent to an understanding of a higher law. Furthermore, by the time the constitution was proposed its framers understood that the obligation to remain subordinate to a higher law was not a fit topic for explicit inclusion in the proposed constitution. But (as the authors carefully pointed out) in no sense should the reader assume that, by separating the political and higher spheres of law, the authors of the Virginia Declaration or, subsequently, the Constitution "underst[ood] or interpret[ed] themselves as less Christian, less committed to the truth of the soul and of society as that truth comes to us through Revelation, than, say, the signers of the Mayflower Compact." *Id.*, at 72.
31. *See generally, id.*, nos. 14, 37, 39, 49, and 51.
32. *See generally,* Federalist, *supra,* note 6, no. 4, at 49; no. 6, at 54–59; no. 9, at 71–76; no. 10, at 81 ("pure democracies").
33. Federalist, *supra* note 6, no. 14, at 101.
34. *Id.*, no. 10, at 81–82, and no. 63, at 387–388.

in a "state of perpetual vibration between the extremes of tyranny and anarchy."[35] Republics could be extended over a larger territory than pure democracies since elected representatives would make public policy decisions instead of all the people assembled in one place; however, most colonialists (particularly among the antifederalists)[36] maintained that republics ought to be confined to a relatively small territory. If they were not so confined, increased size would inevitably lead to the concentration of power believed essential to govern more expansive territory. That in turn would lead to the suppression of individual liberties, to monarchy, and eventually to tyranny.

Antifederalists paradoxically believed that while liberty would most likely flourish in small republics, such states would be by nature short-lived.[37] They inevitably were defeated in war by larger enemies, most frequently those governed by a monarchy or aristocracy, governments that could act vigorously since decision-making power had been lodged in few, and even a single, hands.

For these reasons, even those who understood that monarchical or aristocratic forms of government were inconsistent with the spirit of the Revolution and would never gain the approval of the American people were pessimistic about the future. Even they believed that only such forms offered long-term prospects for a strong and stable national government.

Pure Democracies

Proponents of the constitution viewed democracy's defects differently than did antifederalist opponents. The former not only opposed pure democracy because it was impractical anywhere except in a small territory, but because they believed it was inherently unstable. In such a governmental form, popular passions were often injected immediately and regularly into decision making. That encouraged ill-considered and shortsighted legislation dangerous to the long-term common good. Such governments could not act consistently or with vigor and instead catered frequently to ignorant or erratic majorities. Pure

35. FEDERALIST, *supra* note 6, no. 9, at 71.

36. William B. Allen and Gordon Lloyd comment that the antifederalists "believed that republican liberty was best preserved in small units where the people had an active and continuous part to play in government." ANTIFEDERALIST, *supra* note 25, at xiii.

37. By coopting the term *federalists,* opponents of the proposed constitution were forced to take on the name *antifederalists,* which they insisted was a misnomer. Many antifederalists contended that what the so-called federalists really wanted (but were afraid to admit) was a *national* government, while antifederalists fought for the right of states to retain their traditional sovereignty. Some antifederalists were prepared to grant the national legislature more powers than had existed under the Articles. These different perspectives toward the proposed constitution are of course at the core of the arguments in *The Federalist Papers. See* FEDERALIST, *supra* note 6, at 100, ANTIFEDERALIST, *supra* note 25, at viii, 117–118, and *infra,* comment accompanying note 66.

democracies would inevitably fail to protect both the common good and individual rights (especially those of property). They had a dismal tendency to deteriorate into mobocracies or dictatorships.[38] Publius concisely summarizes the delegates' opposition to this form of government in a most penetrating sentence: "Had every Athenian citizen been a Socrates, every Athenian assembly would still have been a mob."[39]

Republics

Many delegates at the Philadelphia convention also believed that small republics were equally inclined to "folly, feebleness and tyranny;" even worse, that they could not secure their existence for sustained periods.[40] Challenging the view widely shared by antifederalists, proponents of the constitution argued that a well structured republic could be as stable and energetic as any monarchy or aristocracy.[41] They proposed an unprecedented solution—a "compound republic."[42] Thus, they created a new type of government: one that was neither strictly national nor confederal.[43] Unlike prior republics, where at least some portion of power was

38. *Id.*, no. 10, at 81 (such democracies are short-lived). *See also* Willmore Kendall, *The Two Majorities,* 4 Midwest J. Pol. Sci. 317 (1960). Ralph Ketchem, drawing on a seminal article by Martin Diamond (Martin Diamond, *Democracy and* The Federalist: *A Reconsideration of the Framers' Intent,* 53 Am. Pol. Sci. Rev. 52 (1959)) observes that the authors of *The Federalist Papers* contended that they were fulfilling the ideas of the Revolution, not retreating from them. They saw themselves as "wise" democrats and characterized their antifederalist opponents as "foolish" democrats who "merely trumpet . . . the virtues of democracy without taking any account of its difficulties." Ralph Ketchem, *Publius: Sustaining the Republican Principle,* 44 Wm. & Mary Quarterly 576, 576–577 (1987).

39. Federalist, *supra* note 6, no. 55, at 342. *See infra,* chapter 8, text accompanying notes 17–47.

40. *See* Martin Diamond *et al.,* The Democratic Republic 35–36 (2nd. ed. 1966); Federalist, *supra* note 6, nos. 9, 47–49; Montesquieu, The Spirit of the Laws, book 8, at ch. 16, book 9, at ch. 1 (1873).

41. Publius commented "that liberty may be endangered by the abuses of liberty as well as by the abuses of power; that there are numerous instances of the former as well as of the latter, and that the former, rather than the latter . . . [are] apparently most to be apprehended by the United States." Federalist, *supra* note 6, no. 63, at 387–388.

42. "In the compound republic of America, the power surrendered by the people is first divided between two distinct governments, and then the portion allotted to each subdivided among distinct and separate departments. Hence a double security arises to the rights of the people. The different governments will control each other, at the same time that each will be controlled by itself." Federalist, *supra* note 6, no. 51, at 323.

43. Prior to the Philadelphia convention, governments had been characterized either as being national (where all sovereign power was placed in one hand) or confederal (at the time, *federal* was used interchangeably with *confederal*) where important powers were delegated to a common central government (*e.g.,* under the Articles of Confederation). In a confederation, however, sovereignty remained with each of the states. After the Philadelphia convention, the meaning of *federal* was differentiated from *confederal,* the former reflecting the various structures contained in the Constitution: the division of sovereignty between the central government and the states. Amendments passed after the Civil War changed the application of these principles but not the governing principles. The subject will be discussed in chapter 3.

beyond popular control, every part in the proposed constitution was subject to the popular will.[44]

PUBLIUS' CRITIQUE OF THE ARTICLES OF CONFEDERATION

I wish to take a closer look at the context surrounding the constitution's proposal, as seen by its proponents. *The Federalist Papers* begin, not with an eloquent description of the nature and content of individual rights, as one might expect from reading most contemporary literature, but instead with Publius' condemnation of the Articles of Confederation.[45]

Publius immediately concedes that honest disagreements may exist over what course Americans should take. But he also candidly states that he will not hesitate to propose a strong, stable, and efficient government simply because some might try to characterize that proposal as masking a personal desire for power.[46] Publius contends nothing could be further from the truth.[47] As we review Publius' defense of the constitution, readers

44. The Republic created by the Constitution was novel in that, in past republics, at least some power remained beyond popular control (e.g., representation somewhere was based on birth or wealth). In the U.S. Constitution, however, every part of the government ultimately is subject to the people's will. Publius states: "They accomplished a revolution which has no parallel in the annals of human society. They reared the fabrics of governments which have no model on the face of the globe." Federalist, *supra* note 6, no. 14, at 104. Whatever misgivings existed among federalists regarding democracy, in the end all branches of the government charged with making public policy were responsible to and subject to popular will. That attitude may be contrasted with the dominant view today: now, enormous powers in the area of public policy making are invested in the courts and their lack of accountability is largely ignored. *See infra,* chapter 5.

45. Federalist, *supra* note 6, no. 1, at 33 ("after an unequivocal experience of the inefficacy of the subsisting federal government, you are called upon to deliberate on a new constitution for the United States of America").

46. *Id.* Such a clash of such views would provide an excellent example of how different personality types may view one another. "The more extreme feelings types are a bit put off by rule-governed choice, regarding the act of being impersonal as almost inhuman. The more dedicated thinking types, on the other hand, sometimes look upon the emotion-laden decisions and choices as muddle-headed." David Keirsey and Marilyn Bates, Please Understand Me, 20 (1984) [hereinafter Keirsey and Bates]. Allen and Lloyd say the antifederalists understood "the basic choice facing mankind" to be "either republicanism or despotism." Antifederalist, *supra* note 25, at xi. Patrick Henry described the proposed constitution as "a revolution as radical as that which separated us from Great Britain." *Id.,* at 126. Contrast this with the federalist's claim of simply being wise democrats. *See supra,* text accompanying note 38.

47. *Id.,* at 35. Publius observes:

> On the other hand, it will be equally forgotten that the vigor of government is essential to the security of liberty; that, in the contemplation of a sound and well-informed judgment, their interests can never be separate; and that a dangerous ambition more often lurks behind the specious mask of zeal for the rights of the people than under the forbidding appearance of zeal for the firmness and efficiency of government. History will teach us that the former has been found a much more certain road to the introduction of despotism than the latter, and that of those men who have overturned the liberties of republics, the greatest number have begun their career by paying an obsequious court to the people, commencing demagogues and ending tyrants.

Id.

should keep in mind that there were a number of proposals in the air.[48]

Inability to Secure the Safety of Citizens

Publius claims that citizen "safety" is the first task of all governments. That safety would most likely be threatened by wars with foreign powers or by conflicts between two or among more of the thirteen states. Whether either might occur because of "*real or pretended*" causes, or because certain circumstances might arise that "*provoke or invite them,*" a single nation composed of all the former colonies was the most likely successfully to meet such challenges. Publius explains that only the population of a single "united states" could provide the a broad enough base from which competent diplomats might be recruited—skills essential to resolving conflicts between nations or states by measures short of physical force. Similarly, a single interpretation from one union of states would be much preferable to several interpretations from various confederacies and certainly far superior to thirteen. Lastly, since smaller states naturally seek to align themselves with strong foreign powers in an effort to discourage larger neighbors from coveting their territory or resources, one union would eliminate still another frequent source of war. War, Publius observes, unfortunately is related to human nature, and nations wage war whenever there is something to be gained.[49]

In Publius' day, monarchs were particularly notorious for waging wars to satisfy their egos, ignoring both justice or the real interest of their subjects. Publius provides his readers with historical examples.[50] The principle championed then by Publius persists to this day: the United States is far better able to negotiate with other states and to be accorded respect by members of the international community than would several confederacies or thirteen separate states.

Wars with foreign powers did not pose the only danger to citizen safety. Left disunited, the thirteen sovereign states eventually, like all "*bordering* nations . . . would always be either involved in disputes and war, or live in the constant apprehension of them."[51] While citizens of the thirteen states currently enjoy the flush of camaraderie because of their vic-

48. In addition to there being the proposed constitution, antifederalists held a wide range of views on whether or how the Articles of Confederation could be reformed and at the same time retain state sovereignty. There was talk of at least two and perhaps three distinct confederacies.

49. *Id.,* no. 4, at 46. Publius prefaced his comments with this observation: "But the safety of the people of America against dangers from *foreign* force depends not only on their forebearing to give *just* causes of war to other nations, but also on their placing and continuing themselves in such a situation as not to *invite* hostility or insult, for it need be observed that there are *pretended* as well as just causes of war." *Id.*

50. *Id.,* at 47–49.

51. *Id.,* no. 5, at 51.

tory over the British, that would not last for long. Inequalities of population and prosperity soon would divide them, as would disputed territories, surely "one of the most fertile sources of hostility among nations."[52]

There also was the issue of how to pay the debt acquired to fight the Revolution:[53] "for it is an observation, as true as it is trite, that there is nothing men differ so readily about as the payment of money."[54] The more populous states, for example, would press their advantage over the smaller states, which in turn will form alliances among themselves—if not with foreign powers.[55] In the end, even these patriots would turn against one another. Publius again provided several historical examples with which his countrymen were familiar.[56]

We, today, could also provide examples: the American Civil War; the assassination that grew into World War I; the subsequent vindictive peace that sowed the seeds of World War II; the more recent conflict of pride between Iran and Iraq (wherein some one million perished); Gadhafi's never-ending conspiracies, the delusions of Idi Amin or Saddam Hussein or those of Cambodia's Pol Pot. Publius does not fix blame or judge causes and neither will I; he wishes only to remind his readers that all governments must be prepared to deal with such occurrences, and, if the states remained disunited, not only would several or thirteen governments be less likely to deal with them but they would multiply those occurrences. Put concisely, whether the threat to citizen safety came from foreign or domestic causes, it would shape the prospects for citizen liberty. How could it be otherwise? Unless a people are secure from foreign domination or interstate strife, the liberty of all citizens is endangered. Most citizens, if confronted with the prospect that life, liberty, and property will be lost because the government is weak, will place greater emphasis upon the government's ability to win wars, even if by doing so "civil and political rights" may be threatened. "To be more safe, they at length become willing to run the risk of being less free"[57]—as no doubt to-

52. *Id.,* at 60.
53. *Id.,* at 62–65.
54. *Id.,* at 65.
55. *Id.,* at 53.
56. *Id.,* at 55–59.
57. *Id.,* no. 8, at 67. Publius would later observe that "every man the least conversant in Roman history knows how often that republic was obliged to take refuge in the absolute power of a single man, under the formidable title of dictator, as well against the intrigues of ambitious individuals who aspired to the tyranny, and the sedition of whole classes of the community whose conduct threatened the existence of all government, as against the invasions of external enemies who menaced the conquest and destruction of Rome." *Id.,* no. 70, at 423. See *infra,* chapter 6, comment and sources accompanying note 186. (There is some reason to believe that states that did not ratify the Constitution eventually may have been coerced into the Union.)

day would many residents of U.S. cities, confronted as they are by crime seemingly beyond the control of local governments.

Since the stakes would be so high and, without comprehensive union, citizen anxiety so widespread, fortifications would begin to sprout at points of military significance. This soon would lead, as it had in Europe, to state-supported "STANDING ARMIES.[58]" And with the appearance of such armies would come the need for stronger types of government: monarchies. "Thus, we should, in a little time, see established in every part of this country the same engines of despotism, which have been the scourge of the old world."[59]

Inability to Address the Defects of the Republican Form

I already mentioned that at Philadelphia those present had serious reservations about pure democracies and small republics.[60] The matter was so grave that even friends of republicanism suggested that civil liberties might be "inconsistent with the order of society." If the deficiencies described by critics of republican government had been impossible to repair, Publius concedes, then even "enlightened friends of liberty would [be] obliged to abandon the cause of that species of government as indefensible."[61] But fortunately, he contends, the "science of politics" had kept pace and "various principles" had developed that could remedy defects of the republican form. These principles included the separation of powers, the requirement that judges serve only during good behavior, the institution of various checks and balances among executive, legislative, and judicial powers, and representative instead of direct citizen participation in lawmaking. These measures "are means, and powerful means, by which the excellencies of republican government may be retained and its imperfections lessened and avoided."[62]

Publius, admitting that it may appear "novel . . . to some," offers another principle to the ones listed—a republic encompassing all thirteen states—although he acknowledges its suggestion did not sit well with opponents of the proposed constitution.[63] But Publius steadfastly rejects

58. FEDERALIST, *supra* note 6, at 67 (emphasis in original).

59. *Id.*, at 68.

60. *See supra,* text accompanying notes 25–26, 31–44; *infra,* text accompanying notes 68–79.

61. FEDERALIST, *supra* note 6, at 72.

62. *Id.*, at 72–73.

63. *Id.*, at 73 ("ENLARGEMENT of the ORBIT within which such systems are to revolve, either in respect to the dimensions of a single State, or to the consolidation of several smaller States into one great Confederacy"). In this matter, Madison apparently had relied heavily upon the views of David Hume: "Hume's analysis here had turned the small-territory theory upside down: *if* a free state could once be established in a large area, [Hume contended] it would be stable and safe from the effects of faction. Madison had found the answer to Montesquieu." *See* Douglas Adair, *"That*

the conventional wisdom on the appropriate size of a republic. If the republican form is not extended over a large geographical area and states are left independent or grouped into several confederacies, "we shall be driven to the alternative either of taking refuge at once in the arms of monarchy, or of splitting ourselves into an infinity of little, jealous, clashing, tumultuous commonwealths, the wretched nurseries of unceasing discord and the miserable objects of universal pity or contempt."[64] Under the proposed constitution, however, Publius confidently predicts that "the tendency of the Union [will be] to repress domestic faction and insurrection."[65]

What of the contentions that the new central government may have too much power and that the proposed central government is no longer a confederacy but a "*consolidation* of the States"?[66] Publius replies: "So long as the separate organization of

---

Politics May be Reduced to a Science" : David Hume, James Madison, and the Tenth Federalist, 20 HUNTINGTON LIBRARY QUARTERLY 343, 348–355, at 351 (1957).

The view that liberty could flourish only in small republics certainly dominated the antifederalist position. *See generally,* ANTIFEDERALIST, *supra* note 25. "The key criticism [the antifederalists] . . . had with the constitution was the representation issue." *Id.,* at xii. Antifederalists complained that the proposed constitution did not include "the power of recall, frequent elections, and rotation of office," *id.,* at xiii. Antifederalist critics often cited Montesquieu in support, asserting that he would find the proposed constitution defective because, if liberty was the object, it departed from the accepted belief that small republics are to be preferred to larger ones. Publius, however, rejects these criticisms and antifederalist reliance on Montesquieu's arguments since, he noted, the size of republic that Montesquieu had recommended already was smaller than six of the American states, thereby requiring (if such critics remained consistent) that those states be broken up into smaller geographical units—a position no antifederalist advanced. FEDERALIST, *supra* note 6, no. 9, at 73–74.

Upon examining Montesquieu's discussion of confederate republics, Publius concludes that "in the sense of the author who has been most emphatically quoted upon the occasion [*i.e.,* Montesquieu], it would only dictate a reduction of the SIZE of the more considerable MEMBERS of the Union, but would not militate against their being all comprehended in one confederate government." *Id.,* at 74.

64. *Id.,* no. 9, at 73.

65. *Id.* Note Publius' anticipation here (no. 9, usually attributed to Hamilton) that the proposed central government would play a major role in regulating factions (an insight usually noted only with respect to Madison's celebrated no. 10.)

66. *Id.,* at 75. Some antifederalists charged that the federalist position simply amounted to a single government: "'In short, consolidation pervades the whole constitution.'" ANTIFEDERALIST, *supra* note 25, at 61. Others contended that the federalists pursued inconsistent ends: "'We apprehend that two co-ordinate sovereignties would be a solecism in politics.'" *Id.,* at 59. Most antifederalists contended that only two types of government existed, those that operated on "individuals" and those that bound "states and government" together—known as a "*league or confederation.*" They bitterly charged that supporters of the proposed constitution abused political language because in fact so-called federalists were "*national* men." Instead, they contended, the opponents of the proposed constitution were the true federalists. ANTIFEDERALIST, *supra* note 25, at 117–118. Some antifederalists *(e.g., Federal Farmer)* seemed to go so far as to suggest that to be sufficiently federal any central government must be weak: "Every part or branch of the federal head must be feeble, and unsafely trusted with large powers." [*Id.,* at 91]

the members be not abolished; so long as it exists, by a constitutional necessity, for local purposes; though it should be in perfect subordination to the general authority of the union; it would still be, in fact and in theory, an association of states, or a confederacy."[67]

Inability to Control Factions

Only a newly constituted central government would be able "to break and control the violence of faction," which Publius defines as "a number of citizens . . . who are united and actuated by some common impulse of passion, or of interest, adverse to the rights of other citizens, or to the permanent and aggregate interests of the community."[68] Popular governments were so inclined to factions that even respected citizens already had suggested that several of the existing state governments were ineffectual and lacked stability, and Publius concedes that there is some truth to that claim.[69]

The causes of societal factionalism, Publius contends, are in "the nature of man" and all governments must work at eliminating their ill effects. That task might be accomplished either by removing those causes (which he believes would be more harmful to citizens than the disease)[70] or, in two very different situations (when the faction consisted of a minority or a majority), by controlling their effects.[71] In republics, minority factions pose little difficulty because the majority may regularly outvote them.[72] But a faction made up of a majority is an entirely different matter. It can "execute and mask [its] violence under the forms of the Constitution," meaning that a majority faction can do whatever it wants, when it wants to, and still faithfully

67. FEDERALIST, *supra* note 6, at 76. Publius argued that it was clear that state governments were recognized as "constituent parts" of the national government because each state, regardless of population, would possess two votes in the Senate.

68. *Id.,* no. 10, at 77–78. Adair argues that Madison again based his insights on the work of David Hume. See Adair, *supra* note 63, at 355–360. I do not wish, at this point in the text, to draw the reader's attention to the fact that we are here considering the celebrated tenth paper. Publius, however, lists the inability to control factions as only one of many defects in the Articles.

69. *Id.,* at 77. Publius seems to go out of his way to indicate that these criticisms came not from opponents of powerful governments, but from those who were sympathetic to republicanism: "from our most considerate and virtuous citizens, equally the friends of public and private faith and of public and personal liberty." *Id.,* at 77.

70. *Id.,* at 78–79. Publius states that the "two methods of removing the causes of faction [are to first] destroy . . . the liberty which is essential to its existence; the other, by giving to every citizen the same opinions, the same passions, and the same interests." *Id.,* at 78.

71. I make no pretense of offering an analysis of the tenth paper, but I do wish to put that paper in its original context. For a critical appraisal of contemporary misreadings of this paper, *see* Douglas Adair, *The Tenth Federalist Revisited,* 8 WM. & MARY QUARTERLY 48 (1951); James H. Hutson, *supra* note 8, at 310, and GEORGE W. CAREY, IN DEFENSE OF THE CONSTITUTION 75 (1989).

72. *Id.,* at 80. "If a faction consists of less than a majority, relief is supplied by the republican principle, which enables the majority to defeat its sinister views by regular vote." *Id.*

follow every applicable legal procedure.[73]

How then, in republics, can majorities be prevented from abusing the enormous law making powers they possess? If experience is any guide, Publius observes, reliance solely upon either moral or religious constraints, or both, will prove insufficient. Direct democracies are especially vulnerable. In the past they "have ever been spectacles of turbulence and contention; have ever been found incompatible with personal security or the rights of property; and have in general been as short in their lives as they have been violent in their deaths."[74]

Republics, however, enjoy several advantages that pure democracies lack. They often contain more citizens and more territory (diluting the impact of factions) and day-to-day governing responsibilities are delegated to a small number of citizens—which is less likely to lead to the injection of emotion immediately into public policy making.[75]

Publius concedes that, if the preceding analysis is correct, the issue is not whether a pure democracy or a republic is best suited to protect the common good (democracies are clearly unsuited); but instead, what size of republic might to be preferred: a small republic or one more extensive.[76] In his judgement, an extensive republic should be preferred because it would more likely contain more suitable representatives. Each representative—as provided for in the proposed constitution—would be elected from a constituency, not so small as to be manipulated by an astute politician but also not so large so as to prevent that representative from being familiar with local circumstances and needs.[77]

Most important, only a representative form of government would be capable of governing a large number of citizens and an extensive territory—two considerations crucial to any proposed solution of the Articles' defects. "Extend the sphere and you

73. *Id.*, at 80 ("It may clog the administration, it may convulse the society; but it will be unable to execute and mask its violence under the forms of the Constitution"). Publius adds: "When a majority is included in a faction, the form of popular government . . . enables it to sacrifice to its ruling passion or interest both the public good and the rights of other citizens." *Id.*

74. *Id.*, at 81.

75. *Id.*, at 81–82. Madison apparently assumed that, with a more extensive territory, the people in each district might select those with more refined and long-term (aristocratic) views. He certainly assumes that the representative process itself would result in the injection of less passion than if citizens participated directly in public policy making. There is also an underlying belief here (and throughout *The Federalist Papers*) that the people should recognize and admire the more "reasonable" types and that when it came to elections the system should be tilted toward the selection of such people.

76. *Id.*, at 82.

77. *Id.*, at 82–83. There seems to be some empirical evidence to support his contentions, at least if characteristics associated with introversion and intuition are valued. They occur only in 25 percent of the population. See appendix B.

take in a greater variety of parties and interests; you make it less probable that a majority of the whole will have a common motive to invade the rights of other citizens."[78] In sum, Publius argues that just as republics have certain advantages over democracies, the proposed union of all the states possessed advantages over proposals for several confederations or thirteen separate states. He concludes the tenth paper with these words: "In the extent and proper structure of the Union . . . we behold a republican remedy for the diseases most incident to republican government."[79]

Inability to Regulate Commerce

Publius tries to persuade his readers that only a single union can assure future commercial prosperity. European maritime powers remained uncomfortable about America's commercial potential; and those powers, Americans must anticipate, will attempt to divide the states should they remain separate. Three goals motivated European maritime powers: to assure that any of the former British colonies would not intrude on their rights of navigation, to "monopoliz[e] the profits of our trade, and [to] . . . clip . . . the wings by which we might soar to a dangerous greatness."[80] Only by standing united would the several states be able to counter any hostile measures and instead "oblige foreign countries to bid against each other for the privileges of our markets."[81] This analysis by Publius still rings true today for readers acquainted with efforts to revitalize the European Common Market or to enter into periodic trade negotiations with such nations as West Germany, Japan, Eastern Europe, or Russia.

Commercial power, Publius asserts, is integral to the common defense and the general welfare of the nation. The resources of the entire union, notes Publius, will be needed to build a credible navy. And once that navy became operational, any foreign power would fear that, if that navy were added to the navy of one of its competitors, the American navy might determine the outcome of any conflict. Without such a navy, he warns, America could not even hope to remain neutral in commercial disputes. "The rights of neutrality will only be respected when they are defended by an adequate power. A nation despicable by its weakness forfeits even the privilege of being neutral."[82]

Publius drives home the relationship between commercial power, an adequate navy, and the general welfare by contending that, without union and a strong navy, Americans would have little choice but to accept whatever price more powerful na-

78. *Id.,* at 83.
79. *Id.*
80. *Id.,* at 84–85.
81. *Id.,* at 85.
82. *Id.*

tions might put on their commodities. The ability to fish as well as to navigate the Great Lakes and the Mississippi also would be in doubt.[83] Analogous problems persist to this day, and although Americans now may desire to limit fishing (e.g., whaling, trapping dolphins in nets) Publius' conclusions are again undeniable: without the ability to enforce the United States' will, American preferences would be ignored.

Other Defects of the Articles

Up to this point, Publius has defended his position that a single large republic—as proposed in the constitution—is preferable to thirteen independent states or two or three confederacies. Now he shifts ground and takes the offensive, contending that soon citizens will have to go one way or the other because the "major imperfections" contained in the Articles of Confederation inevitably will lead to its collapse and perhaps even to "anarchy."[84] Already, he says, the existing ineffective central government is the object of "national humiliation."[85] Even opponents of the proposed constitution often concede that to one extent or the other, the Articles are defective. Yet, Publius claims, these opponents remain indecisive, unwilling to propose any measures to cure the defects that they admit exist. "They seem still to aim at things repugnant and irreconcilable; at an augmentation of federal authority without a diminution of State authority; at sovereignty in the Union and complete independence in the members."[86] He then identifies many "fundamental errors" in "the first principles and main pillars of the fabric" of the Articles of Confederation.[87] Here I will turn only to the most important of these criticisms.

NO POWER OVER INDIVIDUALS. Under the Articles, the national congress could not reach individuals because it was the states that constituted the heart of the confederation.[88] Since state governments could stand between the acts of the national con-

83. *Id.*, at 87.

84. *Id.*, no. 13, at 97. *But see* Gary B. Nash, *Also There at the Creation: Going beyond Gordon S. Wood,* 46 WM. & MARY QUARTERLY 603, 604 n.5 (1987) (arguing that conditions under the Articles were not as dire as contended by the federalists).

85. FEDERALIST, *supra* note 6, no. 15, at 106.

86. *Id.*, at 108. Publius had listed several particulars: debts that remained unpaid, territories and ports still under foreign power, the inability to navigate the Mississippi River (though entitled to do so under the peace treaty signed with Great Britain), no public credit, declining commerce and land values. *Id,* at 106–107. Publius' characterization here is consistent with a "judger" preference. "The J[udger] is apt to report a sense of urgency until he has made a pending decision, and then be at rest once the decision has been made. The P[erceiver] person, in contrast, is more apt to experience resistance to making a decision, wishing that more data could be accumulated as the basis for the decision." [PLEASE *supra* note 46, at 22.]

87. FEDERALIST, *supra* note 6, at 108.

88. *Id.*

gress and individual citizens, national laws for all practical purposes remained merely recommendatory. That is the worst possible arrangement, claims Publius, because it left the national government only two choices when it came to enforcing its edicts: it had either to threaten force or use it. So, each time the national congress deliberated on what actions to take, it had simultaneously to consider whether it would be necessary to threaten or use force. Being limited to those two choices to effectuate the ordinary will of a government is a sign of poor constitution making because more often than not it would lead to governmental paralysis.[89] But under the proposed constitution, states either obeyed national laws or, they would have to explain their refusal in federal courts.[90]

On first blush, these remarks sound inordinately confrontational, but Publius explains that in the long run the constitution would be far more conducive to effective government and would reduce both the likelihood of confrontations and the frequent need to threaten or use force. He observes that under the Articles it was at times difficult for the national congress to decide when the use of force was appropriate.[91] But under the proposed constitution, he says, states could no longer pretend to want to obey national laws (thereby disarming those who counseled the use of force to obtain compliance) while in fact failing to cooperate. National laws now would operate directly on individual citizens, and so Congress would no longer regularly have to contemplate whether the threat of force or force itself would be necessary to enforce its dictates. It could concentrate on the merits of the legislation because day-to-day enforcement would rest elsewhere: under the proposed constitution, even state judges would be obligated to declare individual or state disobedience "contrary to the supreme law of the land, unconstitutional and void."[92]

Does granting such direct power over individuals cede too much power to this new central government, as claimed by the antifederalists? No, replies Publius, because the people's elected representatives would be passing these laws and they could be held accountable for their decisions.[93] The new federal government would be so much more powerful

89. *Id.*, at 108. Publius adds elsewhere: "[The national government] must, in short, possess all the means, and have a right to resort to all the methods of executing the powers with which it is intrusted, that are possessed and exercised by the governments of the particular states." *Id.*, at no. 16, at 116.

90. *Id.*, at 108–109. *See also Id.*, no. 21, at 138–139.

91. *Id.*, at 112.

92. *Id.*, no. 16, at 117. Publius prefaces his remarks by noting that such judgments would be forthcoming unless "the judges were . . . embarked in a conspiracy with the legislature." *Id.*

93. FEDERALIST, *supra* note 6, at 117 ("the people . . . are . . . the natural guardians of the Con stitution"). In the text, I have simplified Publius' remarks. He notes that attempts to arouse the

than the national congress under the Articles that even very serious disobedience could be handled by the courts. With respect to the most serious disputes, those where not one but many states were involved, Publius' assessment is both realistic and prophetic: "No form of government can always either avoid or control them. It is in vain to hope to guard against events too mighty for human foresight or precaution, and it would be idle to object to a government because it could not perform impossibilities."[94]

LAWS LACKED SUFFICIENT SCOPE. ublius points out that under the Articles the central government simply lacked adequate powers to deal with national problems. Indeed, one of its provisions specifically required "'that each State shall retain every power, jurisdiction, and right, not *expressly*—delegated to the United States in Congress assembled.'"[95] Thus, even if the national government overcame the inherent paralysis already noted above and instead acted energetically as future circumstances demanded, it then could be charged by member states (and rightly so) with acting illegitimately. Publius concluded: "A weak constitution must necessarily terminate in dissolution for want of proper powers, or the usurpation of powers requisite for the public safety."[96]

NO GUARANTEE THAT STATES BE REPUBLICAN. A central government ought to guarantee that each member state maintain a republican form of government. But the Articles did not. Instead, Publius observes, "the liberties of the people" in any particular state could be "trample[d]" while the national government remained legally impotent. Tyranny therefore could take root in one state, adversely affecting or threatening all the states, and under the Articles the national government would remain helpless.

However, Publius points out, some states apparently were apprehensive precisely because under the proposed constitution the power to guarantee republican government was lodged in

people "would not often be made with levity or rashness, because they could seldom be made without danger to the authors, unless in cases of tyrannical exercise of the federal authority." *Id.*

94. *Id.*, at 118. Preceding this conclusion, Publius writes: "And as to those mortal feuds which in certain conjunctures spread a conflagration through a whole nation, or through a very large proportion of it, proceeding either from weighty causes of discontent given by the government or from the contagion of some violent popular paroxysm, they do not fall within any ordinary rules of calculations. When they happen, they commonly amount to revolutions and dismemberments of empire." *Id.*

95. *Id.*, no. 21, at 139 (emphasis added by Publius). I have skipped over some sections here: paper 17 (an attempt to convince his readers that supporters of the proposed constitution did not desire control over local matters); paper 18 (lessons to be learned from the Grecian republics); paper 19 (additional lessons from the Germanic confederations); and paper 20 (more lessons from the Netherlands republics).

96. *Id.*, no. 20, at 136.

the federal government. But Publius counters, "no impediment [is thereby created] to reforming State constitutions by a majority of its people in a legal and peaceable mode." The central government of the union would be prepared to crush only "changes to be effected by violence" in the several states.[97]

POWERLESS TO RAISE ARMIES. During the Revolution, Publius explains, "nothing but the enthusiasm of liberty . . . induced the people to endure" the shameful acts of many states. He recounts how the states had competed for soldiers, offering bounties "until [they] grew to an enormous and insupportable size." State military support also was spotty, and only when British troops clearly threatened self-preservation did states regularly meet their manpower obligations. States distant from the battle fields had consistently dragged their feet. Publius concludes that the military inadequacies that existed under the Articles could never be tolerated again[98]—implying that next time Americans might not be as lucky.

LACK OF A JUDICIAL POWER. The absence of a judicial power, Publius maintains, "crowns the defects" associated with the Articles. "Laws are a dead letter without courts to expound and define their true meaning and operation." Since "uniformity" is so important in such matters "they ought to be submitted, in the last resort, to one SUPREME TRIBUNAL."[99]

CENTRAL GOVERNMENT LACKS AUTHORITY. Again Publius charges that under the Articles the national congress lacked sufficient powers. Only two alternatives existed. If, on the one hand, attempts were made to make the Articles more effective, it was likely that those measures still would fall short, resulting in the collapse of the [at that time existing] Confederation. Hence, Americans again at some future time would have to face the issues that then confronted them, perhaps in much more dire circumstances. On the other hand, if piecemeal attempts to reform the Articles proved temporarily successful, it was likely that the solutions enacted in response to each emergency would result in the national assembly possessing even greater powers, with far fewer restrictions, than were now put before the people in the proposed constitution. Thus, Publius concludes, critics of the proposed constitution may paradoxically "create in reality that very tyranny which the adversaries of the new Constitution

97. *Id.*, at 140. "The natural cure for an ill administration in a popular or representative constitution is a change of men." *Id.* I skip over paper 21, a discussion of the basis upon which states could be taxed equitably.
98. *Id.*, no. 22, at 145.
99. *Id.*, at 150.

either are, or affect to be, solicitous to avert."[100]

Lacks the consent of the whole people. State legislatures, not the people, approved the Articles of Confederation. That fact has raised substantial questions—so much so that "however gross a heresy it may be to maintain that a *party* to a compact has a right to revoke that *compact,* the doctrine itself has had respectable advocates." Thus, in order to solidify the future legitimacy of the government it "ought to rest on THE CONSENT OF THE PEOPLE."[101]

THE FRAMERS' VIEW OF CONSTITUTION MAKING

Publius challenged his antifederalist opponents to address the defects of the Articles of Confederation honestly, because if they did they would come to the realization that any alternate proposal must be at least as comprehensive as the proposed constitution.[102] The central government had to be energetic, stable, republican, and mindful of individual liberty. Without energy, the government could not protect the people either from foreign or domestic threats. Stability was equally essential to secure the people's confidence and to lower their anxiety.[103]

But energy and stability in government were not always compatible. The republican principle (election of accountable representatives) required "that those intrusted with [governmental power] should be kept in dependence on the people by a short duration of their appointments." Yet only longer terms in office assured greater stability. Competing principles such as these confronted delegates at the Philadelphia convention, not to mention the delicate task of marking "the proper line of partition between the authority of the general and that of the state governments."[104] In Philadelphia, both large and small states jockeyed for position, the former lobbying to gain recognition for their "wealth and importance" and the latter proclaiming the necessity for "equality." "Combinations" of smaller and larger states together often struggled against opposing combinations. The differences between such groups were often based on "local position or policy."[105]

What is remarkable, as Publius observes, is not that the proposed constitution lacked perfection but that the delegates overcame so many obstacles. Divergent views, he observes, either were "accommodated" or put aside because of a "deep conviction of the necessity of sacrificing private

100. *Id.,* at 152.
101. *Id.*
102. *Id.,* no. 13, at 97.
103. *Id.,* no. 37, at 226–227 ("among the chief blessings of civil society").
104. *Id.,* at 227.
105. *Id.,* at 229–230.

opinions and partial interests to the public good."[106]

In sum, those at Philadelphia were fully cognizant that they were drafting a constitution: "though it not be perfect in every part, [it] is, upon the whole, a good one; is the best that the present views and circumstances of the country will permit."[107] As we shall see in the next chapter, the framers arranged governmental structures and distributed powers in such a fashion as to assure that Americans could cope with any eventuality. But their work was only a proposal. The American people had to approve it and with ratification of the Constitution of the United States the nation also founded the discipline known today as constitutional law.

106. *Id.*, at 230. Publius adds: "It is impossible for the man of pious reflection not to perceive in it a finger of that Almighty hand which has been so frequently and signally extended to our relief in the critical stages of the revolution." *Id.* A Madison proposal that there be a national veto on state legislation was rejected. *See* Charles Hobson, *The Negative on State Laws: James Madison, the Constitution, and the Crisis of Republican Government* 36 Wm. & Mary Quarterly 215 (1979). But rejection of individual preference was not uncommon. At the convention, Hamilton delivered what was by all accounts a brilliant though ignored speech on a constitutional monarchy. *See* Christopher Collier & James L. Collier, Decision in Philadelphia 76–77 (1986).

107. *Id.*, no. 85 at 523. The Framers apparently were aware of the various balancing of principles required for constitution making. *See* no. 37, at 226 ("Among the difficulties encountered by the convention, a very important one must have lain in combining the requisite stability and energy in government with the inviolable attention due to liberty and to the republican form."); and no. 52, at 326 ("the best that lay within their option").

Describing the tone of the convention, Kendall and Carey write:

> The Federalist . . . is a re-enactment, in miniature, of the miracle of the Philadelphia convention itself—the miracle that produced a document which (a) reflected accurately the deepest convictions of nobody present as to the shape it should have taken, and to which, nevertheless, (b) nearly everybody present . . . was prepared to give his all-out support . . . The Constitution became possible because . . . the delegates were willing to ask themselves not "What do I, personally, think the Constitution ought to be?" but rather "How much of what I think can I insist on with any hope of getting others to go along with me?" and "How much of what we can all get together on is there any hope of getting accepted by the American people?"

Federalist, *supra* note 6, at xii (Introduction). Willmore Kendall and George Carey's essay contained in this edition of *The Federalist Papers (How to Read "The Federalist")*, also may be found in Willmore Kendall, Contra Mundane 403, 409–410 (1971). Onuf concludes that the "*Federalist* . . . appeals for informed consent." Onuf, *supra* note 15, at 366.

CHAPTER TWO

The Framers' Constitutional Design

It has been frequently remarked that it seems to have been reserved to the people of this country, by their conduct and example, to decide the important question, whether societies of men are really capable or not of establishing good government from reflection and choice, or whether they are forever destined to depend for their political constitutions on accident and force.[1]

The delegates at the Philadelphia convention understood that, no matter how painfully achieved or how many times successfully defended, the right to self-government can be lost through a single military defeat. Federalists contended that under the Articles of Confederation the national Congress had failed to defend and secure national borders, and commercial anarchy, if it did not yet exist, was a serious threat. They pointed to several insurrections that had erupted. For these reasons, Publius contended that the Confederation was "a system so radically vicious and unsound" that it could not be repaired by amendment, but instead needed "an entire change in its leading features and character."[2]

GOVERNMENTS MUST POSSESS SUFFICIENT POWER

All legitimate governments (monarchical, aristocratic, or democratic) pursue the common good and, in the interest of all citizens, perform certain essential tasks. Foremost among these tasks is national defense: if a government proves incompetent here, little else matters. Accordingly, Publius specifically raises the issue of how much power ought to be ceded to the proposed central government for purposes of common defense? He pulls no punches:

> These powers ought to exist without limitation, *because it is impossible to foresee or to define the extent and variety of the means which may be necessary to satisfy them.* The circumstances that endanger

1. JAMES MADISON, ALEXANDER HAMILTON, AND JOHN JAY, THE FEDERALIST PAPERS, [hereinafter FEDERALIST], no. 1, at 33.
2. FEDERALIST, *supra* note 1, no. 22, at 152. Antifederalists of course disagreed. *See generally,* WILLIAM B. ALLEN and GORDON LLOYD, THE ESSENTIAL ANTIFEDERALIST 138 (1985) (hereinafter ANTIFEDERALIST).

the safety of nations are infinite, and for this reason no constitutional shackles can wisely be imposed on the power to which the care of it is committed. This power ought to be coextensive with all the possible combinations of such circumstances; and ought to be under the direction of the same councils which are appointed to preside over the common defense.[3]

But the principle is even broader than that task. Publius articulates it: "*The means ought to be proportioned to the end.*"[4] At Philadelphia, that principle had many applications. Which ends, for example, should the national government be assigned in the name of the common good of all Americans? And given those ends, what powers ought to be entrusted to it?[5] Alternatively, which ends should be left in state hands and what powers were crucial to secure them?[6] Finally, considering the preceding questions and given the inability under the Articles of Confederation to so consider them, how could the proposed federal government directly govern individual citizens?[7]

But does not the stated principle also carry with it the considerable danger that the very powers granted to achieve the public good also may be used to oppress the people? Again Publius is frank. That danger must be considered a secondary issue: the powers crucial to advance the public welfare will always have the equal potential of being turned against it.[8]

3. FEDERALIST, *supra* note 1, no. 23, at 153. Publius elsewhere adds:

> With what color of propriety could the force necessary for defense be limited by those who cannot limit the force of offense? If a federal Constitution could chain the ambition or set bounds to the exertions of all other nationals, then indeed might it prudently chain the discretion of its own government and set bounds to the exertions for its own safety.
>
> How could a readiness for war in time of peace be safely prohibited, unless we could prohibit in like manner the preparations and establishments of every hostile nation? The means of security can only be regulated by the means and the danger of attack. They will, in fact, be ever determined by these rules and by no others.

Id. no. 41, at 257 (It should be noted that papers 23 and 41 have different authors). *See also* LEO STRAUSS, NATURAL RIGHT AND HISTORY 160–161 (Publius' position is within the Aristotelian tradition).

4. *Id.*, no. 22, at 153. Publius continues, "The persons from whose agency the attainment of any *end* is expected ought to possess the *means* by which it is to be attained." *Id.*

5. *Id.*, no. 41, at 256. Or, as Publius puts it elsewhere, "whether the power be the necessary means . . . [for] attaining a necessary end." *Id.*, at 255.

6. "Not to confer in each case a degree of power commensurate to the end would be to violate the most obvious rules of prudence and propriety, and improvidently to trust the great interests of the nation to hands which are disabled from managing them with vigor and success." *Id.*, at 155.

7. *Id.*, no. 23, at 154. Always lurking in the background was the question: what changes in governmental structures would the people accept?

8. Publius scolds critics, maintaining that those who oppose the powers granted the federal government "very little considered how far these powers were necessary means of attaining a necessary end." Instead, he charges, they chose "to dwell on the inconveniences which must be unavoidably blended with all political advantages; and on the possible abuses which must be incident to every power or trust of which a beneficial use can be made." He rejects opposition arguments as lacking in "good sense." *Id.*, no. 41, at 255.

Above all else, he explains, citizens are concerned for their safety and that of their loved ones. When their families are threatened, citizens will sanction any measures to relieve that threat, including the government's wielding of powers that were once withheld because of the potential for abuse. Written prohibitions simply will not deter a frightened populace or their elected representatives, and so the fear of abuse must be considered secondary. During periods free from dire exigencies, it is far wiser for constitution makers first to consider "whether such a power be necessary to the public good [and only after granting it then to] . . . guard as effectually as possible against a perversion of the power to the public detriment."[9]

Publius charges that, under the Articles of Confederation, what plagues the national congress is a simultaneous *need for* and *lack of* power. Sooner or later, he says, the Confederation would collapse because either the national congress would be denied the powers it needed or, more probably, that congress will violate the confederation's charter (if something essential had to be done and it technically lacked the power to do it). Thus, however well-intentioned, unrealistic restrictions on governmental powers are doomed to failure. A feeble government is one that will fail to secure citizen safety and with that failure social disorder results. This plants the seeds of tyranny.[10]

THE DIVISION OF POWERS: FEDERAL AND STATE

The assignment of national and local tasks in the Constitution traditionally has been referred to as the division of powers, a matter of deep concern to the Philadelphia convention delegates.[11] At least nine of the thirteen sovereign

9. To quote Publius further:

> It may display the subtlety of the writer; it may open a boundless field for rhetoric and declamation; it may inflame the passions of the unthinking and may confirm the prejudices of the misthinking; but cool and candid people will at once reflect that the purest of human blessings must have a portion of alloy in them; that the choice must always be made, if not of the lesser evil, at least of the GREATER, not the PERFECT, good; and that in every political institution, a power to advance the public happiness involves a discretion which may be misapplied and abused.

Id., no. 41, at 255–256.

10. Publius: "It is in vain to oppose constitutional barriers to the impulse of self-preservation. It is worse than in vain; because it plants in the Constitution itself necessary usurpations of power, every precedent of which is a germ of unnecessary and multiplied repetitions." *Id.*, no. 41, at 257. "Tyranny has perhaps oftener grown out of the assumptions of power called for, on pressing exigencies, by a defective constitution, than out of the full exercise of the largest constitutional authorities." *Id.*, no. 20, at 136–137.

11. *Id.*, no. 14, at 102. Publius certainly contends that the thirteen states would remain independent. FEDERALIST, *supra* note 1, no. 17, at 118. There are many references in the *Papers* to the powers the states would continue to exercise; for example: "The subordinate governments, which can extend their care to all those other objects which can be separately provided for, will retain their due authority and activity." *Id.*, no. 14, at 102. "The variety of more minute interests, which will necessarily fall under the superintendence of the local administrations . . . cannot be particu-

states had to cede powers well beyond those that had been granted to the central government under the Articles of Confederation. Without such ceding, there could be no "more perfect Union."[12] Publius challenges his antifederalist opponents either to explain how any one or more of the powers assigned the federal government are unnecessary or to make their case that all the powers granted the new federal government taken cumulatively are "dangerous to the portion of jurisdiction left in the several States."[13] Which of these powers, he taunts his critics, do they find inconsistent with any of the six tasks entrusted to the federal government; namely: "1. Security against foreign danger; 2. Regulation of the intercourse with foreign nations; 3. Maintenance of harmony and proper intercourse among the States; 4. Certain miscellaneous objects of general utility; 5. Restraint of the States from certain injurious acts; 6. Provisions

larized without involving a detail too tedious and uninteresting to compensate for the instruction it might afford." *Id.*, no. 17, at 119–120. "There is one transcendent advantage belonging to the province of the State governments . . . I mean the ordinary administration of criminal and civil justice. *Id.* at 120. And:

> The powers delegated by the proposed Constitution to the federal government are few and defined. Those which are to remain in the State governments are numerous and indefinite. The former will be exercised principally on external objects, as war, peace, negotiation, and foreign commerce; with which last the power of taxation will, for the most part, be connected. The powers reserved to the several States will extend to all the objects which, in the ordinary course of affairs, concern the lives, liberties, and properties of the people, and the internal order, improvement, and prosperity of the State.

Id., no. 45, at 292–293.

12. U.S. CONST., Preamble. The Preamble specifically provides: "We the People of the United States, in Order to form a more perfect Union, establish Justice, insure domestic Tranquility, provide for the common defence, promote the general Welfare, and secure the Blessings of Liberty to ourselves and our Posterity, do ordain and establish this Constitution for the United States of America." All this, Publius reminds us, "may be considered less as absolutely new than as an expansion of principles which are found in the Articles of Confederation." FEDERALIST, *supra* note 1, no. 40, at 251. Alexander Johnston makes these observations:

> The only method of amendment allowable by the articles of confederation was a unanimous concurrence of the states; but, as the evils of the confederacy became more glaring, the flat impossibility of unanimity among the states became more evident. If such a convention was merely to recommend changes, it must act as a body of private persons, and its recommendations would have no legal or official weight except through the approval of congress. If its recommendations were to be adopted by the ratification of all the states, the convention would plainly do no more than congress had repeatedly and vainly done. If its recommendations were to be adopted by a smaller number than *all* the states, then plainly a real, though peaceable, revolution was to be accomplished, and this was the final result.

ALEXANDER JOHNSTON, *The Convention of 1787,* in CYCLOPEDIA OF POLITICAL SCIENCE, POLITICAL ECONOMY, AND OF THE POLITICAL HISTORY OF THE UNITED STATES, J. J. LALOR, ED., VOL. 1 637 (1883). I am indebted to my colleague Henry Paolucci for bringing this material to my attention. *See infra,* chapter 6, comment accompanying note 186.

13. FEDERALIST, *supra* note 1, no. 41, at 255.

14. *Id.*, at 256.

for giving due efficacy to all these powers."[14] Publius stands firm: every power granted the federal government is a "necessary means of attaining a necessary end."[15]

As to state sovereignty, Publius is never more candid. Again he labels the issue as secondary; in this case because neither the states acting singularly nor confederated under the Articles of Confederation can accomplish the six enumerated tasks.[16] Having admitted as much, his opponents cannot—then—argue that existing state sovereignty should not be diminished. That, says Publius, is putting the cart before the horse.[17]

SEPARATION OF POWERS AND THE TWO FACES OF TYRANNY

With Publius, I have identified one principle and the primary corollary that should guide constitution makers: governments must be afforded sufficient power to accomplish the tasks entrusted to them; and the fear that such powers may be abused must be a secondary consideration. Publius, however, well understood that there is in all governments a tendency toward consolidation of power. "The accumulation of all powers, legislative, executive, and judiciary, in the same hands; whether of one, a few, or many, and whether hereditary, self-appointed, or elective, may justly be pronounced the very definition of tyranny."[18]

Governments not only were likely to be oppressive when making, enforcing, and interpreting the law, were it lodged in a single hand, but such governments most certainly would become "capricious and arbitrary."[19] Publius concedes that when power is more widely distributed, as

15. *Id.,* at 255.

16. *Id.,* no. 45, at 288. It might be incorrectly assumed that this strong nationalistic tone is Hamilton's. It is not. *See* George W. Carey, In Defense of the Constitution 16–31, 75–119 (1989) [hereinafter Defense] (Madison's views on the nature of federalism were not always consistent).

17. Federalist, *supra* note 1, no. 45, at 289.

18. Federalist, *supra* note 1, no. 47, at 301. Although the Constitution guarantees that all states governments be republican (U.S. Const., art. 4, sec 4), there is no explicit separation of powers requirement either for federal or state governments. Adair observes that in monarchies and aristocracies there is "an inveterate and incorrigible tendency to use the apparatus of government to serve the special selfish interests of the one or the few. However, the aristocratic form offered, so it was believed, the best possibility of *wisdom,* in planning public measures, while monarchy promised the necessary *energy, secrecy,* and *dispatch* for executing policy." Douglas Adair, *Experience Must Be Our Only Guide: History, Democratic Theory, and the United States Constitution,* in Ray A. Billington, The Reinterpretation of Early American History 143 (1966).

19. Defense, *supra* note 16, at 57. Carey has convinced me that my earlier discussion of this topic was defective. *See* William Gangi, *Judicial Expansionism: An Evaluation of the Ongoing Debate,* 8 Ohio Northern L. R. 1, 60–62 (1981). *See* George W. Carey, *Separation of Powers and the Madisonian Model: A Reply to Critics,* was originally published in the American Political Science Review (March, 1978).

20. Federalist, *supra* note 1, no. 10, at 80. *See supra,* chapter 2, test accompanying notes 68–79.

in a republic, power is less likely to be concentrated than in a monarchy or aristocracy: republics, however, are prone to a distinct but related defect. When all power is lodged in a single hand, the government oppresses all the governed for the benefit of the rulers; in republics, one faction (the majority) may use the government to suppress another faction (a minority) or the common good.[20] Publius addresses both concerns. Since in some respects dealing with the dangers posed by both governmental tyranny and abusive majority power are at the heart of the Framers' constitutional design, this topic ought to be examined more closely.

Governmental Tyranny

Antifederalists charged that the proposed constitution contained too few precautions against the concentration of power. For authority, these critics cited the respected Montesquieu.[21] Publius categorizes these criticisms as unconvincing and counters that reliance upon Montesquieu is unjustified. Montesquieu, he reports, condemned only the placing of the law-making and law-executing powers in the same hands, or the joining of the legislative and judicial powers. Once that occurred, in Montesquieu's own words, "'the life and liberty of the subject would be exposed to arbitrary control, for *the judge* would then be the *legislator.* [Alternately] . . . were it . . . [joined] to the executive power, the judge might behave with all the violence of an oppressor.'"[22] In both cases, Publius admits, governmental power would be unacceptably concentrated.

But Publius observes that the delegates at Philadelphia carefully considered such issues, certainly more than had any of the states.[23] It is enough, he claims, "that the powers properly belonging to one of the departments ought not to be directly and completely administered by either of the

21. *Id.,* no. 47, at 301. Peter S. Onuf observes that the antifederalists "were troubled by the convention's lack of authority in proposing to abolish the Confederation; they wanted to know whether the Constitution's 'elastic' clauses would sanction a broad interpretation of national powers at the expense of the states and of individual citizens; . . . they wondered why the framers had omitted specific guarantees of individual rights." Peter Onuf, *Forum—Reflections on the Founding: Constitutional Historiography in Bicentennial Perspective,* 46 WM. & MARY QUARTERLY 341, 369 (1989). Some specific antifederalist objections are noted in chapter 1. *See supra,* chapter 1 text and comments accompanying notes 25, 46, 63, and 66. Allen and Lloyd [*See* ANTIFEDERALIST, *supra* note 2], among other things, observe that the antifederalists saw no "need to fundamentally change . . . the Articles of Confederation" and "feared and desired" that no one branch would dominate in the central government and that the Congress would be insufficiently representative. ANTIFEDERALIST, *supra* note 2, at x, xiv.

22. FEDERALIST, *supra* note 1, no. 47, at 302–303.

23. *Id.,* at 304. Publius reports that "there is not a single instance in which the several departments of power have been kept absolutely separate and distinct." His discussion of each state is omitted here. *See id.,* at 304–308.

24. *Id.,* no. 48, at 308. Publius describes the previous paper (no. 47) as having established that the

other departments" and the proposed constitution does that.[24] Additionally, in order that the three types of power remain separated in fact as well as theory, each branch also was given some "constitutional control over the others." Thus, as long as no branch possessed "directly or indirectly, an overruling influence over the others in the administration of their respective powers," Publius concludes that Montesquieu's warning to keep the three distinctive powers in separate branches would have been heeded.[25]

Delegates to the Philadelphia convention understood that separating the powers, while at the same time providing for a competent government, was a complex task. First, the delegates had to decide which tasks should be conferred upon the proposed federal government, which would best be left to the states, and which might be profitably shared by both governments: the division of powers discussed above. Second, delegates had to decide what powers were needed for the federal government to achieve the tasks assigned to it. Third, the delegates had to consider whether each of the powers assigned to the federal government was of a legislative, executive, or judicial character. Only then could the delegates address the "next and most difficult task": how to assure by some practical means that each branch could not jeopardize the exercise of powers granted to another branch.

Having reviewed the work of the convention, Publius raises the issue of how the natural tendency toward the consolidation of power would be thwarted under the proposed constitution. He immediately discards the notion of writing such a prohibition into the constitution itself. Such prohibitions are labeled as mere "parchment barriers"; they may have been useful at one time to hinder monarchs in league with a hereditary legislative branch, and even Americans had sought similar precautions before and immediately following the Revolution because they did not initially conceive of any "danger from legislative usurpation."[26] But since the Revolution, many Americans were more

separation of powers "does not require that the legislative, executive, and judiciary departments should be wholly unconnected with each other." *Id.*, at 308. The purpose of paper 48, he claims, will be "to show that unless these departments be so far connected and blended as to give to each a constitutional control over the others, the degree of separation which the maxim requires . . . can never in practice be duly maintained." *Id.*

25. *Id.*

26. *Id.*, no. 48, at 309. Adair comments:

> A government by the people (so it was thought) always possessed *fidelity* to the common good; it was impossible for a people not to *desire* and to *intend* to promote the general welfare. However, the vices of democracy were that the people, collectively, were not *wise* about the correct measures to serve this great end and that the people could be easily duped by demagogues, who, flattering their good hearts and muddled heads, would worm their way to unlimited power. It was this well-meaning stupidity, the capacity for thoughtless injustice, the fickle instability of the popular will, that led the classical theorists, who the Fa-

wary, witnessing as they had, the tendency of state legislatures to draw "all power into [their] impetuous vortex." Hence, Publius suggests that "the people ought to indulge all their jealousy and exhaust all their precautions" against the prospects of legislative abuses. After all, it is the legislative power that is "at once more extensive, and less susceptible of precise limits," so it can "mask under complicated and indirect measures" the fact that power is consolidating and that executive or judicial independence is being threatened.[27]

In the next two papers (49 and 50) Publius considers and dismisses several possible remedies to reduce the prospects of governmental tyranny. In paper 49, he rejects, for two reasons, Thomas Jefferson's proposal that conventions be called whenever two branches (by a two-thirds vote) believe that constitutional limits have been breached.[28] In paper 50, Publius rejects an alternate proposal that conventions be regularly scheduled.[29]

Publius begins paper 51 by reframing a question that is still actively before us: "To WHAT expedient, then, shall we finally resort, for maintaining in practice the necessary partition of power among the several departments as laid down in the Con-

> thers were familiar with, to designate "pure democracy" as a form doomed to a short existence that tended to eventuate, with a pendulum swing, in the opposite extreme of tyranny and dictatorship.

ADAIR, *supra* note 18, at 142.

27. *Id.*, no. 48, at 310. Publius quotes long passages from Thomas Jefferson's *Notes on the State of Virginia* that support his thesis that the right to elect one's legislators did not diminish the danger posed by the concentration of power; for example, "'One hundred and seventy three despots would surely be as oppressive as one!'" In other quotes, Jefferson claims that the American revolution was not fought in order to create an "'elective despotism,'" but instead to forge a nation where "'the powers of government should be so divided and balanced among several bodies of magistracy as that no one could transcend their legal limits without being effectually checked and restrained by the others!'" Publius shows how Jefferson concluded that while the Articles of Confederation had supposedly lodged the different powers in distinct branches, in fact the "'judiciary and the executive members were left dependent on the legislative for their subsistence in office.'" FEDERALIST, *supra* note 1, no. 48, at 311. Publius also recounts similar experiences in Pennsylvania. *Id.*, at 311–313. From the Virginia and Pennsylvania experiences, Publius concludes that written assurances were inadequate. Paper barriers could not prevent the "tyrannical concentration of all the powers of government in the same hands." *Id.*, at 313.

28. *Id.*, no. 49, at 314–316. Publius observes that such a proposal first fails to address the instance where two departments cooperate in a breach, making it unlikely that a convention would be called; and second, repeated calls for conventions not only would have the net effect of diminishing respect for the proposed constitution (if not inherently defective why would such conventions frequently be necessary?) but also they would raise dangerous public passions. In any event, such conventions would fail to accomplish their intended goal because these conventions would most likely be dominated by forces favoring the legislative branch.

29. *Id.*, no. 50, at 317–319. Publius counters that such conventions were unlikely to provide timely relief and, in support of his contention, he recounts the failure of a similar experiment: the Council of Censors in Pennsylvania.

30. *Id.*, no. 51, at 320.

stitution?" The only viable answer, he says, in a sweeping generalization, lies in "so contriving the interior structure of the government as that its several constituent parts may, by their mutual relations, be the means of keeping each other in their places."[30]

As a practical matter, each branch "should have a will of its own" and, accordingly, be able to select its personnel without interference from another branch.[31] Furthermore, "each department [must be provided with] the necessary constitutional means and personal motives to resist encroachments of the others. Ambition must be made to counteract ambition."[32]

Convention delegates did not deceive themselves. They understood that prudence also required that "auxiliary precautions" be taken.[33] While checks and balances among the three departments were useful, in the final analysis all three branches were not on an equal footing since in "republican government the legislative authority necessarily predominates." Hence, delegates first divided the proposed congress into two distinct parts—House and Senate—and second, "by different modes of election and different principles of action, [rendered them] as little connected with each other as the nature of their common functions and their common dependence on the society will admit."[34]

Delegates still were not satisfied

31. *Id.*, at 321. Publius states this proposition in the text as a general principle, but then modifies it along practical lines. He concludes that since there is but one source of authority, the people, all three branches would have to go back to them for the selection of personnel, but it may not be wise to resort to that authority in the same way in all cases.

> In the constitution of the judiciary department in particular, it might be inexpedient to insist rigorously on the principle: first, because peculiar qualifications being essential in the members, the primary consideration ought to be to select that mode of choice which best secures these qualifications; second, because the permanent tenure by which the appointments are held in that department must soon destroy all sense of dependence on the authority conferring them.

Id., at 321. Publius is preparing the way for a departure from republican principles defended in paper 78.

32. *Id.* Immediately following the words in the text, Publius says:

> The interest of the man must be connected with the constitutional rights of the place. It may be a reflection on human nature that such devices should be necessary to control the abuses of government. But what is government itself but the greatest of all reflections on human nature? If men were angels, no government would be necessary. If angels were to govern men, neither external nor internal controls on government would be necessary. In framing a government which is to be administered by men over men, the great difficulty lies in this: you must first enable the government to control the governed; and in the next place oblige it to control itself.

Id., at 322.

33. *Id.*, at 322.

34. *Id.* Elsewhere, Publius comments:

> It may be suggested that a people spread over an extensive region cannot, like the crowded inhabitants of a small district, be subject to the infection of violent passions or to the danger of combining in pursuit of unjust measures. I am far from denying that this is a

that the precautions taken would thwart the inevitable tendency toward power consolidation, especially with regard to the tendency, in republican governments, for the legislative branch to predominate. Accordingly, they strengthened the executive branch by giving to it a veto power. Finally, Publius explains their creation of a "compound republic": "Hence a double security arises to the rights of the people. The different governments will control each other, at the same time that each will be controlled by itself."[35]

Never, however, from the time Publius began his discussion of governmental tyranny (paper 47), until this point in his analysis, two-thirds of the way into paper 51, is the separation of powers ascribed the purpose many contemporary political scientists and legal scholars confer upon it: "that [it] was intentionally fused into our system to thwart majority rule in one way or another."[36] On the contrary, all of Publius' remarks were directed solely against the danger posed by governmental tyranny: the merging of legislative, executive, and judicial powers. On that score, the delegates clearly favored *structural* remedies such as dividing tasks between the federal government and the states, and, with respect to the powers granted the former, separating them among three distinct branches of government.

I do not for an instant doubt that it was intended that these structural precautions also include an independent judiciary staffed by judges holding office during good behavior. As I will argue shortly, the delegates entrusted to judges not only their ordinary responsibility to interpret the law but also the extraordinary responsibility of enforcing the boundaries of a written constitution. One finds no support for the contention that the delegates believed that the judiciary may set aside unwise, even unethical—though not unconstitutional—exercises of a majority power. We shall shortly see why. Publius considered such laws to be a very different problem from that of the danger of governmental tyranny—a problem to which I now turn. That problem required a very different solution.

Majority Rule and Majority Tyranny

At this juncture in paper 51, Publius shifts his attention from the "first" problem, discussed above, to one he explicitly labels as "second": the

---

distinction of peculiar importance. I have, on the contrary, endeavored in a former paper to show that it is one of the principal recommendations of a confederated republic. At the same time, this advantage ought not to be considered as superseding the use of *auxiliary precautions.* FEDERALIST, *supra* note 1, no. 63, at 385 (emphasis added).

35. *Id.,* no. 51, at 323.

36. DEFENSE, *supra* note 16, at 53. Publius labels the problem of governmental tyranny the *"First"* problem. FEDERALIST, *supra* note 1, no. 51, at 323 (emphasis in original).

37. FEDERALIST, *supra* note 1, no. 51, at 323: "It is of great importance in a republic not only to

prospect that a majority of citizens will use the government to treat minorities unjustly.[37] Publius says there are only two methods to prevent such injustices: the first is to forge "a will in the community independent of the majority—that is, [independent] of the society itself"; the second entails "comprehending in the society so many separate descriptions of citizens as will render an unjust combination of a majority of the whole very improbable, if not impractical."[38]

The first method is unequivocally rejected by Publius. It is, he says, unacceptable in a republic, because removing the right of the legislature—the people—to make final public policy choices *changes the form of government;* from a republican form to one that is not republican. This "independent will" method is more appropriate to "all governments possessing a hereditary or self-appointed authority."[39] Publius concludes that the second method "will be exemplified in the federal republic of the United States."[40] As he elaborates:

> In a free government the security for civil rights must be the same as that for religious rights. It consists in the one case in the multiplicity of interests, and in the other in the multiplicity of sects. The degree of security in both cases will depend on the number of interests and sects; and this may be presumed to depend on the extent of country and number of people comprehended under the same government.[41]

We thus see that the delegates at Philadelphia were fully cognizant of the danger of majority tyranny associated with the republican form of government; and, so cognizant, they did not hesitate in adopting it.[42] They

guard the society against the oppression of its rulers, but to guard one part of the society against the injustice of the other part." Publius also says: "Different interests necessarily exist in different classes of citizens. If a majority be united by a common interest, the rights of the minority will be insecure." *Id.*

38. *Id.,* at 323–324.

39. *Id.,* at 324. Publius describes the nonrepublican approach as "a precarious security," since the "will in the community independent of the majority" might in fact join with the majority or minority. *Id.,* at 323–324. *See* Christopher Wolfe, Judicial Activism: Bulwark of Freedom or Precarious Security (1991) (an evaluation of the pros and cons of contemporary judicial activism).

40. *Id.,* at 324. Publius adds: "Whilst all authority in [the United States] will be derived from and dependent on the society, the society itself will be broken into so many parts, interests and classes of citizens, that the rights of individuals, or of the minority, will be in little danger from interested combinations of the majority." *Id.*

41. *Id.,* at 324.

42. *Id.,* no. 39, at 240–241. Publius claims that "we may define a republic to be, or at least may bestow that name on, a government which derives all its powers directly or indirectly from the great body of the people, and is administered by persons holding their offices during pleasure for a limited period, or during good behavior." *Id.,* at 241.

43. *Id.,* no. 39, at 240. To quote Publius more fully:

had little choice: "No other form [but the republican one] would be reconcilable with the genius of the people of America; with the fundamental principles of the Revolution."[43] Ultimate political power had to be lodged in the hands of the people and their representatives because, as Publius explained "[i]f the plan of the convention . . . is found to depart from the republican character, its advocates must abandon it as no longer defensible."[44]

Convention delegates therefore diligently addressed the defects of the republican form. It is not surprising that Publius rejects as incompatible with their deliberations any institutional check that would set aside the "cool and deliberate sense of the community . . . [from] . . . prevail[ing]."

But is Publius being inconsistent? As noted above, he also had defended an independent judiciary as one of the "auxiliary precaution[s]" necessary to thwart government tyranny.[45] Publius is consistent because the constitutional function of an independent judiciary was a limited function: to assure that the limits on governmental powers constitutionalized by the people would be respected by them, at least until repudiated by amendment.

Delegates unquestionably advocated, defended, and cherished republican rule, but they did not do so blindly. Allegiance to republicanism "does not require an unqualified complaisance to every sudden breeze of passion, or to every transient impulse which the people many receive from the arts of men, who flatter their prejudices to betray their interests."[46] Publius depends upon the multiplicity

> The first question that offers itself is whether the general form . . . be strictly republican. It is evident that no other form would be reconcilable with the genius of the people of America; with the fundamental principles of the Revolution; or with that honorable determination which animates every votary of freedom to rest all our political experiments on the capacity of mankind for self-government.

FEDERALIST, *supra* note 1, no. 39, at 240.

44. *Id.*, no. 39, at 240. In the course of discussing Jefferson's observations on the Virginia state government (see supra text and comment accompanying note 27), Publius observed that "the people are the only legitimate fountain of power, and it is from them that the constitutional charter, under which the several branches of government hold their power, is derived. . . ." *Id.*, no. 49, at 313–314.

45. In paper 39, Publius writes:

> It is true that in controversies relating to the boundary between the two jurisdictions, the tribunal which is ultimately to decide is to be established under the general government. But this does not change the principle of the case. The decision is to be impartially made, according to the rules of the Constitution; and all the usual and most effectual precautions are taken to secure this impartiality. Such tribunal is clearly essential to prevent an appeal to the sword and a dissolution of the compact; and that it ought to be established under the general rather than under the local governments, or, to speak more properly, that it could be safely established under the first alone, is a position not likely to be combated.

FEDERALIST, *supra* note 1, no. 39, at 245–246.

46. *Id.*, no. 71., at 432.

47. U.S. CONST., art. 1, sec. 1. Publius points out that "the essence of the legislative authority is to

of interests to protect minorities from injustice. He understood only too well that, not only would any attempt to prevent injustice by a nonrepublican method eventually fail, but it was tantamount to abandoning the right to self-government won by the Revolution. The structural devices adopted by the delegates (e.g., federalism, separation of powers, checks and balances between and among branches, an independent judiciary, and judicial review) were believed to be prudent and practical means both to reduce the prospects of governmental tyranny and to curtail abusive majorities. Those structures cause delay, and if there is one thing that usually destroys passion, it is delay.

THE THREE BRANCHES OF GOVERNMENT

At the center of the consensus reached at Philadelphia was the belief that whatever powers were granted to the new federal government, they would be distributed among the legislature, the executive, and the judiciary. I will briefly sketch the legislative and executive functions before more thoroughly examining Publius' views on the branch that most concerns the present work: the judiciary.

The Legislature

The Constitution specifies that "[a]ll legislative Powers herein granted shall be vested in a Congress of the United States, which shall consist of a Senate and House of Representatives."[47] Taken together, the powers granted the legislature amount to the responsibility to make national public policy. "The essence of the legislative authority is to enact laws, or, in other words, to prescribe rules for the regulation of the society."[48] The opening sections of article 1 of the Constitution are mostly taken up with mechanics.[49] But if these are set aside, in article 1, section 8, one finds exactly what, in the light of the above discussion, one might expect: the enumeration of those powers thought necessary to achieve the tasks assigned to the federal government.[50]

The Executive

The delegates provided that executive power "shall be vested in a President of the United States of America."[51] Publius observes that "the execution of the laws and the employment of the common strength, either for this purpose or for the common defense, seem to comprise all

enact laws. FEDERALIST, *supra* note 1, at 450.

48. FEDERALIST, *supra* note 1, no. 75, at 450. Elsewhere Publius describes the legislative power as "not only command[ing] the purse but prescrib[ing] the rules by which the duties and rights of every citizen are to be regulated." *Id.*, no. 78, at 465.

49. U.S. CONST., art. 1, secs. 2–7.

50. Please refer to appendix C for the text of the Constitution.

51. U.S. CONST., art. 2, sec. 1.

52. FEDERALIST, *supra* note 1, no. 75, at 450.

the functions of the executive magistrate."[52]

The Constitution specifies that the "President shall be Commander in Chief of the Army and Navy" and that the President "shall take care that the laws be faithfully executed."[53] Publius in turn champions the virtues of an energetic executive. Energy in execution, he says, is crucial to a well functioning government. "A feeble executive is but another phrase for a bad executive and a government ill executed, whatever it may be in theory, must be, in practice, a bad government."[54]

The Judiciary

Turning to the judicial branch, the Philadelphia delegates provided that the "judicial power of the United States, shall be vested in one supreme Court."[55] However that power was to be defined, delegates provided that it would extend to "all Cases in Law and Equity, arising under this Constitution, the Laws of the United States, and Treaties made, or which shall be made." With respect to a short list of instances, the "supreme Court shall have original jurisdiction [while in] all other cases . . . [it] shall have appellate jurisdiction, both as to Law and Fact, with such exceptions, and under such regulations as Congress shall make."[56]

Nowhere in the Constitution is the Supreme Court explicitly granted the power to declare legislative and executive acts void—the power that today we commonly call judicial review.[57] Did the delegates intend to grant such a power to the judiciary, and if so can the purpose and character of such a power be discerned? To pose a further question, would the granting of such a power be consistent both with the principles the delegates applied elsewhere in the Constitution and with its overall design?

Publius addresses each of these questions. Everyone agreed that one of the principal defects of the Articles of Confederation had been the absence of a separate and independent judiciary.[58] Given consensus on that point, Publius maintains that delegates then had to address three practical questions, the most crucial relating to the length of judicial ap-

53. U.S. Const., art. 2, secs. 2, 3.

54. Federalist, *supra* note 1, no. 70, at 423. He adds: "The ingredients which constitute safety in the republican sense are due dependence on the people, and a due responsibility." *Id.,* at 424.

55. U.S. Const., art. 3, sec. 1.

56. *Id.,* secs. 2, 3.

57. Nor does the Constitution specify the number of Supreme Court justices. For thorough discussions of judicial review and related matters, *see generally,* Walter F. Murphy and Herman Pritchett, Courts, Judges, and Politics (1961), Charles S. Hyneman, The Supreme Court on Trial (1963), Raoul Berger, Congress v. The Supreme Court (1969), Henry J. Abraham, The Judiciary: The Supreme Court in the Governmental Process, 11th ed. (1987), and Leonard W. Levy, Original Intent and the Framers' Constitution (1988).

58. Federalist, *supra* note 1, no. 78, at 464. *See supra,* chapter 1, text accompanying note 99.

59. *Id.* The first issue is, "the mode of appointing the judges," which Publius considers as having

pointments.[59] Once delegates resolved the problem of tenure, they could resolve how judicial independence might best be secured and what precautions might be taken to minimize the danger that judicial power might be abused.[60]

The delegates agreed, Publius reports, that the tenure of federal judges ought to be "during good behavior" (that is, that their terms should be for life unless they violated their responsibilities). Such a standard was considered "one of the most valuable . . . modern improvements in the practice of government"—one that should "secure a steady, upright, and important administration of the laws."[61] The delegates thus consciously departed from the republican principle of electoral accountability (in appendix C, readers might contrast the specific terms for members of Congress and the president).[62] But Publius defends that departure on the grounds that judges, unlike legislators or the executive, lack coercive power. The judiciary "may truly be said to have neither FORCE NOR WILL but merely judgment; and must ultimately depend upon the aid of the executive arm even for the efficacy of its judgments." Publius concludes therefore that the judiciary is "beyond comparison the weakest of the three departments of power," specifically quoting Montesquieu's assessment that "'the JUDICIARY is next to nothing.'"[63]

Since the judiciary lacked the power to make or enforce laws, delegates reasoned that it "will always be the least dangerous to the political rights of the Constitution; because it will be least in a capacity to annoy or injure them." Conversely, since judges lacked coercive power the delegates took care to find efficient means "to enable [the judiciary] to defend itself against . . . attacks"; thus, they believed, "the general liberty of the people [would] never be endangered" from the legislative or executive branches.[64]

been already thoroughly discussed, since it "is the same with that of appointing the officers of the Union in general and has been so fully discussed in the two last numbers" (*i.e.*, nos. 76 and 77). The third, "the partition of the judiciary authority between different courts and their relation to each other," he does not discuss until no. 81, and is not at the heart of our inquiry. *Id.*

60. *Id.*, at 464, 465.

61. FEDERALIST, *supra* note 1, at 465. This proposal certainly seems to have been a bold one, given American distrust of monarchical devices. Even more striking is its deviation from the normal inclination to put officials on a short leash; i.e., the requirement that there must be regular elections. As we shall see, Publius makes powerful arguments that the deviation is warranted and is in fact in the common interest.

62. The contrast is even greater when antifederalist sentiment is considered. "Antifederalists noted that under the proposed scheme of representation, the power of recall, frequent elections, and rotation of office were not built into the model." ANTIFEDERALIST, *supra* note 2, at xiii.

63. *Id.*, at 465–466, 466*.

64. *Id.*, at 465–466.

65. *Id.*, at 466.

Publius explains why the creation of a truly independent judiciary was considered by delegates to be in the people's interest and "peculiarly essential in a limited Constitution." He observes:

> By a limited Constitution, I understand one which contains specified exceptions to the legislative authority; such, for instance, as that it shall pass no bills of attainder, no *ex post facto* laws, and the like. Limitations of this kind can be preserved in practice no other way than through the medium of courts of justice, whose duty it must be to declare all acts contrary to the manifest tenor of the Constitution void. Without this, all the reservations of particular rights or privileges would amount to nothing.[65]

Publius brushes aside antifederalist claims that to lodge the power to declare acts contrary to the Constitution void somehow implies "a superiority of the judiciary to the legislative power." To the contrary, all it does is to state the obvious: a Constitution created by an extraordinary act of the people must be considered to be more important than any ordinary statute passed by the people's currently elected representatives. "To deny this would be to affirm that the deputy is greater than his principal; that the servant is above his master; that the representatives of the people are superior to the people themselves; that men acting by virtue of powers may do not only what their powers do not authorize, but what they forbid."[66]

Who, if not the judiciary, would resolve the inevitable questions raised by a limited constitution? Publius asks the question and in answer says that legislators certainly should not determine the extent of their own powers, nor should they be able to bind other branches to their determinations—at least not where the legislative interpretation cannot "be collected from any particular provision in the Constitution." Instead, Publius argues, it is much more appropriate for the courts to serve as "an intermediate body between the people and the legislature in order . . . to keep the latter within the limits assigned to their authority." After all, the "interpretation of the laws is the proper and peculiar province of the courts. A constitution is in fact, and must be regarded by judges as, *a fundamental law* [emphasis added]."[67] Should conflicts arise between the Constitution and legislative acts, the former should be preferred over the latter: "In other words, the Constitution ought to be preferred to the statute, the intention of the people to the intention of their agents."[68]

66. *Id.*, at 467.

67. *Id.*

68. *Id.* When Publius here refers to "the intention of the people," he must be referring to the Constitution's delegates and ratifiers and accordingly he clearly implies that those intentions, should they conflict with ones expressed in ordinary legislation, must be put above "the intention of their

Given Publius' premise that the Constitution is the "fundamental law" and, as such, it must be placed above ordinary legislation repealable by a simple majority vote, Publius contends that the decision of the delegates to place the power to declare contrary acts void in the hands of judges, was logical. Judges deal with analogous issues every time "two contradictory laws . . . clash . . . in whole or part . . . and neither of [those laws] contain . . . any repealing clause or expression." Is it not, Publius asks, "the province of courts to liquidate and fix [the] . . . meaning and operation [of laws]"? In such instances, judges first try to reconcile conflicting laws, but if that proved impossible and one or the other law must be favored, had not judges over the centuries developed different rules to handle different interpretative problems? Publius gives as example that when two laws conflicted, the applicable principle would be that "the last . . . [in] time shall be preferred to the first." While such judicial guidelines are "mere rules[s] of construction" and do not stem from any strict law, Publius claims that they are associated with "the nature and reason" of what judges do. These rules are usually followed because judges have found them to provide a "reasonable" means for resolving "acts of *equal* authority."[69] But when the act of a superior authority conflicts with one by a subordinate authority, delegates therefore expected that "the prior act of a superior ought to be preferred" and "it will be the duty of the judicial tribunals to adhere to the latter and disregard the former."[70]

Antifederalists make another charge: that lodging in judicial hands

---

agents"—the agents being the people's elected representatives. His reference to "the intention of the people" could not have been to the intentions of the current population because such an interpretation would be incompatible with the structures contained in the Constitution. There, by simple majority vote, the current population, without any assistance from the judiciary, could legislate as it saw fit. Similarly, if the Constitution posed some barrier to their will, they could pursue the amendment procedures available to them. In this context, Publius alludes to neither alternative: instead, in his subsequent discussion, he puts forth the proposition that in reviewing legislative acts judges must abide by the "power of the people . . . declared in the Constitution." I will quote the passage in its entirety:

> Nor does this conclusion by any means suppose a superiority of the judicial to the legislative power. It only supposes that the power of the people is superior to both, and that where the will of the legislature, declared in its statutes, stands in opposition of that of the people, declared in the Constitution, the judges ought to be governed by the latter rather than the former. They ought to regulate their decisions by the fundamental laws rather than by those which are not fundamental.

Id., at 467–468.

69. FEDERALIST, *supra* note 1, at 468. "It is a rule not enjoined upon the courts by legislative provision but adopted by themselves, as consonant to truth and propriety, for the direction of their conduct as interpreters of the law." *Id. But see infra* comment accompanying note 79.

70. *Id.*

71. *Id.*, at 468–469.

a power to declare void acts that are contrary to the Constitution would be too dangerous. Judges, they reasoned, could pretend that constitutional infirmities existed; then, with the power granted them, they could declare void whatever legislation they personally disliked.[71] At this juncture, Publius does not deny these possibilities: he simply replies that when the work of the convention is taken in its entirety, the fear is exaggerated.[72] Since every day the people apparently trust judges to interpret ordinary statutes in a principled manner, upon what grounds should the delegates have feared that, when it came to constitutional interpretation, judges would abuse their power? The considerable benefits a truly independent judiciary offered should not be set aside, because if these vague charges "proved anything, [they] would prove that there ought to be no judges distinct from [the legislative] body," a conclusion inconsistent with the acknowledgment that among the Articles of Confederation's major defects was the absence of an independent judiciary.[73]

Publius reminds his readers that while written constitutions seek to secure limits on the exercise of governmental power, those limits are not self-executing. Without an independent judiciary, not only would the prospects of governmental tyranny be increased, it was also unlikely that "the rights of individuals" could practically be secured. In republics, majorities naturally dominate; when elected representatives are faced with a crisis, they are sorely tempted to oppress a "minor party in the community."[74] On the one hand, in republics majorities normally and appropriately define the rights of all citizens; quite rightly, they can "alter [i.e., amend] or abolish the established Constitution," a right Publius describes as "that fundamental principle of republican government." On the other hand, in a republic with a written constitution, even the majority is obliged to honor its provisions. The fact that a majority has the ultimate power to change the constitution does not give them or their elected representatives the right to ignore the meaning it had for those who brought it to life. Nor should members of the judiciary wink at in-

72. Publius: "It can be of no weight to say that the courts, on the pretense of a repugnancy, may substitute their own pleasure to the constitutional intentions of the legislature." FEDERALIST, *supra* note 1, at 469. As we shall see, Publius argues that the delegates took precautions to the degree that they were necessary. This is an opportune place for me again to raise the problem of personality preferences, particularly how thinkers and feelers might evaluate such a situation and the subjective realness of the fear experienced by both.

73. *Id.*, at 469: "The courts must declare the sense of the law; and if they should be disposed to exercise WILL instead of JUDGMENT, the consequence would equally be the substitution of their pleasure to that of the legislative body."

74. *Id.*

75. *Id.*, at 469–470. Publius is being perfectly consistent. If a limited constitution is to endure, it

fractions; rather, as Publius makes clear, "until the people have, by some solemn and authoritative act, annulled or changed the established form, it is binding upon themselves collectively, as well as individually; and no presumption, or even knowledge of their sentiments, can warrant their representatives in a departure from it prior to such an act."[75]

The truly independent judiciary contained in the proposed constitution, could prove to be "an essential safeguard" against "unjust and partial laws" that injure the "private rights of particular classes of citizens [as well as] mitigat[e] . . . the severity and confine . . . the operation of such laws." Publius draws paper 78 to a close with two more points. One, service during good behavior will secure "inflexible and uniform adherence to the rights of the Constitution, and of individuals, which we perceive to be indispensable in the courts of justice." And two, since only a few men are well-suited by training, character, and temperament to perform the judicial function, any alternative design that offered tenure in office less than appointment during good behavior could fail to attract the appropriate caliber of individual, attracting those "less able and less well qualified."[76]

I want now to make five observations regarding the remainder of Publius' discussion of the judiciary—observations that I subsequently will refer back to as the book progresses.

1. He contends that the Convention delegates were not naive in their design. They anticipated, for example, that even explicit constitutional restrictions on the states (e.g., restrictions against the issue of paper money or the taxing of imports) might be violated and some practical means of enforcing such restrictions had to be provided. Publius contends that only two possibilities existed, either the proposed union had to have a "direct negative on State laws" or the "federal courts" had to be capable of overruling any state action "in manifest contravention of the articles of Union."[77]

must be respected by all, including those who would be entrusted with the task of changing it. The capacity of the present generation to amend the Constitution by the procedures provided does not permit them from abandoning those ratified limitations until the change is procedurally enacted. This is a theme I will repeatedly press.

76. *Id.*, at 470.

77. *Id.* At the convention Madison supported a proposal for a federal veto over *state* laws. That veto was rejected and its rejection apparently was linked to the creation of an independent judiciary. On this latter point, Charles Hobson has written:

> That the Supreme Court would be the ultimate line of defense was implicit in the jurisdiction of the federal judiciary as defined in Article III and was made explicit by the twenty-fifth section of the Judiciary Act of 1789, providing for appeals from state tribunals to the Supreme Court. As an additional precaution the framers wrote into the Constitution specific prohibitions and restraints on the states, including an absolute ban on coinage and paper money. Together, the supremacy clause, the judiciary article, and the restrictions on

2. On several occasions Publius specifically refers to the power of Congress to "make . . . exceptions" and "to prescribe . . . regulations." These powers, he observes, should "obviate or remove" whatever "inconveniences" might occur from having granted appellate jurisdiction to the federal courts.[78]
3. In paper 81 Publius elaborates on the position he took in paper 78; namely, that empowering the judiciary to declare void acts contrary to the proposed constitution does *not* make the judiciary superior to the legislature. He reports that antifederalists also claimed that federal judges could construe "the laws according to the *spirit* of the Constitution," since not being elected that document would make them answerable to no one. Judges therefore could "mould [a law] into whatever shape it may think proper; especially as its decisions will not be in any manner subject to the revision or correction of the legislative body." In sum, Publius observes, antifederalists charged that the judicial power created by

---

the states constituted the judicial substitute for the legislative negative on state laws. Charles Hobson, *The Negative on State Laws: James Madison, the Constitution, and the Crisis of Republican Government,* 36 WM. & MARY QUARTERLY 215, 228–229 (1979) [hereinafter Hobson]. Hobson describes Madison as being "disappointed with the Convention's final draft." Hobson at 216. In their introduction to *The Federalist Papers,* Kendall and Carey observe: "The Constitution was made possible . . . first and foremost because in the course of its proceedings the individual delegates became increasingly willing to 'write off' their own pet ideas, to subordinate their personal preferences, to the overriding necessity of arriving at a *consensus.*" FEDERALIST, *supra* note 1, at xii.

78. *Id.,* at 480–481. Publius is referring to the constitutional language in art. 3, sec. 2.2, which provides for appellate jurisdiction "with such Exceptions, and under such Regulations as the Congress shall make." FEDERALIST, *supra* note 1, no. 80, at 481. In paper 81, Publius specifically quotes the applicable constitutional text, observing that "the Supreme Court would have nothing more than appellate jurisdiction 'with such exceptions and under such *regulations* as the Congress shall make.'" FEDERALIST, *supra* note 1, no. 81, at 488. Several pages later he repeats the point, claiming that it is only proper that a power first be couched in broad terms and then provide "that this jurisdiction shall be subject to such *exceptions* and regulations as the national legislature may prescribe." *Id.,* at 490. The purpose for doing so is also clearly described: "This will enable the government to modify [jurisdiction] in such a manner as will best answer the ends of public justice and security." *Id.,* at 490. His complete statement reads: "To avoid all inconveniences, it will be safest to declare generally that the Supreme Court shall possess appellate jurisdiction both as to law and fact, and that this jurisdiction shall be subject to such exceptions and regulations as the national legislature may prescribe." *Id.* Two paragraphs later, for the fourth time Publius refers to the power to regulate and make exceptions to the appellate jurisdiction. The context of these remarks leaves little doubt that it was Publius' belief that, given the impressive precautions taken against the possible abuse of judicial power, the nation had much more to gain than to fear from the creation of a truly independent judiciary: "that an ordinary degree of prudence and integrity in the national councils will insure us solid advantages from the establishment of the proposed judiciary without exposing us to any of the inconveniences which have been predicted from that source." *Id.,* no. 81, at 491.

79. FEDERALIST, *supra* note 1, no. 81, at 482. Allen and Lloyd provide the following from a promi-

convention delegates was "'as unprecedented as it is dangerous.'"[79]

Publius, dismisses these antifederalist objections on the grounds that "[t]here is not a syllable in the plan under consideration which *directly* empowers the national courts to construe the laws according to the spirit of the Constitution." He says that his proposition about the power to declare legislative acts void, however, was consistent with "the general theory of a limited constitution."[80] "It may," he says,

> in the last place be observed that the supposed danger of judicial encroachments . . . is in reality a phantom. Particular misconstructions and contraventions of the will of the legislature may now and then happen; but they can never be so extensive as to amount to an inconvenience, *or in any sensible degree to affect the order of the political system.* This may be inferred with certainty from the general nature of the judicial power, from the objects to which it relates, from the manner in which it exercised, from its comparative weakness, and from its total incapacity to support its usurpations by force.[81]

4. Publius carefully points out that an "important check" against the possibility of judicial abuse is the fact that judges may be impeached. The political procedures contained in the proposed constitution should give judges pause: the House would indict and the Senate would try potential usurpers. "This is alone a security. There never can be danger that the judges, by a series of deliberate usurpations on the authority of the legislature, would hazard the united resentment of the body intrusted with it, while this body was possessed of the means of

nent antifederalist, who wrote under the name Agrippa:

> "I appeal to the knowledge of everyone, if it does not frequently happen, that a law is interpreted in practice very differently from the *intention* of the legislature. Hence arises the necessity of acts to amend and explain former acts. This is not an inconvenience in the common and ordinary business of legislation, but is a great one in a constitution. A Constitution is a legislative act of the whole people. It is an excellence that it should be permanent, otherwise we are exposed to perpetual insecurity from the fluctuation of government."

ANTIFEDERALIST, *supra* note 2, at 45 (emphasis added). Agrippa's words imply that even antifederalists viewed a written constitution as being superior to ordinary legislation; and that, with respect to both, they considered judges to be bound by the lawgivers' will.

80. FEDERALIST, *supra* note 1, at 482. Publius contends that the proposed solution, a completely independent judiciary, is preferable to the British model. In fact, since more of the American states use a model similar to the one proposed at Philadelphia, the proposed constitution is in this respect not "as novel and unprecedented" as its critics suggest. *Id.,* at 483. Publius goes on to give his reasons for reaching these conclusions. See *id.,* at 483–484. It should be kept in mind that Publius' analysis in all the papers is made in the absence of a Bill of Rights, a situation which would have added to the number of prohibitions to be monitored by the judiciary.

81. *Id.,* at 484–485. Emphasis added.

82. *Id.,* at 485.

punishing their presumption by degrading them from their stations."[82]

5. In paper 83 Publius clearly demonstrates the awareness of the delegates that interpretative rules were considered to be an essential part of the judicial craft; and that those rules would both increase the consistency of law application and reduce the discretion of individual judges.[83] In referring to such rules[84] he uses words such as a "rule of interpretation," "rules of legal interpretation,"[85] and "rules."[86] At other times he uses "rules of construction"[87] and "*legal maxims.*"[88] The most complete description he offers is that "rules of legal interpretation are rules of *common sense,* adopted by the courts in the construction of the laws."[89] Clearly, the delegates understood both that rules of interpretation were an integral part of the judicial craft and that these rules could be manipulated and used inappropriately.[90]

83. *See id.,* no. 83. In paper 82 Publius discusses the relationship between the newly created federal judiciary and that of the state judiciaries, a subject not immediately pertinent to the inquiry in this book. Of interest, however, is this statement: "I shall lay it down as a rule that the State courts will *retain* the jurisdiction they now have, unless it appears to be taken away in one of the enumerated modes." *Id.,* no. 82, at 492.

84. In paper 83 (see below) Publius recognizes that such rules can be abused, but he says that is no reason to deny their usefulness. As noted in the text, he states that "certain *legal maxims* . . . [could be] perverted from their true meaning." *Id.,* no. 83, at 496. Furthermore, as will be discussed shortly, Publius is consistent on this throughout his discussions, arguing that the potential for abuse is not in itself an adequate reason to deny a needed power. Peter S. Onuf observes that the "Federalists . . . emphasized the document's similarity to the state constitutions, promising that traditional canons of construction would be applied to its provisions." Onuf, *supra* note 21, at 369.

85. FEDERALIST, *supra* note 1, no. 32, at 201; and FEDERALIST, *supra* note 1, no. 83, at 496. In an article, Allen specifically discusses paper 83 to demonstrate [her contention] that the framers' understanding of the "plain meaning rule" was more sophisticated than had been characterized by other scholars. Anita L. Allen, *The Federalist's Plain Meaning: Reply to Tushnet,* 61 S. C. L. REV. 1701, 1712–1713 (1988).

86. *Id.,* no. 41, at 263.

87. *Id.,* no. 40, at 248; no. 78, at 468.

88. *Id.,* no. 83, at 496.

89. *Id.* Throughout the *Papers,* Publius provides examples of such rules: (1) "NEGATIVE PREGNANT," *Id.,* no. 32, at 200; (2) "every expression ought, if possible, to be allowed some meaning," *Id.,* no. 40, at 248; (3) "where the several parts cannot be made to coincide, the less important should give way to the more important part," *Id. See also* no. 41, at 263, no. 83, at 497; (4) "the last in order of time shall be preferred to the first," *Id.,* no. 78, at 468, no. 83; (5) "'A specification of particulars is an exclusion of generals,'" *Id.,* no. 83, at 496. *See also* no. 41, at 263.

90. In paper 83 Publius denies that the proposed constitution abolished or could be interpreted to abolish state jury trial in civil cases. Paper 83, at 496. "The dispute did not exist according to [Publius] because . . . the text was perfectly clear when read in accordance with the rigors of common sense, logic, and traditional maxims of legal construction, correctly applied," Allen, *supra* note 84, at 1712. In paper 83, while Publius admitted that interpretative rules sometimes had "a precise technical sense," he maintained that these critics had gone out of their way to misconstrue a rule's application. Applied to a constitution "the natural and obvious sense of its provisions,

To sum up this section on the judicial branch, the convention created an independent judiciary and empowered it to declare void acts contrary to the Constitution. The context of that decision consists of the clauses that provide for judicial tenure during good behavior and a guarantee that judicial salaries could not be decreased.[91]

Publius defends the work of the convention on several grounds. There is nothing to fear from an independent judiciary because it lacks any real or coercive power; it commands no army; it has no money: it is a passive institution. Issues come before the judiciary through the ordinary processes of law—in cases. Thus, judicial decisions are only as effective as they are reasonable; and those decisions are still dependent on the executive for enforcement. Because of the nature of the power of interpretation, Publius maintains, this power can safely be lodged in judicial hands. The interpretative power is different from physical coercive power. If judges themselves possessed the physical power to coerce, how would the interpretive power entrusted to them differ from that assigned to the legislature and executive branches? Coercive power itself lodged in judicial hands would only evoke a coercive response—civil war being the most natural result. But judicial decisions based on reason obligate all parties (i.e., legislators, executives, and citizens) to defend the Constitution.

Not only will judicial independence enable judges to perform the ordinary task of interpreting the law (i.e., to fix its meaning) without fear of legislative or executive retribution;

---

apart from any technical rules is the true criterion of construction." In demonstration he points out that Congress was granted only specific powers. Publius comments: "This specification of particulars evidently excludes all pretension to a general legislative authority, because an affirmative grant of special powers would be absurd as well as useless if a general authority was intended." Paper 83, at 497. *See also* Charles F. Lofgren, *The Original Understanding of Original Intent,* 5 Constitutional Commentary 77, 89 (1988) (Publius contended that acquired expertise in the law should not be used to undermine common sense interpretation). Lofgren maintains that "a key question in interpreting the Constitution [for Publius] becomes whether common sense and reason would direct attention to ratifier intent in order to determine the 'will . . . of the people declared in the Constitution.'" *Id.,* at 89. I concur. Publius then draws a parallel, pointing out that the proposed constitution similarly declares that only in certain types of cases would the federal judiciary have jurisdiction. He observes: "The expression of those cases marks the precise limits beyond which the federal courts cannot extend their jurisdiction, because the objects of their cognizance being enumerated, the specification would be nugatory if it did not exclude all ideas of more extensive authority." Paper 83, at 497. Publius concludes by saying that critics had applied the wrong rule or applied a sound rule inappropriately: the proposed constitution did not preclude jury trials in civil cases and it cannot be fairly interpreted to do so.

91. *See supra,* text and comments accompanying notes 91–92. See also U.S. Const., art. 3, sec. 1 (providing that the compensation of judges shall not be diminished during their continuation in office).

92. *See supra,* text accompanying note 39.

it will also make it safe for judges to be entrusted with an extraordinary application of the interpretative task: the power to declare void laws contrary to the Constitution. In a limited government, that power must exist somewhere; what better place than with the judiciary? They already possess familiarity with the interpretive task and the Constitution has been structured to permit them to withstand executive or legislative retribution.

Publius is staunch in his defense of an adequately empowered independent judiciary, but his remarks cannot be fairly construed as sanctioning the exercise by the judiciary of either legislative or executive powers—powers that have a nature different from the judiciary's. In the Constitution, the delegates specifically assigned the legislative and executive powers to other departments. By describing the ordinary judicial function and by his other observations, Publius leaves little doubt that the judicial role he defends is a limited one. He explicitly rejects an institutional check on the legitimate exercise of legislative power.[92]

The convention thus applied to the responsibilities of the judicial branch the same principles they had applied to the legislative and executive branches.[93] Publius had contended that when a written constitution purports to establish a government with limited powers there must be some means to keep the most likely violators of its provisions, the legislative and executive branches, within the declared limits. Delegates believed the judiciary was particularly well-suited to the task since judges interpret the law all the time; and declaring acts to be unconstitutional is akin to that task. Traditional rules of construction also would help to reduce arbitrariness.[94]

Publius rejects all contentions that possible abuses of judicial power (e.g., that judges would substitute their personal views for those of the legislature; that they would be guided by the spirit of the laws;[95] or that they would inappropriately use rules of construc-

93. *See supra,* text accompanying notes 4–9. The most important of these principles bear repeating: "Not to confer in each case a degree of power commensurate to the end would be to violate the most obvious rules of prudence and propriety." FEDERALIST, *supra* note 1, no. 23, at 153.

94. Publius apparently viewed judicial review as a veto power akin to that granted to the executive. U.S. CONST., art. 1, sec. 7.2. *Cf.* FEDERALIST, *supra* note 1, no. 73 (executive veto). Several distinctions are made: the president is authorized to veto any legislation he considers either unconstitutional or unwise ["to increase the chances in favor of the community against the passing of bad laws, through haste, inadvertence, or design"] (FEDERALIST, *supra* note 1, no. 73, at 443), but judges were not similarly authorized. As noted earlier, Publius states that the judiciary should declare an act of the legislature void only if it exceeded its powers and the abuse was "manifest." Judges, he says, are not entitled to "substitute their own pleasure to the constitutional intentions of the legislature." [*Id.*, no. 78 at 468–469]. On the contrary, as long as the legislature does not clearly overstep its powers, the judiciary has no cause to intervene. That is the only possible interpretation of Publius' remarks. I contend that the delegates specifically denied the judiciary a general revisionary power, and the special power granted—the judicial power—is neither a general power to

tion) offer sufficient cause to deny an admittedly necessary power: to keep the branches of government within the ratified bounds.[96] Any power employed for the public good also holds the potential for abuse—that is the nature of power. He drives that point home in a sentence stating that if the mere possibility of abusing granted power constitutes an adequate cause for denying a needed power, then "there ought to be no judges distinct from [the legislature]."[97] In short, the same fears could be raised against all judges and the very power of interpretation itself.

Publius discusses the theoretical and practical controls that may be directed at possible judicial abuses, and on several occasions he specifically alludes to the congressional power to control and regulate the appellate jurisdiction of the federal courts. Thus, judicial review is defended by Publius as a republican cure for a republican disease.

THE BILL OF RIGHTS

The *Federalist Papers* are nearly at an end and not once has Publius systematically addressed antifederalist demands for a bill of rights—a failure of the convention that some contemporary historians label a "grievous and obvious . . . error."[98] Antifederalists had suggested that another con-

legislate nor does it extend to matters of wisdom or morals. The only authority to which the justices legitimately may appeal to supersede that of the legislature is the people; not, as already noted, the *current* population, who may themselves at any time employ article 5, but rather in the sense of the intentions of those who ratified the Constitution. *See supra* comment accompanying note 68.

The judicial veto, like the executive veto, also may be overturned by the legislature. But the two vetoes address different purposes, and legislative revision must be consistent both with the different functions served by each branch and the need to maintain independent executive and judicial departments. Publius concedes that there is nothing in the proposed constitution that prohibits "revisal of a judicial sentence by a legislative act," but the revision of cases already decided by the judiciary would, he says, be highly irregular. Publius concludes: "The impropriety of the thing, on the general principles of law and reason, is the sole obstacle." FEDERALIST, *supra* note 1, no. 81, at 484. Publius explicitly states that the Constitution provides a cure wherever particular judicial decisions are distasteful. Should they cause "some partial inconveniences . . . it ought to be recollected that the national legislature will have ample authority to make such exceptions and to prescribe such regulations as will be calculated to obviate or remove those inconveniences." *Id.*, no. 80, at 481. Publius goes on explicitly to affirm what had earlier been merely deduced: "The possibility of particular mischiefs can never be viewed, by a well-informed mind, as a solid objection to the general principle which is calculated to avoid general mischiefs and to obtain general advantages." *Id.*, no. 80, at 481.

95. *See supra* text accompanying note 63.

96. Publius is being consistent. If a limited constitution is to endure, it must be respected even by those *authorized* to change it. The capacity of the present generation to change a constitution does not warrant it (or its elected representatives) from abandoning the ratified limitations. That principle states a fairly conventional view. As we shall see, it is only when that principle is applied equally to the judiciary that a controversy ensues.

97. *See supra* text accompanying notes 72–73.

98. CHRISTOPHER COLLIER AND JAMES L. COLLIER, DECISION IN PHILADELPHIA: THE CONSTITUTIONAL CONVENTION OF 1787, 333 (1986) [hereinafter cited DECISION].

99. *Cf.* DECISION, *supra* note 98, at 332–350; REX E. LEE, A LAWYER LOOKS AT THE CONSTITU-

vention be held to draft a bill of rights prior to any attempt to ratify the constitution proposed at Philadelphia or, alternatively, for states to ratify the proposed constitution only conditionally until a bill of rights was added. Both suggestions were opposed by federalists and ratification was not forestalled.[99] The Constitution was fully functional for several years before a bill of rights was added.

To what should we attribute the cavalier treatment of antifederalist demands? To the rush of events? Or to the desire of federalists to avoid the matter? At least some federalists promised during the ratification debates that if the constitution was approved they subsequently would support the addition of a bill of rights (as they in fact did).[100] But such explanations seldom recount that a proposal specifically calling for a bill of rights was *specifically and unanimously* defeated during the Philadelphia convention,[101] the delegates concluding that a bill of rights was "not merely unnecessary but unwarranted."[102] Curiously, the delegates reached that conclusion despite the fact that many of them "had helped to write their own states' bills of rights, and nearly all had taken part in the ongoing debate over the nature of human rights and government."[103]

Publius on Bills of Rights

Publius explains the federalists' refusal to add a bill of rights, although his defense, in paper 84, is rarely if ever discussed in contemporary literature. He begins by pointing out that despite the clamoring of antifederalists in New York for a national bill of rights, not only did their own state lack one but the proposed federal constitution contained more important

TION 17–25 (1981) [hereinafter LEE] *with* WILLMORE KENDALL AND GEORGE CAREY, THE BASIC SYMBOLS OF THE AMERICAN POLITICAL TRADITION 119–136 (1971) [hereinafter BASIC] and James H. Hutson, *The Drafting of the Bill of Rights: Madison's "Nauseous Project" Reexamined, III BENCHMARK* 309–320 (1987). Kendall claims that "the anti-bill-of-rights men won the [First Congress] elections hands down, and . . . completely dominated the First Congress." WILLMORE KENDALL, *supra* note CONTRA MUNDUM 307 (1971) [hereinafter CONTRA] 77, at 307.

100. *Id.,* at 303–325 (a still provocative examination of these contentions).

101. LEE, *supra* note 99, at 18. Collier and Collier add:

> Not surprisingly, it was Elbridge Gerry who supplied the motion Mason wanted [*i.e.,* to add a bill of rights]. Mason seconded it. Only Sherman spoke. He said, "The state Declarations of Rights are not repealed by this Constitution; and being in force are sufficient." The national legislature could not impinge on the rights of the people because its powers were limited to those enumerated. Mason protested that the new government would be paramount to the state constitutions and could override state bills of rights. Nobody agreed. On the vote, the state delegations voted unanimously against a bill of rights. Neither Gerry nor Mason could carry with them the delegates from their own states.

DECISION, *supra* note 98, at 338–339.

102. DECISION, *supra* note 98, at 332.

103. LEE, *supra* note 99, at 18.

104. FEDERALIST, *supra* note 1, no. 84, at 510–511. Publius characterizes such rights "perhaps

rights than did the New York constitution (e.g., habeas corpus, prohibitions of ex post facto laws, or the granting of titles of nobility).[104] Furthermore, the federal rights would not be mere "parchment" (i.e., existing only on paper without an adequate means of securing them), as so often was the case, according to Publius, with respect to state bills of rights. The proposed constitution would create a powerful national government fully capable of enforcing its provisions.[105]

Publius points out that bills of rights traditionally were agreements between kings and an aristocracy and such restrictions "have no application to constitutions, professedly founded upon the power of the people and executed by their immediate representatives. Under the constitutional proposal, the people surrender nothing; and as they retain everything they have no need of particular reservations."[106] After quoting a portion of the proposed preamble,[107] he puts forth this conclusion: "Here is a better recognition of popular rights than volumes of those aphorisms which make the principal figure in several of our State bills of rights and which sound much better in a treatise of ethics than in a constitution of government."[108]

greater securities to liberty and republicanism than any [that the New York constitution] contains."

105. *Id.,* at 511–515. With respect to parchment barriers, Kendall observes that "the Virginia Declaration of Rights [was] not regarded as part of the constitution of that State but rather as . . . a statement of ideals that the citizens are understood to entertain in common but know not to be immediately applicable." CONTRA, *supra* note 77, at 313. Consistent with that position, Publius makes several disparaging remarks about parchment barriers: *e.g.,* no. 25, at 67 ("unequal parchment provisions"); no. 48, at 308 ("parchment barriers"); no. 73, at 443 ("mere parchment delineation"). *See supra,* text accompanying note 26. Elsewhere [paper 24, at 159*] Publius' remarks hint that at least some state bills of rights provisions contained language specifying only that something "OUGHT NOT" be done, and he describes such an approach as "in truth, rather a CAUTION than a PROHIBITION." At the same place he observes that in other states prohibitions were qualified by this provision: "WITHOUT THE CONSENT OF THE LEGISLATURE." Paper 24, at 159*. He then states: "New York has no bill of her rights, and her constitution says not a word about the matter. No bills of rights appear annexed to the constitutions of the other States, except the foregoing, and their constitutions are equally silent. I am told, however, that one or two States have bills of rights which do not appear in this collection; but that those also recognize the right of the legislative authority in this respect" [Publius here is referring to state bills of rights that prohibited standing armies in time of peace. He finds only two states with such a precaution; in others he found silence or "the right of the legislature to authorize their existence"]. Paper 24, at 159, 159*. *See also* BASIC, *supra* note 99, at 61–74.

106. *Id.,* at 513. Kendall observes that "it was the Federalist not the Anti-Federalist who used the 'democratic' argument, the put-your-confidence-in-the-people argument, in the controversies over a bill of rights." CONTRA, *supra* note 77, at 310.

107. FEDERALIST, *supra* note 1, no. 84, at 513. Publius' exact words are: "'WE, THE PEOPLE of the United States, to secure the blessings of liberty to ourselves and our posterity, do *ordain* and *establish* this Constitution for the United States of America.'" *Id.* I assume that Publius gives this shortened version of the proposed constitution's preamble due to either reliance on an earlier draft, poetic license, or less rigid rules regarding quotations.

108. *Id.,* at 513.

109. *Id.,* at 513 (emphasis added).

Still not satisfied, Publius presses a point that evidently gave pause to representatives to the first Congress: "A minute detail of particular rights is certainly far less applicable to a Constitution like that under consideration, which is merely intended to regulate the *general political interests of the nation,* than to a constitution which has the regulation of *every species of personal and private concerns.*"[109] Such a statement of rights should instead be added to state constitutions where they could have an immediate impact on the daily lives of their citizens.[110]

Taking the offensive, Publius characterizes antifederalist demands for bills of rights as "not only unnecessary in the proposed Constitution but . . . dangerous. They would contain various exceptions to powers which are not granted [and as such] would afford a colorable pretext to claim more than were granted. For why declare that things shall not be done [for] which there is no power to do?"[111] He takes as an example the proposals to guarantee the liberty of the press.[112] What is to be gained by providing that "the liberty of press shall not be restrained, when no power is given by which restrictions may be imposed?"[113]

110. *Id.*

111. *Id.* Publius contends that once a bill of rights was added, those so inclined might use its provisions to claim that, by its addition, the powers granted the federal government had been increased. In his words:

> I will not contend that such a provision would confer a regulating power; but it is evident that it would furnish, to men disposed to usurp, a plausible pretense for claiming that power. They might urge with a semblance of reason that the Constitution ought not to be charged with the absurdity of providing against the abuse of an authority which was not given, and that the provision [for example] against restraining the liberty of the press afforded a clear implication that a power to prescribe proper regulations concerning it was intended to be vested in the national government. This may serve as a specimen of the numerous handles which would be given to the doctrine of constructive powers by the indulgence of an injudicious zeal for bills of rights.

Id. at 514.

112. In discussing "liberty of the press," Publius mentions that this freedom was not protected under the New York constitution. Those who urged adding a bill of rights in the proposed constitution often looked to the New York constitution as a model. He remarks rather acidly, whatever "has been said about [freedom of the press] . . . in . . . any State [constitution] amounts to nothing." Federalist, *supra* note 1, no. 84, at 514. Freedom of the press could not be defined without "leav[ing] the utmost latitude for evasion." *Id.* Instead, he suggests protection of that right "must altogether depend on public opinion and on that general spirit of the people and of the government." *Id. See also* Contra, *supra* note 77, at 320–325 and Hudson, *supra* note 99, at 316–320.

113. Federalist, *supra* note 1, no. 84, at 513–514. I am not familiar with all the suggestions that may have been made by antifederalists for inclusion in a bill of rights. Some opponents of the constitution obviously suggested that a provision be added that prohibited standing armies. It evidently was an important matter since it took four papers (24 to 28) for Publius to explain his rejection. As noted, Publius replied: leave such decisions to the people by empowering the legislature. Publius' treatment of so sensitive a subject sets the tone for his position that a bill of rights was unnecessary.

The matter is more complex than commonly assumed. Different suggestions were made by dif-

Publius concludes his remarks in paper 84 with the contention "that the Constitution is itself, in every rational sense, and to every useful purpose, A BILL OF RIGHTS." He explains:

> And the proposed Constitution, if adopted, will be the bill of rights of the Union. Is it one object of a bill of rights to declare and specify the political privileges of the citizens in the structure and administration of the government? This is done in the most ample and precise manner in the plan of the convention; comprehending various precautions for the public security which are not to be found in any of the State constitutions. Is another object of a bill of rights to define certain immunities and modes of proceeding, which are relative to personal and private concerns? This we have seen also have been attended to in a variety of cases in the same plan. Adverting therefore to the substantial meaning of a bill of rights, it is absurd to allege that it is not to be found in the work of the convention. It may be said that it does not go far enough though it will not be easy to make this appear; but it can with no propriety be contended that there is no such thing.[114]

Relationship to the Constitution

Why then shortly after ratification of the Constitution did the First Congress propose a bill of rights?[115] Was Publius' defense of the convention's action subsequently repudiated? I do not think so. Since several future

---

ferent parties, and even antifederalist forces were far from unified over the need for a bill of rights. Publius observes, that some opponents did "not object to the government over individuals, or to the extent proposed, but to the want of a bill of rights." Others, however, apparently concurred "in the absolute necessity of a bill of rights, but contend . . . that it ought to be declaratory, not of the personal rights of individuals, but of the rights reserved to the States in their political capacity." Still others were of the "opinion that a bill of rights of any sort would be superfluous and misplaced, and that the plan would be unexceptionable, but for the fatal power of regulating the times and places of election." FEDERALIST, *supra* note 1, No. 38, at 235. Madison eventually distilled the Bill of Rights as we know it from some two hundred suggestions. See DECISION, *supra* note 98, at 332–350; LEE, *supra* note 99, at 25, and CONTRA, *supra* note 77, at 305, 319–320.

114. FEDERALIST, *supra* note 1, no. 84, at 515. It is beyond the scope of this book to examine issues such as the importance of the omission of a bill of rights, or the federalist promises to add a bill of rights once the proposed constitution was ratified. *See* LEE, *supra* note 99, at 18–22. Hutson hints that support for a bill of rights was significant (*see* Hutson, *supra* note 99, at 319), while in *Contra Mundum* Kendall flat-out maintains that such support enjoyed minority support. *See* CONTRA, *supra* note 77, at 307.

115. Hutson comments: "So abrupt a change on so fundamental a matter is incredible and suggests that the account of rights in revolutionary America, as we now have it, is seriously flawed." Hutson, *supra* note 99, at 319. He suggests that promises made during the ratification debates were significant. *See* Hutson, *supra* note 99, at 319. Kendall suggests that any concessions were offered only to increase the margin of victory (*See* CONTRA, *supra* note 77, at 307), and federalists elected to the First Congress hardly made consideration of a bill of rights their first priority. See LEE, *supra* note 99, at 24 ("took up every matter of business other than a bill of rights") and BASIC, *supra* note 99, at 128 ("a Bill of Rights . . . was far from being the first concern of those who first met under the authority of the Constitution"). *See also* CONTRA, *supra* note 77, at 308.

116. LEE, *supra* note 99, at 20. Kendall has this assessment:

discussions in this book hinge on a proper understanding of this matter, it is best that the subject be broached now. I want to address the change of heart that to some might initially appear to be a desire to modify the Constitution.

The key to understanding this change is to recognize that many federalists "did not necessarily oppose some of the ideas behind a bill of rights, if that is what people wanted; rather, they objected to the timing."[116] Once antifederalist pleas for the addition of a bill of rights, or for another convention to draft one, failed to delay ratification, both the stakes and the issues changed. Proponents of a bill of rights now faced *unorganized and disunited* opposition. Even some federalists had promised to support a bill of rights once a constitution was ratified,[117] believing, as one scholar describes it, that such an addition was good "public relations."[118]

Federalists and antifederalists agreed about some rights, particularly those rooted in English and American common law.[119] Convention delegates apparently opposed bills of rights proposals mostly as a matter of strategy. Only two significant arguments raised by Publius in paper 84 had to be neutralized: that bills of rights befit a monarchical form of government, more than a re-

> Indeed I have come to the conclusion that if a draft *had* been prepared and adopted by a nation-wide anti-Federalist organization, and *if* that draft had limited itself to the common-law rights, there need have been no controversies. The Federalists would have said, would have *had* to say, "Ah! If *that* is all you mean, let us by all means have your bill of rights." They were not going to take the public position that they wished the new government to have the power to make unreasonable searches and seizures, or to force witnesses to testify against themselves, or to try accused persons a second time for one and the same offense.

Contra, *supra* note 77, at 305.

117. Onuf, *supra* note 21, at 371 ("The challenge then was to keep the founders true to their words."); *see* Hutson, *supra* note 99, at 314 ("Federalists . . . obliged to promise . . . that they would sponsor amendments"). Kendall suggests, however, that Madison had to work very hard to sell his federalist colleagues on the need for a bill of rights. *See* Contra, *supra* note 77, at 316–320.

118. Suzanna Sherry, *The Founders' Unwritten Constitution,* 54 U. Chi. L. Rev. 1127, 1166 (1987).

119. Hutson comments that much of contemporary literature fails "to distinguish between [the framers'] attitudes towards bills of rights and rights." Hutson, *supra* note 99, at 317. Many of the framers considered bills of rights not only to be ineffective but believed that they created a false sense of security: "Inscribing a list of rights on paper and declaring them to be sacrosanct had not prevented legislative majorities from regularly trampling on them." *Id.*, at 317. I differ from Hutson insofar as I believe common-law rights were of greater concern to more Americans than the more abstract rights of man. With respect to the latter, or at least those Kendall puts in that category, Kendall describes federalist reasoning as follows: "Once, in your listing of rights, you go beyond the common-law rights, you kiss good-bye to the sanction of tradition; as a people we *have* no tradition of free speech, or free press, or freedom of conscience—not even a tradition of having no established church. Gentlemen, you wish to launch us on uncharted seas, and we will have none of it." Contra, *supra* note 77, at 312–313.

120. Basic, supra note 99, at 129. The Ninth Amendment states: "The enumeration in the Con-

public; and that the addition into the Constitution of specific prohibitions could be confusing if not "dangerous." The Bill of Rights affirms the convention delegates' position that the powers granted to the federal government were limited. This explicitly addresses antifederalist concerns. Madison observed that when the Bill of Rights was proposed "'the most plausible'" argument that had been made against antifederalist proposals for such a bill was that, if certain rights were specified, this might be used to disparage other rights not named. Madison informed the House that in order to discourage possible misconstructions, he had taken a preventive measure: the Ninth Amendment.[120] Additionally, while the Tenth Amendment[121] may well have been legally "'superfluous'"[122] (i.e., merely repeating explicitly what the delegates at the convention had assumed implicitly), Madison believed a positive statement would serve to "quiet that anxiety which prevails in the public mind."[123]

Only the objection that bills of rights are not appropriate in a republic had to be addressed. But that objection requires the weighing of the benefits of having a bill of rights against the liabilities of not having one:[124]

stitution, of certain rights, shall not be construed to deny or disparage others retained by the people." U.S. CONST., Amend. 9. *See* Sherry, *supra* note 118, 1162–1166 ("The House solved that problem by including what became the ninth amendment.") *id.*, at 1164; Henry Monaghan, *Our Perfect Constitution,* 56 N.Y.U.L. REV. 353; 365 ns. 78, 81; 367 n. 86 (1981) ("The scant legislative history of the ninth amendment indicates that it was intended to counter an objection to the bill of rights."), *id.*, at 367, n. 86, and Raoul Berger, *The Ninth Amendment,* 66 CORNELL L. Q. REV. 1 (1980).

121. The Tenth Amendment states: "The powers not delegated to the United States by the Constitution, nor prohibited by it to the States, are reserved to the States respectively, or to the people." U.S. CONST., amend. 10.

122. Hutson, *supra* note 99, at 316. Hutson notes: "In 1787 there was an overwhelming consensus among the Framers that the Bill of Rights was superfluous. Undoubtedly many who voted for it two years later still considered it unnecessary legally, however desirable it might be politically." *Id.*, at 316. Elsewhere Hutson observes that at the time there was some dispute regarding "whether State bills of rights would have been superseded by the Federal Constitution had a Federal Bill of Rights exempting the States not been adopted." Hutson, *supra* note 99, at 318. Hutson maintains that Madison's description of the Bill of Rights as providing "'a double security' implies a conviction that State bills of rights were not intended to be superseded." *Id.*, at 318, n. 88.

123. ROBERT CORD, SEPARATION OF CHURCH AND STATE 6 (1982). *See also* LEE, *supra* note 99, at 24 ("During the ratification struggle . . . [Madison] gradually became convinced that a bill of rights would help gain support for the new government."); Hutson, *supra* note 99, at 316 (Madison described putting together the Bill of Rights as a "nauseous project"), and Kendall describes Madison's concern "that the proposed Amendments will make [in Madison's words] 'the Constitution better in the eyes of those who are opposed to it, without weakening its frame or abridging its usefulness.'" CONTRA, *supra* note 77, at 317.

124. During the ratification debates, this point was made by A Columbian Patriot (Mercy Otis Warren). In her words:

> But the gentleman goes on to tell us, "that the primary object is the general government, and that the rights of individuals are only incidentally mentioned, and that there was a clear impropriety in being very particular about them." But, asking pardon for dissenting

this is a question of prudence.[125] Some counseled for, others against. Those voting for a bill of rights said they thought it might remove lingering reservations in the minds of those who had lost the ratification battle; might help turn a new nation's attention from the past to the future.[126] Madison wrote that "'I have favored [a bill of rights] because I suppose it might be of use, and if properly executed could not be of disservice.'" Later, in the House, he repeated his position that while its absence had not justified opposing ratification of the proposed constitution, "at the same time, I always conceived, that in a certain form, and to a certain extent, such a provision was neither improper nor altogether useless."[127]

When the Bill of Rights was ratified—the point cannot be overemphasized—*it in no way modified either the purposes for which the Constitution was adopted or the powers that were granted the federal government.* Madison explicitly contended that a bill of rights[128] "will not 'endanger

---

> from such respectable authority, who has been led into several mistakes, more from his predilection in favour of certain modes of government, than from a want of understanding or veracity. The rights of individuals ought to be the primary object of all government, and cannot be too securely guarded by the most explicit declarations in their favor. . . . no republic ever yet stood on a stable foundation without satisfying the common people.

A Columbian Patriot, *Observations on the New Constitution, and on the Federal and State conventions,* THE OLD SOUTH ASSOCIATION 498 (1955).

125. Prudence is an acquired habit perhaps more related to personality type than to intellect. Have intuitive and sensible types been different in their views on the question of whether a bill of rights should be adopted? Kiersey and Bates comment:

> The sensation types notice the actual and want to deal with that. They focus on what actually happened rather than worrying too much about what might have been or what will be in the future. They usually are accurate in observing details, perhaps because, when a sensible type approaches something, his eyes tend to pick up a specific element.
>
> The intuitive acts as if he is an extraterrestrial, a space traveler engaged in explorations beyond the realities of the present and the past. The possible is always in front of him, pulling on his imagination like a magnet. The future holds an attraction for the intuitive which the past and the actual do not. . . . He operates in future time, sees "around corners."

DAVID KEIRSEY AND MARILYN BATES, PLEASE UNDERSTAND ME 17–18 (1984).

126. Hutson remarks that contemporary scholars are divided on "the intellectual credibility of the Federalists' argument that bills of rights were unnecessary in a government in which the sovereign people granted only limited, enumerated powers to the magistracy and retained the remainder itself." Hutson, *supra* note 99, at 319. I also want to reiterate here that, in putting forth the idea for a bill of rights, antifederalist forces were hardly unified as to such a bill's content. *See supra,* comment accompanying note 113. *See* Allen and Lloyd, *supra* note 2, at 54–56, 61, 71, 93, 101, and 130. McDonald reports that when Madison began compiling suggestions, the numbers were impressive. "In all, the various proposals encompassed 186 amendments, or 210 if the twenty-four preamble-type amendments offered by the New York convention are included." FOREST MCDONALD, E. PLURIBUS UNUM 368 (1965) [hereinafter MCDONALD].

127. William Van Alstyne, *Interpreting This Constitution: The Unhelpful Contributions of Special Theories of Judicial Review,* 35 U. FLA. L. REV. 209, 211 (1983).

128. Twelve amendments were proposed, but "the first two, concerning the number and salaries of congressmen, were never ratified." MCDONALD, *supra* note 126, at 369. Our first amendment,

the beauty of Government [i.e., the Constitution] in any one important feature, even in the eyes of its most sanguine admirers."[129] Madison's change, from opposing a bill of rights before ratification to championing one afterward, entailed no abandonment by the "father"[130] of the Bill of Rights of principles that he had once defended as Publius.[131]

Some other considerations remain. Almost all of the ratified Bill of Rights provisions consisted of well-known common law rights. Many of them already were contained in state laws—common and statutory—or constitutions. The people were familiar with what these provisions meant and none were thought to inhibit governmental energy or stability.

Additionally, ratification of the Bill of Rights had no direct impact on the states. Its provisions applied only against federal officials and unless those provisions also existed separately in state law, state officials could and did treat their citizens differently.[132] For example, states could and did establish religions[133]—action that was prohibited for the federal government by the First Amendment.

The Impact on Congressional Power

Was the Bill of Rights of good republican lineage? Insofar as its provisions were understood by its ratifiers as having restricted congressional power, a statute inconsistent with that understanding should never be enacted. In the event that one is, it should be declared void by federal courts. But the Bill of Rights certainly did not modify the republican character of the regime established by the Constitution. Nor did it modify the fundamental fact that in republics, as noted above, "the legislature not only commands the purse but prescribes the rules by which the du-

hence, had been the third proposed.

129. Basic, *supra* note 99, at 128–129. *See also* McDonald, *supra* note 126, at 366–369.

130. Basic, *supra* note 99, at 128.

131. *See* Hutson, *supra* note 99, at 315–318. My comments are not inconsistent with Hutson's. Publius had stated the principle: "The intrinsic difficulty of governing THIRTEEN STATES at any rate, independent of calculations upon an ordinary degree of public spirit and integrity, will, in my opinion, constantly *impose* on the national rulers the *necessity* of a spirit of accommodation to the reasonable expectations of their constituents." Federalist, *supra* note 1, no. 85, at 525.

132. When the proposals were first drafted in the House they "were designed to apply to state governments as well as the national government." The Senate, however, "removed the applicability of the bill of rights to the states." McDonald, *supra* note 126, at 369. Kendall suggests that Madison knew that the Senate would not approve of applying the bill of rights against the states. Contra, *supra* note 77, at 320: "Of course that provision was, as Madison must have known it would be, duly struck out in the Senate; on Madison's own showing, the idea of a bill was to please the objecting minority, who were above all anti-consolidators, anti-centralizers, States' righters."

133. McDonald, *supra* note 126, at 369 ("states remained free to tax all citizens for the support of established churches, as Connecticut did until 1818 and Massachusetts did until 1833").

134. Federalist, *supra* note 1, no. 78 at 465.

ties and rights of every citizen are to be regulated."[134] This topic will be discussed more thoroughly later.

THE FRAMERS AS CONSTITUTION MAKERS

If a reader puts down *The Federalist Papers* and picks up the Constitution, that reader finds exactly what might be expected: detailed descriptions of legislative, executive, and judicial governmental structures. It becomes obvious that the Constitution's words were carefully chosen. Each word seems to have been put there to convey as clearly as possible some meaning for those asked to read and decide whether or not to ratify it. For example, members of the House of Representatives shall be elected "every second Year," no more, no less.[135] Neither the House nor the Senate might adjourn for more than three days, no more, no less.[136] The strictures go on and on. Although there are instances of ambiguity, each seems consistent with the nature of the item being discussed and the delegates' evident desire to enable their successors to meet yet unknown circumstances. Thus, when powers are listed it is not surprising to see them couched in broad language: "To lay and collect taxes"; "to provide and maintain a Navy."[137] On the other hand, when experience dictated caution, qualifiers were added: "to raise and support Armies, but no appropriation of money to that use shall be for a longer term than two years."[138]

A written constitution is a collection of specific decisions about governance (ends, means, and structures) and delegates were not wishy-washy about republican government. They not only insisted that it be guaranteed,[139] they also took preventive measures, prohibiting both federal and state governments from granting titles of nobility.[140]

The people's ability to adopt a constitution or amend it is the essence of republican self-government—an understanding shared even by antifederalists.[141] One generation announces to future ones that "this is what we

135. U.S. Const., art. 1, sec. 2.1.

136. *Id.,* at art. 1, sec. 5.4.

137. *Id.,* at art. 1, sec. 8, paras. 1, 13.

138. *Id.,* art 1, sec. 8.12. This same reluctance to box in their successors led them to reject a provision they considered imprudent, though then popular: the prohibition of standing armies.

139. U.S. Const., art. 4, sec. 4. The Constitution is understood to prohibit any state from adopting a monarchical or oligarchic form of government.

140. *Id.,* art. 1, secs. 9.8 and 10.1. "Nothing need be said to illustrate the importance of the prohibition of titles of nobility. This may truly be denominated the cornerstone of republican government; for so long as they are excluded there can never be serious danger that the government will be any other than that of the people." Federalist, *supra* note 1, no. 84, at 512.

141. Statements such as those in the text are at the heart of an acquired habit toward self-government—an attitude that permeates not only *The Federalist Papers* but antifederalist statements as well: "You are then under a sacred obligation to provide for the safety of your posterity, and would you now basely desert their interests, when by a small share of prudence you may transmit to them

believe; this is what we think is important; this is what we fought and died for; this is the legacy and wisdom passed to you with the hope that you will preserve, protect and pass it on to your children and their children. Or not! The "or not" is important, for that same ability accords each generation the absolute right to reject, modify, or add to what our predecessors have handed down to us; the right to discard even the most treasured beliefs of our forefathers. In the midst of so doing each generation simultaneously affirms their ancestors' sacrifices and continues their legacy: the right to self-government.

Constitutionalism—the commitment to be governed by law and not the arbitrary will of men—is also about self-restraint.[142] Generations of citizens voluntarily agree not to exercise unlimited political power that has been won by their predecessors by the force of arms; they embrace the belief that unlimited political power, like total freedom, is an illusion. Both tempt the body and soul but more often than not lead to abuses, to self and others. Constitution makers identify and prevent the most predictable types of abuses, and even before the Bill of Rights was added the delegates at Philadelphia had incorporated the more obvious ones: e.g., "No Bill of Attainder or *ex post facto* Law shall be passed."[143] Similarly, when extraordinary circumstances might demand extraordinary measures, delegates expressed concern about those abuses, but proceded cautiously: e.g., "[t]he privilege of the Writ of Habeas Corpus shall not be suspended, unless in cases of rebellion or invasion the public safety require it."[144] Surely these provisions had specific meaning for those who authored and ratified them.

The delegates to the convention were concerned with the tendency of all governments to consolidate legislative, executive, and judicial power into a single hand—what they labeled as tyranny. This concern is clearly reflected in the Constitution. It is impossible to read either *The Federalist Papers* or the Constitution and remain unimpressed with the attention and intricate care its authors gave to explaining what responsibilities the federal government ought to have, and why; how the powers granted are necessary to the responsibilities given; why particular struc-

a beautiful political patrimony, which will prevent the necessity of their travelling through seas of blood to obtain that, which your wisdom might have secured" Cato, in ANTIFEDERALIST, *supra* note 2, at 160. Surely, the specific constitutional requirement that all officials "shall be bound by Oath or Affirmation, to support this Constitution" is significant? U.S. CONST., art. 6, sec. 3. *See* William Gangi, *The Supreme Court: An Intentionist's Critique of Non-Interpretive Review,* 28 THE CATHOLIC LAWYER, 253, 313–314 (1983).

142. STRAUSS, *supra* note 3, at 132–133.

143. U.S. CONST., art. 1, sec. 9.3.

144. *Id.,* art 1, sec. 9.2.

145. FEDERALIST, *supra* note 1, no. 16, at 117 (judges "would pronounce the resolutions of such a

tures were proposed and how they were to work; and for what reasons certain prohibitions ought to be included or foresworn.

Publius defended a judicial power to declare void acts contrary to the Constitution as being both *necessary* and *consistent* with the theory of a limited and republican government.[145] It was *necessary* because the Constitution was understood to provide rules that would govern successive generations of Americans. The Constitution places specific restrictions on the federal government, the states, or both. Being both precise and prudent, the delegates often used well-known common-law phrases, and by doing so they raised the commonly understood protection afforded by their equivalents in common or statutory law to constitutional status.[146] That is, they created constitutional rights that were no longer revisable by simple legislative majorities. When they wished to deviate from the way words were used in common law, the delegates specifically signalled this.[147] Bear in mind that elevated status distinguishes a superior command (constitutional) from an inferior one (statute or common law);[148] and that

majority to be contrary to the supreme law of the land, unconstitutional, and void"); *Id.*, no. 22, at 150 ("To produce uniformity in these determinations, they ought to be submitted, in the last resort, to one SUPREME TRIBUNAL."); *Id.* no. 37, at 229 (adjudication serves to clarify meaning); *Id.* no. 39, at 245–246 (disputes between states and federal government are to be settled by national tribunal "according to the rules of the Constitution."); *Id.* no. 73, at 446–447 (inappropriate for judges to participate in council of revision); *Id.* no. 78, at 466 (duty of courts "to declare all acts contrary to the manifest tenor of the Constitution void."); *Id.* no. 80, at 476 ("manifest contravention").

146. The common and statutory law provisions could be revised by simple majority vote; the constitutional provisions could be revised only by the amendment process. *See* RAOUL BERGER, DEATH PENALTIES: THE SUPREME COURT'S OBSTACLE COURSE 63 n.19 (1982) [hereinafter DEATH]; RAOUL BERGER, GOVERNMENT BY JUDICIARY 366–367 (1977) [hereinafter GOVERNMENT]. Berger notes: "The Founders resorted to a written Constitution the more clearly to limit delegated power, to create a fixed Constitution; and an important means for the accomplishment of that purpose was their use of common law terms of established and familiar meaning." DEATH, at 61. As Justice Story stated, "the common law 'definitions are necessarily included, as much *as if they stood in the text* of the Constitution.'" DEATH, at 63 (quoting United States v. Smith, 18 U.S. [5 Wheat.] 153, 160 [1820].

147. Berger writes: "So completely did the Framers assume that the terms they employed would be accompanied by their common law meaning that they defined treason narrowly in order to restrict its excessive scope at common law." DEATH, *supra* note 146, at 62–63. Berger adds:

> Justice James Iredell . . . earlier wrote that the Framers sought "to define with precision the objects of the legislative power, and to restrain it within *marked and settled* boundaries." In Jefferson's graphic phrase, "It is jealousy and not confidence which prescribes limited Constitutions to *bind down* those whom we are obliged to trust with power"; they should be bound "down from mischief by the chains of the Constitution." The means the Founders employed to forge the "chains," to fashion a "fixed and permanent" Constitution, were words, common law terms of established meaning.

Id., at 65 (quoting Iredell, J., Calder v. Bull, 3 U.S. 386, 399 (1978) and 4 Elliot 543).

148. Article 5 of the Constitution (the amendment procedures) provides successive generations the opportunity to evaluate the wisdom of their predecessors (or to depart from their folly) *insofar as any relevant judgments have been constitutionalized.* Otherwise, legislators by simple

the Constitution contains choices, such as its preference for the republican form of government or, as expressed in the Bill of Rights, the preference for freedom of press, speech, and religion over repression and suppression. When delegates elevated the meaning of common-law rights to constitutional status, they did not thereby preclude subsequent congressional participation in either defining what specific conduct was or was not protected or in determining what punishments were appropriate for violations.[149]

As to *consistency* with the Constitution's overall design and the people's right to self-government, Publius argued that locating the power of judicial review in the hands of life-tenured judges was indeed consistent. Such a power, he reasoned, had to be located *somewhere,* and the delegates thought the judiciary well-suited to playing a guardian role. Consistent with how they handled similar concerns in the other branches, the delegates entrusted the judiciary with sufficient independence and power to accomplish its tasks.

The judiciary's ordinary power—to interpret the laws, generally, and its more extraordinary application (i.e., judicial review), were considered by the delegates to be subordinate powers—very important powers, but not so important as being able to change the form of government.[150]

Nowhere in *The Federalist Papers* or elsewhere is there support for the view that judges may legitimately declare void legislative policy choices because they consider them to be unwise, immoral, or unethical. I argue in the remainder of this book that judges may not expand or increase the restrictions contained in the Constitution through an imaginative interpretation of the text because they (the judiciary) believe more or additional restrictions are in the public in-

---

statute may enact any and all laws "thought meet and convenient for the general good" Mayflower Compact (1620). I like the symbolic simplicity of the phraseology, but the Preamble to the Constitution is more precise.

149. *See generally,* Bradford Wilson, *The Fourth Amendment as More Than a Form of Words: The View from the Founding,* in THE BILL OF RIGHTS 151 (Eugene W. Hickok, Jr., ed., 1991). (The framers assumed that common-law remedies would be available for rights violations, but that statutory rights could be provided and would supersede common-law remedies).

150. Berger sums up this issue with the words:

> What then is the proper role of the Court? It is not wrapped in mystery. Fearful of the greedy expansiveness of power, the Founders sought to confine their delegates to the power conferred. To insure that their delegates would not "overlap" those bounds, the courts were designed to *police* those boundaries. No reference to judicial review beyond that policing function is to be found in the records of the several conventions; there is not the slightest intimation that the courts might supersede the legislature's exercise of power *within* its boundaries.

DEATH, *supra* note 146, at 86–87 (emphasis in original; footnotes omitted).

151. FEDERALIST, *supra* note 1, no. 51, at 323–324.

terest. Judges cannot multiply or redefine the restrictions contained in the Constitution simply because appointment during good behavior as a practical matter insulates them from most political pressure. If judges multiply or redefine the restrictions from what they had been understood to mean when they had been consented to by the constitution's ratifiers, they transform the American society from a republic to some other form of government, regardless of how well that shift is disguised or how often it is ignored by judges who were particularly charged with preserving our heritage. As we have seen, the delegates to the convention rejected giving judges such power because it is, as Publius noted, one that only "prevails in . . . governments possessing an hereditary or self-appointed authority."[151] So, too, should Americans reject it today.

CHAPTER THREE

Early Cases Decided by the Supreme Court

This original and supreme will organizes the government, and assigns to different departments their respective powers. It may either stop here, or establish certain limits not to be transcended by those departments.[1]

I wish to convince the reader that the design of the Philadelphia convention, defended by Publius in *The Federalist Papers,* actually was instituted. Chapter 3 examines six Supreme Court cases decided between 1800 and 1854: *Marbury v. Madison* (1803), *M'Culloch v. State of Maryland* (1819), *Gibbons v. Ogden* (1824), *Barron v. Baltimore* (1833), *Luther v. Borden* (1848) and *Dred Scott v. Sandford* (1856).

For the most part, these cases are put forth without commentary. I sought a middle ground: to provide enough details for a nonexpert reader to become familiar with the constitutional principles referred to in the remainder of the book; but not to cram in so much detail as to try the patience of those with more background in the field. I preferred, however, the risk of boring the expert over leaving the novice ill-equipped.

These Supreme Court cases are widely recognized as containing important constitutional principles and they add weight to Publius' judgments recounted in the first two chapters. These opinions also provide, in as economical a fashion as is possible, authority for opinions of mine that will be aired later in the book.

MARBURY V. MADISON (1803): JUDICIAL REVIEW

In this case the issue was whether or not a person named Marbury, appointed by an outgoing administration, could go directly to the Supreme Court of the United States to obtain a judicial order, specifically, a writ of mandamus, to compel the secretary of state of an incoming administration, James Madison, to give him his commission as a judge.[2]

Chief Justice John Marshall deliv-

1. Marbury v. Madison, 1 Cranch 97, 176 (1803) (J. Marshall) (hereinafter Marbury).

2. *Id.,* at 166. The Court believed three questions had to be answered. First, whether Marbury had a right to the commission; the Court decided he did. Second, given that he possessed the right to the commission, whether "the laws of his country afford him a remedy"; again the Court found for Marbury. And third, if the law afforded a remedy, is the Supreme Court the proper place for Marbury to obtain it; this the Court denied. Marshall quotes Blackstone: "'where there is a legal right, there is also a legal remedy.'" *Id.,* at 163 (quoted from COMMENTARIES, 3rd Vol, at 23). Pub-

ered the opinion of the Court. In refusing to give Marbury his commission, the chief justice observed that in the Constitution "original" jurisdiction—the authority to hear a case—was extended to the Supreme Court only in a specified number of situations.[3] Marbury's position—that Congress might add other instances of original jurisdiction, as it purported to do in the Judiciary Act of 1789—was not convincing because it would ignore "the distribution of jurisdiction, made in the constitution."[4]

The Constitution contains "fundamental" principles that may be repudiated only by the same process that brought them to life; and until that time any inconsistent congressional act cannot "become the law of the land." The principles ratified had been "designed to be permanent" ones.[5] Chief Justice Marshall continued:

> The powers of the legislature are defined and limited; and that those limits may not be mistaken or forgotten, the constitution is written. To what purpose are powers limited, and to what purpose is that limitation committed to writing, if these limits may, at any time, be passed by those intended to be restrained? The distinction between a government with limited and unlimited powers is abolished, if those limits do not confine the persons on whom they are imposed, and if acts prohibited and acts allowed, are of equal obligation.[6]

In other words, Americans cannot have it both ways. The chief justice added: "The Constitution is either a superior paramount law, unchangeable by ordinary means, or it is on a level with ordinary legislative acts, and, like other acts, is alterable when

---

lius expresses the same view: "there ought always to be a constitutional method of giving efficacy to constitutional provisions." JAMES MADISON, ALEXANDER HAMILTON, AND JOHN JAY, THE FEDERALIST PAPERS, no. 80, at 475 [hereinafter FEDERALIST]. *See generally,* Bradford Wilson, *The Fourth Amendment as More Than a Form of Words: The View from the Founding,* in THE BILL OF RIGHTS 151, 153–156 (Eugene W. Hickok, Jr., ed., 1991) (judicial discretion controlled by legislative oversight). I return to this topic in subsequent chapters.

Marshall reasons that since we are "a government of laws, and not of men" such remedies should be forthcoming "for the violation of a vested legal right," by which he presumably meant one already established in law. He adds: "The province of the court is, solely to decide on the rights of individuals, not to inquire how the executive, or executive officers, perform duties in which they have a discretion. Questions in their nature political, or which are, by the constitution and laws, submitted to the executive, can never be made in this court." Marbury, *supra* note 1, at 170.

3. *Id.,* at 173. *See* U.S. CONST., art. 3, sec. 2.2 ("In all cases affecting ambassadors, other public ministers and consuls, and those in which a State shall be a party, the Supreme Court shall have original jurisdiction.") *See* William W. Van Alstyne, *A Critical Guide to Marbury v. Madison,* in LOUIS FISHER, AMERICAN CONSTITUTIONAL LAW 66–71 (1990). *But see* comment accompanying note 76, ch. 5, *infra.*

4. *Id.* Marshall went on: "Affirmative words are often, in their operation, negative of other objects than those affirmed; and in this case, a negative or exclusive sense must be given to them, or they have no operation at all."

5. *Id.,* at 175.

6. *Id.,* at 176–177.

the legislature shall please to alter it." Otherwise, "written constitutions are absurd attempts, on the part of the people, to limit a power, in its own nature, illimitable."[7]

While it is true that "the province and duty of the judicial department [is] to say what the law is," that does not mean the Supreme Court might turn a blind eye to constitutional requirements. Ignoring constitutional provisions would be to ignore what Americans have for some time considered one of the greatest advancements in governing: a written constitution.[8]

Finally, Marshall points to other instances in the Constitution where the specific language would leave the Court little choice but to declare its clear meaning even in the face of contrary congressional legislation: e.g., a tax on exports, or a law passed making it possible to convict for treason upon the testimony of only one witness instead of the two required by the Constitution.[9] He concludes:

> From these, and many other selections which might be made, it is apparent, that the framers of the constitution contemplated that instrument as a rule for the government of courts, as well as of the legislature. Why otherwise does it direct the judges to take an oath to support it? This oath certainly applies in an especial manner, to their conduct in their official character. How immoral to impose it on them, if they were to be used as the instruments, and the knowing instruments, for violating what they swear to support![10]

M'CULLOCH V. STATE OF MARYLAND (1819): FEDERAL-STATE RELATIONS

In this case the Supreme Court addressed two issues: whether the creation of a national bank was within the powers delegated to the federal government and, if it was, whether that bank might be taxed by a state? Chief Justice Marshall delivered the

7. *Id.*

8. *Id.,* at 177–178. Marshall: "That it thus reduces to nothing, what we have deemed the greatest improvement on political institutions, a written constitution, would, of itself, be sufficient, in America, where written constitutions have been viewed with so much reverence, for rejecting the construction." *Id.,* at 178. Later Marshall again turns to the intentions of those who framed and ratified the Constitution: "Could it be the intention of those who gave this power, to say, that in using it, the constitution should not be looked into? That a case arising under the constitution should be decided, without examining the instrument under which it arises? . . . And if they can open it at all, what part of it are they forbidden to read or to obey?" *Id.,* at 179. The chief justice specifically uses the example cited by Publius: the instance where two laws conflict. *Id.,* at 177. *See supra,* chapter 2, text accompanying note 69.

9. *Id.,* at 179. Regarding the criteria for treason, he says: "Here, the language of the Constitution is addressed especially to the courts. It prescribes, directly for them, a rule of evidence not to be departed from. If the legislature should change that rule, and declare one witness, or a confession out of court, sufficient for conviction, must the constitutional principle yield to the legislative act?"

10. *Id.,* at 178.

opinion of the Court. He observed that this was the second time Congress had chartered a national bank. Congress had vigorously debated but approved the first national bank and by again enacting such legislation it had reaffirmed its belief that such a power was proper. Unless the Court had some independent reason for denying it, in such matters the judgement of Congress "ought not to be lightly disregarded."[11]

Marshall denied that the powers delegated to Congress were somehow inherently limited by those powers still retained by the states. Calling that contention "difficult to sustain," he observed that once the Constitution had been ratified by three-quarters of the ratifying conventions, congressional authority "proceed[ed] directly from the people."[12] While good faith interpretive disagreements undoubtedly would continue to exist, that did not mean that interpretive guidelines were totally lacking. For example: "If any one proposition could command the universal assent of mankind, we might expect it would be this—that the government of the Union, though limited in its powers, is supreme within its sphere of action."[13]

Marshall thus dismissed the contention that the power to create a bank must be denied because that specific power was not explicitly contained in the Constitution. Constitutions, he noted, frequently omit "incidental or implied powers," and what particularly undermines Maryland's position in this instance was the fact that the convention had omitted the restrictive language contained in the Articles of Confederation.[14]

Constitutions, Marshall observed,

11. M'Culloch v. State of Maryland, 17 U.S. 316 (1819) (hereinafter M'Culloch). The chief justice mentioned, however, that the Court might not so easily acquiesce where the matter was less clear or that the Court would resist some "bold and daring usurpation . . . [even] after an acquiescence still longer and more complete than this." *Id.,* at 401.

12. *Id.,* at 402–403. Marshall continues: "The assent of the States, in their sovereign capacity, is implied in calling a Convention, and thus submitting that instrument to the people." *Id.,* at 404. By this I understand him to mean that had a state, as a state, objected to a possible revision of its sovereign power, then its legislature ought not have assented to the calling of a convention in which the people of that state ratified a change in the nature of the sovereignty that state heretofore had exercised. Marshall concludes: "But the people were at perfect liberty to accept or reject it; and their act was final. It required not the affirmance, and could not be negatived, by the State governments. The constitution, when thus adopted, was of complete obligation, and bound the State sovereignties." *Id.,* at 403.

13. *Id.,* at 404–405. Marshall continues: "This would seem to result necessarily from its nature. It is the government of all; its powers are delegated by all; it represents all, and acts for all." *Id.,* at 405. Marshall claims that not only is that conclusion drawn from the nature of the document, but that it is explicitly declared in the supremacy clause and the provision that members of state legislatures, must "take the oath of fidelity to it." *Id.,* at 406.

14. *Id.,* at 406. The Articles of Confederation read: "Each state retains its sovereignty, freedom, and independence, and every Power, Jurisdiction and right, which is not by this Confederation *expressly* delegated to the United States, in Congress assembled." W. SWINDLER, SOURCES AND DOCUMENTS OF UNITED STATES CONSTITUTIONS 1491–1800 335 (1982) (article 2) (emphasis

never include every detail. If they did, they would grow too long and too complex, obscuring the most important principles contained therein, thus making it impossible for average citizens to understand. As a result, citizens would not be able to decide whether or not to adopt such a constitution.[15] He notes, for example, that very specific restrictions on congressional powers appear in the Constitution in the ninth section of article 1.[16] Hence, given both the language of and the experience under the Articles of Confederation, had the delegates to the convention believed that a more generalized restriction was appropriate, they certainly would have known how to express that belief. But they did not, and when "considering this question, then we must never forget, that it is *a constitution* we are expounding."[17]

Marshall cautions, however, against possible misconstructions of his remarks. The enumerated powers (e.g., to lay taxes, regulate commerce, and so on) do not "draw after them other powers of an inferior importance, merely because they are inferior."[18] That view would be inconsistent with the fact that the national government possessed only limited powers.

> But it may with great reason be contended, that a government, entrusted with such ample powers, on the due execution of which the happiness and prosperity of the nation so vitally depends, must also be entrusted with ample means for their execution. The power being given, it is the interest of the nation to facilitate its execution.[19]

The Court, he continues, is not compelled to reach a conclusion solely on "general reasoning." In article 1, section eight of the Constitution, the delegates at Philadelphia added a power to make "'all laws which shall be

added). Marshall also engaged in some speculation but labeled it as such. "The men who drew and adopted this amendment [*i.e.*, the Tenth] had experienced the embarrassments resulting from the insertion of the word [*i.e., expressly*] in the articles of confederation, and probably omitted it to avoid those embarrassments." M'Culloch, *supra* note 11, at 407.

15. M'Culloch, *supra* note 11, at 407. Marshall observes that with respect to a constitution "only its great outlines should be marked [and] its important objects designated." Once that is done, "minor ingredients" might be deduced, and that is precisely what the framers did. *Id.*

16. Article 1, section 9 of the Constitution contains a lengthy list of specific restrictions on the congressional powers that had been granted in article 1, section 8. These restrictions include a specific prohibition on the importation of persons (*i.e.*, slaves), a limit on the ability to suspend the writ of habeas corpus, prohibition of bills of attainder, ex post facto laws, and so on.

17. M'Culloch, *supra* note 11, at 407.

18. *Id.*, at 408.

19. *Id.* Marshall does qualify these words: "Can we adopt that construction (unless the words imperiously require it) which would impute to the framers of the instrument, when granting these powers for the public good, the intention of impeding their exercise by withholding the choice of means?" *Id.* He later notes to the contrary: "Those who contend that [the government] may not select any appropriate means, that one particular mode of effecting the object is excepted, take upon themselves the burden of establishing that exception." *Id.*, at 410.

necessary and proper, for carrying into execution the foregoing powers, and all other powers vested by this constitution, in the government of the United States, or in any department thereof.'"[20] But Maryland contended that the terms "necessary" and "proper" should be interpreted very strictly—that in order to meet that test any law should be "an absolute physical necessity." The chief justice rejected that view on the grounds that the ordinary use of the word *necessary* fails to support such an interpretation. Instead, he claimed the word frequently imports no more than the connotation that something is convenient or useful, or essential to another.[21] For example, he points to another instance in the Constitution where the delegates had used the word, "necessary," but they had carefully added a modifier so as to leave little doubt as to their more restrictive intent.[22] Thus, the word *necessary* "like others, is used in various senses; and, in its construction, the subject, the context, the intention of the person using them, are all to be taken into view."[23] In this particular instance, the Court concluded that "it must have been the intention of those who gave these powers, to assure, as far as human prudence could insure, their beneficial execution . . . [because this Constitution was] intended to endure for ages to come, and, consequently, to be adapted to the various *crises* of human affairs."[24]

In the end Marshall decided that Maryland's position, that the necessary and proper clause should be narrowly and strictly read, was contrary to "the intention of the Convention."[25] In addition to the preceding arguments he observes that the necessary and proper clause in article 1, section 8 had been placed among Congress's enumerated powers, not in article 1, section 9 which contained a list of restrictions on Congress's powers. Hence, the clause obviously constituted an apparent effort by the convention to "enlarge, not to diminish the powers vested in the government. . . . [and no] reason has been, or can be assigned for thus concealing an intention to narrow the discretion of the national legislature under the words that purport to enlarge it."[26] Lastly, while the clause ultimately does not add to the powers delegated to Congress, it certainly should not be interpreted to "restrain" the powers granted to it or to "impair" the right of Congress to

20. *Id.*, at 411–412.
21. *Id.*, at 413.
22. "No state shall . . . lay any imposts or duties on imports or exports, except what may be *absolutely necessary* for executing its inspection laws." U.S. CONST., article 1, sec. 10, para. 2 (emphasis added).
23. *Id.*, at 414–415.
24. *Id.*, at 415.
25. *Id.*, at 419.
26. *Id.*, at 419–420.

select the means it judges the most appropriate to the ends sought.

> We admit, as all must admit, that the powers of the government are limited, and that its limits are not to be transcended. But we think the sound construction of the constitution must allow to the national legislature that discretion, with respect to the means by which the powers it confers are to be carried into execution, which will enable that body to perform the high duties assigned to it, in the manner most beneficial to the people. Let the end be legitimate, let it be within the scope of the constitution, and all means which are appropriate, which are plainly adapted to that end, which are not prohibited, but consist [*sic*] with the letter and spirit of the constitution, are constitutional.[27]

Having concluded that Congress had the authority to incorporate a bank, the chief justice turned to the second issue, whether or not Maryland might tax a branch of that bank. He decided that it could not. While both the federal and state governments possessed a taxing power, the power of the latter must give way to the power of the former if it was inconsistent with "the constitutional laws of the Union."[28] Congress must have the power to protect what it creates; otherwise its destiny would be left in state hands. The "great principle is, that the constitution and the laws made in pursuance thereof are supreme; that they control the constitution and laws of the respective States, and cannot be controlled by them."[29]

While Maryland did not contend it could "resist a law of Congress," it contended sovereign states should be able to exercise their taxing powers at least until such time that its exercise was found to be demonstrably contrary to the welfare of the Union.[30] But for several reasons the chief justice concluded that position was inconsistent with the subordinate position states must play in a union created to serve all the people.[31] On the one hand, if state legislators abuse their unlimited power to tax, the people of that state could elect new legislators. On the other hand, the taxing power granted the federal government was granted "by the people of all the states. They are given by all, for the benefit of all—and upon [that] theory, should be subjected to that government only which belongs to all."[32] Thus, only Congress is empowered to enact as well as to repeal

27. *Id.*, at 426.
28. *Id.*, at 425. Marshall apparently evokes a common canon of construction: "A law, absolutely repugnant to another, as entirely repeals that other as if express terms of repeal were used." *Id.*, at 425–426.
29. *Id.*, at 425–426.
30. *Id.*, at 427.
31. *Id.*, at 428.
32. *Id.*, at 428–429.

national taxes. No one state or group of states should be permitted to undermine a congressional decision.

The Court's conclusion that a state cannot tax a bank created by the United States is not only consistent with the division of powers contained in the Constitution, it also would relieve the judiciary from having to consider "the perplexing inquiry, so unfit for the judicial department, [of] what degree of taxation is the legitimate use, and what degree may amount to the abuse of the power."[33] Hence, Maryland's suggestion that the states would not abuse their taxing power to interfere with congressional policies misses the point. The issue was not one of confidence; rather, it was the fact that, just as no state would be comfortable granting another state control over its important affairs, the Union cannot be placed in a similar position.[34] "In the legislature of the Union alone, are all represented. The legislature of the Union alone, therefore, can be trusted by the people with the power of controlling measures which concern all, in the confidence that it will not be abused."[35] If the Court sanctioned a state power to tax the federal government, before long the Union would become subordinate to the states; since if the state may tax a bank they might also tax any other instrument of the national government—the mails, the coining of money, the granting of patents, and so on. "[T]hey may tax all the means employed by the government, to an excess which would defeat all the ends of government. This was not the constitutional design put forth at Philadelphia and subsequently approved by the American people. They did not design to make their government dependent on the States."[36] The bottom line is the issue of "supremacy."[37] While a concurrent (i.e., a power exercised by

33. *Id.*, at 430.

34. Maryland had conceded that "the power to tax involves the power to destroy," but it had suggested that there must be a showing of actual abuse before its taxing power was restricted. *Id.*, at 431.

35. *Id.*

36. *Id.*, at 432.

37. *Id.*, at 432–433. In defense of its contentions, Maryland had cited *The Federalist Papers.* Marshall concedes that the authority of the *Papers* ordinarily must be accorded great weight, but he insists that it is the Court that must decide whether or not that authority had been used appropriately. In this instance, he concludes that it had not. *Id.*, at 432–433. Marshall quotes a passage from THE FEDERALIST PAPERS, supra note 2, no. 31, at 195–196, that summarizes the antifederalist position that the necessary and proper clause, coupled with an unlimited power to tax, could lead to the "'destruction of the state governments.'" M'Culloch, *supra* note 11, at 433–434. Marshall dismisses that contention on the grounds that it was not on point. He concludes that *The Federalist Papers* could not be read in such a manner as to "place within the reach of the states those measures which the government might adopt for the execution of the own powers." M'Culloch, *supra* note 11, at 435. Marshall does not, however, recount Publius' candid remarks on the subject:

> The preceding train of observations will justify the position which has been elsewhere laid down that "A CONCURRENT JURISDICTION in the article of taxation was the only admissible substitute for an entire subordination, in respect to this branch of power, of State

both the federal government and the states) power to tax certainly existed, the federal government and states cannot exercise that power in identical ways.[38]

GIBBONS V. OGDEN (1824): FEDERAL POWER OVER COMMERCE

The state of New York had granted to Robert R. Livingston and Robert Fulton an exclusive right to navigate by boat all its territorial waters—a right that eventually passed into the hands of Ogden. Gibbons also, however, subsequently was licensed under a congressional act to operate a ferry between New York and New Jersey—a licence that undermined the exclusive right granted by New York to Ogden. The New York courts upheld Ogden's exclusive right to a monopoly and Gibbons appealed to the United States Supreme Court.[39] The attorney-general for the United States argued that state monopolistic laws such as that passed by New York "were precisely [like] those . . . [that had] led to the adoption of the constitution."[40] He informed the Court that New York, New Jersey, and Connecticut were "almost on the eve of war" and pleaded "that if [the Court did] not interpose [its] friendly hand, and extirpate the seeds of anarchy which New York has sown, you *will* have civil war. The war of legislation . . . will . . . become a war of blows."[41]

Chief Justice John Marshall delivered the opinion of the Court.[42] Because, before the Constitution was adopted, the states had been completely sovereign there were those who continue to argue that the limited powers granted the Congress "ought to be construed strictly." Why, he asks, is "a strict construction" required? Certainly an "enlarged construction, [one that] would extend words beyond their natural and obvious import," was unacceptable to all concerned. And considerable room for good faith differences of opinion remained whenever a delegated power was applied to particular circumstances. But the Court could not "per-

---

> authority to that of the Union." Any separation of the objects of revenue that could have been fallen upon would have amounted to a sacrifice of the great INTERESTS of the Union to the POWER of the individual States. The convention thought the concurrent jurisdiction preferable to that subordination; and it is evident that it has at least the merit of reconciling an indefinite constitutional power of taxation in the federal government with an adequate and independent power in the States to provide for their own necessities. There remain a few other lights in which this important subject of taxation will claim a further consideration.

FEDERALIST, *supra* note 2, no. 34, at 211.

38. M'Culloch, *supra* note 11, at 435. The chief justice adds: "This opinion does not deprive the States of any resources which they originally possessed." *Id.*, at 436.

39. Gibbons v. Ogden, 22 U.S. 1 (1824) [hereinafter Gibbons].

40. *Id.*, at 180.

41. *Id.*, at 184–185.

42. *Id.*, at 186. The opinion comes after nearly two hundred pages of fascinating argument by counsels.

ceive the propriety of [any] strict construction [that] would cripple the government, and render it unequal to the object for which it is declared to be instituted, and to which the powers given, as fairly understood, render it competent."[43]

Constitutional interpretations (like statutory interpretations), maintained the Chief Justice, should proceed along familiar lines. For example, unless contrary evidence can be found the Court must assume that the words selected by delegates for inclusion in the Constitution "most directly and aptly express the ideas [the delegates] intend[ed] to convey." Similarly, it also must be assumed that delegates "employed words in their natural sense, and to have intended what they have said." Should doubts still persist then "it is a well settled rule, that *the objects for [the power had been granted]*, especially when those objects are expressed in the instrument itself, should have great influence in the construction."[44]

Marshall quotes the pertinent text[45] and begins his analysis with the observation that at the time of ratification commerce was perceived in broad terms: it was "intercourse." The chief justice notes that "the power over commerce, including navigation, was one of the primary objects for which the people of America adopted their government."[46] He then puts forth this rule of statutory construction: "The exceptions from a power mark its extent." In other words, unless the Constitution contained some other specific language that limited the application of the power, that power should be construed as broadly as possible in order to permit Congress to secure the object entrusted into its care.[47] Moreover, the words "among the several states" implied

43. *Id.,* at 187–188. I have somewhat manipulated the text but do so, I trust, without distorting the chief justice's meaning.

44. *Id.,* at 188–189 (emphasis added). The chief justice's remarks in full read:

As men, whose intentions require no concealment, generally employ the words which most directly and aptly express the ideas they intend to convey, the enlightened patriots who framed our constitution, and the people who adopted it, must be understood to have employed words in their natural sense, and to have intended what they have said. If, from the imperfection of human language, there should be serious doubts respecting the extent of any given power, it is a well settled rule, that the objects for which it was given, especially when those objects are expressed in the instrument itself, should have great influences in the construction. . . . We know of no rule for construing the extent of such powers, other than is given by the language of the instrument which confers them, taken in connexion with the purpose for which they conferred.

Id., at 188–189.

45. "Congress shall have power to regulate commerce with foreign nations, and among the several States, and with the Indian tribes." U.S. CONST., art. 1, sec. 8.3.

46. Gibbons, *supra* note 39, at 189–190. Publius also used the term *intercourse* in the context of improving interstate and foreign commerce. FEDERALIST, supra note 2, no. 14, at 102.

47. Gibbons, *supra* note 39, at 190. Marshall explores the meaning of the provision in art. 1, sec. 9 (placing limitations on federal powers granted) that specifies the following: "No Preference shall be given by any Regulation of Commerce or Revenue to the Ports of one State over those of

that "[a] thing which is among others, is intermingled with them. Commerce among the States, cannot stop at the external boundary line of each State, but may be introduced to the interior." Conversely, the language implied that the federal commerce power did not extend to "completely internal" commerce because "such a power would be inconvenient, and is certainly unnecessary."[48]

But the question remains: How far may Congress go when exercising its power to regulate commerce? The chief justice responds that, like all other powers granted Congress, the commerce power "is complete in itself, may be exercised to its utmost extent, and acknowledges no limitations, other than are prescribed in the constitution." In sum, just as the power to declare war is solely within Congress's power, so is the exercise of other powers delegated to it. The "wisdom and the discretion of Congress" is for the people to decide at election time—that is "the sole restraint . . . on which [the people] have relied, to secure them from its abuse."[49] Gibbons was validly licensed by Congress to conduct interstate commerce and any contrary New York legislation and judicial decrees must be put aside.[50]

BARRON V. BALTIMORE (1833): THE BILL OF RIGHTS

Barron owned "an extensive and highly productive wharf," but as a result of Baltimore's "paving of streets,

another, nor shall Vessels bound to, or from, one State, be obliged to enter, clear, or pay Duties in another." *Id.*, at 191.

48. Gibbons, *supra* note 39, at 194–195. He states: "Comprehensive as the word 'among' is, it may very properly be restricted to that commerce which concerns more States than one." *Id.*, at 194.

49. *Id.*, at 196–197. Marshall rejects as faulty an analogy between the power to tax retained by the states and Congress's exercise of the commerce power. Taxes are "indispensable" to the state, and may be collected by different sovereigns for different purposes. "But when a State proceeds to regulate commerce with foreign nations, or among the several States, it is exercising the very power that is granted to Congress, and is doing the very thing which Congress is authorized to do. There is no analogy, then, between the power of taxation and the power of regulating commerce." *Id.*, at 199–200. Marshall also dismisses as untimely the question of whether states may regulate commerce affecting other states if no congressional legislation exists. *Id.*, at 197–99, 209–211. In this case, as noted, congressional legislation authorized the granting of a license to ply interstate waters. *Id.*, at 200. *See also* Cooley v. Board of Wardens of Philadelphia, 53 U.S. 299 (1851).

50. *Id.*, at 240. Mr. Justice Johnson wrote in a concurring opinion:

> In attempts to construe the constitution, I have never found much benefit resulting from the inquiry, whether the whole, or any part of it, is to be construed strictly, or literally. The simple, classical, precise, yet comprehensive language, in which it is couched, leaves, at most, but very little latitude for construction; and when its intent and meaning is discovered, nothing remains but to execute the will of those who made it, in the best manner to effect the purpose intended.

Id., at 223. Johnson strongly advocated (also at 223) that commerce was at the very center of the framers' concern and hence he claimed that even the fact that Gibbons had obtained a license under an act of Congress should not be crucial to the Court's determination that states may not monopolize interstate commerce. *See id.*, at 231.

and regulating grades for paving," over a six-year period silt deposits eventually rendered the wharf practically useless.[51] The city of Baltimore never offered to compensate Barron and when sued by him for damages the city sought only to prove that its actions were within the authority granted it by the Maryland legislature.[52] A Baltimore jury, however, found for Barron and awarded him $4,500. That verdict was subsequently reversed by a higher Maryland court and Barron then appealed to the United States Supreme Court. He contended, among other things, that the powers granted to the mayor and city council were contrary to "the fifth article of the amendments to the constitution, which declares that "'private property shall not be taken for public use without just compensation.'"[53]

Chief Justice Marshall maintained that before the Court could consider Barron's contention on its merits, it first had to establish whether or not it possessed jurisdiction. Barron claimed that federal courts had jurisdiction because a Fifth Amendment right had been denied: He contended that "this amendment, being in favor of the liberty of the citizen, ought to be so construed as to restrain the legislative power of a state, as well as that of the United States."[54]

But, responded Marshall, if his contention was without merit the Court would lack jurisdiction. "The question thus presented is . . . of great importance, but not of much difficulty" since it was commonly understood that the Constitution of the United States was created by the whole people only to secure national purposes. When the people had ratified the Constitution they had lodged certain powers in the federal government, while in other instances they had imposed restrictions. Neither situation is applicable in this case, however, because Barron's complaint ultimately is with either the city of Baltimore or the state of Maryland, or both, but certainly not with the federal government.[55]

Marshall explained that after adopting the Constitution the people of each state remained free to draw up state constitutions in which they could place whatever "limitations and restrictions . . . [their] judgment[s] dictated." Barron's assumption "that the constitution was intended to secure the people of the several states against the undue exer-

51. Barron v. The Mayor and City Council of Baltimore, 32 U.S. (7 Pet.) 243 (1833) [hereinafter Barron].

52. *Id.,* at 243–244.

53. *Id.,* at 244, 246. The Fifth Amendment to the United States Constitution in part provides: "nor shall property be taken for public use, without just compensation." U.S. Const., Amend. 5.

54. Barron, *supra* note 51, at 247.

55. *Id.,* ("the fifth amendment must be understood as restraining the power of the general government, not as applicable to the states.")

cise of power by their respective state governments; as well as against that which might be attempted by their general government," lacked support.[56]

On the contrary, advised the chief justice, the ninth and tenth sections of article 1 of the United States Constitution, containing the only restrictions on federal and state legislative power, "afford . . . a strong if not a conclusive argument in support of the [conclusion]" that the Fifth Amendment is not applicable against the states. The ninth section enumerated "in the nature of a bill of rights" particular restrictions on the federal government. Similarly, the tenth section "proceeds to enumerate those [restrictions] which were to operate on the state legislatures," explicitly stating in each instance that "no State shall" do such and such. By incorporating those restrictions into the Constitution, the delegates at Philadelphia clearly sought to prevent states from undermining any of the responsibilities assigned to the federal government (e.g., states are prohibited from making treaties with foreign powers or coining money).[57] Such restrictions on state power were strenuously opposed by many and in most state ratifying conventions "amendments to guard against the abuse of power [had been] recommended." But in no instance were any of the suggested amendments directed at possible abuses by *state* legislatures.[58] He concluded:

> We are of the opinion that the provision in the fifth amendment to the constitution, declaring that private property shall not be taken for public use without just compensation, is intended solely as a limitation on the exercise of power by the government of the United States, and is not applicable to the legislation of the states. We are therefore of the opinion that there is no repugnancy between the several acts of the general assembly of Maryland . . . and the constitution

56. *Id.,* at 247–248.

57. *Id.,* at 248–249.

58. *Id.,* at 250. Marshall implies that any abuses at the state level could be addressed by the people of that state because the federal government guaranteed that states had to have republican government. He goes on to say:

> The unwieldy and cumbrous machinery of procuring a recommendation from two-thirds of congress, and the assent of three-fourths of their sister states, could never have occurred to any human being as a mode of doing that which might be effected by the state itself. Had the framers of these amendments [*i.e.* the Bill of Rights] intended them to be limitations on the powers of the state governments, they would have imitated the framers of the original constitution, and have expressed that intention. Had congress engaged in the extraordinary occupation of improving the constitutions of the several states by affording the people additional protection from the exercise of power by their own governments in matters which concerned themselves alone, *they would have declared this purpose in plain and intelligible language.*

Id. (emphasis added).

of the United States. This court, therefore, has no jurisdiction of the cause; and it is dismissed.[59]

LUTHER V. BORDEN (1848): POLITICAL QUESTIONS

In this case[60] the Court was called upon to determine which of two competing Rhode Island governments was the legitimate one. On the one hand, there was a so-called Charter government, represented by Governor King. Even after the American Revolutionary War Rhode Island never formally adopted a constitution and simply modified the original Charter granted by the British King. This government declared independence from Britain, fought the Revolution, and ratified the Constitution. At no time, however, did the Charter contain any amendment procedure and it also required that one had to own land (be a freeholder) in order to vote.[61]

On the other hand, there was a so-called popularly elected government represented by Governor Dorr. This government had been created by citizens who considered the legislature of the Charter government unresponsive to calls to revoke the freeholder requirement. Reform-minded citizens formed private associations that advocated suffrage reform and eventually held unauthorized elections to send representatives to an equally unauthorized constitutional convention. That convention in turn crafted and submitted for ratification by the people a new constitution—one that not only guaranteed suffrage for all resident males, twenty-one and over, but even declared those individuals eligible to vote on ratification. This same convention had declared that a majority of Rhode Island citizens had approved the new constitution, and hence that it had become the paramount law of the state. Accordingly, they called upon the existing Charter government to follow its precepts. In the end, there were two legislatures and two governors.[62]

The events that brought the issue before the Supreme Court occurred when one Luther (aligned with the Dorr faction) claimed that Borden (aligned with the King faction) had illegally entered his house. Defending himself, at his trial, against the charge of trespass Borden claimed that Luther had been aiding and abetting an armed insurrection; that Rhode Island's legitimate general assembly (along with Governor King) had declared martial law, and that he in the capacity of a militiaman, under military orders, had broken into and entered Luther's house to arrest him.

59. *Id.*, at 250–251.
60. Luther v. Borden, 7 How. 1 (1849) [hereinafter Luther].
61. *Id.*, at 35.
62. *Id.*, at 35–36.
63. *Id.*, at 19–20. Much of this language parallels the Declaration of Independence (1776).
64. *Id.*, at 20.

Luther, however, moved that the trial judge should instruct the jury that the people of Rhode Island had established a new constitution and a new legislature (led by Governor Dorr); that the Dorr government should be considered the legitimate one and, hence, that Borden's actions constituted an illegal trespass because his behavior had not been authorized by the legitimate government. The trial judge and higher Rhode Island courts refused to permit such jury instructions, and Luther appealed to the Supreme Court of the United States.

Before the Supreme Court, Luther reasserted that the Dorr and not the King government was the legitimate one. He argued:

> That this conclusion also follows from one of the foregoing fundamental principles of the American system of government, which is, that government is instituted by the people, and for the benefit, protection, and security of the people, nation, or community. And that when any government shall be found inadequate or contrary to these purposes, a majority of the community hath an indubitable, inalienable, and indefeasible right to reform, alter, or abolish the same, in such manner as shall be judged most conducive to the public weal.[63]

Furthermore, Luther contended that certain premises and conclusions also stemmed from the foregoing theory of popular sovereignty: that "the people are capable of self-government,"[64] that they can alter and abolish such governments at will, "[t]hat where no constitution exists, and no fundamental law prescribes any mode of amendment . . . [the people] must adopt a mode for themselves;[65] and the mode they do adopt, when adopted, ratified, or acquiesced in by a majority of the people, is binding upon all."[66]

In reply, Borden's counsel maintained "that the question to be decided was, whether a portion of the voters of a State, *either the majority or minority,* whenever they choose, assembling in mass meeting without any law, or by voting where there is no opportunity of challenging votes, may overthrow the constitution and set up a new one?"[67] Put another way, the idea "that the people can get together, call themselves so many thou-

65. The Charter, issued in 1664, was subsequently modified by the Rhode Island legislature so as to be in accord with the Declaration of Independence, the Articles of Confederation, and the Constitution of the United States, but no constitution had been put before Rhode Island citizens for their consent.

66. *Id.*, at 24.

67. *Id.*, at 27 (emphasis added). Among specific contentions made by Borden's counsel was one claiming that "there is no such thing as a natural right to vote. . . . If it was a natural right, it would appertain to every human being, females and minors" *Id.*, at 28. Counsel also challenged Luther's unqualified reliance upon "this vaunted American doctrine of popular sovereignty," noting that the presidential veto and the amendment process could clearly deny the majority will. *Id.*

sands, and establish whatever government they please [must be rejected because] . . . others must have the same right. We have then a stormy South American liberty, supported by arms to-day and crushed by arms to-morrow."[68]

Chief Justice Roger B. Taney delivered the opinion of the Court. He noted, among other things, that the Charter government claimed that a majority of citizens had supported its declaration of martial law (under which Borden had acted), and that the militia of the Charter government had defeated the troops headed by Mr. Dorr, who eventually was tried and convicted of treason. Thereafter, the Rhode Island Charter legislature had sanctioned a constitutional convention and that convention had drawn up a constitution which was ratified under the procedures specified by the Charter legislature. Rhode Island has since operated under that constitution.[69]

Hence, as the chief justice explained, the crucial issue is which government was the legitimate one at the time of the claimed trespass. If the Charter government was the lawful one, then the breaking and entering of Luther's residence by Borden may have been authorized; if not, then "the laws passed by [the Charter government's] legislature . . . [are] nullities . . . and the officers who carried their decisions [e.g., Borden are] answerable as trespassers, if not in some cases as criminals."[70]

When the Supreme Court is confronted with such high stakes it must "examine very carefully its own powers before it undertakes to exercise jurisdiction." Whether or not a constitution or amendment has been approved by a population usually is decided by the "political departments," not the judiciary. Many state courts, including those in Rhode Island, followed that practice, and when a claim similar to the one made here by Borden had been made in a related case (i.e., the prosecution of Thomas W. Dorr for treason), Rhode Island courts had declared that subject a political one. After all, the very existence of a court system presumes the existence of a legitimate government and it is that government that authorizes legislators to legislate and judges to adjudicate. Although courts interpret the law, that function must be authorized; and the very moment a court finds that the fundamental law under which it acts is illegitimate, it too ceases to function, having itself declared that the right and power it had exercised until that moment is now illegitimate.[71]

68. *Id.*, at 31. This portion of the argument was made by a Mr. Webster.

69. *Id.*, at 37–38. The Court does not mention what reforms were included in the constitution eventually adopted—specifically, whether it retained suffrage for resident males aged twenty-one as had the constitution under the Dorr government.

70. *Id.*, at 38–39.

71. *Id.*, at 39–40.

In this context "it is a well settled rule . . . that the courts of the United States adopt and follow the decisions of the State courts in question which concern merely the constitution and laws of the State."[72] When that rule is applied here, pertinent decisions of the Rhode Island courts leave little doubt that the only legitimate qualifications to vote had been created under the Charter government, the very same authority that gave legitimacy to its courts. In sum: "It is the province of a court to expound the law, not to make it. And certainly it is no part of the judicial functions of any court of the United States to prescribe the qualification of voters in a State."[73]

The chief justice then observed that insofar as the Constitution of the United States "provided for an emergency of this kind, and authorized the general government to interfere in the domestic concerns of a State . . . [it] has treated the subject as political in its nature, and placed the power in the hands of [the political departments]." For example, the federal government guarantees each state a republican form of government and protection from foreign invasion. But in each instance the crucial determinations are left in the hands of the political branches. Congress must decide which government is the legitimate one before it can decide whether that government is republican, and both houses of Congress directly address that issue when they decide which individuals are to be seated as representatives and senators. These decisions are "binding on every other department of the government, and could not be questioned in a judicial tribunal."[74] An analogous situation exists with respect to the Constitution's guarantee regarding civil strife and, in fact, Congress had passed pertinent legislation.[75] If under such legislation the president takes action (i.e., sends troops), is it appropriate for a federal court to determine the correctness of those actions, especially in the midst of armed conflict?

> If it could, then it would become the duty of the court (provided it came to the conclusion that the President had decided incorrectly) to discharge those who were arrested or detained by the troops in the service of the United States or the government which the President was endeavoring to maintain. If the judicial power extends so far, the guarantee contained in the Constitution of the United States is a guarantee of anarchy, and not of order. Yet if this right does not reside in the courts when the conflict

72. *Id.,* at 40.
73. *Id.,* at 41.
74. *Id.,* at 42.
75. *Id.,* at 42–43. The chief justice quoted a 1795 act that authorized the executive to call out the militia of several states upon the application of the legislature, or when the legislature was not convened, the executive of the state. *Id.,* at 43.

> is raging, if the judicial power is at that time bound to follow the decision of the political [branch], it must be equally bound when the contest is over. It cannot, when peace is restored, punish as offenses and crimes the acts which it before recognized, and was bound to recognize, as lawful.[76]

Although in this instance the federal militia had not been called out by the president, he was prepared to do so to support the Rhode Island Charter government. Knowing that fact, no court can support the claims of the Dorr government. "In the case of foreign nations, the government acknowledged by the President is always recognized in the courts of justice. And this principle has been applied by the act of Congress to the sovereign States of the Union." The fact that presidents may abuse this power is irrelevant since the "ordinary course of proceedings in courts of justice would be utterly unfit for the crises."[77]

The chief justice concluded that it was not the function of the Court to express opinions on "political rights and political questions." On the contrary, he said, the function of the Supreme Court is to decide whether the actions of the state or those of the federal legislature or its executive "are beyond the limits of power marked out for them respectively by the Constitution of the United States. This tribunal, therefore, *should be the last to overstep the boundaries which limit its own jurisdiction*."[78] While the Supreme Court must answer any question appropriately put before it, it also should "take care not to involve itself in discussions which properly belong to other forums."[79]

> No one, we believe, has ever doubted the proposition, that, according to the institutions of this country, the sovereignty in every State resides in the people of the State, and that they may alter and change their form of government at their own pleasure. But whether they have changed it or not by abolishing an old government, and establishing a new one in its place, is a question to be settled by the political power. And when that power has decided, the courts are bound to take notice of its decision, and to follow it.[80]

DRED SCOTT V. SANDFORD (1856): CITIZENSHIP

In this case,[81] Chief Justice Taney described the issue before the Court:

> The question is simply this: Can a negro, whose ancestors were im-

76. *Id.*, at 43.
77. *Id.*, at 44.
78. *Id.*, at 47 (emphasis added).
79. *Id.*
80. *Id.*, at 47.
81. Dred Scott v. Sandford, 60 U.S. (19 How) 393 (1856) (hereinafter Dred Scott).

> ported into this country, and sold as slaves, become a member of the political community formed and brought into existence by the Constitution of the United States, and as such become entitled to all the rights, and privileges, and immunities, guarantied by that instrument to the citizen? One of which rights is the privilege of suing in a court of the United States in the cases specified in the Constitution.[82]

More particularly, the chief justice said the Court had to decide "whether the descendants of such slaves, when they shall be emancipated, or who are born of parents who had become free before their birth, are citizens of a State, in the sense in which the word citizen is used in the Constitution of the United States."[83]

Taney's analysis begins by equating the term *citizen* with the idea of the "people of the United States": those "who hold the power and conduct the Government through their representatives."[84] He said he was satisfied that slaves or their descendants never had been and could not now be considered part of the "people," citing for support various state statutes, the Declaration of Independence, and the text of the Constitution.[85]

The chief justice conceded that a few free blacks (Taney, of course, used the contemporary word *negroes,* throughout) had existed at the time of the Declaration of Independence, and that in a few states—where he says slavery was found unsuitable or not as productive as free labor—there had been some movement toward its abolition. But he denied that a state could make a citizen of the United States those "who were not intended to be embraced in this new political family, which the Constitution brought into existence, but were intended to be excluded from it."[86] He supported his conclusion by pointing out that even in states such as Connecticut where the slave trade had been abandoned, legislation condemned miscegenation and blacks were denied rights enjoyed by other citizens.[87] Taney further observed:

82. *Id.,* at 403.

83. *Id.* The chief justice distinguished blacks from American Indians, who were "a free and independent people." Taney noted that American Indians were treated more like inhabitants of foreign nations than citizens. *Id.,* at 403–404.

84. *Id.,* at 404–405. In full, he states:

> On the contrary, [slaves] were at the time [the Constitution was adopted] considered as a subordinate and inferior class of beings, who had been subjugated by the dominant race, and, whether emancipated or not, yet remained subject to their authority, and had no rights or privileges but such as those who held the power and the Government might choose to grant them.

85. *Id.,* at 406.

86. *Id.*

87. *Id.,* at 412–415. Maine is excepted but no details are provided. *Id.,* at 416. However, Publius gives some hint that the distaste for slavery was wider than Taney indicates: "Is the Importation of slaves permitted by the new Constitution for twenty years? By the old it is permitted for-

It cannot be believed that the large slave-holding States regarded [slaves] as included in the word citizens, or would have consented to a Constitution which might compel them to receive them in that character from another State. For if they were so received, and entitled to the privileges and immunities of citizens, it would exempt them from the operation of the special laws and from the police regulations which they considered to be necessary for their own safety. It would give to persons of the negro race, who were recognized as citizens in any one State of the Union, the right to enter every other State whenever they pleased, singly or in companies, without pass or passport, and without obstruction, to sojourn there as long as they pleased, to go where they pleased at every hour of the day or night without molestation, unless they committed some violation of law for which a white man would be punished; and it would give them the full liberty of speech in public and in private upon all subjects upon which its own citizens might speak; to hold public meetings upon political affairs, and to keep and carry arms wherever they went. 'And all of this would be done in the face of the subject race of the same color, both free and slaves, and inevitably producing discontent and insubordination among them, and endangering the peace and safety of the State.[88]

Shifting ground, the chief justice conceded that by ratifying the Constitution the right to naturalize and define national citizenship had been ceded by the states to Congress. But even then, he claimed, Congress's power to grant citizenship was limited to those "born in a foreign country, under a foreign Government. It does not include the power to raise to the rank of a citizen any one born in the United States, who, from birth or parentage, by the laws of the country, belongs to an inferior and subordinate class."[89] Furthermore, the Court ruled that no state could grant national citizenship to blacks and thereby compel another state to recognize that status.[90] While the chief justice acknowledged that Congress could utilize its power to naturalize "anyone, of any color, who was born under allegiance to another Government," he concluded that naturalization statutes had thus far been so confined "to white persons."[91]

---

ever." FEDERALIST, *supra* note 2, no. 38, at 238. Thus, Publius seems both to recognize that such importation is regrettable and at the same time argue that the restriction at least is an improvement over the situation under the Articles of Confederation.

88. Dred Scott, *supra* note 81, at 417.

89. *Id.*

90. *Id.*, at 418. Taney distinguishes between (1) the use of the privileges and immunities clause in the Articles of Confederation and (2) its use in the Constitution. The former specified *free inhabitants;* the latter stated *citizenship.* He did not offer extrinsic evidence to support this distinction.

91. *Id.*, at 419.

Rights associated with citizenship are distinct from those granting "political power." For example, white women, or male and female minors, may be citizens entitled to certain rights but still may be denied the right to vote. Similarly, a "State may give the right [to vote] to free negroes . . . but that does not make them citizens of the State, and still less of the United States. And the provision in the Constitution giving privileges and immunities in other States, does not apply to them."[92] Any other interpretation "is evidently not the construction or meaning of the [privileges and immunities clause] contained in the Constitution."[93] He observed:

> No one, we presume, supposes that any change in public opinion or feeling, in relation to this unfortunate race, in the civilized nations of Europe or in this country, should induce the court to give the words of the Constitution a more liberal construction in their favor than they were intended to bear when the instrument was framed and adopted. Such an argument would be altogether inadmissible in any tribunal called on to interpret it. If any of its provisions are deemed unjust, there is a mode prescribed in the instrument itself by which it may be amended; but while it remains unaltered, it must be construed now as it was understood at the time of its adoption. It is not only the same in words, but the same in meaning, and delegates the same powers to the Government, and reserves and secures the same rights and privileges to the citizen; and as long as it continues to exist in its present form, it speaks not only in the same words, but with the same meaning and intent with which it spoke when it came from the hands of its framers, and was voted on and adopted by the people of the United States. Any other rule of construction would abrogate the judicial character of this court, and make it the mere reflex of the popular opinion or passion of the day. This court was not created by the Constitution for such purposes. Higher and graver trusts have been confided to it, and it must not falter in the path of duty.[94]

92. *Id.,* at 422.
93. *Id.,* at 423.
94. *Id.,* at 426. For support, Taney turns to *The Federalist Papers,* where Publius characterizes the acquisition and regulation of territories acquired as a result of the Revolution as having been beyond the competency of powers ceded by the states to the Confederation. From that discussion, the chief justice concludes that Publius "urges the adoption of the Constitution as a security and safeguard against such an exercise of power." Dred Scott, *supra* note 81, at 447. Curiously, having just warned his readers of the danger of taking remarks out of context (Dred Scott v. Sandford, *supra* note 81, at 442–445), Taney does just that. In *paper* 38, Publius had scolded antifederalist critics: they wished for a strong central government but were unwilling to give the new national government sufficient powers to accomplish national ends. Thus, Publius concludes (speaking about actions of the confederate congress with regard to the acquired territories) that "all this has been done; and done without the least color of constitutional authority." FEDERALIST, *supra* note

After reviewing other portions of the Constitution, the Court concluded that should a citizen of the United States move into a territory acquired by the United States, Congress, in exercising its delegated powers, could not deny a citizen the property rights he would otherwise enjoy. Congress therefore may not liberate a legally owned slave, but instead must act "within the scope of its constitutional authority."[95] Just as other parts of the Constitution prohibited Congress from establishing a national church or denying a citizen the right to a jury trial in a criminal case, so too, the Fifth Amendment protects citizens from being denied their property (slaves being property and recognized as such in the Constitution) "without due process of law."[96] All contrary congressional acts must be declared void. The opinion concludes:

> Upon these considerations, it is the opinion of the court that the act of Congress which prohibited a citizen from holding and owning property of this kind in the territory of the United States . . . is not warranted by the Constitution, and is therefore void;[97] and that neither Dred Scott himself, nor any of his family, were made free by being carried into this territory; even if they had been carried there by the owner, with the intention of becoming a permanent resident.

2, no. 38, at 239. Publius' remarks seem to imply that, in contrast, any new constitution ought to be prepared to deal with such matters from the very beginning. Taney's interpretation implies Publius' overall disapproval, but that is not confirmed by Publius' concluding paragraph, which is *ignored* by Taney:

> I mean not by anything here said to throw censure on the measures which have been pursued by [the Confederate] Congress. I am sensible they could not have done otherwise. The public interest, the necessity of the case, imposed upon them the task of overleaping their constitutional limits. But is not the fact an alarming proof of the danger resulting from a government which does not possess regular powers commensurate to its objects? A dissolution or usurpation is the dreadful dilemma to which it is continually exposed.

FEDERALIST, supra note 2, no. 38, at 239–240. The entire context of Publius' remarks leads me to believe that Taney's very narrow reading of the clause in question may not reflect the Philadelphia convention's intent as much as Taney's preference. Certainly Publius' remarks—as Taney suggests—cover the Northwest Territories, but so to confine them would be to ignore Publius' words about "the danger resulting from a government which does not possess regular powers commensurate to its object." Taney's interpretation leaves the Union Congress in the same boat as the Confederation congress. It also ignores chief Justice Marshall's advice that where doubtful intent exists, courts ought to defer to *legislative* interpretation. I share that view.

Taney also did not challenge the power of Congress to expand the United States by adding new states, but since "no express regulation" is contained in the Constitution to define that power, he contended that "the court must necessarily look to the provisions and principles of the Constitution, and its distribution of powers, for the rules and principles by which its decision must be governed" Dred Scott, *supra* note 81, at 447.

95. *Id.*, at 447–448.

96. *Id.*, at 450.

97. *Id.*, at 452. The law to which he refers is the Missouri Compromise of 1820. *Id.*, at 455 (Wayne, J., concurring).

PART II.

THE DECLINE OF SELF-GOVERNMENT

CHAPTER FOUR

The Rise of Modern Judicial Power

It is not the province of the court to decide upon the justice or injustice, the policy or impolicy, of these laws. The decision of that question belonged to the political or law-making power; to those who formed the sovereignty and framed the Constitution. The duty of the court is, to interpret the instrument they have framed, with the best lights we can obtain on the subject, and to administer it as we find it, according to its true intent and meaning when it was adopted.[1]

I hope the reader found as fascinating as I did the six cases presented in the preceding chapter. Every decade of American history has its share of such cases: they are part of the legacy of constitutional law. Now, for practical reasons, I must turn to less detailed descriptions of post–Civil War developments. Constitutional law textbooks covering the same time frame as this book typically consists of some fifteen hundred pages—and this is not intended to be a textbook. My objective is to convince the reader that judges today are abusing their power and to achieve that objective I regrettably had to abandon any idea of recounting particular cases or of paying much attention to the economic, historical, political, and social contexts of cases.

This chapter is noticeably more polemic than those in part 1. Broad conclusions must be stated in clear and unequivocal terms: they do not permit the recounting of twists and turns that might serve only to confuse the reader. But I stand by the judgments made in this chapter, believing them sound and clearly supported by the evidence. While readers may not concur in every pronouncement, I trust they will acknowledge that my statements are reasonable, even where they are not convincing.

The chapter covers a substantial

1. Dred Scott v. Sandford. 60 U.S. (19 How) 393, 405 (1856) (Taney, C. J.).

time frame, ranging from passage of the Civil War amendments in the mid-1860s to the stewardship of Chief Justice Warren Burger in the 1970s. The subject matter reviewed is equally comprehensive: it begins with the rise of judicial power in the post–Civil War period and continues to the seven premises that underlie the contemporary exercise of judicial power in the United States.

CIVIL WAR AMENDMENTS: THE ORIGINAL UNDERSTANDING

This much is certain, the Civil War decided the slavery issue very differently than did the Court majority in *Dred Scott.* It was inevitable that *Dred Scott* would be formally excised from the corpus of constitutional law and in 1865 slavery was constitutionally abolished by ratification of the Thirteenth Amendment.[2] That abolition, however, as important as it was, resolved only that slavery was illegal. The Thirteenth Amendment did not otherwise modify state power or the right of a majority of a state's citizens to define civil, political, and social rights. Accordingly, after the end of military hostilities, most former confederate state legislatures passed statutes called Black Codes. Charles Fairman has described their purpose:

> The Negroes' place was made clear: he was to be a laborer, chiefly a plantation laborer, bound by the year; his wage would, in practice, be set by the employers; to be without employment would lead to severe sanctions. It was not contemplated that the Negro would progress, for the roads were barred. No public education was provided. Poor relief was a charge only upon the Negroes.[3]

In 1866, in response to the enactment of such state statutes, Congress passed a Civil Rights Act,[4] designed to secure for the newly freed black slaves a limited but crucial, body of specific rights—to be known as civil rights—including the rights to inherit, buy, lease, sell, and convey property, to make contracts, to sue and to be sued, and the pivotal right to testify in a court of law (though not to serve on a jury).[5] Nevertheless, in

2. Amendment Thirteen (1865) reads: "Neither slavery nor involuntary servitude, except as a punishment for crime whereof of the party shall have been duly convicted, shall exist within the United States, or any place subject to their jurisdiction."

3. Charles Fairman, Reconstruction and Reunion 1864–88, Part I., 115 (1971). Charles Fairman provides detailed information on the Black Codes. *Id.,* at 110–117. He notes that such codes blatantly legalized a double standard of conduct for whites and blacks. Such codes, for example, prohibited blacks from owning property and "being witnesses in any case whatsoever, except for or against each other." *Id.,* at 112.

4. 42 U.S.C. secs. 1981–1988.

5. Raoul Berger, Government By Judiciary: The Transformation of the Fourteenth Amendment 25 (1977). Belz concludes: "The Civil Rights Act [of 1866] was not intended to confer political rights, nor to create total racial equality by prohibiting all forms of discrimination,

and out of Congress grave reservations persisted with respect to the statute's constitutionality. Where, in the Constitution, had Congress been authorized to interfere with what until 1866 had been considered a matter between the citizens of each state and their elected representatives? Many believed that the Thirteenth Amendment simply made slavery illegal but did not in any other way curtail state power.[6]

By 1868 the political climate was changing and it was anticipated that before long the former confederate states would regain the congressional voting rights denied them since their attempt to secede from the Union.[7] But since the Thirteenth Amendment in effect had repealed the Philadelphia convention's three-fifths compromise, once Southern representatives were again seated in Congress those states would enjoy even greater representation than when they had taken up arms.[8] This infuriated radical Republicans, who feared that these new southern representatives, joined by northern Democrats unsympathetic to the blacks' plight, might by a simple majority vote repeal the 1866 Civil Rights Act.[9] In

---

whether at the hands of state governments or private individuals" Herman Belz, *Equality and the Fourteenth Amendment: The Original Understanding,* 4 BENCHMARK 329, 343 (1990).

6. See FAIRMAN, *supra* note 3, at 1172–1182; BERGER, *supra* note 5, at 113–114 and Belz, *supra* note 5, at 338–345.

7. Herta Meyer describes the political situation as "logically absurd":

> The Southern states were both outside and inside of the Union at the same time. They were outside because they were excluded from all representation in Congress, and because certain conditions imposed by Congress must be met before they could reenter. One of these conditions was that they assist the northern states in adopting a Fourteenth Amendment to the Constitution of the United States! Otherwise, they must remain outside of the Union. They were inside of the Union, because the Amendment could not become part of the Constitution without their favorable action.

HERTA MEYER, THE HISTORY AND MEANING OF THE FOURTEENTH AMENDMENT 3–4 (1977).

8. U.S. CONST., art. 1, sec. 2, para. 3 (the three-fifth's compromise). In the 1787 Constitution, every five slaves were to be counted as three persons for purposes of representation and taxation. *See* MEYER, *supra* note 7, at 2–3.

9. Belz, *supra* note 5, at 344 (Doubts existed over whether the Thirteenth Amendment "was a sufficient source of authority" for the 1866 Civil Rights Act and the Fourteenth Amendment was proposed "in order to constitutionalize the Civil Rights Act"). *Id.* During this period Radical Republicans also feared that the Supreme Court would declare many of the Reconstruction acts, including the Civil Rights Act of 1866 unconstitutional—a fear that grew when the Court first heard oral arguments in *Ex parte* McCardle, 74 U.S. (7 Wall) 506 (1868), and then rescheduled that case for additional oral arguments in the following term. But before the Court reconvened for the fall term, Congress enacted legislation removing jurisdiction in such cases and in McCardle, the Court recognized its power to do so. Raoul Berger, recounting the research of Fairman, also points out that while the McCardle case was being heard, "a bill that 'would declare the reconstruction Acts were political in character and that *no court* was competent to question their validity' [was introduced by Senator Trumbell]. Fairman comments that 'This bill was like a cocking of a gun, audible in the nearby Supreme Court Chamber.'" RAOUL BERGER, DEATH PENALTIES: THE SUPREME COURT'S OBSTACLE COURSE 169 (1982) (citations omitted). For a complete discussion, see FAIRMAN, *supra* note 3, at 437–501.

order to elevate the protections contained in the 1866 act from statutory to constitutional status, Radical Republicans proposed the Fourteenth Amendment. The first section of this amendment reads:

> All persons born or naturalized in the United States and subject to the jurisdiction thereof, are citizens of the United States and of the State wherein they reside. No State shall make or enforce any law which shall abridge the privileges or immunities of citizens of the United States; nor shall any State deprive any person of life, liberty, or property, without due process of law; nor deny to any person within its jurisdiction the equal protection of the laws.[10]

The first sentence of the amendment was intended unequivocally to reject the most important distinction made by Chief Justice Roger B. Taney in *Dred Scott v. Sandford;* namely, that blacks could never become citizens.[11]

In the second sentence, the phrase *privileges or immunities* probably was used by its framers to convey only the substantive rights associated with United States citizenship. Those rights were understood to consist of no more and no less than those that had been enumerated in the Civil Rights Act of 1866; generally, those relating to "(1) personal security; (2) freedom of locomotion; and (3) ownership and disposition of property."[12] Very similar language had existed in the 1787 Constitu-

10. U.S. Const., amend. 14, sec. 1. *See* Belz, *supra* note 5, at 342.

11. *See supra,* chapter 3, text accompanying notes 84–94.

12. Berger, *supra* note 5, at 21, 20–36 passim. *See supra,* chapter 8, text accompanying notes 4–5. Meyer observes that "there seemed to be general agreement that the major purpose of the first section was the protection of the Civil Rights Act of 1866, because its constitutionality had been in doubt from the start." Meyer, *supra* note 7, at 91. She describes the purpose of the civil rights bills as being "to secure to Negroes and others the same 'civil rights or immunities' as belonged to whites. 'Civil rights' were defined in both bills to include 'the right to make and enforce contracts, to sue, be parties, and give evidence, to inherit, purchase, lease, sell, hold and convey real and personal property'." Meyer, *supra* note 7, at 91–92.

Belz contends that more contemporary views of race relations distort our understanding of their intent. He comments:

> To put the matter plainly, it was not racial prejudice and discrimination in general that the framers of the Reconstruction amendments intended to eradicate. Racial distinctions were a part of the historic social order, if not of the natural order, and could hardly be categorically eliminated. The framers and supporters of the Fourteenth Amendment acted to protect civil rights not because they believed in racial equality; they did so despite a belief in racial *inequality.* . . . Racial classification and discrimination were to be restricted and declared wrong insofar as they led to the denial of fundamental rights to which all persons were entitled by natural law.

Belz, *supra* note 5, at 345. *See also* Raoul Berger, *The Scope of Judicial Review: An Ongoing Debate,* 6 Hast. Const. L. Q. 527, 552, 623 (1979) [hereinafter *Ongoing*] and Raoul Berger, *The Fourteenth Amendment: Light from the Fifteenth,* 74 NW. L.Rev. 311 (1979) (hereinafter *Fourteenth*). Raoul Berger is most associated with the contemporary assessment of the intent of those who framed the Fourteenth Amendment.

tion[13] but, given the way it was understood, its application proved to be of limited value to the former slaves.[14] Thus, by elevating these fundamental *civil rights* to constitutional status (incorporating them within the meaning of "privilege or immunities") the framers of the Fourteenth Amendment clearly wished to broaden the reach of congressional power over the states beyond the scope contemplated in 1787 by the delegates at Philadelphia.[15] But beyond fundamental civil rights they did not go; for example, into the area of social rights, such as the regulation of marriage. Even after adoption of the Fourteenth Amendment, state legislatures could still discriminate among their citizens. The states continued to legislate without federal interference on matters such as segregated schools and interracial marriage.[16]

Similarly, the Fourteenth Amendment did not disturb the state power to regulate political rights among its citizens (e.g., voter qualifications).[17] The amendment's second section empowers Congress only to invoke a

13. U.S. CONST. ART. 4, sec 2. ("The Citizens of each State shall be entitled to all Privileges *and* Immunities of Citizens in the several States") *(emphasis added).* That language in turn had been borrowed from the Articles of Confederation, art. 4 ("shall be entitled to all privileges and immunities of free citizens in the several states"). WILLIAM F. SWINDLER, SOURCES AND DOCUMENTS OF UNITED STATES CONSTITUTIONS, SECOND SERIES, NATIONAL DOCUMENTS 1492–1800 336 (1982). Meyer observes that proponents of the Fourteenth Amendment distinguished, "'privileges or immunities of citizens' which [they] . . . said were secured in article 4, section 2 [of the Constitution from] 'rights' secured in the first eight amendments." MEYER, *supra* note 7, at 119.

14. Herta Meyer describes the impact of the original clause contained in the 1787 Constitution:

> If a white married woman went into another state, she was entitled only to such privileges and immunities which that other state accorded to its own white married women, not to those which it accorded to the white males. By parity of reasoning, if a free Negro went into another state, he could claim only such privileges and immunities to which the free Negroes in that state were entitled. But most states did not confer citizenship on Negroes. A Negro who claimed a citizenship in his home state would then have to be given the privileges of white citizens by such other state, even though his own state excluded him from most of those privileges. This the other states were not prepared to do. It appeared to them more logical to look at the factual situation, namely whether the home state accorded to its free Negroes the privileges and immunities customarily connected with citizenship. If it did not, another state would see no reason to recognize him as a citizen. Obviously, the problem could only be solved by entitling all free native-born Negroes to citizenship in all the states of the Union, and thereby to citizenship of the United States. But this had to wait until the adoption of the fourteenth amendment.

MEYER, *supra* note 7, at 39.

15. Meyer contends, however, that the language of the amendment, not provisions of the original Constitution, "prevents the states from discriminating between their own citizens, and they have to extend to the citizens of another state no greater rights. . . . A state . . . may still regulate the substantive civil rights—such as the right to make contracts . . . differently for different population groups, such as for males and females, for adults and children, and for whites and other races." MEYER, *supra* note 7, at 100.

16. BERGER, *supra* note 5, at 123–124, 161–163.

17. *Id.,* at 32–33.

penalty should it find that a state denied or abridged the right of twenty-one-year-old males to vote (i.e., Congress could reduce representation in violating states). But the amendment did not directly prohibit restrictions on voting; nor did it authorize a federal takeover of state voting standards.[18] Even after the Fifteenth Amendment was adopted in 1870, directly placing specific restrictions on state power to define voting qualifications, that power was not generally diminished. The Fifteenth prohibited legislation based on "race, color, or previous condition of servitude," but states still could and did deny women and minors the right to vote.[19]

But to return to the Fourteenth Amendment's first section: in addition to the privileges or immunities language already discussed, the two remaining pivotal phrases in this section—the due process and equal protection clauses—have been characterized by Raoul Berger as being only adjective in nature. That is, both phrases describe certain conditions that have to be satisfied before something substantial could be done. For example, the due process clause guarantees only that common-law *procedures* will be employed before life, liberty, and property would be modified or lost. Such procedural protections addressed *how* life, liberty, or property could be lost, not *whether* it could be lost.[20] The equal protection clause was understood by its framers to be "wedded and confined to those enumerated rights" subsumed in the privileges and immunities clause.[21] The contention that the framers of the Fourteenth Amendment, by use of

18. Sec. 2 of the amendment, as already noted, modified the three-fifths compromise contained in the original constitution of 1787. Sec. 2 also specifies that "when the right to vote" for national political offices is denied to twenty-one-year-old males, "or in any way abridged" (with certain reasonable exceptions), "the basis of representation therein shall be reduced in the proportion which the number of such male citizens shall bear to the whole number of male citizens twenty-one years of age in such state." Sec. 3 in effect prohibits (without Congressional approval) anyone from holding political or other office of trust in the United States who had in the past taken that oath and violated it by supporting the southern cause. Sec. 4 prohibits any court from questioning the debt incurred in pursuing the Civil War, and absolves the Union from any debt incurred by the Confederate states. Meyer contends that the second section of the amendment was considered more important than the first section. "It seems that the Republicans who dominated the Thirty-ninth Congress were much more interested in finding ways to reduce the congressional representation of the South and to exclude the Confederate leaders altogether than in a thorough discussion of the language of the first section." MEYER, *supra* note 7, at 90.

19. The Fifteenth Amendment states in sec. 1: "The right of citizens of the United States to vote shall not be denied or abridged by the United States or by any State on account of race, color, or previous condition of servitude." U.S. CONST., amend. 15 (1870).

20. BERGER, *supra* note 5, at 197. "Summing up 400 years of history, [Alexander] Hamilton said, 'The words "due process" have a precise technical import, and are only applicable to the process and proceedings of the courts of justice; they can never be referred to an act of the legislature.'" *Fourteenth, supra* note 12, at 334. *See also* MEYER, *supra* note 7, at 140–149.

21. Raoul Berger, *The Fourteenth Amendment: Facts vs. Generalities,* 32 ARK. L. REV. 280, 286 (1978) [hereinafter *Facts*].

the equal protection language, intended that all people in the future could or would have to be treated equally in all things, finds little support.[22] Indeed, Chief Justice Taney's contention in the *Dred Scott* decision that civil rights were considered distinct from social and political rights was apparently accepted by those who framed and ratified the amendment.[23]

The fifth section of the Fourteenth Amendment and the second section of the Fifteenth Amendment declare only that Congress "shall have power to enforce this article by appropriate legislation." The clause did not compel Congress to take any actions, nor did it empower the judiciary to do so.[24]

In sum, the post–Civil War amendments obliterated *Dred Scott v. Sandford*.[25] The framers of these amendments had limited objectives in mind:[26] That is the conclusion that seems most consistent with Reconstruction and subsequent history, and with past and recent scholarship.[27] Some scholars disagree with that assessment;[28] others claim that it is impossible for us to know with certainty what the framers' purpose was;[29] still others assert that, whatever the

22. BERGER, *supra* note 5, at 166–169.
23. *See supra* chapter 3, text accompanying note 92.
24. U.S. CONST., amend. 14, sec. 5. I concur in Berger's conclusion that the language of the fifth section only specifies that Congress "shall have power to enforce"—not Congress *shall* enforce: the discretion is Congress's." BERGER, *supra* note 9, at 171–172. The Fourteenth Amendment, therefore, adds nothing to the judicial power as it had existed in article 3. Given the status of the Supreme Court after its decision in Dred Scott, it would take a considerable body of evidence to reach the conclusion that the framers of the Fourteenth Amendment sought to *increase* judicial power!
25. Easterbrook, *Approaches to Judicial Review,* in POLITICS AND THE CONSTITUTION: THE NATURE AND EXTENT OF INTERPRETATION, NATIONAL LEGAL CENTER FOR THE PUBLIC INTEREST 22–23 (1990) [hereinafter POLITICS]. "They gave Congress and the Court power against the states, but there is no clue that they expand the Court's power against Congress or justify innovative theories. Their principal aim, after all, was to get rid of *Dred Scott,* not to enlarge the Court's discretion." *Id.* Belz adds: "The persistence of strong racist attitudes in the northern public thus imposed political limits on Republican civil rights proposals and the meaning of equality as a constitutional concept." Belz, *supra* note 29, at 339.
26. Belz, *supra* note 5, at 343–345. *See supra* comment accompanying note 5. For more particulars on reaching that conclusion, *see* William Gangi, *Judicial Expansionism: An Evaluation of the Ongoing Debate,* 8 O. N. U. L. R. 1, 55–56 (1981). Of course, what the framers of that amendment wished to accomplish is distinct from the question of whether or not we remain bound to them today.
27. *See* Charles Fairman, *Does the Fourteenth Amendment Incorporate the Bill of Rights? The Original Understanding,* 2 STAN. L. REV. 5 (1949); Stanley Morrison, *Does the Fourteenth Amendment Incorporate the Bill of Right? The Judicial Interpretation,* 2 STAN. L. REV. 140 (1940); LOUIS LUSKY, BY WHAT RIGHT (1975); FAIRMAN, *supra* note 3; BERGER, *supra* note 5; MEYER, *supra* note 7.
28. *See, e.g.,* MICHAEL K. CURTIS, NO STATE SHALL ABRIDGE: THE FOURTEENTH AMENDMENT AND THE BILL OF RIGHTS (1986). For an extensive discussion, SEE 6 HAST. CONST. L. Q. 1 (1979) (Symposium on Raoul Berger's GOVERNMENT BY JUDICIARY).
29. *See, e.g.,* Judith A. Baer, *Reading the Fourteenth Amendment,* in POLITICS, supra note 25, at 75. "The congressional debates on the Fourteenth Amendment support Chief Justice Earl Warren's

framers of the Fourteenth Amendment meant, that need not concern us today.[30] All remain unconvincing; or they raise issues that are discussed later.

THE RISE OF LAISSEZ-FAIRE

The decade preceding the Civil War was a time of intellectual excitement. Science was being redefined and this opened up new vistas for understanding the universe.[31] In England, Herbert Spencer, Darwin's most important advocate, sought to transform "biological laws into social 'laws.'"[32] He contended that various animal species had evolved through the process of natural selection, guaranteeing "the survival of the fittest." Just as man had not intervened in that process, if governments adopted a similar perspective, not only would greater progress ensue in that society,[33] but human perfection would be inevitable.[34] "The intellectual powers of the race would become cumula-

---

characterization as "'at best . . . inconclusive.'" *Id.*, at 75 (citing and quoting Brown v. Board of Education, 347 U.S. 483, 489 [1954] (Warren, C.J).

30. For example, there are the following remarks by Michael Perry:

> I wonder which is stronger among contemporary constitutional theorists: the belief that the Supreme Court should maintain a strict fidelity to the original understanding of the fourteenth amendment or the desire to have the Court continue to answer "fourteenth amendment" questions by reference to traditional and emergent societal ideals. . . . My guess (hope?) is that most constitutional theorists will forsake the belief that the Court should be faithful to the original understanding. While they may not forsake it openly, many will do so silently, by declining to call for the Court to overturn all fourteenth amendment doctrine plainly not rooted in the decidedly limited original understanding of the amendment.

Michael Perry, book review, 78 COLUM. L. REV. 685, 704 (1978).

31. *See* ERNEST TUVESON, MILLENNIUM AND UTOPIA (1964) (Between the 15th and 17th centuries our contemporary idea of progress was created from the combination of increased knowledge of the natural sciences and changes in theological perspectives. By the mid-nineteenth century, however, progress's theological roots had been lost.) For a more detailed discussion, including sources, *see* William Gangi, *The Supreme Court: An Intentionist's Critique of NonInterpretive Review,* 28 THE CATHOLIC LAWYER 253, 257–260 (1983) [hereinafter Gangi].

32. ERIC GOLDMAN, RENDEZVOUS WITH DESTINY 90–91 (1966). Herbert Spencer and Auguste Comte were the originators of modern sociology. *See also* RICHARD HOFSTADTER, SOCIAL DARWINISM IN AMERICAN THOUGHT 38–51 (rev. 1959). Contrary to Herbert Spencer, Auguste Comte contended that in his *science* of sociology a planned and controlled society was required. *Id.* James Wilson comments that even today the two different approaches put forth by Spencer and Comte still influence modern sociological theory. *See* JAMES Q. WILSON, THINKING ABOUT CRIME 62–63 (1975).

33. My colleague Henry Paolucci has brought to my attention a letter from Karl Marx to Friedreich Engels (18 June 1862):

> Darwin, whom I have looked up again, amuses me when he says he is applying the "Malthusian" theory also to plants and animals, as if with Mr. Malthus the whole point were not that he does not apply the theory to plants and animals but only to human beings—and with geometrical progression—as opposed to plants and animals. It is remarkable how Darwin recognizes among beasts and plants his English society with its division of labour, competition, opening-up of new markets, "inventions," and the Malthusian "struggle for existence." It is Hobbes's *bellum omnium contra omnes,* and one is reminded

tively greater, and over several generations the ideal man would finally be developed."[35]

Even before the influence of Charles Darwin began to be felt, English and French political economists had recommended that the only way to improve the human condition was for governments to stop interfering with economic competition. These laissez-faire theorists contended that the "natural laws" of the marketplace (e.g., supply and demand and business cycles of expansion and contraction) eventually, if left alone, would lead to ever increasing economic prosperity because an "invisible hand," unknown to the competitors, guided their selfish pursuit of individual profit toward the realization of the common good.[36] Not all Americans embraced such theories, but the new ideas captured the imagination of many of the most influential members of U.S. society. Laissez-faire economic assumptions, supported by Darwinian "science," seemed to both embody and reflect America's individualistic, frontier spirit. Social Darwinism became a powerful social force in the United States in the post–Civil War period and many individuals and the nation prospered.

In this Age of Faith, as Grant Gilmore has called it, the legal profession, too, sought to be more scientific, applying to the study of law the methodology that had proved so fruitful in the biological sciences.[37] These legal theorists soon viewed the "law library . . . [as a] laboratory" and "printed case reports" became "experimental materials."[38] Treatises

---

of Hegel's *Phenomenology,* where civil society is described as a "spiritual animal kingdom," while in Darwin the animal kingdom figures as civil society.

KARL MARX: SELECTED WRITINGS 526 (DAVID MCLELLAN, ed., 1977).

34. HOFSTADTER, *supra* note 32, at 40.

35. *Id.,* at 39. "'The ultimate development of the ideal man is logically certain. . . . Progress . . . is not an accident, but a necessity. Instead of civilization being artificial, it is a part of nature . . . [like] the development of the embryo or the unfolding of a flower.'" *Id.,* at 40, footnote omitted; (quoting H. SPENCER, SOCIAL STATICS 79–80 [1850]). Once one comes under the spell of progress a *new man* is always just around the corner.

36. Gangi, *supra* note 31, at 258–260n. 30.

37. GRANT GILMORE, THE AGES OF AMERICAN LAW 42–43 (1977). Gilmore points out that many legal theorists believed that "there [was] such a thing as the one true rule of law which, being discovered [would] endure, without change, forever." *Id.,* at 43. *See also* MORTON HORWITZ, *The Conservative Tradition in the Writing of American Legal History,* 17 AM. J. LEGAL HIST. 275, 280 (1973) (the American ideology since the 19th century has been "that law is a science discoverable by reason and that its scientific character is what distinguishes law from politics." *Id.*). For an overview, *see Recent Trends in American Legal History,* 4 BENCHMARK 217 (1990) [hereinafter *Recent Trends*] (articles by Stephen B. Presser, Kermit L. Hall, Herman Belz, Morris S. Arnold, Robert W. Gordon, William E. Nelson, and Maxwell Bloomfield).

38. GILMORE, *supra* note 37, at 47. Christopher Columbus Langdell, the first dean of Harvard Law School, epitomized the "law as a science" age (*see id.* at 42), and was the originator of the case method of teaching. *Id.* at 125n. 3.

fell out of favor and some precedents were viewed as "useless."[39] Case reporting—a "new type of legal literature"—emerged, drawing a line "between the correct cases and the vast majority of worthless ones."[40]

In this climate, some judges contended that when the framers of the Bill of Rights and the Fourteenth Amendment had used terms such as "liberty" and "due process" they had intended to secure certain *natural* individual economic rights from the possibility of federal or state legislative interference. These rights were not procedural but *substantive* and as such they were entitled to absolute protection. Upon such principles the Supreme Court subsequently struck down state and federal legislation designed to ameliorate the growing hardships associated with industrial revolution, recession, and eventual depression.[41]

This laissez-faire thinking (and its judicial support) did not pass out of fashion suddenly, but a growing body of citizens began to question it. They noted that some of their fellow citizens survived in both good economic times and bad and began to understand that this was due, not to the fact that these survivors were the most fit but to the fact that they were the most cunning, crude, greedy, and, at times, the most arrogantly mean-spirited. Business cycles, it was also noticed, did not always lead to increased prosperity, at least not for the many; and, more importantly, business downturns adversely affected more decent citizens than those above-mentioned survivors. Why, it was asked as the gap between social classes widened, did society as a whole suffer ill effects under the purportedly beneficent guidance of the Invisible Hand? Citizens began to raise serious questions about how the economic and political systems worked, or failed to work. Other citizens expressed concern over the effects laissez-faire assumptions were having on American society, asking if the values fostered by those assumptions were consistent with others—concepts of fairness, proportionality, and Christianity.

These early challenges to laissez-faire thinking failed miserably. They were easily suppressed since belief in

39. *Id.*, at 58. Gilmore recounts the unique role play by the West Publishing Company, which "made a contribution to our legal history which, in its importance, may have dwarfed the contributions of Langdell, Holmes, and all the learned professors on all the great law faculties." *Id.* at 59.

40. *Id.* Case reporters, Gilmore informs us, were not obliged to publish every case adjudicated, and in fact "string citations of the wrongly decided cases . . . not infrequently outnumbered the parallel strings of correct cases." *Id.*

41. *See* GILMORE, *supra* note 37, at 64–65; Horwitz, *supra* note 37, at 278. *See, e.g.*, Lochner v. New York, 198 U.S. 45 (1905); Bailey v. Drexel Furniture Co., 259 U.S. 20 (1922); Adkins v. Children's Hospital, 261 U.S. 525 (1923); Schechter Poultry Corp. v. United States, 295 U.S. 495 (1935); Carter v. Carter Coal Co., 298 U.S. 238 (1936), and United States v. Butler, 297 U.S. 1 (1936).

the Invisible Hand still remained strong among the population generally—particularly among the intelligentsia.[42] The dominant, powerful faithful suppressed these questions by continuing to rely on the very premises that were being questioned: Do nothing and things will work out.[43] Faiths do not evaporate overnight. Many reformers were themselves believers, and they attempted only to eliminate the more obvious and perhaps curable evils.[44] Even then they were labeled Socialists or Communists by those who, as if in a dream, ignored the economic dislocations surrounding them.

By the late 1880s, critics bitterly charged that under the rubric of constitutional interpretation judges had imposed their personal economic beliefs upon the country. Instead of looking at all the precedents in an evenhanded manner, they claimed, some judges had selected only those precedents that supported their predilections. These critics charged that not only did the Constitution not bar needed economic and social welfare reform legislation, but that the courts should accord the federal and state legislatures greater discretion in the clash between capital and labor.[45]

THE PROGRESSIVIST REVOLT: CARDOZO

One of the leading critics of laissez-faire oriented adjudication was Benjamin Cardozo. In his book, *The Nature of the Judicial Process,* he argued that "a constitution is not intended to embody a particular economic theory, whether of paternalism and the organic relation of the citizen to the state, or of laissez faire":[46] it was the legislature, not the judiciary, that

42. The matter of attitudes (acquired through habit) and the difficulty of changing them is discussed in Appendix A.

43. Eric Voegelin, Science, Politics and Gnosticism 44 (1968). "But we now see more clearly that an essential connection exists between the suppression of questions and the construction of a system. Whoever reduces being to a system cannot permit questions that invalidate systems as a form of reasoning." *Id.*

44. Eric Voegelin concisely summarizes the tactics used during this period:

> Hence, the . . . adherents of a System will develop the well-known variety of devices which are meant to protect the respective System against the inevitable friction with reality. There is the just-mentioned device of "revision," frequently used to preserve the plausibility of the System, though it may lead to dissent among the adherents and to angry redefinitions of orthodoxy and dissent. There is the fundamental taboo on questions concerning the premises of the eristic fusion. . . . There is the dignified tactic of not taking cognizance of fatal criticism, and the less dignified procedure of personally defaming the critic.

Eric Voegelin, Anamnesis 143–146 (1978). Do any of the above criteria sound vaguely familiar to students of current legal literature? *See* Gangi, *supra* note 26, at 32n. 272; 62–63n. 472.

45. One might similarly charge Chief Justice Marshall of putting forth his personal agenda. *See* Stephen Presser, *Confessions of a Rogue Legal Historian: Killing the Fathers and Finding the Future of the Law's Past,* IV Benchmark 217 (1990), and Christopher Wolfe, The Rise of Modern Judicial Review 63 (1986).

46. Benjamin Cardozo, The Nature of the Judicial Process 75, 75–79 (1921) [hereinafter Cardozo] (citing Lochner v. New York, *supra* note 41, at 75 [Holmes, J., dissenting]).

must set societal goals. Legislatures should craft broad policy in goal-oriented statutes; then judges in applying the law in different circumstances ought to keep those goals in mind.[47] Cardozo contended that American society was moving in the "direction of a growing liberalism" and that what he called a "new spirit" had slowly evolved. Only in retrospect, he claimed, has the progress made so far become apparent. This "progress" was difficult to discern since common-law legal terms had remained the same while their underlying meaning had changed. Judges must now be guided by the societal goals of legislatures, not by the meanings these common-law terms once had: "The juristic philosophy of the common law is at bottom the philosophy of pragmatism. Its truth is relative, not absolute."[48]

No longer should judges pretend that the legal principles they articulate had been shared by the framers of the Constitution or its amendments; instead, Cardozo contended, judges should analyze operative facts and implement the lawgivers' will. Once judges proceeded in that manner, all law would soon be "reduced to statutory form with most of the significant continuing problems being committed to administrative agencies." As that goal was achieved, he said, the judicial role "was bound to become progressively more modest, more mechanical, more trivial."[49] In his book, *The Ages of American Law,* Grant Gilmore has concluded that "realists" such as Cardozo sought to "strip . . . judges of their trappings of black-robed infallibility and reveal . . . them to be human beings whose decisions were motivated much more by irrational prejudice than by rules of law."[50]

Realist legal theory eventually merged with practical and successful progressivist politics: both influenced the administration of Franklin D. Roosevelt. The Realist-Progressivist coalition derided those judges who claimed to have found economic rights in the Constitution. These critics accused judges of *creating* such rights. They insisted that judges once again must consider *all* precedents—not simply those that fit into the

47. *Id.*, at 98–101 *passim.* The approach suggested by Cardozo became known as the Sociological School.

48. Cardozo, *supra* note 46, at 101–102.

49. Gilmore, *supra* note 37, at 92. With respect to Cardozo's reliance on sociological jurisprudence Horwitz observes: "The principle argument is that there is some sort of inevitable and necessary unfolding of different stages of legal ideas." Horwitz, *supra* note 37, at 279. These stages were described by Roscoe Pound, another leading theorist of the period, as consisting of (a) archaic law; (b) strict law; and (c) liberalization. *See Id.* Horwitz notes, however, that "never are we told why the second stage becomes the third or, indeed, which social forces gain and which lose by this transition." *Id.* Pound's threefold theoretical division dates back to the thirteenth century. *See* Gangi, *supra* note 31, at 257n. 23.

50. Gilmore, *supra* note 37, at 92.

laissez-faire framework.[51] Faced with unprecedented economic dislocation, critics grew intolerant of interference from judges who did not have to be elected: "Judicial power was [to be] a relic of the dead past."[52]

POSTWAR TRANSITION: THE FRANKFURTER CRITERION

By the mid-1930s, under considerable political pressure and with the country in the midst of a severe economic depression, the Supreme Court reevaluated the relationship between constitutional law and laissez-faire economic theory;[53] nevertheless, thirty more years would pass before the justices explicitly acknowledged that it had abandoned judicial review as a means of overseeing national economic policy.[54]

In 1939, Felix Frankfurter, an influential New Deal thinker, was confirmed as an associate justice of the Supreme Court.[55] He put forth the view that while the Supreme Court

51. *Id.*
52. *Id.,* at 70–71, 79.
53. NLRB v. Jones & Laughlin Steel Corp., 301 U.S. 1 (1937) ("When industries organize themselves on a national scale, making their relation to interstate commerce the dominant factor in their activities, how can it be maintained that their industrial labor relations constitute a forbidden field into which Congress may not enter when it is necessary to protect interstate commerce from the paralyzing consequences of industrial war?"). *Id.,* at 41. As Bernard Schwartz recounts, this change in the majority's perspective took place without any change in court personnel. Given the political climate and F. D. Roosevelt's court reorganization plan, the change in the Court's perspective is referred to as "'a switch in time saved Nine.'" BERNARD SCHWARTZ, THE SUPREME COURT: CONSTITUTIONAL REVOLUTION IN RETROSPECT 16 (1957).
54. The Court explicitly rejects a role for itself in economic policy in Ferguson v. Skrupa, 372 U.S. 726, 729 (1962). *See generally* WILLIAM LOCKHART, YALE KAMISAR and JESSIE CHOPER, CONSTITUTIONAL LAW 127–128 (5th ed., 1980) (description of political climate in which the Court reversed its due process approach) [hereinafter CONSTITUTIONAL LAW]. Gilmore observes that the change from laissez-faire thinking to a New Deal philosophy was "not much more than a changing of the guard . . . a change of course, not a change of goal." GILMORE, *supra* note 37, at 87, 100. This much is clear: "The slogan 'law is a science' became 'law is a social science.' Where Langdell had talked of chemistry, physics, zoology, and botany as disciplines allied to the law, realists talked of economics and sociology not merely as allied disciplines but as disciplines which were in some sense part and parcel of the law." *Id.,* at 87. During this period it was fashionable for liberals and progressivists to view the states as social laboratories. *Id.,* at 91. *See also* Maurice Holland, *American Liberals and Judicial Activism: Alexander Bickel's Appeal from the New to the Old,* 51 IND.L.R. 1025, 1036 n.28 (1976).

While the Realist-Progressivist movement rejected the substitution of judicial preferences for those of the legislature with respect to national economic policy, within several years, as we shall see shortly, they began to use judicial power to set national policy goals in three other areas: the rights of criminal defendants, race relations, and voting rights. In the remainder of this chapter, I choose to concentrate on the first area—the rights of criminal defendants—because my own expertise lies in that area and the literature regarding the other two areas is extensive and complex and has been profitably explored by other scholars. My analysis, however, is equally applicable to the other areas mentioned and when developments in the other areas are pertinent they will be noted.
55. Holland explains that Felix Frankfurter was one of the formulators of "Robert La Follette's platform plank in 1924 which called for a constitutional amendment giving Congress power to override Supreme Court invalidation of federal statutes by a two-thirds vote. Frankfurter even ad-

should respect the states' "own notion of what will best further [their] own security in the administration of justice . . . the history of liberty has largely been the history of observance of procedural safeguards."[56] Thus, the Court could not sanction "[police] methods that may fairly be deemed in conflict with deeply rooted feelings of the community."[57] He concluded, for example, that the "[j]udicial supervision of the administration of criminal justice in federal courts implie[d] the duty of establishing and maintaining civilized standards of procedure and evidence."[58]

In this manner Justice Frankfurter sanctioned judicial involvement in public policy areas unrelated to the national economy. Among other things, he advocated that the Court develop criminal prosecution safeguards that "not only . . . assure[d] protection for the innocent but also . . . secure[d] conviction of the guilty by methods that commend themselves to a progressive and self-confident society."[59] Over several decades, he contended that to do otherwise would be to "disregard standards that we cherish as part of our faith in the strength and well-being of a rational, civilized society."[60] Police, he said, should not be permitted to use "authoritarian methods";[61] and in order to "remove the inducement to resort to such methods . . . [the Court should deny] the use of the fruits of illicit methods."[62] He believed that illicit police methods violated the "underlying principle of our enforcement of the criminal law. Ours is the accusatorial as opposed to the inquisitorial system."[63] In an accusatorial system, the burden of proof is on society to prove its case, not out of the accused's "own mouth" but, by "evidence independently secured through skillful investigation."[64] Americans, Frankfurter claimed, had embraced that system "not out of tenderness for the accused but because we have reached a certain stage of civilization."[65]

While the states were primarily responsible for protecting their citizens from crime, Frankfurter contended

---

vanced the modest proposal of excising the due process clause from the fourteenth amendment." Holland, *supra* note 54, at 1026n. 3 (1976). Frankfurter served on the Court until 1962.

56. McNabb v. United States, 318 U.S. 332, 340, 347 (1943).

57. Haley v. Ohio, 332 U.S. 596, 604 (1947). I find Frankfurter's early formulation here interesting because it clearly conveys that the basis for his reasoning rests not on law—constitutional or statutory—but on custom or sentiment: on community support. His approach parallels the views of the sociological school described earlier.

58. McNabb v. United States, *supra* note 56, at 340.

59. *Id.,* at 344.

60. Haley v. Ohio, *supra* note 57, at 606.

61. Fikes v. Alabama, 352 U.S. 191, 199 (1957) (Frankfurter, J., concurring).

62. Haley v. Ohio, *supra* note 57, at 607.

63. Watts v. Indiana, 338 U.S. 49, 54 (1949).

64. *Id.*

65. Stein v. New York, 346 U.S. 155, 200 (1953) (Frankfurter, J., dissenting).

that the adoption of the Fourteenth Amendment had "severely" restricted state control over their administrations of criminal justice.[66] In defending that position, he characterized the content of the Fourteenth Amendment as "generalities circumscribed by history and appropriate to the largeness of the problem of government with which they were concerned."[67] Furthermore, since the due process clause of the Fourteenth Amendment was of constitutional stature, he and the other justices could not "escape" their duty to decide whether existing state criminal procedures were consistent with those constitutional standards.[68] Frankfurter observed that in the 1940s the justices concluded that "coercive police methods . . . tend to brutalize habits of feeling and action on the part of police, thereby adversely affecting the moral tone of the community."[69] The Supreme Court had to condemn these illicit police practices, because if they failed to do so it would have been a "retrogressive step in the administration of criminal justice."[70]

Hindsight makes clear that in the post–New Deal and World War II periods the justices of the Supreme Court demoted economic rights and elevated personal rights, among which may be counted those of criminal defendants. Stated broadly, the rationale went something like: "To encourage societal progress, it is important . . . to protect 'those liberties of the individual which history has attested as the indispensable conditions of an open as against a closed society.'"[71]

Within this theoretical framework, subsequent Supreme Court majorities

66. Watts v. Indiana, *supra* note 63, at 50.

67. Malinski v. New York, 324 U.S. 401, 412–416 *passim* (1944). In that case Frankfurter asserted that the Fourteenth Amendment embodied a demand for "civilized standards," and that to deny that "independent function" of the Fourteenth Amendment in favor of specific provisions of the Bill of Rights (as then being advocated by Justices Black and Douglas), would be detrimental to the "fabric of Law" in the several states. *Id.* For a more thorough discussion of these matters, see William Gangi, *A Critical View of the Modern Confession Rule: Some Observations on Key Confession Cases,* 28 Ark. L. Rev. 1, 32–33 (1974).

68. Watts v. Indiana, *supra* note 63, at 50.

69. Stein v. New York, *supra* note 65, at 199–200.

70. *Id.,* at 201.

71. Robert G. McCloskey, *Economic Due Process and the Supreme Court: An Exhumation and Reburial,* 1962 Sup. Ct. Rev. 34, 34–36 (quoting Kovacs v. Cooper, 336 U.S. 77, 95 [1949] Frankfurter, J., concurring). *See also* Lusky, *supra* note 27, at 113. The open-society concept—one discussed more fully later in this chapter—is intimately related to the preferred freedom doctrine which seeks to grant the "fullest liberty of professing and discussing . . . any doctrine, however, immoral it may be considered." Willmore Kendall, *The 'Open Society' and Its Fallacies,* 54 Am. Pol. Sci. Rev. 972 (1960) (quoting J. John Mill, On Liberty and Considerations on Representative Government 14 [R. McCallum ed. 1946]. Open-society proponents generally argue that as a nation we failed to live up to the commitment first expressed in the Declaration of Independence and later infused in the Bill of Rights and Civil War amendments, until the emergence of the Warren Court, when, as noted in text below, the Supreme Court took a more active role in realizing such ideals.

developed a multifaceted double standard in order to explain different treatment of economic and personal rights. They contended first that, with respect to economic policies, the federal and state legislatures were better equipped to discern the people's will and judges ought to defer to that will. But the judiciary was far better suited than legislatures to articulate and defend personal civil liberties.[72] Second, because of America's commitment to an open society, personal civil liberties should always expand and never be permitted to contract. Accordingly, the Supreme Court took a closer look at the traditional doctrine of stare decisis (respect for precedents), concluding that while the Court should respect and uphold those precedents that created new (or expanded old) ideas of civil liberties, those that inhibited either should be treated with suspicion.[73] Lastly, while at one time progressivists defended considerable state discretion in conducting economic and social experiments (viewing the states as social laboratories), the justices now concluded that the Constitution did not permit experimentation with respect to personal liberties.[74] Former Justice Arthur Goldberg explains:

> While practical considerations counsel against a too rude or too rapid assertion of the power of supervision over the states, common sense reinforces the command of stare decisis not to give back to the states any of their previously asserted power to curtail fundamental liberties—power which was denied to them by the Fourteenth Amendment. Nothing is to be gained by overruling those cases which caused wounds to state sensibilities that have already healed.[75]

THE WARREN AND BURGER COURTS

Warren Court Implementation

Beginning in 1960, Justice Frankfurter's "evolving standards of decency . . . of a maturing society" took on more specific meanings than he could have anticipated.[76] For example, borrowing Frankfurter's exact language, Chief Justice Earl Warren contended that in interpreting the Constitution the justices "must draw

72. It is sufficient to note here that defenders of this dichotomy, among other things, claim that since the federal judiciary is unelected, they can better resist popular prejudices or constituent pressures.

73. Arthur Goldberg, Equal Justice 85 (1971) ("expansion of an individuals' rights is based on the fact that under our constitutional scheme these rights do and should expand. Overruling is therefore permissible, or rather intrinsically necessary, to facilitate this beneficial expansion, which I have shown to be sanctioned by tradition and reason.") *Id.*, at 85.

74. *Id.*, at 86–97. After mentioning Justice Brandies's perception of the federal system as laboratories, permitting state social welfare experimentation, Justice Goldberg said in one of his opinions: "'I do not believe that this includes the power to experiment with the fundamental liberties of citizens safe-guarded by the Bill of Rights.'" *Id.* at 95 (quoting Pointer v. Texas, 380 U.S. 400, 413 [1965]).

75. *Id.*, at 95.

76. McNabb v. United States, *supra* note 56, at 344. For an excellent summary of the Warren

[their] meaning from the evolving standards of decency that mark the progress of a maturing society."[77] Warren concluded further that "as important as it is that persons who have committed crimes be convicted, there are considerations which transcend the question of guilt or innocence."[78] Thereafter, Supreme Court majorities decided that "evolving standards of decency" now required that certain Bill of Rights guarantees be made applicable to the states. Once declared incorporated (i.e., applicable to the states), such guarantees would apply to the states in the same manner as they had been defined in federal courts.[79]

The Supreme Court role was a difficult one, the chief justice explained. The justices often are "forced to resolve a conflict" between our society's need for effective law enforcement and an individual's right not to be subjected to "unconstitutional methods of law enforcement."[80] But, he concluded, the Court is obliged to take a long view of societal needs;

Court's impact on criminal justice, see CRIMINAL LAW REPORTER, THE CRIMINAL LAW REVOLUTION AND ITS AFTERMATH: 1960–1970 (1972) (briefs of relevant cases).

77. Trop v. Dulles, 356 U.S. 86, 101 (1958) (Warren, C. J.). Chief Justice Earl Warren does not quote Frankfurter's *McNabb's* language but one need *not* accuse the chief justice of plagiarism, only note that such a criterion was widely believed—which is to say that by this time it had become a deeply embedded attitude in liberal circles.

78. Blackburn v. Alabama, 361 U.S. 199, 206 (1959) (opinion, Warren C. J.).

79. The assertion that the framers of the Fourteenth Amendment had intended to make the first eight amendments applicable to the states first was enunciated in Betts v. Brady, 316 U.S. 455 (1942) and Adamson v. California, 332 U.S. 46, 68 (1947) (Black, J. dissenting). This "total" incorporation theory, however, never was accepted by a Court majority and at the time was severely criticized by a majority of scholars (including Frankfurter). *See* Fairman, *supra* note 27, and Morrison, *supra* note 27. As Meyer points out, almost all of Justice Black's reasoning relied on comments made on the first and rejected draft of the Fourteenth Amendment. MEYER, *supra* note 7, at 115–124. She concluded that "only one proviso of the Federal Bill of Rights was incorporated into the text of the fourteenth amendment and made applicable to the states, namely the due process clause of the fifth amendment." *See id.*, at 124. But after recounting the history of that phrase (id., at 125–149) she concluded that "it meant that a person's life, liberty, or property may not be taken away without his first having had a trial in accordance with procedural rules applicable to all alike." *Id.*, at 149. Berger adds weight to Meyer's conclusions. *See* BERGER, *supra* note 5, at 20–36 (privileges and immunities) and 193–200 (due process guarantees only procedure). Nevertheless, as this chapter makes clear, since the Civil War such provisions have been viewed by laissez-faire proponents and progressivists alike as containing generalities, providing all such justices with a powerful means for redefining constitutional law.

Despite the fact that *total* incorporation was rejected as historically untenable, since 1947 various Court majorities have accepted in its place the even more absurd doctrine of "selective incorporation": the idea that only some amendments or provisions thereof of the Fourteenth Amendment were intended by its framers to apply to the states. If, as certainly is the case, there is little historical support for the total incorporation theory, historical support for selective incorporation is nonexistent. *See generally,* Raoul Berger, *Incorporation of the Bill of Rights in the Fourteenth Amendment: A Nine-Lived Cat,* 42 OHIO ST. L. J. 435 (1981) (various doctrines of incorporation are without historical foundation).

80. Spano v. New York, 360 U.S. 315, 315 (1959) (opinion, Warren C. J.).

hence, the justices must look beyond what impact the Court's decisions might have on a particular defendant. Echoing Justice Frankfurter, Warren suggested that there were "deep-rooted feelings that the police must obey the law while enforcing the law; that in the end life and liberty can be as much endangered from illegal methods used to convict those thought to be criminals, as from the actual criminals themselves."[81] Hence, the Court could not "escape the demands of judging or of making the different appraisals inherent in determining whether constitutional rights have been violated."[82]

Warren's colleague, Justice Arthur Goldberg, contended that the Constitution's framers had entrusted the Supreme Court with the responsibility of keeping the Bill of Rights meaningful in changing circumstances.[83] Justice Frankfurter was echoed again when Goldberg argued that "our Constitution, unlike some others, [struck] the balance in favor of the right[s] of the accused."[84] Two years later, a Warren Court majority favorably quoted this formulation of the various competing principles: "'The quality of a nation's civilization can be largely measured by the methods it uses in the enforcement of its criminal laws.'"[85]

Warren Court majorities also often contended that their conclusions were steeped in historical experience. Take, for example, Justice Goldberg's recounting of coerced confession history:

> We have learned the lesson of history, ancient and modern, that a system of criminal law enforcement which comes to depend on the "confession" will, in the long run, be less reliable than a system which depends on extrinsic evidence independently secured through skillful investigation. . . . We have also learned the companion lesson of history that no system of criminal justice can, or should survive if it comes to depend for its

81. *Id.* at 320–321.
82. Haynes v. Washington, 373 U.S. 503, 515 (1963). (Goldberg, J.).
83. The former justice explained how he had viewed the Court's role as follows: "The Court plays a most important role in expressing the essential morality inherent in the Constitution. It is the voice not only of what the Constitution commands but also of what it inspires. This responsibility counsels against contracting fundamental rights, since the signal of the nation—the moral message of a reversal of the trend—will be damaging." GOLDBERG, *supra* note 73, at 93. Justice William Brennan, also frequently a member of the majority during this period, more recently has provided this illustrative formulation: "The prohibitions of the Fourth Amendment are not, however, limited to any preconceived conceptions . . . instead we must apply the constitutional language to modern developments according to the *fundamental principles* that the Fourth Amendment *embodies.*" United States v. Jacobson, 80 L. Ed. 2d 85, 109 (1984) (Brennan, J., dissenting) (emphasis added).
84. Escobedo v. Illinois, 378 U.S. 478, 488 (1964) (Goldberg, J.).
85. Miranda v. Arizona, 384 U.S. 436, 480 (1966) (Warren, C.J.) (quoting Walter Schaefer, *Federalism and State Criminal Procedure,* 70 HARV. L. REV. 29 [1956]).

> continued effectiveness on the citizens' abdication through unawareness of their constitutional rights. No system worth preserving should have to *fear* that if an accused is permitted to . . . [exercise his rights], he will become aware of, and exercise, these rights. If the exercise of constitutional rights will thwart the effectiveness of a system of law enforcement, then there is something very wrong with that system.[86]

Warren Court admirers subsequently argued that the Supreme Court injected new life into the Bill of Rights, making those amendments again pertinent to twentieth-century realities. "We have emerging a concept that the accusatorial system must be enforced . . . because the *nature* of a free society demands it and because anything less jeopardizes that society itself."[87] They insisted that in the mid-twentieth century Warren Court decisions only made more practical and accessible American ideals of liberty and equality.[88]

To summarize, the Warren Court majority criminal justice legacy may be reduced to four components. First, the justices sought to make the rights of criminal defendants easier to exercise and harder for police to circumvent.[89] Second, they worked systematically to flesh out in considerable detail what Justice Frankfurter had called an accusatorial system—a "due Process Model" as Herbert Packer subsequently labeled it.[90] In that model, factual determinations of guilt (i.e., whether the accused actually committed the crime) became less important than the goal of imposing proper rules of conduct on police, prosecutors, and lower courts—rules

86. Escobedo v. Illinois, *supra* note 84, at 488–490. For a critical appraisal of these remarks, see Gangi, *supra* note 67, at 44–50.

87. *Escobedo in the Courts,* 19 Rutgers L. R. 111, 137 (1965) [hereinafter Escobedo].

88. *See supra* chapter 1, text accompanying note 1 for a discussion of the "official literature". Alexander Bickel characterized it somewhat differently:

> The Justices of the Warren Court thus ventured to identify a goal. . . . And the Justices steered by this goal . . . in the belief that progress, called history, would validate their course, and that another generation, remembering its own future, would imagine them favorably. . . . On such a faith . . . was built the Heavenly City of the Twentieth-Century Justices.

Alexander Bickel, The Supreme Court and the Idea of Progress 13–14 (1970). Although Bickel's confidence in the Court declined significantly before his untimely death, earlier he had been a strong proponent, if not the originator of the ideas that the constitutional text should be interpreted in open-ended fashion and that the Court should be a "prophet and shaper" whose duty it was "to create moral principles and give them substance." *Id.,* at 11–42, 108–168. *See* also John H. Ely, The Supreme Court 1977 Term—Forward: *On Discovering Fundamental Values,* 92 Harv. L. Rev., 54–55 (1978); Holland, *supra* note 54, at 1026–1028; Edward A. Purcell, *Alexander M. Bickel and the Post-Realist Constitution,* 11 Harv. C.R.–C.L.L. Rev. 521, 32–33, 537–538 (1976).

89. Goldberg, *supra* note 73, at 20.

90. *See* Herbert Packer, *Two Models of the Criminal Process,* 113 U. Pa. L. Rev. 1 (1964).

that in the future would have a beneficent impact on society. *Legal guilt* took precedence over the more traditional emphasis on *factual guilt.* The former, unlike the latter, elevated the determination of whether or not factual guilt had been established "in a procedurally regular fashion and by authorities acting within competencies allocated to them"; and for the justices, the "integrity of the process" became more important than the conviction and punishment of any particular factually guilty defendant.[91] Third, the justices increasingly sanctioned use of an exclusionary rule to bar the admissibility of evidence they believed had been acquired in an inappropriate manner—a sanction they considered crucial if the previously noted procedural integrity of the criminal justice system was to be preserved. By implementing the Due Process Model and the exclusionary sanction, the Warren Court majority believed that the rights of criminal defendants would be more widely respected. Lastly, the Warren Court demanded more rigorous use of specified procedures (e.g., warrants), tightening judicial standards governing police discretion (e.g., probable cause to search), and in the end ultimately promulgated legislative-type rules to prevent police from circumventing the rules created (e.g., the *Miranda* warnings).[92]

The Burger Court Retrenchment

Congress was not entirely pleased with the Warren Court's criminal justice decisions. Following *Escobedo* (1964) and *Miranda* (1966),[93] legislators concluded that, despite what the justices thought, police custodial interrogation continued to be an important practical tool for effective law enforcement, and that the Court had unduly reduced its effectiveness.[94] Congress enacted the Omnibus Crime Control and Safe Streets Act to rebalance the competing considerations[95] and expressed its assessment of the competing considerations: "[We feel] that society is entitled to the use of confessions and incriminating statements. . . . The committee also feels that a civilized society could not be more fair to persons accused of crime, as the constitutional rights of defendants in criminal cases would be fully protected

91. *Id.,* at 16–17.

92. Escobedo v. Illinois, *supra* note 84; and Miranda v. Arizona, *supra* note 85. For a review of the relevant cases, *see* Criminal Law Reporter, *supra* note 76.

93. 2 U.S. Code Cong. & Ad. News 2113–2133, 2212–2215 (1968). *See* The Impact of Supreme Court Decisions 48–49 (W. Murphy, ed. 1969).

94. 2 U.S. Code Cong. & Ad. News 2127–2128, 2132 (1968). *But see id.,* 2212–2215.

95. *See* Comment, *Title II of the Omnibus Crime Control Act: A Study in Constitutional Conflict,* 57 Geo. L. Rev. 438, 439–441 (1968) [hereinafter *Title*]; Comment, *Title II of the Omnibus Crime Control and Safe Streets Act of 1968 As It Affects the Admissibility of Confessions and Eyewitness Testimony,* 40 Mis. L. Rev. 257, 270–285 (1969) [hereinafter Admissibility]; and Comment, *The Six-Hour Delay: A Confession Killer,* 33 U. Pitt. L. Rev. 341, 351 (1971) [hereinafter Delay].

and respected by the safeguards in this proposed legislation."[96]

Congress defended this legislation on the grounds that Chief Justice Warren himself had invited congressional participation in the formulation of proper criminal procedures, reasoning that his invitation had been extended because "Congress is better able to cope with the problems of confessions, than is the Court."[97] Unlike courts, Congress made clear it could (and did) hold hearings, subpoena witnesses, and, in general, collect more complete data from a variety of sources. It insisted that "passage of this bill with all of its legislative history—the record of the subcommittee hearings and all of the underlying social policies bearing on this issue and taken into account by Congress—will furnish an excellent record that will hopefully make an impression on some of the Supreme Court justices."[98]

But bigger changes were to intervene. Crime rates and crime control emerged as important issues during the 1968 presidential election and the successful candidate, Richard M. Nixon, nominated Warren E. Burger to be chief justice.[99] Burger wasted little time reevaluating his predecessor's legacy.[100] Before long, critics were contending that the progress made under the Warren Court had come to a screeching halt under the new chief justice. They accused the Burger Court of going backwards because of its preoccupation "with accurate results in individual cases . . . [and its] disregard [for] . . . procedures that protect[ed] the integrity of the process in ways unrelated to factfinding."[101] The Supreme Court, they contended, was "no longer a bold, innovative institution and . . . keeper of the nation's conscience";[102] beneath Burger's public rhetoric about a new era of judicial restraint, said critics, the Court was as activist as had been the Warren

96. 2 U.S. Code Cong. & Ad. News 2137 (1968). *But see* Alvin Goldstein, *Miranda v. Arizona: A Reply to Senator Ervin,* 5 Am. Crim. L. Q. 173 (1967).

97. 2 U.S. CODE CONG. 7 AD. News 2132 (1968).

98. *Id.,* at 2133.

99. Warren E. Burger replaced Chief Justice Earl Warren, and Harry A. Blackmun replaced Justice Tom Clark. Subsequently, Lewis F. Powell, Jr. and William H. Rehnquist were appointed to fill the vacancies created by the resignation of Justices John M. Harlan and Hugo Black.

100. *See* Harris v. New York, 401 U.S. 222 (1971); and Bivens v. Six Unknown Fed. Narcotics Agents, 403 U.S. 388 (1971).

101. Edward Chase, *The Burger Court, The Individual, and the Criminal Process: Directions and Misdirections,* 52 N.Y.U.L. Rev. 518, 519 (1977). Commentators who use Warren Court precedents as a benchmark surely engage in what Morgan amusingly refers to as "the higher Chutzpah" [the classic description being the child, who after murdering his parents, pleads for mercy before the court on the grounds that he is an orphan!]. Richard E. Morgan, in *Symposium: Constitutional Scholarship: What Next?,* 1 Constitutional Commentary 17, 66 (1988) [hereinafter *Symposium*].

102. Donald E. Wilkes, *The New Federalism in Criminal Procedure: State Court Evasion of the Burger Court,* 62 Ky. L. J. 421 (1974).

Court. But under Burger the Court "simply has different goals in mind."[103] Finally, no longer able to depend on Supreme Court majorities to defend their viewpoint, supporters of the Warren approach suggested that a new emphasis be put on state judges and state constitutional protections.[104]

CONTEMPORARY JUDICIAL POWER: UNDERLYING PREMISES

I will conclude here my discussion of post–Civil War developments in constitutional law. For practical reasons, it is time again to enlarge the discussion. For more than a century now Supreme Court majorities have set national priorities and each time they have done so a succeeding majority has characterized those priorities as being rooted in their predecessor's predilections—not the Constitution. One theme has remained constant, however—an ever expanding judicial power and the proportionate diminution of the right to self-government. The situation did not materially change after the Burger Court retrenchment, and so I postpone until the final chapters the stewardship of Chief Justice William Rhenquist. I want to conclude this chapter by identifying seven premises that to this day form the foundation for how many contemporary scholars view judicial power.

The Symbol of an Open Society

An open society is one in which barriers to free expression and individual self-realization are systematically eliminated.[105] Rights must be considered inherently personal, not conferred by the community, and once the society recognizes some rights to be fundamental, not even the legislature may dilute or take them away.[106] With its emphasis on liberty and equality,

103. *Id.*, at 488. Chase comments: "The Burger Court has chosen to disregard legal guilt . . . as the dominant focus for the resolution of issues of criminal procedure." Chase, *supra* note 101, at 519. It "has refused to go forward, and indeed has retreated." *Id.*, at 595.

104. William Brennan, *State Constitutions and the Protection of Individual Rights,* 90 Harv. L. Rev. 489 (1977). *See, e.g.,* Wilkes, *supra* note 102; and Alan Dershowitz and John H. Ely, *Harris v. New York—Some Anxious Observations on the Candor and Logic of the Emerging Nixon Majority,* 80 Yale L. J. 1198 (1971).

105. *See e.g.,* Lawrence Tribe, American Constitutional Law 16–25, 1063 (1978) [hereinafter Tribe]; and John H. Ely, *Constitutional Interpretivism: Its Allure and Impossibility,* 53 IND. L.J. 399, 404–05 (1978). One commentator conceives an open society as fostering man's "moral evolution." *See* Michael Perry, *Non-Interpretation Review in Human Rights Cases: A Functional Justification,* 56 N.Y.U.L.R. 278, 292 (1981) [hereinafter Perry].

106. Louis Lusky, *Government by Judiciary: What Price Legitimacy?,* 6 Hast. C. L. Q. 403, 417 (1979). To believers in an open society a correlation apparently exists between the openness of a society's beliefs and a presumed faith in progress. *See* McCloskey, *supra* note 71, at 46–48. Monaghan reports that Dean Redlick argued "that 'the textual standard should be the entire Constitution' and its 'image of a free and open society.'" Henry Monaghan, *Our Perfect Constitution,* 56 N.Y.U.L. Rev. 353, 367 (1981) (quoting Norman Redlick, *Are There 'Certain Rights . . . Retained By the People'?,* 37 N.Y.U.L. Rev. 787, 810 [1962]).

the Declaration of Independence unequivocally establishes that Americans have always believed that their society was an open one and, after the Revolution, the American people's continued commitment to societal openness was demonstrated by the addition of a Bill of Rights to the Constitution, often viewed as part of a Lockean social contract in which certain natural rights became inviolable.[107]

It is at this juncture that the connection between the open society symbol and the modern rise of judicial power becomes clearer. "Open society" subscribers contend that the framers created an independent federal judiciary not simply to assure that legislative majorities would not abandon Bill of Rights requirements, but to assure that the people's commitment to the premises of an open society would continue and intensify in the future. "Everything about the prohibitions in the Bill of Rights points to the propriety of their being construed with extreme breadth . . . and the job of so construing them, and enforcing them as construed, is *properly the job of the Court.*"[108] American dedication to an open society was strengthened considerably by the addition of the Civil War amendments.

Open societies are not viewed then as being static; rather they are seen as being inherently progressive.[109] How far a particular society has progressed can be measured by seeing how open that society really is in practice.[110] Hence, a society continuously must work to remove barriers (created either by private or governmental actions) that deny individuals, or identi-

107. *See* Avian Soifer, *Protecting Civil Rights: A Critique of Raoul Berger's History,* 54 N.Y.U.L. Rev. 651, 661, 674, 682 (1979). *But see* Raoul Berger, *Soifer to the Rescue of History,* 32 S.C.L. Rev. 427, 459 (1981). *Cf. supra,* chapter 1, text accompanying note 20.

108. Charles S. Hyneman, The Supreme Court on Trial 231 (1963) (quoting Charles L. Black, Jr., The People and the Court 96 [1960]) (emphasis added). Professor Black had continued: "Everything points to the propriety of high judicial vigilance in these areas, and of unembarrassed judicial courage in acting where these considerations compel action." *Id.,* at 108.

109. Bryden observes that such an approach poses "the perpetual danger of equating the progress of liberty with the progress of the law." David P. Bryden, supra note 101, at 73. *See e.g.,* Zechariah Chafee, *The Progress of the Law, 1919–1922,* 35 Harv. L. Rev. 428 (1922). Robert Bork refers to this view in which rights only expand and never contract as a "liberal rachet." Robert H. Bork, The Tempting of America 92 (1989).

110. *See* Soifer, *supra* note 107, at 651, 682, 705–706. *But see,* Berger, *supra* note 107, at 458–460, and Michael Perry, *Interpretivism, Freedom of Expression, and Equal Protection,* 42 Ohio St. L.J. 261, 285, n. 100, 286–287 (1981). David M. O'Brien comments:

> It was with the generations that came of age in the late 1950s, 1960s and early 1970s that liberal legal scholars . . . turned toward 'abstract beliefs about morality and justice,' the teachings of natural law and human dignity, the 'voice of reason,' 'a moral patrimony' implicitly in 'our common heritage,' 'the circumstances and values of the present generation,' 'constitutional morality,' 'fundamental values,' the 'essential principles of justice,' and even the idea of progress.

O'Brien, in *Symposium, supra* note 101, 109, at 58.

fiable groups, appropriate procedures or substantive rights enjoyed by others. An example of such a view can be seen in the approach taken by Michael Perry, who argues that such barriers are viewed as "inhibit[ing] man's moral evolution."[111] In another approach, First Amendment freedoms must be accorded a preferred status.[112] However, all open society subscribers apparently agree, that it was not until the emergence of the Warren Court that Bill of Rights and Fourteenth Amendment provisions were given more practical application. Until then, the American people had largely failed to live up to the commitments made in the Declaration of Independence and the Bill of Rights, and subsequently enhanced by the Civil War amendments.[113]

Methodology

Those who envisioned the Supreme Court as the ultimate protector, implementor, and expander of open society values had to challenge the traditional view that the judicial power to interpret the law had been a limited and passive power. Accordingly, they substituted the "idea of a permanent constitution . . . [with] the idea of a living constitution, a constitution whose substantive meaning [would depend] more upon time and circumstance than upon clearly discernable political principles."[114]

A more suitable interpretative meth-

111. Michael Perry, *Noninterpretive Review in Human Rights Cases: A Functional Justification,* 56 N.Y.U.L. Rev. 278, 292 (1981).

112. The preferred freedom doctrine usually refers to "freedom of expression and association, rights of political participation, rights of religious autonomy, and rights of privacy and personhood." Tribe, *supra* note 105, at 564. Origination of the doctrine is usually attributed to Justice Stone's opinion in United States v. Carolene Products Co, 304 U.S. 144, 152n.4 (1938). *See* Lusky, *supra* note 27, at 112. A classic statement may be found in Zechariah Chafee, Free Speech in the United States (1954). More absolutist approaches may be found in Alexander Meiklejohn, *The First Amendment is an Absolute,* 1961 Sup. Ct. Rev. 688 (1961); Edmond Cahn, *Justice Black and First Amendment 'Absolutes': A Public Interview,* 37 N.Y.U.L. Rev. 549 (1962); George Anastaplo, The Constitutionalist (1971); and, Nat Hentoff, The First Freedom: The Tumultuous History of Free Speech in America (1980).

As early as 1963 Charles S. Hyneman concluded that after 1937 the Supreme Court apparently substituted preferred freedoms over the property rights favored by their predecessors. In either case the presumption that legislative acts were constitutional began to erode; instead, statutes affecting rights in the preferred area began to be treated with suspicion, if not being presumed to be unconstitutional. Hyneman, *supra* note 108, at 226. One sample of what he found will suffice (he is quoting Jerome Frank):

> "I suggest that the following proposal would bring us a little closer to the plan of the fathers. . . . The doctrine of presumption should be completely eradicated in cases involving basic liberties. In that area, a presumption of unconstitutionality should prevail. In free speech cases, in particular, the Supreme Court has no business paying 'great deference' or indeed any deference to the judgment of the legislature. It should do the exact opposite."

Hyneman, *supra,* at 227, in Supreme Court and Supreme Law (Edmond Cahn, ed., 1954).

113. *See infra,* chapter 6 (under *individual rights*).

114. Gary L. McDowell, The Constitution and Contemporary Constitutional Theory 13 (1985). *See infra,* chapter 6 (under *Remain Adaptable*).

odology emerged after World War II. The first, crucial step required that a "right" be identified. Such rights might be found to be more appropriate to American society's contemporary commitment to racial equality (e.g., prohibiting racial segregation in public schools);[115] or deduced from textual language (e.g., a right to have illegally obtained evidence excluded from a defendant's trial—a right deduced from, among other textual provisions, the Fourth Amendment guarantee against unreasonable searches and seizures);[116] or based on explicit constitutional language (e.g., the Fifth Amendment proviso that no person "shall be compelled" to be a witness against himself);[117] or because the right was now associated with the "emanations" or the "penumbras" of other constitutional provisions (e.g., privacy).[118]

Neither the specific content nor the justifications offered for such rights need concern us here. The key to understanding the change in methodology in each instance is that the constitutional text must be approached at the proper level of generality or abstraction.[119] One scholar provides this illustration: "The practice of denying blacks the legal right to contract could be described, at one level of generality, as 'racial discrimination' and at higher levels of generality, as 'discrimination based on morally irrelevant characteristics,' 'unjust discrimination,' and 'injustice.'"[120] Details are again unnecessary. Once the preferred level of generality or abstraction is conceptualized and selected, in the next step a judge may conclude that if the identified right is not being exercised in a meaningful fashion (an assessment reached by the same judge), that constitutional provision has become meaningless. Hence, drawing on the examples previously noted, Supreme Court majorities have ruled that police interrogation must cease at the defendant's request otherwise his right to silence (a right itself derived from the prohibition against self-incrimination) would not be practically preserved; or, if even improperly obtained reliable evidence is not excluded from a

115. Brown v. Board of Education, 347 U.S. 483 (1954).
116. Mapp v. Ohio, 367 U.S. 643 (1961).
117. Miranda v. Arizona, 384 U.S. 436 (1966).
118. Roe v. Wade, 410 U.S. 113 (1973); United States v. Katz, 389 U.S. 347 (1967); and Griswold v. Connecticut, 381 U.S. 479 (1965).
119. *See, e.g.,* Paul Brest, *Who Decides?*, 58 So. Cal. L. Rev. 661, 662 (1985) ("levels of generality"); and Frederick Davis, *Symposium: Judicial Review and the Constitution—The Text and Beyond,* 8 U. Dayton L. Rev. 443, 452 (1983) ("higher and higher levels of generality"); Terrance Sandalow, *Constitutional Interpretation,* 79 Mich. L. Rev. 1033, 1035, 1045 (1981) (different levels of generality" and "right level of generality"); and Owen Fiss, *Objectivity and Interpretation,* 34 Stan. L. Rev. 739, 742 (1982) ("general language"); and Richard H. Fallon, *Constructivist Coherence Theory of Constitutional Interpretation,* 100 Harv. L. Rev. 1189, 1245 (1987) ("historical intent may be fixed at highly varied levels of abstraction").
120. Davis, *supra* note 119, at 452.

defendant's trial, then all citizens' future Fourth Amendment rights would be jeopardized; or that the decision to abort a fetus must substantially remain between a woman and her physician so that her right of privacy is preserved. Although in each instance the competing interests might be weighed differently by legislators, these judicial *interpretations* are not viewed as mere public policy preferences but instead as *constitutional commands* without which the rights in question (e.g., right against compulsory self-incrimination, to silence, to the exclusion of illegally obtained evidence, and to privacy), would be reduced to a "'mere form of words.'"[121]

Subscribers to this new methodology defend such judicial pronouncements on the grounds that they constitute nothing more than the *enforcement* of promises initially made by the American people in the Constitution and its subsequent amendments; which is to say, affirmations of their commitment to an open society. Thus, contemporary judicial interpretations, including the creation of rights not found in the explicit language of the text or which were unknown to the framers, must be obeyed and respected equally by all Americans and the other political branches as if they had been explicitly written into the Constitution. In this view, the framers lodged the crucial power of judicial review in the hands of one Supreme Court so that they could adapt the Constitution to changing circumstances.[122]

The Proper Role of the Supreme Court

As already mentioned in passing, subscribers to the new methodology, frequently inspired by the vision of an open society, assert that until the mid-twentieth century, an acute gap existed between the ideals that the American people professed (i.e., liberty and equality) and the nation's history—one marked by racial, gender, and economic discrimination. Even after World War II, when the need for "long-range . . . social reform" had become blatantly apparent,[123] needed reforms were blocked due to the misfeasance, nonfeasance, or malfeasance of often archaic and sometimes repressive state executives and legislatures.[124] They charge that elected officials simply proved ill-equipped or unwilling to embark on unpopular reforms or

121. Mapp v. Ohio, *supra* note 77, at 648–649. *See* chapter 6 *infra,* text accompanying note 99.

122. Oliver v. United States, 80 L. Ed 2d 214, 229–230 (1984) (Marshall, J.). *But see* William Gangi, *O What a Tangled Web We Weave . . .*, 19 The Prosecutor 15, 26 (1986). These premises are associated under *Remain Adaptable* in chapter 6, *infra.*

123. William Forrester, *Are We Ready for Truth in Judging?* 63 A.B.A.J. 1215, 1216 (1977).

124. These arguments are related to the existence of an alleged vacuum (*i.e.,* the failure of a representative institution to act when, according to its critics, it should have) and will be discussed in chapter 6, *infra,* under *Vacuum.*

reforms that were opposed by entrenched economic interests. Thus, elected officials were perceived as part of the problem, not the solution.[125]

Proponents of increased judicial power contend that the traditional democratic remedy for an unresponsive government—electing those more responsive—had become inoperative either because the right to vote itself was being severely circumscribed, if not altogether denied, or the individuals denied rights were members of permanent minorities (e.g, racial minorities or criminal defendants). Thus, prejudiced constituents repeatedly elected prejudiced officials who passed prejudicial laws. In this context, traditional theories of democratic electoral accountability fell short (or perhaps worked too well). Similarly, cumbersome amendment processes proved equally ineffective as instruments of needed reform, being more responsive to majority desires than providing relief to insular and isolated minorities. As one scholar observed: "We [scholars] simply do not believe that 'majorities' and legislatures are willing or able to engage in serious, reflective moral discourse. . . . The scholar's implicit message is that if the Supreme Court does not take rights seriously, no one will."[126]

Upon such assumptions, the American legal intelligentsia has favored the expansion of judicial power and today judges must be acknowledged as important, and at times even decisive, public policy makers. Judicial power provides an acceptable and more efficient means for addressing

125. *See infra,* chapter 6 for further discussion of the *Best Suited* symbol. *Cf. e.g.,* Paul Brest, *The Misconceived Quest for the Original Understanding,* 60 B.U.L. REV. 204, 227–229 (1980), *with* Raoul Berger, *Paul Brest's Brief for an Imperial Judiciary,* 40 MARYLAND L. REV. 1, 24–26 (1981).

Since the decline of the Warren Court and the emergence of the Burger-Rhenquist courts, an increasingly radicalized legal literature has become hostile to many of the liberal assumptions made in the text. Supporters of the Warren Court thus find themselves criticized by both conservative commentators and those critical of the entire legal system (*e.g.,* the Critical Legal Studies Movement). *See e.g.,* Allen C. Hutchinson and Patrick J. Monaghan, *Law, Politics, and the Critical Legal Scholars: The Unfolding Drama of American Legal Thought,* 36 STAN. L. REV. 199, 199 (1984) (Critical Legal Theory "adherents do not simply contest the practical policies yielded by traditional legal theory; they reject the very basics of the theory itself"); Roberto Unger, *The Critical Legal Studies Movement,* 96 HARV. L. REV. 563, 563 (1983) (The "critical legal studies movement has undermined the central ideas of modern legal thought and put forth another conception of law [that] . . . implies a view of society and informs a practice of politics"); and, Duncan Kennedy, *Form and Substance in Private Law Adjudication,"* 89 HARV. L. REV. 1685 (1976). *But see* Charles Fried, *Jurisprudential Responses to Legal Realism,* 73 CORNELL L. REV. 331 (1988). Tushnet, for example, claims that continued attempts to legitimize the Warren Court decisions by some commentators "result from an unconscious recognition that liberal political theory has failed, and from a desperate effort to suppress that recognition." Mark Tushnet, *Legal Realism, Structural Review, and Prophecy,* 8 U. DAYTON L. REV. 809, 809 (1983).

126. Paul Brest, *The Fundamental Rights Controversy: The Essential Contradictions of Normative Constitutional Scholarship,* 90 YALE L. J. 1063, 1106 (1981). *See infra,* chapter 6, for further discussion of the *Cumbersome* symbol.

contemporary societal conflicts and achieving desired results. The judiciary is now viewed as a bulwark of personal liberties—a "Supreme Administrative Agency,"[127] if not a "LegisCourt."[128]

A Constitutional Right To Meaningful Court-Created Remedies

Based on the three preceding premises, a new judicial duty emerged: to make certain that for each identified constitutional violation courts would provide a practical and meaningful remedy. Justice Goldberg, for example, summed up the Warren Court's criminal defendant decisions as "introduc[ing] an entirely new principle—a new promise—that where there is a right, that right will not remain unenforceable because of the defendant's poverty, ignorance, or lack of remedy."[129] Judge Richard A. Posner recently concluded that "federal courts have learned in recent years how to legislate, adjudicate, and (through broad interpretations of their equity powers) execute public policy."[130]

The Constitution As Open-Ended

Earlier we noted that at the heart of the new methodology is the belief that the Constitution must be capable of being applied to changing circumstances. Proponents defend that perspective by contending that the delegates at Philadelphia intentionally used "language which was almost certainly selected for its open-endedness and its capacity for redefinition over time."[131] Andizej Rapaczynski, for example, claims that with respect to interpreting the Constitution there is "no textual provision *by itself* [that] seriously constrains how [the Constitution] is going to be interpreted. This . . . is true not only about the open-ended provisions but quite generally, about all textual provisions."[132] Another scholar explains

127. Gary Leedes, *The Supreme Court Mess,* 57 Texas L. Rev. 1361, 1361 (1979).

128. Forrester, *supra* note 123, at 1216. *See infra,* chapter 6 for further discussion of the *Results* (where the Supreme Court legislates new rules on criminal interrogation, death penalties, or abortion), *Accepted* and *Legiscourt* symbols.

129. Goldberg, *supra* note 73, at 20.

130. Richard A. Posner, *The Separation of Powers,* in Politics, supra note 25, at 43. Some scholars contend that this new judicial role merely extends the common-law power of judges, and, in that respect, the new court role "closely resembles common-law adjudication." Brest, *supra* note 126, at 1068. The point need not be belabored here: whether through an expanded application of the interpretative power or through higher levels of abstraction [*See* comment accompanying note 118, *supra*] all such contentions amount to mere variants of the "landmarks" discussed in the text. For a more recent and ambitious variant, *see* Stephen Munzer, A Theory of Property (1990). *See* chapter 6 *infra,* discussion of the influence of Justice Cardozo.

131. Alan Dershowitz, *The Sovereignty of Process: The Limits of Original Intention,* in Politics, *supra* note 25, at 12.

132. Andrezej Rapaczynski, *The Ninth Amendment and the Unwritten Constitution: The Problem of Constitutional Interpretation,* 64 Chicago-Kent L. Rev. 177, 177 (1988).

that the courts "serve as speech writers continually updating [the Framers' 'sublime oration on the dignity of man'] . . . symbolized—and only symbolized—by the Constitution."[133] Or to give yet another example: "The open-ended clauses of Section 1 [of the Fourteenth Amendment] . . . 'Privileges or immunities,' 'liberty,' 'due process,' and 'equal protection' do not interpret themselves."[134]

Advocates of open-endedness usually contend that the "meaning [of constitutional phrases], cannot [or rather should not] be determined by reference to text or history" [i.e., what those phrases meant to those who ratified them].[135] Instead, the phrases' meaning must be approached in the context of whether or not they pose a barrier to open society ideals.[136] A few commentators justify this approach on the narrow ground that the Court should be "entitled . . . to seek out the sorts of evils the framers meant to combat and to move against their twentieth century counterparts."[137] Far more frequently, however, commentators go considerably further, describing the Constitution as containing words or phrases that are "general and leave room for expanding content as time passes and conditions change."[138] Some scholars even "view the Constitution as authorizing

133. Edward J. Erler, in *Symposium, supra* note 101 at 52 (quoting Brennan, J.) (citations omitted).
134. Baer, in Politics, *supra* note 29, at 70. *See also* Henry S. Commager, *The Constitution and Original Intent,* 19 The Center Magazine 4, 5 (1986) (The Constitution contains "inevitable ambiguities, some of which were included quite deliberately"). This assumption, that at least several clauses were designed by the framers to be open-ended, is distinct from another related assumption (*e.g.,* that clauses may be interpreted at higher and higher levels of generality). *See* accompanying note 118, *supra.* The contention about open-endedness seems either to attribute that purpose to the framers or to say that the incorporation of such general phrases is a part of good constitution making. There are strong progressivist assumptions associated with the generality point of view attributed to certain constitutional phrases by thinkers such as Roscoe Pound, Benjamin Cardozo, and Felix Frankfurter who made that approach popular. *See supra* chapter 4, text and comments accompanying notes 46–52. William Van Alstyne's criticism should suffice: "Given suitable ingenuity, perhaps the whole of the constitution could be reduced to a single paragraph and still not lose any of the judicial glossing it has received." William Van Alstyne, *Interpreting **This** Constitution: The Unhelpful Contribution of Special Theories of Judicial Review,* U. Fla. L. Rev. 209, 219 (1983).
135. Joseph D. Grano, *Ely's Theory of Judicial Review: Preserving the Significance of the Political Process,* 42 Ohio St. L. J. 167, 168–169 (1981).
136. See John H. Ely, *The Wages of Crying Wolf: A Comment on Roe v. Wade,* 82 Yale L. J. 920, 945 (1973); Brest, *supra* note 125, at 205.
137. Ely, *supra* note 136, at 929.
138. Robert H. Bork, *Neutral Principles and Some First Amendment Problems,* 47 Ind. L. J. 1, 13 (1971) (quoting Herbert Wechsler, *Toward Neutral Principles of Constitutional Law,* in Principles, Politics, and Fundamental Law 3, 43 (1961). *See also* William Rehnquist, *The Notion of a Living Constitution,* 54 Texas L. Rev. 693, 695 (1976) ("living Constitution" justifies judicial action when other branches fail to act), and Terrance Sandalow, *Judicial Protection of Minorities,* 75 Mich. L. Rev. 1162, 1162 (1977) (post-Warren Court majorities create uncertain constitutional protections). Allied expressions include the belief that constitutional provisions "exist on a spectrum ranging from the relatively specific to the extremely open-textured," (Ely, *supra* note

courts to nullify the results of the political process on the basis of general principles of political morality not derived from the constitutional text or the structure it creates."[139]

Although some proponents claim to limit judicial adaptation to "inferences from the values the Constitution marks as special,"[140] they also frequently advocate modifying the framers' original understanding of those principles, or substitute judicial assessments for legislative ones.[141] In the end, many legal scholars today put in the hands of the judiciary the power to create new individual rights and provide remedies for their violation—a power that is not traceable to the constitutional text, the historic milieu at the time of adoption, nor the framers' understanding of the judicial power.[142]

The most prestigious law reviews are characteristically filled with disagreements among the proponents of various views, each author advising judges on how constitutional phrases should be reinterpreted in order to create new personal rights, or to enhance the application of traditional rights; or how both may be applied more effectively; or their exercise made less dependent on an individual's or group's economic status.[143] Each year these "special theories of judicial review"[144] grow bolder and more numerous.[145] Several generalizations should be sufficient to orient

---

105, at 413) or are "difficult to read responsibly as anything other than open and across-the-board invitations to import into the constitutional decision process considerations that will not be found . . . in the Constitution." *Id.,* at 415.

139. Monaghan, *supra* note 106, at 353.

140. *See* Ely, *supra* note 136, at 935 (emphasis omitted). For example, although he would personally approve of such *legislation,* Ely had this to say about the Court's decision in *Roe v. Wade:* "[My] point is that the prior decisions, including those that have drawn the most fire, at least started from a value singled out by, or fairly inferable from, the Constitution as entitled to special protection." *Id.,* at 936 n. 97.

141. *See* Bork, *supra* note 138, at 17. Nagel provides this analysis of one variant of such constitutional theory: "The preferred method of analysis is to examine text, history, political theory, social facts, and other sources in order to identify a value that should be accorded constitutional status. Because constitutional significance is not tied to specific language or history, the value is necessarily both important and vague; hence, almost any issue can have constitutional dimensions, and the value alone cannot explain case outcomes." Robert Nagel, book review, 127 U. PA. L. REV. 1174, 1178 (1979) (reviewing TRIBE, *supra* note 105).

142. *See* Ely, *supra* note 136, at 946.

143. It is beyond the scope of this book to provide an exhaustive list of the main protagonists in such disputes, but the following brief list should enable the interested reader to pursue the matter: JOHN RAWLS, A THEORY OF JUSTICE (1971); ROBERT NOZICK, ANARCHY, STATE, AND UTOPIA (1974); RONALD DWORKIN, TAKING RIGHTS SERIOUSLY (1978) [hereinafter SERIOUSLY]; RONALD DWORKIN, LAW'S EMPIRE (1986) [hereinafter EMPIRE]; Fallon, *supra* note 119; JOHN H. ELY, DEMOCRACY & DISTRUST (1980); MICHAEL PERRY, THE CONSTITUTION, THE COURTS AND HUMAN RIGHTS (1982) and MUNZER, *supra* note 130.

144. Van Alstyne, *supra* note 134.

145. *See* Robert W. Gorden, *The Politics of Legal History and the Search for a Usable Past,* and William Nelson, *New Directions in American Legal History,* in *Recent Trends, supra* note 37.

the reader: on the one hand, some commentators advocate open-ended interpretation of constitutional provisions to obtain, secure, and expand only *procedural or process oriented rights* (i.e., rights that promise to increase access to or participation in, or criticism of, the political processes);[146] on the other hand, other commentators believe that courts should use those techniques only to increase or expand important *substantive rights* (e.g., to abortion, to speech, and to more equitable distributions of property).[147]

At times these two positions appear irreconcilable, but they share the common belief that the judiciary should be ceded enormous and unprecedented power.[148] Substance proponents are perhaps more elitist, because they favor direct judicial implementation of their views.[149] More often than not, however, both camps go "beyond an emphasis on structure, process and participation."[150] Nagel, for example, offers this observation: "The Constitution . . . [they] suggest, necessarily must address the most serious public concerns, and must achieve a result that can be seen as virtuous in order to be worthy of its fundamental status. Any 'imperfections' in the document must be remedied by interpretation."[151] And so it is to contemporary views of interpretation that I now turn.

Interpretive v. Noninterpretive Views of Interpretation

Have you ever discussed a movie or book with friends only to find that you disagreed with them about the meaning of the plot? Or about what motivated the main characters or another major point? Some contemporary scholars contend that constitutional interpretations should be viewed no differently than other types of interpretation,[152] or semiotics,[153] or

146. *See, e.g.,* Ely, *supra* note 143.
147. *See supra,* comment accompanying note 125.
148. *See, e.g.* Richard Neely, How Courts Govern America 5–7 (1981) (vague constitutional issues provide the Court with an exclusive vehicle to effect changes on individuals and state agencies often without warning). See *infra* chapter 7, for specific examples.
149. *See e.g.,* James B. White, *Reflections on the Role of the Supreme Court: The Contemporary Debate and the "Lessons" of History,* 63 Judicature 162, 171 (1979).
150. *Id.*
151. Nagel, *supra* note 141, at 1179–1170 (reviewing Tribe, *supra* note 105. *See also* Monaghan, *supra* note 106.
152. Empire, *supra* note 143, at 59. Gordon Wood states that "deconstruction and reception theory remind us that books or texts do not belong to their authors." Gordon Wood, *Ideology and the Origins of Liberal America,* 44 The Wm. & Mary Quarterly 628, 628 (1987). Paul Bator understands Stanley Fisk to believe that "every text is the creation of the reader." Paul Bator, *Discussion-Jurisprudential Responses to Legal Realism,* 73 Cornell L. Rev. 341, 344 (1988). *But see id.,* at 346.
153. Semiotics is "a general philosophical theory of signs and symbols that deals esp[ecially] with their function in both artificially constructed and natural languages and comprises the three branches of syntactics, semantics, and pragmatic." 3 Webster's Third New International Dictionary of the English Language, Unabridged 2064 (1971).

hermeneutics.[154] Judicial interpretation is viewed as analogous to literary criticism, "teasing out the various dimensions of value in a complex play or poem."[155] Within this framework, subscribers to this view can freely admit that a constitutional provision might have had a specific meaning for the delegates at Philadelphia, while simultaneously declaring that judges today need not be confined by that meaning.[156] Generally, these scholars are referred to as deconstructionists.[157] They contend that the "Constitution means whatever we want it to mean. Of course, we cannot attribute any meaning we want and expect to get away with it. We have to convince others of our 'true' interpretation, and if we can convince enough people that that is the 'true' meaning, then so it becomes."[158]

There are also other positions,[159] but over the past decade two main

154. Hermeneutics is "the study of the methodological principles of interpretation and explanation; . . . [more specifically] the study of the general principles of biblical interpretation." Webster, *supra* note 153, at 1059. *See, e.g.,* Anthony Giddens, Profiles and Critiques in Social Theory (1982) (*But see* William Gangi, book review, 13 Perspective 60 [1984]); John L. Hodge, *Democracy and Free Speech: A Normative Theory of Society and Government,* in The First Amendment Reconsidered: New Perspectives in the Meaning of Freedom of Speech and Press 148–80 (1982); Peter Goodrich, *Language, Test and Signs in the History of Legal Doctrine,* 8 Liverpool L. Rev. 95, 95–96 (1984) and Timothy Reiss, The Uncertainty of Analysis: Problems in Truth, Meaning, and Culture (1988). *See infra,* chapter 6, text and comments accompanying notes 67–71, for additional discussion on the contemporary use and abuse of "symbols" and "models". (I would like to express my appreciation to Edward McGowan, research associate at St. John's University, for bringing many of the works mentioned in this note and in note 119, chapter 5, *infra* to my attention.)

155. Empire, *supra* note 143, at 228. *See also* Easterbrook, in Politics, *supra* note 25, at 118–119 (discussing deconstruction and New Criticism interpretive techniques).

156. Of course, earlier discussions on generality, abstraction, and open-ended approaches to the constitutional interpretation are pertinent at this juncture. Easterbrook comments: "New Critics are uninterested in what the writers may have wanted to convey. Readers, not writers, are sovereign. Just as people may find unexpected meaning in a painting or discover in a photograph something the photographer did not know was in the frame, so interpreters may attribute new meaning to texts." Easterbrook, in Politics, *supra* note 25, at 18.

157. "Deconstructionists exalt the creative and subjective dimension of interpretation [and] deny that an interpretative community possesses the necessary authority to confer the rules that might constrain the interpretation and constitute the standards of evaluation." Fiss, *supra* note 119, at 746. John McArthur maintains that such advocates "reject . . . altogether the possibility of settled textual reading." John B. McArthur, *Abandoning the Constitution: The New Wave in Constitutional Theory,* 59 Tulane L. Rev. 280, 298 (1984). For additional sources *see* Fiss, *supra* note 119, 746n. 9 and Christopher D. Stone, *Introduction: Interpreting the Symposium,* 58 Sou. Cal. L. Rev. 1, 5 (1985).

158. Wood, *supra* note 152, at 632. Wood may be reporting, not advocating, here.

159. Alexander suggests that a "sound theory of interpretation would tell us not only what the Framers did, but also why what they did is authoritative, and to what extent." Larry A. Alexander, *Painting Without the Numbers: Noninterpretive Judicial Review,* 8 U. Dayton L. Rev. 447, 453–454 (1983). *But see* William Rehnquist, "The Nature of Judicial Interpretation," in Politics, *supra* note 130, at 3–4.

groups have emerged: the interpretivists and the noninterpretivists.[160] Apparently Thomas Grey first used the terms,[161] but they are most frequently employed today with the specificity added by John Hart Ely, who defined interpretivism to mean "that judges deciding constitutional issues should confine themselves to enforcing *values* or *norms* that are stated or very clearly implicit in the written Constitution." Ely defined noninterpretivism as the belief that "courts should go beyond that set of references and enforce *values and norms* that cannot be discovered within the four corners of the document."[162]

Michael Perry, however, offers the

160. Brest employed the term "originalism" to convey what other commentators call interpretivism and "moderate originalism" for what others call noninterpretivism. *See* Brest, supra note 136. Walter B. Michaels describes Brest's "originalism . . . [as the] belief that the provisions of the Constitution should mean throughout history whatever they meant in 'the original understanding.'" Walter Michaels, *Response to Perry and Simon,* 58 SO. CAL. L. REV. 673, 673 (1985). Clinton, who provides extensive source materials, defines originalism as "the view that the Constitution or any amendment thereto should be interpreted as its spirit and language were understood when the relevant provision was drafted rather than in light of new and different meanings that later generations have created and supplied." Robert N. Clinton, *Original Understanding, Legal Realism, and the Interpretation of 'This Constitution'*, 72 IOWA L. REV. 1177, 1179 (1987). Accordingly, Gunther describes the works of Raoul Berger as "advocating simply reading the legislative debates of the Constitutional Convention to define what the Framers would have said about all the problems this Constitutional polity has faced over the years." Gunther, in Commager, *supra* note 134, at 8.

The above descriptions are inadequate because the framers viewed the Constitution as being both fixed and capable of meeting new developments. Some of the above descriptions of interpretivism (originalism) also come dangerously close to equating it with literalism, a kind of constitutional fundamentalism. *But see infra,* chapter 5, comment accompanying note 118. Michael rightly points out that in principle at least interpretivists as such make "no claim about what the Constitution 'should mean', [they only claim] . . . that the Constitution—*can only mean* what it originally meant." Michaels, id., at 673. Other scholars see themselves as somewhere between the two camps. Gunther comments:

> Many constitutional scholars, including I, believe that neither pure originalism nor complete open-endedness is the true guide to the Constitution. It is something in between these extremes that provides guidance. Permissible guidelines can be found in the text, history, and structure of the Constitution. These are far superior to simply reading political mores or contemporary intellectual views into the Constitution.

Gunther, in Commager, *supra* note 134, at 9. *See also* Clinton, *supra,* at 1278. While the possibility of "a third way" cannot be foreclosed, by the same token just as Parmenides maintained that one cannot simultaneously contend something is and is not (see *infra* chapter 5, comment accompanying note 4), the literature is replete with attempts to do just that, embracing Publius' design for a republic while at the same time locating the amending power in the hands of the Supreme Court. In any event, the terms *interpretive* and *noninterpretive* will be used in the text because they appear more frequently in the literature than do those put forth by Brest.

161. Thomas Grey, *Do We Have an Unwritten Constitution?*, 27 STAN L. REV. 703, 706n. 9 (1975). Grey ultimately rejected interpretivism on the ground that it cannot obtain the results he believed desirable. *Id.*, at 714. Furthermore, he apparently argued that since contemporary Supreme Court opinions have not employed interpretivism, it should be discarded on historical grounds: it did not last. *Id.*, at 717.

162. Ely, *supra* note 105, at 399 (emphasis added). Ely's distinctions also fall short because he

clearest distinctions between interpretivists and noninterpretivists.[163] He maintains that the two groups look very differently at *the power of judicial review.* Interpretivists see the Constitution as consisting "of a complex of value judgments the *Framers wrote into the text of the Constitution and thereby constitutionalized.*"[164] In one category Perry puts the "structure of American government"; namely, the division and separation of powers;[165] in a second category he puts "aspects of the relationship that shall exist between the individual and government," which he maintains the Constitution "specifies."[166] Interpretivists, Perry concludes, decide specific questions by depending on the "character" given by the framers to "one of the value judgments" contained in the Constitution.[167] In contrast, noninterpretivists proceed quite differently, since to them the Supreme Court may determine that an issue is of constitutional character even though it is based on "value judgment[s] *other* than one[s] constitutionalized by the Framers."[168] For this reason Perry specifically identi-

---

uses open-ended textual explications with both terms, freeing the adherents of both groups from the meaning which certain terms acquired through historical usage. He also often engages in speculation, and his usage of certain terms cannot be reconciled with traditional concepts of judicial review and democratic theory. *See* Grano, *supra* note 135, at 171. Other commentators point to the fact that Ely's support of judicial intervention in freedom of expression and equal protection cases lacks historical support. See Bork, *supra* note 109, at 178–185; Fallon, *supra* note 119, at 1217–1223; Perry, *supra* note 110, at 270–275; McDowell, *supra* note 114, at 14–20; Brest, *supra* note 126, at 1080–1085 and Monaghan, *supra* note 106, at 356–357.

163. Perry, *supra* note 110. Other scholars also contributed to the defining of these terms. See Larry A. Alexander, *Modern Equal Protection Theories: A Metatheoretical Taxonomy and Critique,* 42 Ohio St. L.J. 3 (1981).

164. Perry, *supra* note 110, at 263–264 (emphasis added). See Bork, *supra* note 109, at 159 ("The interpretation of the Constitution according to the original understanding, then, is the only method that can preserve the Constitution, the separation of powers, and the liberties of the people").

165. Perry, *supra* note 110, at 264.

166. *Id.*

167. *Id.* Perry also mentions that such judgments need not be explicitly contained in "some particular provision" or the "overall structure." *Id.* That position seems defensible, for example, since neither the separation of powers or judicial review is explicitly contained in the Constitution. *See infra,* chapter 5, comment accompanying note 118.

168. *Noninterpretive, supra* note 111, at 265 (emphasis added). Perry acknowledges, however, that "the Court may explain its decision with rhetoric designed to create the illusion that it is merely 'interpreting' or 'applying' some constitutional provision." *Id.* at 264–265. Elsewhere he adds that there is "no harm" in such deception "as long as the justice candidly admits that he or she does not mean that the action offends the original understanding of the clause (the value judgment constitutionalized by the Framers), but that it contravenes the Court's developing equal protection doctrine." *Id.* at 350–351, n. 272. Perry apparently argues that the Court should be entrusted with our "moral evolution," [*id.* at 291–292] and that almost all knowledgeable individuals, including the justices, know that the intentions of the framers are rarely at issue. From my own perceptive, however, Perry claims we live in an advanced moral era but it is an era, in which the justices knowingly violate what in a less advanced stage of civilization was considered one of the first

fies the "legitimacy of noninterpretive review [as] the central problem of contemporary constitutional theory."[169]

Perry, however, rejects the interpretivist's perspective that "all . . . noninterpretive review is illegitimate,"[170] although he concedes that "the decisions in virtually all modern constitutional cases of consequence . . . cannot plausibly be explained except in terms of noninterpretive review, because in virtually no such case can it plausibly be maintained that the Framers constitutionalized the determinative value judgment."[171] Nevertheless, noninterpretive theories have "becom[e] . . . the coin of the realm."[172]

The Assumption That Democratic Institutions Are Inadequate or Have Failed

When all of the prior premises are considered cumulatively, it is abundantly clear that many supporters of contemporary judicial power contend that the Constitution crafted in Philadelphia was seriously flawed. While some of these flaws were at least partially addressed in subsequent amendments, others persist. Elected officials, for example, often have proved unwilling to pursue wise or moral public policies in areas that touch upon race, the poor, criminal defendants, and other disadvantaged groups,

---

moral principles (i.e., lying). This fact calls into question Perry's apparent faith in man's moral evolution. See also McArthur, *supra* note 157, at 295–305 ("The New Wave: Noninterpretivism as Progressive Ideology").

169. Perry, *supra* note 110, at 263.

170. Perry, *supra* note 110, at 265.

171. *Id. See also* Perry, *supra* note 110, at 301. Powell, often a critic of the interpretivist approach, admits that "if 'the Constitution' means nothing more than whatever a legislative majority of five Supreme Court Justices prefer, then the American experiment in a constitutional polity that combines democracy and limited government has failed." H. Jefferson Powell, *Constitutional Law as Though the Constitution Mattered,* 5 DUKE L.J. 915, 927 (1986) (emphasis added).

172. McArthur, *supra* note 157, at 305. McArthur claims that "liberals and conservatives alike share the same prognosis . . . [and thereby] encourage the idea that noninterpretivism is a proven theory, one that is neutral, objective and value-free." *Id.* Perry admonishes critics of interpretivism, "those who seek to defend noninterpretive review—'judicial activism'—do it a disservice when they resort to implausible textual or, more commonly, historical arguments; nothing is gained but much credibility is lost when the case for noninterpretive review is built upon such frail and vulnerable reeds." Perry, *supra* note 110, at 275. Perry himself puts forth what he considers is a justification that could legitimize recent court decisions, a topic beyond the scope of this book. *See generally, Noninterpretivism, supra* note 111. *But see* William Gangi, *The Supreme Court: An Intentionist's Critique of Noninterpretive Review,* 28 THE CATHOLIC LAWYER 253, 275–284 (1983). But Tushnet hints that Perry's support for interpretivist critics of other noninterpretivists is necessary for Perry to put forth his justification. Tushnet, *supra* note 125, at 811 ("The upsurge of interest in constitutional theory [such as evidenced in Perry's works] is plainly designed to protect the legacy of the Warren Court").

because either they share the prejudices of their constituents or fear being defeated at the polls should they take unpopular, though more morally correct, positions.[173] Some scholars go considerably further, viewing law qua law as prettifying the domination of the have-nots by the haves.[174]

If reminded that the delegates at the Philadelphia convention never envisioned the judicial role championed today, or that the people never have consented to a redefining of the judicial power, noninterpretivists typically respond by redefining the meaning of consent. Paul Brest, for example, asserts that "actual consent is not . . . a practicable measure of the legitimacy of any system of government."[175] Other noninterpretivists justify locating the ultimate governing power in the hands of nonelected judges on the grounds that public opinion polls frequently indicate that legislatures are unrepresentative.[176]

So, this is where we find ourselves today: one noninterpretive group urges judicial action on behalf of the democratic process, while the other

173. See *supra* text accompanying notes 123–128. Charles Hyneman summed up this line of reasoning as follows:

> The judicial branch thus becomes a backstop for the legislature and Executive. When the latter fail to read the public mind correctly, the judges are authorized to come in with a correct reading. When the political departments read correctly but fail to respond to the instructions they read, the judges may order those departments to act, or may even formulate and announce the policies which they suspect they can never force from the elected officials.

HYNEMAN, *supra* note 108, at 262.

174. See e.g., Richard D. Parker, *The Past of Constitutional Theory—And Its Future,* 42 OHIO ST. L. J. 223, 257–259 (1981); Hall, in Symposium, *supra* note 101, at 41 ("Constitutional historians need to relearn the old lesson of the Progressive Era that economic interests often drive rather than are driven by ideological concerns"); Kermit and Hall, *American Legal History as Science and Applied Science,* in *Recent Trends, supra* note 37, at 238 ("American history had been a continuous social struggle in which a small elite succeeded repeatedly in frustrating the much larger majority").

175. Brest, *supra* note 136, at 226. But see BORK, *supra* note 109, at 112: "'The intellectual class has found a vehicle for giving its values the force of law, without bothering to take over the political authority of the state'" (quoting Herbert Schlossberg). For additional details *see infra,* chapter 6, under Accepted.

176. Critics of American republicanism often cite national polls in support of their contention that elected representatives do not adequately reflect the will of the American people: e.g., where numerical majorities evidently express views different than those expressed by legislative majorities. *See infra,* chapter 8, test and comments accompany notes 70–73. Compare Tushnet, *supra* note 125, at 811–813 (citing the failure of the equal rights amendment, favored by a national popular majority), with BORK, *supra* note 109, at 153 ("The Constitution . . . holds that we govern ourselves democratically, except on those occasions, few in number though crucially important, when the Constitution places a topic beyond the reach of majorities"), and Perry, who rejects such arguments on the grounds that at least legislative bodies are electorally accountable; their "degree of responsiveness" should be deemphasized because it is being compared to the judiciary, which is "not electorally accountable at all." Perry, *supra* note 110, at 279–280.

noninterpretive group urges judges to create new substantive rights.[177] Both groups accuse one another of imposing personal preferences on the American people.[178] Both groups concede, even at times express concern, that some judicial impositions surely constitute an abuse of the judicial power. Yet neither group considers such admissions fatal, and both process[179] and substantive[180] proponents continue to strive to expand the judicial power.[181] Hence, under the stewardship of three distinctly different chief justices (Earl Warren, Warren Burger, and William Rhenquist), for one purpose or another and in varying degrees the federal judiciary has in some respects become this nation's ultimate public policy maker, reversing the New Dealers' hard-won battle against a laissez-faire judiciary.[182]

177. See Grano, *supra* note 135, at 170 and *supra,* text accompanying notes 146–152.
178. See, e.g., Fallon, *supra* note 119, at 1204 ("Value arguments are even more prominent; indeed, they enjoy almost total predominance, in much of the most respected modern constitutional scholarship").
179. See Alexander, *supra* note 159, at 44–51; George D. Braden, *The Search for Objectivity in Constitutional Law,* 57 Yale L.J. 571, 573–574 (1948) (procedural limitations include jurisdiction over persons and subject litigants). *Id.,* at 574.
180. See Leedes, *supra* note 127, at 1372–1376. (The use of substantive due process by courts to legislate is evident from its discretionary use and development of rules, principles, standards and values). *Id.,* at 1372. To the extent that equal protection is used to set a standard of moral worth it is unquestionably substantive. Alexander, *supra* note 159, at 45.
181. For comments regarding the evidently similar positions of Dworkin and Rawls, see Leedes, *supra* note 127, at 1378, 1396.
182. Compare "Back to the Constitution," address delivered by the Solicitor General, Robert H. Jackson, before the Section of Public Utility Law at San Francisco, July 10, 1939. 25 American Bar Association Journal 745 (1939).

PART III.

THE ROAD DIVIDES

CHAPTER FIVE

Interpretation and the Constitution

Powerful and ingenious minds . . . may, by a course of well digested, but refined and metaphysical reasoning, . . . explain away the constitution of our country, and leave it, a magnificent structure indeed, to look at, but totally unfit for use. They may so entangle and perplex the understanding, as to obscure principles, which were before thought quite plain, and induce doubts where, if the mind were to pursue its own course, none would be perceived. In such a case, it is peculiarly necessary to recur to safe and fundamental principles to sustain those principles, and, when sustained, to make them the tests of the arguments to be examined.[1]

Sooner or later every traveler approaches a fork in the road: "Right or left, which road will take me to my destination?"[2] Should the journey be an unfamiliar one, or directions be lacking or confusing, for most of us such situations surely evoke anxiety, especially if a decision to take one road or the other must be made quickly. And should the journey be in a foreign country, the failure to understand road signs might tempt the traveler to abandon the journey and return home.

For some readers this chapter may be somewhat analogous to confronting a fork in the road in a foreign country. There may be times when the principles being discussed seem like signposts written in a foreign language, causing anxiety and tempting the reader to abandon the journey altogether. That is understandable. Many of our forefathers undoubtedly were similarly confused and sorely tempted to do nothing when asked to chose between the federalists' and antifederalists' visions of America's future. Fortunately, the reader is not forced to make a hasty decision. Indeed, I encourage readers to linger as long as necessary.

1. Gibbons v. Ogden, 22 U.S. 1, 222 (1824) (Marshall, C.J.).

2. The imagery is as old as Parmenides. *See* Werner Jaeger, The Theology of the Early Greek Philosophers 99 (1947).

But a more systematic inquiry into the nature of interpretation can no longer be postponed: it is necessary preparation for the remainder of the journey. As I observed at the end of the last chapter, two views of interpretation dominate today. In one camp are so-called interpretivists who believe, as did Publius, that the delegates to the Philadelphia convention envisioned only a limited role for the judiciary. The chapter's first section will provide a systematic review of that position.[3] In the other camp are the noninterpretivists, those contending that for one reason or another—contrary to interpretivists claims—judges should not be confined by what the ratifiers of the Constitution or any of its subsequent amendments understood their provisions to mean. In the preceding chapter, the underlying premises of noninterpretivists were explored and I concluded that their views more often than not were means to ends that transcended issues of interpretation. For that reason, as well as those of economy, the noninterpretivist defense of extensive judicial power will largely be ignored here. It will be thoroughly presented in the next chapter. In this chapter it is noninterpretivist criticisms of the interpretivist position that must be put squarely before the reader and it is these criticisms that the reader must stop and evaluate. The reader may again anticipate that the polemic will increase another notch.

Some scholars may assert that the choice put before the reader is contrived; that in fact the reader has alternate routes available; or that it is possible to travel along both the interpretivist and noninterpretivist roads simultaneously.[4] I do not think those options are viable, but admittedly I have reached that conclusion only after a decade of having journeyed down many of the suggested alternate roads—side trips fully recounted in the next chapter. Thus, while I consider it imperative for each reader eventually to come to a conclusion regarding my thesis—that today courts deny Americans the full measure of their right to self-government—I agree that some will wish to reserve judgment until after exploring all the arguments still before them. In this

3. *See supra,* chapter 1, text, comment, and sources accompanying notes 2–16. In attempting to sustain the literary fork-in-the-road device, I was sorely tempted to have one road (*i.e.,* the road favored by most contemporary supporters of judicial power) go to the left while the road to the right would be the one favored by Publius. Evidence certainly exists to sustain such a distinction. But to do so not only would be inaccurate (*e.g.,* when convenient, some conservatives appear to be as willing to use techniques to increase judicial power as are liberals), but it would trivialize the options before the reader, and the choices before the reader are what is important.

4. "Though Parmenides . . . suggested that there are only two 'conceivable ways of inquiry,' either a thing is or it is not . . . this utterly false way can be, and constantly is, so combined with the true way that a third way, a compromise between the other two, a thing both is and is not, comes into the picture. This third way is the way on which 'ignorant mortals wander two-faced' . . . because . . . 'they combine contraries.'" Geoffrey S. Kirk and J. E. Raven, The Presocratic Philosophers 271 (1966).

chapter, however, it must only be determined whether or not noninterpretive criticisms of interpretivism are compelling.

PUBLIUS ON THE POWER OF INTERPRETATION

As noted earlier, Publius described "interpretation of the laws" as "the proper and peculiar province of the courts." He also contended that the will of the ratifiers of the Constitution must stand on higher ground than any contrary expression supported by legislative majorities.[5] By so arguing, concludes Lofgren, Publius "defended constitutional supremacy rather than judicial supremacy."[6] This power to declare void acts contrary to the Constitution was considered by Publius as only an extraordinary application of an ordinary judicial interpretive task: e.g. being akin to the chore of resolving a conflict between "two contradictory laws."[7]

Paper 78 of *The Federalist Papers* came to life in *Marbury v. Madison,* which in all important respects paralleled Publius' discussion.[8] Chief Justice John Marshall described the

5. James Madison, Alexander Hamilton, and John Jay, the Federalist Papers [hereinafter Federalist] no. 78, at 467. *See also supra,* chapter 2, text and comments accompanying notes 67–68.

6. Charles Lofgren, *The Original Understanding of Original Intent?,* 5 Constitutional Commentary 77, 88 (1988). Publius put it this way: "The genius of republican liberty seems to demand on one side not only that all power should be derived from the people, but that those intrusted with it should be kept in dependence on the people by a short duration of their appointments; and that even during this short period the trust should be placed not in a few, but a number of hands." Federalist, *supra* note 5, no. 37, at 227.

7. Federalist, *supra* note 5, at 468. *See chapter 2 supra,* text accompanying note 69. Publius certainly was aware of the difficulties surrounding the interpretive task:

> All new laws, though penned with the greatest technical skill and passed on the fullest and most mature deliberation, are considered as more or less obscure and equivocal, until their meaning be liquidated and ascertained by a series of particular discussions and adjudications. Besides the obscurity arising from the complexity of objects and the imperfections of the human faculties, the medium through which the conceptions of men are conveyed to each other adds a fresh embarrassment. The use of words is to express ideas. Perspicuity, therefore, requires not only that the ideas should be distinctly formed, but that they should be expressed by words distinctly and exclusively appropriate to them. But no language is so copious as to supply words and phrases for every complex idea, or so correct as not to include many equivocally denoting different ideas. Hence it must happen that however accurately objects may be discriminated in themselves, and however accurately the discrimination may be considered, the definition of them may be rendered inaccurate by the inaccuracy of the terms in which it is delivered. And this unavoidable inaccuracy must be greater or less, according to the complexity and novelty of the objects defined. . . .
>
> Here, then, are three sources of vague and incorrect definitions: indistinctness of the object, imperfection of the organ of conception, inadequateness of the vehicle of ideas. Any one of these must produce a certain degree of obscurity. The convention, in delineating the boundary between the federal and State jurisdictions, must have experience the full effect of them all.

Federalist, *supra* note 5, no. 37, at 229.

8. Marbury v. Madison, 1 Cranch 97 (1803). See *supra,* chapter 3, for a discussion of Marbury.

function of the courts as "to decide on the rights of individuals" and not to decide issues "in their nature political."[9] Elsewhere, he described "the judicial power . . . [as] never exercised for the purpose of giving effect to the will of the judge; always for the purpose of giving effect to the will of the legislature."[10] Similarly, Chief Justice Taney later described "the province of [the] Court . . . [is] to expound the law, not make it";[11] and again, as "not . . . to decide upon the justice or injustice, the policy or impolicy, of . . . [the] laws [but] to interpret [the Constitution] with the best lights we can obtain on the subject . . . according to its true intent and meaning when it was adopted."[12]

Publius contended that judges were particularly well-suited to decide whether the legislature or executive had exceeded the powers granted them because of their expertise in interpreting the law.[13] But for Publius, as well as the delegates at Philadelphia (even the antifederalists) the power to interpret the law certainly could never be confused with making or executing the laws. These were essentially different tasks that had been clearly assigned to the two electorally accountable branches of government.[14] Publius makes it clear that the power to interpret the law did not confer on judges an unlimited power to create law or to evoke its spirit—a power by which judges would substitute their views for the will of the ratifiers, or of elected representatives. Aside from seeing the many problems that the granting of such power would have entailed for a republican schema, one may turn to the convention's rejection of a council of revision; and Publius' rejection of similar antifederalist assertions.[15]

9. *Id.,* at 170. *See,* chapter 3, comment accompanying note 2, *supra.*
10. Osborne v. Bank of the U.S., 22 U.S. (9 Wheaton) 738, 866 (1924).
11. Luther v. Borden, 7 How. 1, 41 (1849). See *supra,* chapter 3, for a discussion of Luther.
12. Dred Scott v. Sandford, at 404–405. See *supra,* chapter 3, for a discussion of Dred Scott.
13. Federalist, *supra* note 5, no. 78, at 468.
14. There is of course some mixing of powers (*e.g.,* the presidential veto) in the Constitution. But those are exceptions, and Publius deals with them, explaining why each is necessary in the context of the whole. Raoul Berger, for example, notes that "John Adams' 1780 Massachusetts Constitution made the separation of power explicit, forbade each branch to exercise the power of another, and particularized that the "'[judiciary shall] never exercise the legislative . . . powers . . . [so that this] may be a government of laws, and not of men.'" Raoul Berger, *Scope of Judicial Review: An Ongoing Debate,* 6 Hast. Const. L.Q. 527, 540 n. 8 (1979) [hereinafter *Scope*].
15. *See supra,* chapter 2 for a summary of Publius' views. James Wilson's proposal for a single executive meet with considerable opposition at the Philadelphia convention. Roger Sherman, for example, contended that "the executive should do no more than carry out the will of the legislature, and that therefore the Congress ought to be able to make it one or several as it suited them at the moment." Christopher Collier and James L. Collier, Decision in Philadelphia: The Constitutional Convention of 1787 291 (1986). As the convention deliberated on the matter, Sherman suggested that he "would support a single executive, if there was some sort of council that he would have to consult before he acted." *Id.,* at 292. The convention proceeded to approve

The Matter of Intent

Jefferson Powell quite rightly notes that "only the text can claim the dignity of *being* 'the Constitution' [while all other statements about it, whether made by Publius, the justices of the Supreme Court or a law student] are at most *about* 'the Constitution.'"[16] Many contemporary scholars therefore consider any exploration of the framers' intent as conceptually

---

the idea of a single executive, leaving aside the issue of whether a council of revision, possessing undetermined powers, would also be approved. At the time of the convention, apparently all the states had such councils, "with greater or lesser control over the executive," because there was a widespread desire to curb executive power. *Id.,* 292–293. For example, under the Virginia Plan proposed at the convention, such a "council of revision" consisted of "'the executive and a convenient number of the national judiciary,' which could veto legislative acts." *Id.,* at 293. Collier and Collier comment:

> Elbridge Gerry . . . raised a critical point. He doubted that the judiciary ought to be part of any council of revision, as they would already have the power to decide on a law's constitutionality. Gerry's fellow delegate from Massachusetts, Rufus King, said the same: "Judges ought to be able to expound the law as it should come before them, free from the bias of having participated in its formation."

Id., at 293. It is not at all likely that the participants at the Philadelphia convention believed that the power of judicial review *included* the power to revise legislative policy. *See* Raoul Berger, Government by Judiciary 300–306 (1977). The convention's rejection of a council of revision as a check on the executive seems to stem from the fact that such a council was unwieldy and likely to cancel any of the benefits that would accrue from having a single executive. But more to the point, there was the belief that members of the judiciary should be excluded from ordinary policy making. That belief was not thought inconsistent with judicial review, and those at the convention simultaneously rejected judicial involvement in policy making, while supporting judicial review. For example, as Berger recounts:

> When . . . George Mason argued for judicial participation in the presidential veto, [Mason] recognized that judges already 'could declare an unconstitutional law void. But with regard to every law *however unjust oppressive* or pernicious, which did not come plainly under this description, they would be under the necessity as Judges to give it a free course. He wished further use to be made of the Judges, of giving and in *preventing every improper law.*

Id., at 301. Similarly, when James Wilson argued against inclusion of the judiciary, he acknowledged that judges could not refuse to give effect to constitutional laws that were within the competency of Congress. ("Laws may be unjust, may be unwise, may be dangerous, be destructive, and yet not be so unconstitutional as to justify the Judge in refusing to give them effect.") *Scope, supra* note 14, at 628. Berger contends that even with the support of such advocates as Edmund Randolph, George Mason, and James Madison for including members of the judiciary on the council of revision, it failed to gain support. "Nathaniel Gorham saw 'no advantage of employing the Judges in this way. As Judges they are not to be presumed to possess any peculiar knowledge of the mere policy of public measures.'" Similarly, Elbridge Gerry, clearly a supporter of judicial review argued:

> It was *quite foreign* from the nature of ye office to make them *judges of the policy* of public measures. . . . It was making Statesmen of the Judges; and setting them up as the guardians of the Rights of the people. He relied for his part on the Representatives of the people as the guardians of their Rights and Interests. It was making the Expositors of the Laws, the Legislators which ought never to be done.

Berger, *supra* at 301.

16. H. Jefferson Powell, *Parchment Matters: A Meditation on the Constitution as Text,* 71 Iowa L. Rev. 1427, 1433 (1986).

sterile.[17] As will be explored more systematically later in the chapter, such scholars have substantial reservations about employing the idea of intent. They contend, among other things, that often the framers' intent is impossible to discern; that different framers expressed different intent on the same subject; or that the same framers expressed different intent at different times. Other critics charge that confining an inquiry to the framers' intent is misleading since it is the ratifiers' *understanding* that is more important; or that there is no agreed upon approach on how to ascertain the framers' intent (e.g., some scholars allege that it can be discerned solely from the text of the Constitution, or from debates at the Philadelphia convention, or from state ratification debates). Still other scholars contend that it is debatable whether intent may ever be ascribed to any group action. And as seen earlier, there are scholars who maintain that even if the framers' intent could be discerned, it would not be binding on judges today.

By any reasonable measure, these scholars certainly raise serious questions about the matter of intent and these questions ought to be addressed. By the same token, the reservations expressed by contemporary scholars apparently were not shared, or at least not considered insurmountable, by Publius or judges during the early days of the Republic.[18] As already recounted, Publius spoke comfortably of the "intention of the people" and left little doubt that he considered the articulation of that intent, the Constitution, to be binding upon both judges and future generations.[19] Chief Justice Marshall, among others, also made repeated references to intent. Sometimes Mar-

17. There is something to be said for substituting in the text the word *understanding* for intent, as suggested by Lofgren (Lofgren, *supra* note 6, at 78), and from time to time I do just that. The word *intent* or *intention,* however, also is used in the text because Publius and early judicial decisions used it, and because the literature continues to employ it, though a certain hostility to that usage is detectable. I have reservations, however, about another expression suggested by Lofgren, *expectations,* which I will explain later. The entire subject can use more systematic exploration.

18. Lofgren points out that "the Federalists never explicitly and unambiguously stated that future interpreters should resort to ratifier intent." Lofgren, *supra* note 6, at 93. But he then provides several reasons to explain why they did not (*id.* at 92–93). 43 *See also* Robert N. Clinton, *Original Understanding, Legal Realism, and the Interpretation of 'This Constitution'*, 72 Iowa L. Rev. 1177, 1186–1213 (1987).

19. *See supra* chapter 2, text and comment accompanying note 68. Gary McDowell comments: "Original intention and original meaning were held to be the primary means by which the written Constitution could be kept a *limited* Constitution. In this belief, men as politically opposed as Thomas Jefferson and John Marshall could stand united." Gary L. McDowell, The Constitution and Contemporary Constitutional Theory 11 (1985). Walter B. Michaels adds that "my argument is that interpretation is impossible without the invocation of context, that context is an account of the author's intention, and, therefore, that interpretation is an account of the author's intention." Walter Michaels, *Response to Perry and Simon,* 58 So. Cal. L. Rev. 673, 676 (1985). Judge Robert H. Bork concludes: "A theory of Constitutional law must . . . set limits to judicial powers as well as to legislative and executive powers; there is no theory of Constitutional

shall referred to the intent of "the framers of the instrument,"[20] and at other times, when speaking of the interpretative craft, to "the intention of the person" in the use of particular words.[21] In another instance, he concluded that "it must have been the intention of those who gave these powers, to assure, as far as human prudence could insure, their beneficial execution" since this Constitution "is intended to endure for ages to come, and, consequently, to be adapted to the various *crises* of human affairs."[22] In still another case, he referred to the "intention of the Convention," and in the same breath declared that it would be inappropriate for the Court to assume "an intention to narrow the discretion of the national legislature under the words that purport to enlarge it."[23] Marshall is representative of the traditional judicial approach of the importance of intent that existed well into this century.

While Marshall, as did Publius, assumed that the Constitution was superior to statutes, both understood that constitutional interpretation would parallel the interpretation of statutes.[24] Delegates to the Philadelphia convention therefore anticipated that the interpretation of the Constitution might require the discernment of the author's intent, either contained explicitly in textual language or by applying interpretive guidelines.[25] Accordingly, unless some contrary evidence existed, Marshall declared that judges were to presume that the words the framers selected for inclusion in the Constitution "most directly and aptly express the ideas [they] intend[ed] to convey."[26] Elsewhere, he stated that the Court must presume the framers "intended what they have said," and if doubts persisted "it is a well settled rule, that the objects for which it was given, especially when those objects are expressed in the instrument itself,

---

adjudication that can set limits to judicial power other than the philosophy of original intent." Robert H. Bork, The Tempting of America 111 (1989).

20. *See supra,* chapter 3, note 19.

21. *See supra,* chapter 3, text accompanying note 22.

22. M'Culloch v. Maryland, 17 U.S. 316, 415 (1819).

23. *See supra,* chapter 2, text accompanying note 26.

24. Powell concludes that "by 1787, the English legal system had produced a wealth of reflection on the process of construing normative documents. Moreover, the common law considered these canons of interpretation to be themselves a part of the law, and to be equally binding on the maker and the interpreter of a document." H. Jefferson Powell, *The Original Understanding of Original Intent,* 78 Harv. L. Rev. 885, 894 (1985).

25. *Cf.* Powell, *supra* note 24, and H. Jefferson Powell, *The Modern Misunderstanding of Original Intent,* 54 U. Chi. L. Rev. 1513 (1987), *with* Raoul Berger, *"Original Intention" in Historical Perspective,* 54 The Geo. Wash. L. Rev. 296 (1986), and Raoul Berger, *The Founders' Views—According to Jefferson Powell,* 67 Texas L. Rev. 1033 (1985). *See also* Lofgren, *supra* note 6, Clinton, *supra* note 18, at 1186–87, 1192–94, and William Gangi, *On Raoul Berger's Federalism: The Founders' Design,* 13 Law and Social Inquiry 801 (1988).

26. Gibbons v. Ogden, 22 U.S. 1, 188–89 (1824).

should have great influence in the construction."[27]

Justice Johnson put the matter this way: "The simple, classical, precise, yet comprehensive language, in which [the Constitution] is couched, leaves, at most, but very little latitude for construction; and when its intent and meaning is discovered, nothing remains but to execute the will of those who made it, in the best manner to effect the purpose intended."[28]

Hence, while considerable difficulties undoubtedly surround the discernment, use and abuse of the framers' intent,[29] and several shall be examined shortly, for the delegates at Philadelphia and early justices of the Court, those issues remained manageable.[30] Put another way, the "core

27. *Id.* Berger observes: "'The intention of the lawmaker is the law. . . . [A] thing which is within the letter of the statute, is not within the statute, unless it be within the intention of the makers.'" [Raoul Berger, *Lawyering vs. Philosophizing: Facts or Fancies,* 9 U. Dayton L. Rev. 171, 197 (1984) (quoting Hawaii v. Mankichi, 190 U.S. 197, 212 [1903], quoting Smythe v. Fiske, 90 U.S. (23 Wall) 374, 380 [1874]). Herman Belz makes the following distinction:

> Purpose and intent are related but distinguishable terms that it is necessary to define in analyzing the original understanding of constitutional provisions. The purpose of an amendment is the main relevant reason why the amendment appears in the Constitution. It may be thought of as external to construction of the text, in contrast to intent which is internal to the document, and as providing a standard of choice between two competing interpretations of meaning. Purpose refers to the political and institutional context in which an amendment is proposed.

Herman Belz, *Equality and the Fourteenth Amendment: the Original Understanding,* 4 Benchmark 329, 339n.43 (1990).

28. Gibbons v. Ogden, *supra* note 26, at 223. Monaghan observes that "all law, the constitution not expected, is a purposive ordering of norms. Textual language embodies one or more purposes, and the text may be understood and usefully applied only if its purposes are understood. . . . from any relevant sources, including its 'legislative history.'" Henry Monaghan, *Our Perfect Constitution,* 56 N.Y.U.L. Rev. 353, 374–375 (1981).

29. *See infra,* text accompanying notes 104–134. Bork provides one of the most systematic critiques of the noninterpretivist position that inquiry into the framers' intent is not an appropriate standard for judicial decisions. In his book he raises and rejects the following claims: that original understanding is unknowable; that the Constitution must change as society changes; that there is no real reason the living should be governed by the dead; that the Constitution is what the judges say it is; that the philosophy of original understanding involves judges in political choices; and that clause-bound interpretation is impossible. Bork, *supra* note 19, at 161–179. *See also* Clinton, *supra* note 18, at 1180–1182n. 4. *See infra,* chapter 6, where arguments such as those are placed in the context of a debate.

30. Bork provides these conclusions:

> We must not expect too much of the search for original understanding in any legal context. The result of the search is never perfection; it is simply the best we can do; and the best we can do must be regarded as good enough—or we must abandon the enterprise of law and, most especially, that of judicial review. Many cases will be decided as the lawgivers would have decided them, and, at the very least, judges will confine themselves to the principles the lawgivers intended. The precise congruence of individual decisions with what the ratifiers intended can never be known, but it can be estimated whether, across a body of decisions, judges have in general vindicated the principle given into their hands. If they accomplish that, they have accomplished something of great value.

Bork, *supra* note 19, at 163.

question remains: do the basic postulates of the constitutional order require that the court undertake the task of ascertaining original intent, *as best it can*?"[31] I believe an affirmative response is much more sustainable than a negative one. Charles Lofgren reflects my reasoning: while "historical intent might not be easily reconstructed" where it could be determined it is "dispositive in the resolution of textual ambiguities."[32] Gary L. McDowell offers a more general conclusion: "The original intention of the Framers . . . is the first rule of constitutional interpretation."[33] But no one puts the matter more directly than Henry P. Monaghan: "For I would insist that any theory of constitutional interpretation which renders unimportant or irrelevant questions as to original intent, *so far as that intent can be fairly discerned,* is not, given our traditions, politically or intellectually defensible."[34]

A Limited Constitution

Publius not only argued that an independent judiciary would help control the tendency of all governments toward tyranny; as noted earlier, he specifically maintained that such a body was especially well-suited to the task of protecting a written constitution, "one which contains specified exceptions to the legislative will."[35] He believed that such limits "can be preserved in practice no other way than through the medium of courts of justice, whose duty it must be to declare all acts contrary to the manifest tenor of the Constitution void."[36] That precise point was made by Chief Justice Marshall in *Marbury v. Madison,* when he described "a written constitution . . . [as the] great-

31. Monaghan, *supra* note 28, at 377.
32. Lofgren, *supra* note 6, at 97. Clinton observes: "The Framers' focus on language, however naive it may appear today, apparently assumed that words have a relatively fixed and unchanging meaning." Clinton, *supra* note 18, at 1193. *But see supra* comment accompanying note 7 (framers aware of interpretative problems caused by language). Belz provides this summary:

> Although understood as the embodiment of fundamental political principles, the American Constitution from the outset was construed in the manner of legal documents in the anglo-American common law tradition. The authors of the Constitution were presumed to have said what they meant to say in the document itself. At times, however, the correct interpretation of the document may depend on the use of sources external to it. With the Constitution, therefore, as with other legal documents, the search for the meaning of the text can become a search for the author's intentions, or the intent of the framers.

Belz, *supra* note 27, at 329.
33. McDowell, *supra* note 19, at 8.
34. Henry Monaghan, *The Constitution Goes to Harvard,* 13 Harv. Civ. Rights—Civ. Lib. L. Rev. 117, 124 (1978). In another article Monaghan observes: "It is, rather, a way of thinking about constitutional 'meaning' that follows from the basic concepts that legitimate judicial review itself. The root premise is that the supreme court, like other branches of government, is constrained by the written constitution." Monaghan, *supra* note 28, 375–376.
35. Federalist, *supra* note 5, no. 78, at 465–466.
36. *Id.,* at 466.

est improvement on political institutions" and observed that Americans viewed such constitutions "with . . . much reverence."[37] The American forefathers demanded a written constitution *precisely because* they wished to remove as much doubt as humanly possible regarding the principles that governed their nation[38]—so "that those limits may not be mistaken or forgotten."[39] If constitutions do not stand on higher ground than simple statutes reversible by a simple legislative majority, then "written constitutions are absurd attempts, on the part of the people, to limit a power, in its own nature, illimitable."[40] As Allen concludes, "the guiding assumption of *The Federalist* was that the Constitution—'the intention of the people'—is to be 'regarded by the judges as, a fundamental law' for the advancement of the public good and individual rights."[41]

Accordingly, those who find vagueness in the Constitution where Publius or early judicial decisions suggest none exists, as John Marshall concluded, must take on a significant burden of proof.[42]

Fixed Meaning

Those who framed and ratified the Constitution believed it had fixed meaning and their understanding was not as rigid as noninterpretivist critics today make it out to be.[43] Gary McDowell states:

37. Marbury v. Madison, *supra* note 8, at 178. *See supra* chapter 3, note 8. Clinton adds: "The ultimate faith of the framers of the Constitution in the power of the written word is not surprising . . . [given the tradition] in which written documents played powerful roles in controlling human behavior and shaping the structure of, and limits on, governmental power." Clinton, *supra* note 18, at 1187.

38. "The interpretation of the Constitution according to the original understanding, then, is the only method that can preserve the Constitution, the separation of powers, and the liberties of the people." Bork, *supra* note 19, at 159.

39. Marbury v. Madison, *supra* note 8, at 176 (C.J. Marshall). H. Jefferson Powell comments: "This unbreakable link that the text forges between present and past is the kernel of truth in the delusive pursuit of the 'original intent'." Powell, *supra* note 17, at 1431.

40. Marbury v. Madison, *supra* note 8, at 177.

41. Anita L. Allen, *Comment: The Federalist's Plain Meaning: Reply to Tushnet,* 61 Southern Cal. L. R. 1701, 1715 (1988). Allen does not directly say so, but her usage seems to reflect my earlier expressed conclusion, that the intentions noted by Publius are those of the ratifiers of the Constitution, not the current population. *Compare supra,* chapter 2, text and comment accompanying note 68.

42. M'Culloch v. Maryland, 17 U.S. (4 Wheat.) 316, 410 (1819) ("those who contend that [the Government] may not select any appropriate means . . . take upon themselves the burden of establishing that exception.") *See supra,* chapter 4, comment accompanying note 19.

43. *See supra,* chapter 2, text accompanying notes 146 and 147. Lofgren constructs this response from "a puzzled Federalist" who was asked "about the future status of ratifier intent":

> "What? Are you hinting that the Constitution will not mean in the future what it says and what its structure implies? That's a strange position. I don't understand the suggestion that we are ratifying something other than the system that common sense discloses to us. Yes, there may be a few ambiguities. Remember, though, that if the officials of the new govern-

> To the Founders the Constitution's principles, though fixed, were of a nature sufficient to allow for *political* changes under them. What the ideology of a 'living' constitution argues is not that the Constitution—by its own terms and language—allows political solutions to the exigencies time inevitably will bring, but that the terms and language of the Constitution itself must be understood as changing.[44]

The issue then is not whether the Constitution should remain adaptable—of course it should—but rather which institution was charged with that responsibility. I will explore a little more thoroughly noninterpretivist charges that a constitution with fixed meaning is an inflexible one.

THE POWERS CONFERRED. When the Constitution was adopted, everyone understood the federal government to be one of limited powers and those powers were to be exercised in the context of the objectives set forth in the Preamble.[45] Publius kept those objectives in mind and, as already detailed, so did Chief Justice Marshall. Marshall concluded that while the powers granted in the Constitution had been specifically enumer-

---

> ment fail to give effect to what we ratifiers see in the document, there are correctives."
> Which is, of course, very nearly what some Federalists did say.

Lofgren, *supra* note 6, at 93. Lofgren's conclusion seems perfectly consistent with the conclusion reached in chapter 2, *supra* text accompanying notes 135–151 and the remarks of Publius, comment accompanying note 7, *supra*.

44. McDowell, *supra* note 19, at 28. Erler adds: "The permanent principle of the Constitution must, of course, be adapted and applied in different ways in order to meet changing exigencies. But this adaptation and application does not alter or change the principles themselves." Edward J. Erler, in *Symposium: Constitutional Scholarship: What Next?,* 1 Constitutional Commentary 17, 54 (1988) [hereinafter Symposium]. Commager, after referring to the Preamble of the Constitution, observes that in the Constitution "we do not find confusion, obfuscation, or contradiction. We find clarity and specificity, whenever these are called for, and broad general terms, when those are called for." He then goes on to describe federalism, concluding that on such matters "these distinctions could never be clear, nor were they, nor could they ever be, fixed and rigid." Henry S. Commager, *The Constitution and Original Intent,* 19 The Center Magazine 4, 5 (1986) I do not find Commager's description inconsistent with the position taken in the text; rather, as noted by Lofgren, particularly with respect to the defining of federal-state boundaries, the framers believed such matters "would only be determined by future adjudication." Lofgren, *supra* note 6, at 85. *See* Clinton, *supra* note 18, at 1190–1192. *See infra,* chapter 7, for concrete examples.

45. The Preamble of course cannot itself be viewed as granting sweeping powers to the federal government. The Preamble comes before and is not part of the Constitution. Any other view seems hopelessly inconsistent with the specific powers granted in article 1, section 8 and applicable canons of construction. *See,* for example, Federalist, *supra* note 5, no. 83, at 497. The Preamble, however, helps us grasp the whole: the purposes for which the instrument was proposed. Study of the Preamble should be one of several considerations in the interpretative process when a judge must inquire into the extent of the powers delegated, which is to say what Marshall did in M'Culloch. *See supra* chapter 4, comment accompanying note 92. Lofgren comments: "The Federalists . . . examined [the Constitution] in light of its purposes and the deficiencies it was designed to remedy; they analyzed its structure and harmonized its parts." Lofgren, *supra* note 6, at 85.

ated, Congress could chose to exercised each of these powers in plenary fashion: the matter was one of legislative and not judicial discretion.[46] Thus, on the one hand, the delegates understood the powers delegated to the federal government to be *fixed;* meaning that subsequently Congress could *not* add powers. On the other hand, when the delegates enumerated the powers they did, they used broad language, enabling future legislators to expand or contract the exercise of those powers as circumstances might require.[47] Any other explanation seems inconsistent with the framers' oft-repeated desire to assure that the federal government remain competent in the areas entrusted to it. Their approach, to paraphrase Publius, enabled the people to live under the rule of law and still avail themselves of the experience and reason of elected and thereby accountable representatives.[48]

The delegates at Philadelphia un-

46. *See supra,* chapter 2, text accompanying note 4 (Publius) and, for example, chapter 3, text and comments accompanying notes 43–47 (C. J., Marshall in Gibbons).

47. Lofgren comments that "a desire for clarity in language is not antithetical to recognition that future interpreters might resort to subjective or historical intent to clarify any remaining obscurities." Lofgren, *supra* note 6, at 80. *See also* comment accompanying note 7, *supra,* and these remarks by Publius:

> In the first place it is to be remembered that the government is not to be charged with the whole power of making and administering laws. Its jurisdiction is limited to certain enumerated objects, which concern all the members of the republic, but which are not to be attained by the separate provisions of any. The subordinate governments, which can extend their care to all those other objects which can be separately provided for, will retain their due authority and activity. Were it proposed by the plan of the convention to abolish the governments of the particular States, its adversaries would have some ground for their objection; though it would not be difficult to show that if they were abolished the general government would be compelled by the principle of self-preservation to reinstate them in their proper jurisdiction.

FEDERALIST, *supra* note 5, no. 14, at 102. *See also* id., no. 46 at 295 (Even if citizens become more confident in the national than state governments, it is only within a "certain sphere that the federal government can . . . be advantageously administered"); *see id.,* at 297 (although some "sacrifices" have been made by the states, close attention was paid to "local prejudices, interests, and views of particular States"); *see id.,* at 297–298 (unpopular federal policies will be met with state resistance); *see id.,* no. 51, at 320 (constitutional structure will be maintained "by so contriving the interior of the structure of the government as that its constituent parts may, by their mutual relations, be the means of keeping each other in their proper places"). One of Publius' clearest statements is as follows:

> That we may form a correct judgment on this subject, it will be proper to review the several powers conferred on the government of the Union; and that this may be the more conveniently done they may be reduced into different classes as they related to the following different objects: 1. Security against foreign danger; 2. Regulation of the intercourse with foreign nations; 3. Maintenance of harmony and proper intercourse among the States; 4. certain miscellaneous objects of general utility; 5. Restraint of the States from certain injurious acts; 6. Provisions for giving due efficacy to all these powers.

FEDERALIST, *supra* note 5, no. 41, at 256.

48. FEDERALIST, *supra* note 5, no. 23, at 153.

derstood that none of the enumerated powers could or should for all time be definitively defined. Any attempt to do so would jeopardize the ability of future legislators to accomplish the very objectives for which the Constitution was proposed. Instead, they granted to Congress these broad powers and relied on the courts to thwart any clear departures from them.[49] But the delegates authorized judicial interventions only if Congress violated the ratifiers will (e.g., intentions of the people). Upon what other ground would a court be justified in substituting its judgment for that of the people's elected representatives? That understanding is precisely the one put forth by the Supreme Court in *M'Culloch v. Maryland*.[50]

RESTRICTIONS ON GOVERNMENTAL POWER. Delegates at the Philadelphia convention approached restrictions on governmental power somewhat differently than they had approached grants of power. As already noted the purpose of the latter was to assure governmental competency even in unforeseen circumstances, but the purpose of the former was to curtail known types of governmental abuses; that is, wishing to deny the federal government or state governments, or both, certain prerogatives. Both governments, for example, were prohibited from passing bills of attainder and ex post facto laws; or from granting titles of nobility—"forever."[51] Commenting on the last item, Publius explained that "for so long as [titles of nobility] are excluded there can never be serious danger that the government will be any other than that of the people."[52]

Here I will lay some foundation for the position I take in subsequent chapters—that a narrow reading of the Constitution's restrictive clauses is more consistent with the delegates' design than would be a broad one; and why a broad reading of the Constitution's grants of power is more appropriate than a narrow one. The unifying theme is the delegates' desire to establish a competent government.[53]

49. *See supra* chapter 2, text accompanying note 65.
50. M'Culloch v. Maryland, *supra* note 42, at 426. For the full text *see supra,* chapter 3, text accompanying note 92.
51. U.S. CONST., art 1, sec. 9, paras. 3, and 8; and sec 10, para. 1. The text concentrates on the 1787 Constitution but the discussion that follows in the text is equally applicable to all parts of the present amended Constitution.
52. FEDERALIST, *supra* note 5, no. 84, at 512. Publius had made the connection earlier: "Could any further proof be required of the republican complexion of this system, the most decisive one might be found in its absolute prohibition of titles of nobility, both under the federal and the State governments; and in its express guaranty of the republican form to each of the latter." *Id.,* no. 39, at 242.
53. *See infra,* chapter 7, text and comments accompanying notes 4–18; chapter 8, text and comments accompanying notes 38–42. Robert Bork states "that abstinence has the inestimable value of preserving democracy in those areas of life that the Founders intended to leave to the people's self-government." BORK, *supra* note 19, at 163.

Surely, the inclusion of prohibitions (such as against granting titles of nobility) conveys to any reader of the Constitution that those who proposed it believed that legislators and judges could recognize a federal or state statute that granted what was prohibited. Yet, I do not recall any instance in *The Federalist Papers* where Publius defines the meaning of the phrase "title of nobility"; or for that matter "ex post facto laws" or "bills of attainder." Yet both federalists and antifederalists alike, as well as those asked to ratify the proposed constitution, must have understood the kinds of things that those clauses prohibited. So if today Congress or a state legislature proposed a statute clearly violating that understanding, should not conscientious legislators oppose it on the grounds that it is unconstitutional? Should either proposal nevertheless become a law, should not a judge set it aside for the same reason, as presumably it would have been set aside had it been passed the day after the Constitution was ratified?

Or take a somewhat different situation. The Constitution provides that "no person shall be convicted of Treason unless on the Testimony of two Witnesses to the same overt act, or on Confession in open Court."[54] Given how such subjects had been handled in England and at common law, those at Philadelphia evidently wished to depart from how these matters had been handled in the past. Why otherwise would they specifically stipulate that "two" (and not one, as had been English practice) witnesses would be necessary for conviction? And why, elsewhere, add the stipulation that Congress may not "work Corruption of Blood, or Forfeiture except during the Life of the Person attainted"?[55] Is it not reasonably clear that, when the drafters of the Constitution specifically sought to deviate from English common law or American practice, they did so for the obvious purpose of better protecting themselves and their children's children?[56]

What then, if today, Congress nevertheless authorized doing something that could be reasonable construed to

54. U.S. CONST., art. 3, sec. 3, para. 1.

55. *Id.*, sec. 3, para. 2. *See also* FEDERALIST, *supra* note 5, no. 43, at 273; no. 74, at 448–449. Chief Justice Marshall, as noted earlier, specifically quotes this passage and describes it as "addressed especially to the courts. . . . [providing the justices with] a rule of evidence not to be departed from." Marbury v. Madison, *supra* note 8, at 178.

56. *See, e.g.* RAOUL BERGER, DEATH PENALTIES (1982). Berger provides yet another example in his discussion of the "benefit of clergy . . . which [under common law] exempted any one who could read from the death penalty." [*id.*, at 42]. He concludes:

> So completely did the Framers assume that the terms they employed would be accompanied by their common law meaning that they defined treason narrowly in order to restrict its excessive scope at common law. So too . . . the First Congress provided for capital punishment without 'benefit of clergy,' as did a number of earlier State statutes, in order to insure that the english exculpation would not apply.

Id., at 62–63.

violate the ratifiers' understanding of these provisions; but the proposed statute did not exactly match what the ratifiers understood as having been prohibited? Such a statute certainly would raise interpretive questions; and fully understanding that fact Publius anticipated that a judicial interpretation would "liquidate and fix . . . [its] meaning and operation."[57] Interpretivists have no quarrel with such exercises of judicial power. But today such interpretive problems are a far cry from the power that noninterpretivists accord judges, for many noninterpretivists go far beyond such situations and instead defend a judicial power unknown to the framers, some even suggesting that judges today are not bound even should the ratifiers' understanding be clearly discernible.

A Common Grammar[58]

Publius, as seen earlier, stated that the nature of the judicial profession steeped judges in a long tradition and well-developed rules of their craft.[59] Recently one scholar has called these rules "a professional grammar" that "discipline[s]" and "constrain[s]" the interpreter."[60] Publius illustrates the ratifiers' anticipation that the Constitution would be interpreted according to rules of "common sense."[61] His anticipation was not misplaced.

57. FEDERALIST, *supra* note 5, no. 78, at 468. For text *see supra,* chapter 2, text accompanying note 65.

58. Powell: The Constitution provides "a common set of terms and expressions, almost a vocabulary and grammar for political debate." Powell, *supra* note 17, at 1429.

59. *See supra,* chapter 2, text and comments accompanying notes 69–70, 83–89. Justice Story commented: "where its words are plain, clear, and determinate, they require no interpretation . . . Where the words admit of two senses, each of which is conformable to general usage, that sense is to be adopted, which without departing from the literal import of the words, best harmonizes with the nature and objects, the scope and objects, the scope and design of the instrument." McDowell, *supra* note 19, at 12 (citations omitted). Allen adds: "For Publius, the meaning of written law is plain, but only when texts are well-drafted in modes of discourse open to discernment, reason and common sense, and when those who purport to apply the texts rely on true and proper maxims of construction." Allen, *supra* note 41, at 1715.

60. Owen Fiss, *Objectivity and Interpretation,* 34 STAN. L. REV. 739, 744–745 (1982).

61. *See supra,* chapter 2, text accompanying note 89. Publius understood that such rules could be abused: "certain legal maxims . . . [could be] perverted from their true meaning." FEDERALIST, *supra* note 5, No. 83, at 496. *See supra,* chapter 2, text and comment accompanying note 90; chapter 3, comment accompanying note 37 (Marshall, C.J., rejects misreading of the FEDERALIST PAPERS). *See generally,* James G. Wilson, *The Most Sacred Text: The Supreme Court's Use of* THE FEDERALIST PAPERS, *1985 BRIG. Y. L. REV. 65* (1985). Lofgren quotes a long letter from James Madison to M.L. Hurlbert (May 1830), from which the following is excerpted:

> As there are legal rules for interpreting laws, there must be analogous rules for interpreting const[itutio]ns and among the obvious and just guides to the Const[itutio]n of the U.S. may be mentioned—
>
> 1. The evils & defects for curing which the Constitution was called for & introduced.
> 2. The comments prevailing at the time it was adopted.
> 3. The early, deliberate & and continued practice under the Constitution, as preferable

Again and again the Supreme Court applied canons,[62] refining them so as to provide a consistent framework for constitutional interpretations.[63]

Canons isolate relevant questions, distinguish one interpretive problem from another, and provide rules by which similar types of issues can be approached uniformly no matter what clause in the Constitution is addressed; or at least can be addressed more uniformly than if the canons did not exist. Justice Joseph Story observed:

> Let us now proceed to consider the rules, by which [the Constitution] ought to be interpreted; for if these rules are correctly laid down, it will save us from many embarrassments in examining and defining its powers. Much of the difficulty which has arisen in all public discussions on this subject, has had its origin in the want of some uniform rules of interpretation, expressly or tacitly agreed on by the disputants.[64]

Such canons always were considered "only an aid to fulfilling the legislature's intent; as such [they were] always rebuttable by more specific matter from the statutory text or from legislative history."[65] Hence, even the consistent application of canons can not eliminate all interpretive disputes, although it undoubtedly tends to narrow them and a judge's discretion.[66] Canons are to judges what hand tools are to carpenters: both si-

---

> to constructions adopted on the spur of occasions, and subject to the vicissitudes of party or personal ascendencies.

Lofgren, *supra* note 6, at 110 (citations omitted). Lofgren also maintains that H. Jefferson Powell "omit[ed] the sentences in which Madison explicitly endorsed ratifier intent." *Id.,* at 104.

62. *See* Christopher Wolfe, The Rise of Modern Judicial Review 41–50 (1986) and *Christopher Wolfe, John Marshall & Constitutional Law,* 15 Polity 5, 7–11 (1982).

63. For specific examples *see also supra* chapter 3, text and comments accompanying notes 4, 8, 9 (Marbury); notes 13, 16, 19, and 28 (M'Culloch); notes 44, 48, and 50 (Gibbons); note 56 (Barron); and note 93 (Dred Scott).

64. Joseph Story, Commentaries on the Constitution of the United States 134–162 (1983) (discussing the application of various canons).

65. Willard Hurst, Dealing with Statutes 56–57 (1982).

66. Fiss observes that "[n]othing I have said denies the possibility of disagreement in legal interpretation." Fiss, *supra* note 60, at 747. It seem to me, however, that some noninterpretative approaches raise issues of legitimacy when they amount to "an attack on the current constitutional order" (John B. McArthur, *Abandoning the Constitution: The New Wave in Constitutional Theory,* 59 Tulane L. Rev. 280, 313 (1984); then, "the interpreter isn't interpreting an old text, but either writing a new one, or imagining someone else has written it." Michaels, *supra* note 19, at 678. Such interpreters "'propose the destruction of an existing community, established by our laws and constitution.'" William Van Alstyne, *Interpreting **This** Constitution: The Unhelpful Contribution of Special Theories of Judicial Review,* U. Fla. L. Rev. 209, 217 n.27 (1983) (quoting James B. White, *Law as Language: Reading Law and Reading Literature,* 60 Texas L. Rev. 415, 442–43 [1982]). For that reason alone, the fruits of such theorizing must be rejected as a possible "third way" since some *other* regime is substituted for the republic to which the people consented (*see* comment accompanying note 4, *supra*).

In an insightful article, however, Fallon argues that under his concept of "commensurability," a

multaneously enable the task to be performed while limiting the performance of the task. The better and more specialized the tools, the easier the task and the more craftsmanlike the product.[67]

Justice Story later listed nineteen rules that today could continue to provide an excellent jumping-off point for contemporary scholarship. From that list, Christopher Wolfe has distilled four basic tenets:

> First, the interpreter should start with the plain and common meaning of words, which are the best expression of the lawgiver's intention, in this case, the intention of the people, who adopted the Constitution on a "just survey" of its text. Yet words may be ambiguous, or of doubtful meaning and so recourse must be had to other rules. Thus, the second rule is that doubtful words may be clarified best by looking to the nature and design, the scope and objects of the instrument. . . . The third rule . . . is that the nature of the Constitution is a frame or fundamental law of government, which requires a reasonable interpretation giving to the government efficacy and force, with respect to its apparent objects. The powers of the government are to be neither narrowed, because of probable conjectures about their impropriety, or fear of abuse, nor enlarged beyond their limitations because of fear that these limitations are impolitic. The fourth and final rule is that rules of verbal criticism and particular maxims arising from the use of words in practical life, shall be used to assist the interpretation of the instrument, insofar as their use stands well with the context and subject matter.[68]

Perhaps particular examples of canon application will add weight to judgments already made and advance the discussion:

Definition By Exclusion. One can get a better idea of what legislators are trying to accomplish by examin-

---

theory of interpretation must encompass all the past decisions of the Court whether or not they may be rooted in the framers' understanding. Richard H. Fallon, *Constructivist Coherence Theory of Constitutional Interpretation,* 100 Harv. L. Rev. 1189, 1189 (1987) But should a concept of *his* creation be accorded greater weight than the design defended by Publius, however imperfect? To encompass decisions just because a majority of the Court has approved them circumvents the legitimacy issue and the purpose of a written constitution—though, as noted subsequently, judges, unlike scholars, are and should be constrained by prudence.

67. Fiss adds that the existence and acceptance of such rules creates "an interpretive community, which recognizes those rules as authoritative." Fiss, *supra* note 60, at 744. He adds that "the disciplining rules operate similarly to the rules of language: which constrain the users of the language, furnish the standards for judging the uses of language, and constitute the language." *Id.,* at 745.

68. *See* Christopher Wolfe, *A Theory of U.S. Constitutional History,* 43 J. POL. 292, 294–295 (1981). For additional discussions of interpretive canons, *see* Fiss, *supra* note 60 and McArthur, *supra* note, 66, at 306–307. With respect to the ranking of various interpretive arguments, *see* Fallon, *supra* note 66.

ing what changes were made between earlier and final draft.[69] For example, early drafts of the Fourteenth Amendment contained broad language that could be construed to authorize federal control over state political and social rights, as well as civil rights. Since that broad language was dropped in the final draft, it significantly reduces the likelihood that a broad interpretation can be attributed to the narrower language of the final draft.[70]

THE GREATER INCLUDES THE LESSER. The congressional power over interstate commerce may be exercised in plenary fashion and comprehends even the authority to prohibit it altogether.[71] Similarly, aware of malapportionment abuses the Framers of Fourteenth amendment nevertheless left control of suffrage issues in state hands.[72] If framers of the Fourteenth Amendment had attempted to do otherwise, it is more probable than not that the Fourteenth Amendment would not have been ratified even in many states that during the Civil War had remained in the Union.[73]

ENUMERATION EXCLUDES THE NON-MENTIONED. Once a specific meaning is attributed to words or phrases, that specific meaning must exclude any broader interpretation of those words of phrases.[74] A contemporary application of this canon has gener-

69. Raoul Berger, *The Fourteenth Amendment: Light from the Fifteenth,* 74 NW.L.REV. 311, 356 (1979) [hereinafter *Fourteenth*]; Raoul Berger, *Government by Judiciary: Some Countercriticism,* 56 TEXAS L.R. 1125, 1131 (1978) [hereinafter *Government*].

70. RAOUL BERGER, GOVERNMENT BY JUDICIARY 16–17, 27–28, 120–122 (1977); HERTA MEYER, THE HISTORY AND MEANING OF THE FOURTEENTH AMENDMENT 107–111 (1977); *Scope, supra* note 14, at 551–552, 571–572; Michael Perry, book review, 78 COLUM.L.REV. 685, 689 (1978). In this regard, Belz points to "the *rejection* by the House of Representatives of a provision stating 'that there shall be no discrimination in civil rights or immunities among the inhabitants of any state or Territory of the United states on account of race, color, or previous condition of slavery.'" Belz, *supra* note 27, at 343. But *see* Clinton, *supra* note 18, at 1256–1259.

71. Champion v. Ames, 188 U.S. 321 (1903) (Lottery Case).

72. *See supra,* chapter 3, text and comments accompanying note 92; *See also* BERGER, *supra* note 70, at 69–77 and Fallon, *supra* note 66, at 1255.

73. BERGER, *supra* note 70, at 60–68 and Raoul Berger, *The Fourteenth Amendment: Facts vs Generalities,* 32 ARK.L.REV. 280, 285 (1978) [hereinafter *Facts*].

74. BERGER, *supra* note 70, at 28; Scope, *supra* note 14, at 551; Facts, *supra* note 73, at 285. Belz concludes:

> The framers of the Fourteenth Amendment did not intend to introduce into the Constitution an open-ended principle for the attainment of total racial equality; nor for the prohibition of all unfair classification, racial as well as nonracial; nor the prohibition of racial classifications that stigmatize a group. The amendment was designed to confer limited absolute equality, or a guarantee of fundamental rights of person and property under state authority without distinction of color. Equality in basic rights was justified on the ground that all individuals have natural rights. The Fourteenth Amendment did not embody the general principle that racial discrimination is categorically wrong.

Belz, *supra* note 27, at 345. For additional detail, *see supra,* chapter 4, text and comments accompanying notes 2–30.

ated significant controversy, as may be illustrated by contrasting the views of Raoul Berger (who contends that the framers of the Fourteenth Amendment did not intend to prohibit state control over suffrage or prohibit segregation) with those of other scholars who concede that he is right only in a "negative" sense (i.e., while the amendment does not specifically mention suffrage and segregation, the evidence Berger presents fails to provide positive proof that the framers intended to exclude them, or that its provisions may not be reinterpreted today to do so).[75]

Berger replies that his Fourteenth Amendment conclusions, as those of other scholars, were based on the unequivocal statements of the amendment's framers. But even had they not been, because the Constitution granted only limited powers to the federal government (a principal reaffirmed by the addition of the Tenth Amendment), the burden of proof—the obligation to present concrete evidence of intended change—squarely falls on those suggesting that a radical departure beyond the announced objects for which the amendment was proposed was intended.[76] That burden of proof is particularly high in such instances because its framers' clearly expressed only the desire to constitutionalize the Civil Rights Act of 1866 and rejected earlier drafts of the amendment, that had been broader in scope. In such instances, sound interpretive principles require that any conclusion regarding their intentions "should be expressed in plain and explicit terms."[77]

75. *See supra,* chapter 4, text and sources accompanying note 119 (generality), (Civil War amendments), and notes 131–151 (open-ended adjudication).

76. *Berger, supra* note 70, at 52–68, 117–133; Raoul Berger, *The Scope of Judicial Review and Walter Murphy,* 1979 Wis.L.Rev. 341, 343–347 (1979) (hereinafter *Murphy*); Perry, *supra* note 70, at 689–691. Publius explained the rationale of this canon as follows:

> For what purpose could the enumeration of particular powers be inserted, if these and all others were meant to be included in the preceding general power? Nothing is more natural nor common than first to use a general phrase, and then to explain and qualify it by a recital of particulars. But the idea of an enumeration of particulars which neither explain nor qualify the general meaning, and can have no other effect than to confound and mislead, is an absurdity.

Federalist, *supra* note 5, no. 41, at 263. Publius is quite explicit on the point:

> Having now seen that the maxims relied upon will not bear the use made of them, let us endeavor to ascertain their proper use and true meaning. This will be best done by examples. The plan of the convention declares that the power of Congress, or, in order words, of the *national legislature,* shall extend to certain enumerated cases. This specification of particulars evidently excludes all pretension to a general legislative authority, because an affirmative grant of special powers would be absurd as well as useless if a general authority was intended.

Id., no. 83, at 497. In the next paragraph Publius applies the principle of enumeration to the jurisdiction granted federal courts: "specification would be nugatory if it did not exclude all ideas of more extensive authority." *Id.*

77. United States v. Burr, 25 F. Cas. 55, 165 (C.C.D. VA 1807) (No. 14, 693). Monaghan concluded:

The most important interpretative rule is intellectual integrity, a quality some noninterpretivists find onerous today because scholars such as myself insist that it be placed even on a higher plane than good results.[78] The only means of enforcing that integrity is by a consensus of the scholarly community. While attempting to make this point to a colleague, I used the analogy of an outfielder who, in making a daring catch, knows that he trapped, rather than caught, the ball before it touched the ground. My colleague responded that the call was the umpire's and not the outfielder's to make. But what if the outfielder insists on telling the truth? Truth-telling is a matter of habit and his desire to confess might be rooted in acquired attitudes toward sportsmanship—those that teach that a dishonest victory is ultimately unsatisfying, damaging to the soul and self-esteem, and to the sport. A dishonest victory is wrong. Scholarly integrity is likewise a matter of acquired habit, of putting that integrity even above personal preference on public policy. The habit is so strong that it precedes rational choice. Lawyers are advocates; scholars are not.[79] Truth has a role to play in constitutional scholarship as it does in criminal law.[80]

> I find too little in the relevant source material, including the constitutional text, to think it more probable than not that any such sweeping change in the governmental structure was intended. Moreover, and more importantly, I am unable to believe that in light of the then prevailing concepts of representative democracy, the framers or ratifiers of [sec.] 1 intended the *courts* (rather than the national legislature pursuant to [sec.] 5) to weave the tapestry of federally protected rights against state government.

Monaghan, *supra* note 34, at 127–28.

78. McDowell, *supra* note 19, at vii ("it is not too much to say that the preference for the rule of law over the rule of men depends upon the intellectual integrity of interpretation"); *Compare, e.g.,* J. Skelly Wright, Professor Bickel, *The Scholarly Tradition, and the Supreme Court,* 84 Harv. L. Rev. (1971) with Aileen S. Kraditor, *On Curiosity: or the Difference Between an Ideologue and a Scholar,* The Intercollegiate Review 95 (Spring 1980). With respect to those scholars who continue to strive to keep such integrity alive, *see* John H. Ely, The *Wages of Crying Wolf: A Comment on Roe v. Wade,* 82 Yale L. J. 920, 945 (1973), or this comment by Gerald Gunther who, like Ely, personally favors abortion legislation but who nevertheless describes Roe v. Wade as "an abomination, an outrage, one of the worst Supreme Court decisions in terms of constitutionally mandating what ought to be legislatively mandated responses to political pressures." Gunther, in Commager, *supra* note 44, at 17. *See infra,* chapter 8, text accompanying notes 52–64.

79. *See e.g.,* Fallon, *supra* note 66, at 1281 ("Bickel concluded that it was at least plausible that the framers deliberately chose language capable of supporting a gradual expansion of the jurisprudence of equality.") Bickel did so, even though he recognized that the evidence he collected would fail to sustain a statute (*see* comment accompanying note 125, *infra*). *See also* Randall W. Bland, Private Pressure on Public Law: The Legal Career of Justice Thurgood Marshall, Revised Edition (1992).

80. William Gangi, *The Exclusionary Rule: A Case Study in Judicial Usurpation,* 34 Drake L. Rev. 33 (1985) (exclusionary rule imposed on American people). Upon what other ground may a judge rightly set aside a nine-year conviction? *See* "DNA Frees Convicted Rapist After 9 Years." N.Y.T. (August 1, 1991), p. B1 (judge sets aside conviction of guilt after DNA test, unavailable at the time of trial, proves that defendant's semen was not that found on victim's underpants).

PROBLEMS OF INTERPRETATION ASSOCIATED WITH INTENT

Many scholars today equate concern for the framers' intent with a denial of the present (and those who live in it) in favor of a dead past. There is considerable merit for their concern. Those attending the Philadelphia convention certainly could not have anticipated present circumstances or contemporary public policy disputes and, even if they offered suggestions to deal with either, those suggestions, quite frankly, may not be desirable.

Thus far I have sidestepped problems associated with attempts to discern the ratifiers' intent. I did so, firstly, because those problems had been obviously insufficient to deter Publius and others from ascribing intent; secondly, because such problems hardly seem crucial, given the chasm that separates interpretivists and noninterpretivists; and finally, because while some of the problems already mentioned in passing raise intriguing questions, none seemed weighty enough to justify departing from the ratifiers' understanding of judicial power. Thus, I thought it more appropriate to delay considering those problems until after setting out the ratifiers' understanding of judicial power and the nature of interpretation. I make no claim to having resolved the problems in the pages that follow, but the problems must be acknowledged if for no other reason than to retain the reader's confidence.

I begin with the charge that renewed interest in the framers' understanding of the Constitution has its roots in politics;[81] specifically, in the administration of President Ronald Reagan and a speech delivered by Attorney General Edwin Meese,[82] the thrust of which quickly was challenged by Justice William J. Brennan, Jr.[83] Meese also was chastised for not approaching "the Constitution . . . as an erudite scholar searching for the origin and history of each word, but as a politician, and [the fact] that . . . [a] dispute over interpretation concerns political and philosophical issues."[84]

I concede such charges and state them even more broadly: American politicians have always and will always attempt to get what they want by citing for authority—properly or improperly—the framers' or ratifiers' will. Such misrepresentations have occurred from the earliest days of the

81. Commager, *supra* note 44, at 7.
82. Address by Attorney General Edwin Meese, *American Bar Association* 4, 11 (July 17, 1985) (available in U.S. Dep't of Justice, Current Documents, 1985 Fiche No. 116. *See also* Edwin Meese, *Politics and the Constitution,* in POLITICS AND THE CONSTITUTION: THE NATURE AND EXTENT OF INTERPRETATION 53 (1990) [hereinafter POLITICS]. ("In most political disputes, the Constitution does not take sides"). *Id.,* at 54. *But see* Robert Glennon, *Will the Real Conservatives Please Stand Up,* ABA JOURNAL 49 (August, 1990). *See also* Clinton, *supra* note 18, at 1182n. 5.
83. William Brennan, *Guaranteeing Individual Liberty,* 115 U.S.A. TODAY 40 (1986).
84. Commager, *supra* note 44, at 7 (quotes are out of order).

Republic and the only hope seems to be today what it always has been—greater vigilance: to challenge false claims on their merits within a principled set of shared interpretative guidelines. But to reject on the level of principle the authority of the ratifiers' will, once established, seems to me to be tantamount to rejecting constitutionalism. Above all else, a written constitution embodies a people's promise to remain faithful to that constitution's original meaning until the people decide to change it.[85] Abuse of interpretive tools is not new and it does not justify ignoring those tools.[86] Nor is there much merit in the argument that some of those who

85. As Monaghan points out, many noninterpretivists prefer to make imaginative end runs around the intent problem. Many of them do not argue that the framers' original understanding cannot be ascertained, but "rather . . . [to seek] to sterilize the concept, most typically by conceptualizing original intent at a level of abstraction that, in effect removes it as an interpretation constraint." Monaghan, *supra* note 28, at 378. I suggest that such an approach is to maintain that something simultaneously is and is not. *See supra,* comment accompanying note 4.

86. *See, e.g.,* chapter 3, text accompanying notes 37 (Marshall, C. J.) and 93 (Toney, C. J.). *But see* Levy's observation:

> [In fact], Bork and Rehnquist, like any other originalist judge, are every bit as subjective as Brennan and Marshall. Their manipulation of the rules of construction achieves whatever result they seek. What they attribute to the Framers derives from their own moral reasoning. No credence can be given to Bork's contention that 'only by limiting themselves to the historic intentions underlying each clause of the Constitution (where is that to be found in) can judges avoid becoming legislators, avoid enforcing their own moral predilections, and ensure that the Constitution is law.'

LEONARD LEVY, ORIGINAL INTENT AND THE FRAMERS' CONSTITUTION 384 (1988). *But compare* Raoul Berger, *Original Intent and Leonard Levy,* 42 RUTGERS L. REV. 255 (1989). John Roche, with his typically penetrating irreverence, further claims that because of renewed interest in the framers' understanding, "psychoanalyzing the dead became a growth industry" and that the logical culmination of such inquiries would be to find out what every individual believed who voted for delegates to each state ratification convention. John Roche, in *Symposium, supra* note 44, at 22–23. *But see* Clinton, *supra* note 18, at 1180 n. 4 ("Very few originalists literally desire to psychoanalyze the members of the Philadelphia Convention or any other set of relevant framers. Instead, they focus on ascertaining the reasonable meanings that might be attributed to such framers in light of the surviving primary historical materials.").

Two other articles must be noted. The first, by Richard H. Fallon, Jr. (Fallon, *supra* note 66), who establishes a hierarchy of argumentative authority: "1. Arguments from text. . . . 2. Arguments of historical intent. . . . 3. Arguments of theory. . . . 4. Arguments from precedent. . . . 5. Arguments of value. *Id.,* at 1244–46. I have not given the matter sustained attention, but I am leery about being dependent upon higher levels of generality or abstraction, evidently accepted by Fallon. *See supra* comment accompanying note 66. I find such an approach, along with Fallon's theory and value arguments (3 & 5), most often are simply a means to reach a desired result [*see infra* chapter 6, discussion of the *results* symbol] or the means by which more contemporary and expanded views of judicial power may be substituted for those of Publius. Fallon's own descriptions of those items seem consistent with that assessment. Fallon, *supra* note 66, at 1199.

The second article, by H. Jefferson Powell, is in many ways penetrating and deserves close reading by anyone thinking about the Framers' intent, and how it may be properly as well as improperly pursued. *See* H. Jefferson Powell, *Rules for Originalists,* 73 VIRGINIA L. REV. 659 (1987). Even if the appropriateness of the rules Powell proposes were accepted by all parties concerned, however, disagreements still would persist because different interpreters may disagree

resort to the framers' intent distort it or close doors that should remain open.[87] Such arguments again appear to counsel greater vigilance, not abandonment of the approach. Such abuses must be expected, and any other expectation seems unrealistic, an attitude preference for perfection where none may be found.[88] Why should it be assumed that the power of interpretation will be pursued any differently than the exercise of any other governmental power?[89] The only response, imperfect as it may be, is the one suggested by Publius: to construct devices that minimize such abuses without eliminating the power that is admitted as being necessary. Thus, with the admission that any inquiry into the ratifiers' intentions is fraught with possibilities of abuse, I turn to particulars.

The Meaning of Intent

What is meant by intent? Intent usually refers to a speaker's public explanations (for example, in conventions or legislative sessions) of what the speaker understands by a constitutional provision or law, or that provision's purpose. Presumably, should a speaker express a misconception about a proposed constitutional amendment or statute, that misconception would be challenged or addressed by other speakers.[90] Related

---

with respect to how and which rules should apply in particular circumstances or how they should be ranked. For example, on several occasions in the text that follows I accept the rule he propounds but find his examples unconvincing. Thus, like canons of construction, Powell's rules can only aid in interpretation, they do not substitute for it. Space does not permit a full treatment of Powell's provocative article but in the discussion that follows I attempt to incorporate some, though not all, of the issues he raises. My estimate of his article parallel's his comment on one of Monaghan's articles: "While [at times] I strongly disagree with [it] . . . I think [the criteria he raises] . . . [are] profoundly correct. Powell, *supra* note 17, at 1432n.12.

87. Powell observes: "Intentionalism itself . . . is fundamentally antitextual, for it treats the document as a mere occasion for a partial and always distorted re-creation of what certain individuals wanted the text to accomplish." *Meditation, supra* note 16, at 1431.

88. *See generally,* Appendix A; and Monaghan, *supra* note 28. *See also* Robert Waelder, *The Concept of Justice and the Quest for an Absolutely Just Society,* 57 J CRIM. L., C & P.S., 1 (1966).

89. *See supra,* chapter 2, text and comments accompanying notes 21–36.

90. Berger defines "the original intention [as meaning] the draftsman's explanation of what he intended to accomplish by the words he used." Raoul Berger, *Robert Bork's Contribution to Original Intention,* 84 NORTHWEST. U. L. REV. 1167, 1178 (1990). Lofgren adds: "Saying that an improper meaning had been attributed to the sources is different from suggesting that the sources had been invented." Lofgren, *supra* note 6, at 99. *But see* Moore, who concludes "that no concept of legislative intention is appropriate to legal interpretation." Michael S. Moore, *A Natural Law Theory of Interpretation,* 58 SO. CAL. L. REV. 279, 338 (1985). The difficulty with Moore's article is that, like the works of so many other scholars, it creates a closed system upon no other authority than Moore's imagination and often relies more upon its own internal coherence than on how such things as interpretation take place, however imperfectly, in the real world. In the end, Moore seems to deny what, in fact, occurs: legislators make laws and people more or less follow them, and whatever problems may arise regarding the specific meaning of those laws, they pale in significance when compared with the obvious truth that people who pass laws do so for a purpose. Moore evidently favors the rule of the just man over the rule of law. Moore, *supra* note 90,

corollaries suggest that the understanding of the *proponents* of an amendment or statute generally is accorded greater weight than the understanding put forth by its opponents.[91] The next corollary counsels that statements made by those responsible for the actual drafting of an amendment or statute generally are to be accorded greater weight than those who merely voted for the measure, since the former are presumed to have a better understanding of the purpose of the measure. A final corollary holds that publicly expressed, *contemporaneous* understandings are always to be accorded greater weight than understandings put forth at a later date.[92]

Intent, therefore, should refer only to the publicly conveyed understanding of the meaning of a proposed statute or amendment (e.g., how it is supposed to work; why it is needed). But what about the speaker having motives other than those made public—ulterior reasons for voting for the measure, or some unexpressed understanding, or judgments based on considerations of expediency (e.g., a desire to be reelected)?[93] Such considerations are not considered by interpretivists as part of intent, though there are noninterpretivist scholars who think they ought to be; or who think the word *motive* may be used interchangeably with *intent.*[94] Such scholars contend that legislators, perhaps constituting a majority, frequently vote for proposals for reasons other than those given in public debate (i.e., for motives never expressed).[95]

Such observations may contain a good deal of truth, but if they are pursued in a rarified, theoretical context, they lead to the experientially absurd (though logically-demanded) conclu-

at 354. But the American people have not consented to such a rule; they have consented to a republican one.

91. Experience demonstrates that opponents tend to exaggerate the proponents' purpose or the impact of an amendment or statutory proposals in order to scare away possible supporters.

92. Although participants at an event (*e.g.,* at the Philadelphia convention) would logically be expected to know more about the purpose of a provision than someone who did not attend, or others who are trying to discern the document's meaning solely from the text, it is possible that the passage of time can dim even the participants' understanding; or that hindsight or subsequent political considerations might prompt participants to recast earlier explanations. *See e.g.,* George W. Carey, *James Madison on Federalism: The Search for Abiding Principles,* 3 BENCHMARK 27 (1987). *See generally,* BERGER, *supra* note 70, at 157, 189; *Facts, supra* note 73, at 282; *Scope, supra* note 14, at 493–494, 615–616.

93. *See* Monaghan, *supra* note 28, at 375. Monaghan claims, and I concur, that "original intent theory is not concerned with the hidden intent of the Framers." *Id.,* 375 n. 30 (quoting for support Gibbons v. Ogden, *supra* note 1, at 188 ["the Framers and ratifiers 'must be presumed to have intended what they said'"]).

94. *See, e.g.,* Walter Murphy, book review, 87 YALE L. J. 1752, 1756 (1978) and Moore, *supra* note 90, who generally seems to blend the two.

95. RONALD DWORKIN, LAW'S EMPIRE 313–317 (1986); *see also e.g., Appendix to the Opinion of the Court,* 6 HAST. CONST L. Q. 455 (1979), and Murphy, *supra* note 94, at 1755.

sion that all deliberative processes are incomprehensible: we never can know with certitude what a majority consensus believed.[96] And it is upon that conclusion that noninterpretivists assert that any appearance of the ratifiers' or legislators' consensus may be safely ignored. In its place, and on a staggering array of grounds, partial evidence, and speculation, noninterpretivists justify their departure from the framers' design; instead they offer imaginative and often novel interpretation of constitutional provisions. Hence, there is no Constitution; rather, it is in a state of becoming. One prominent scholar has sworn to forego reading such literature;[97] another has concluded that the literature has become "energized by a growing sense of desperation";[98] hence, many noninterpretivists, convinced that the deliberative processes is incomprehensible (or, if comprehensible, not particularly binding) have become increasingly preoccupied with constructing logically coherent systems[99] that are capable of achieving presupposed desirable results,[100] rather than trying to understand constitution-making, the understanding of the Constitution, or politics as detailed by Publius.[101]

Legislators regularly reach resolutions on public policy issues and, when judicial interpretations are required, the discernment of the ratifiers' or legislature's intent still is accorded greater weight than their possible motives; certainly it is accorded greater weight than *speculations* regarding such motives. Assuming that for the delegates to the Philadelphia convention unsubstantiated ulterior motives had greater influence on their decisions than the identified weaknesses of the Articles of Confederation is unacceptable.

96. Bork, *supra* note 19, at 163 ("Any modern congressional majority would divide over particular applications of a statute its members had just enacted").

97. Bork, *supra* note 19, at 255 ("It is my firm intention to give up reading this literature").

98. Allan Hutchinson, *Alien Thoughts: A Comment on Constitutional Scholarship,* 58 Sou. Cal. L. Rev. 701, 701 (1985).

99. *See, generally,* Dworkin *supra* note 143; Moore, *supra* note 90; Fallon, *supra* note 66; and Suzanna Sherry, *The Founders' Unwritten Constitution,* 54 U. Chi. L. Rev. 1127 (1987). *See infra,* chapter 6 (use of analogies, models, and symbols).

100. *See infra* chapter 6 (use of the *Results* symbol). I take exception, for example, to Fallon's apparent approval of the conclusion reached by Archibald Cox (Cox, The Role of the Supreme Court in American Government, 1976), who admits that "despite the linguistic oddness of finding substantive rights protected by the due process clause, the Supreme Court's 'persistent' invocation of substantive due process notions 'for almost a century attests the strength' of the natural law impulse supporting the concept, such that it would be 'unwise as well as hopeless to resist it.'" [Fallon, *supra* note 66, at 1253 n.257]. On the contrary, such history helps scholars discern the exact age of the disease, and while it may be hopeless, constitutionalists are very wise in their continued opposition, for the same reason that only persistence eventually repudiated the abuses of a laissez-faire dominated judiciary. *See supra,* chapter 3, and *infra,* chapter 6 (use of the *Irreversible* symbol).

101. *See, generally,* Monaghan, *supra* note 28 and Van Alstyne, *supra* note 66.

One should discount possible motives because what is unknown or unexpressed cannot be said to have been considered or approved.[102] Publius' assessment is as accurate as it is concise: "The moment we launch into conjecture . . . we get into an unfathomable abyss and fairly put ourselves out of reach of all reasoning."[103]

The Application of Intent

After defeating the British forces Americans became their own lawgivers and, perhaps paradoxically, thereafter only they could bind themselves.[104] The people created state constitutions, the Articles of Confederation and, "in Order to form a more perfect Union,"[105] the Constitution of the United States. Through the regular rhythm of electoral accountability on the federal and state level public policy decisions were made, modified, and repudiated.[106]

All laws in the United States are interpreted on the statutory and constitutional levels, and the issue now is how intent—the lawgivers' will—applies to those subjects. Statutes demand similar behavior from all like-situated citizens (e.g., those driving horsedrawn carriages must conduct themselves in a particular way) and they are passed by simple majorities.[107] Since constitutions put forth fundamental principles, however, the processes used to change them usually are more difficult than those used to pass statutes.

In seeking to interpret the ordinary, day-to-day (statutory) or extraordinary (constitutional) expressions of the people's will, judges first must establish that they have jurisdiction (i.e., have authority to hear the case). Once jurisdiction has been ascertained judges begin with the text, whether that text be a statute or the

102. *Cf.* Raoul Berger, *The Fourteenth Amendment: Light from the Fifteenth,* 74 NW. L. REV. 311, 367 (1979); BERGER, *supra* note 70, at 157n.2 *with supra,* chapter 4, text and comments accompanying notes 2–30. In the context of a written Constitution, one providing for its amendment, it cannot be maintained that the people approved a fundamental change about which they never were informed or to which they never consented. That certainly is the position taken by Publius. *See supra* chapter 2, text accompanying note 74. Are we to attribute a lesser standard of disclosure with respect to constitution making than for the purchase of a consumer item? The common-law maxim of the marketplace, "Let the buyer beware," may be modified by the legislature, but are judges entitled to employ its interpretive equivalent: let the ratifier beware of what judges may *interpret* the Constitution to mean?

103. FEDERALIST, *supra* note 5, no. 31, at 196. *Compare* Moore, *supra* note 90, at 339–352.

104. *See supra* chapter 3, text accompanying note 56. (Marshall, C. J.). Self-government is apparently akin to self-discipline, which in the framers' view was as natural as freedom. SEE LEO STRAUSS, NATURAL RIGHT AND HISTORY 132–133 (1952).

105. U.S. CONST., Preamble.

106. Speaking of the House of Representatives, Publius observes: "All these securities, however, would be found very insufficient without the restraint of frequent elections. Hence . . . the House of Representatives is so constituted as to support in the members an habitual recollection of their dependence on the people." FEDERALIST, *supra* note 5, no. 57, at 352.

107. EMPIRE, *supra* note 95, at 100.

Constitution. Next, they attempt to discern the will of the legislature that enacted that statute or those who had ratified the constitutional provision. Such attempts may proceed either from the text directly or, as has become more prevalent in recent years, through extrinsic sources (e.g., legislative history).[108] To guard against possible misconstructions, judges must presume that the lawgivers meant what they said, that words ordinarily should not be taken out of context or given technical or esoteric construction instead of their commonly-understood meaning, and that "when the intention is clear it is as good as written into the text."[109] Below I apply these principles to both the interpretation of statutes and the Constitution.

THE STATUTORY LEVEL. Circumstances change: take, for example, the time period between the passage of laws regulating horsedrawn carriages and the advent of the automobile. Conflicts ensued between these two modes of transportation.[110] Some legislatures responded by passing laws to govern automobile usage (perhaps inhibiting, perhaps encouraging); others did not. In some states, judges reinterpreted horsedrawn carriage usage statutes, perhaps applying them more broadly than had been envisioned by legislators who originally had passed the statute: *interpreting* the statutory language to include a new means of "transportation."

Such reinterpretations of statutes are representative of the common law (judge-made law) and have been one means by which American society has adapted to changing circumstances.[111] At least two options exist. Judges can ask, "When the legislature passed this statute, what was it trying to accomplish?" In the example cited, if automobiles can be brought within the purview of that purpose, without materially changing it, then judges may interpret the statute's language to cover automobiles. But another judge, after inquiring into the legislature's original intent, might conclude that for one reason or another an expansive reading of the statutory language is not permissible. This judge might find that the two means of transportation are so radically different that, in practice, issues such as which vehicle should have right of way cannot be easily reconciled. Such a judge might reason that it is more appropriate for the legislature to reconcile any conflicts between the two modes of transportation and so refuse to expand the application of statutory language. Such refusals often prompts fresh legislative consideration. Then

108. *See infra* text accompanying notes 135–144.

109. *Scope, supra* note 14, at 620–621. *See also* sources collected at note 25.

110. The discussion in the text parallels Ronald Dworkin's example. *See generally,* DWORKIN, *supra* note 95 and HURST, *supra* note 65.

111. *See* OLIVER W. HOLMES, JR., THE COMMON LAW (1881).

again, it may not, for various reasons: because legislators are indecisive about going one way or the other; or because the legislature is dominated by horsedrawn carriage interests; or because legislators believe they have far more important things to consider and prefer to wait until decisive action is clearly required. Whatever their reasoning, however, if and when they eventually decide, a simple majority could accept, reject, or modify whatever judicial "interpretations" already had been made. Statute law takes precedence over judge-made law. Judges then would be obliged to obey the legislative will, regardless of personal disagreements with it, at least until another interpretive opportunity comes before them: a new case.

THE CONSTITUTIONAL LEVEL. Constitutions assume that a bond exists between those who create them and others, including their descendants.[112] But interpretative choices also arise on the constitutional level, as they did on the statutory level. The Constitution, for example, grants to Congress the power "to raise and support Armies"[113] and "to provide and maintain a Navy."[114] The question may be posed: May Congress subsequently "raise and support" or "provide and maintain" an *air force,* something the framers obviously never contemplated?[115] Given the framers' clear purposes to protect the United States from foreign enemies or domestic insurrections, as well as the inclusion of the necessary and proper clause, may a judge legitimately interpret *army* and *navy* broadly, say in terms of *national defense forces,* and conclude that an air force falls within the framers' intent? I think so.[116]

112. For those who find that bond too confining, Robert Bork reminds us that "the dead-men argument proves too much" since no part of the Constitution is excepted from such reasoning, including the Bill of Rights. BORK, *supra* note 19, at 173. This proposition is of course related to the *Adaptable* symbol, discussed in chapter 6, *infra.*
113. U.S. CONST., art 1, sec. 8, para. 12.
114. *Id.,* art. 1, sec. 8 para. 13.
115. Powell puts forth this rule: *"Arguments from silence are unreliable and often completely ahistorical."* He identifies two broad categories. In the first would be "situations where the issues of contemporary importance could have been raised by the founders"; and in the second category "situations in which our issue could not have been raised." Powell, *supra* note 86, at 671. In the first situation "it is possible that the combined weight of the founders' conceptual framework, contemporaneous word usage, cultural setting, and so on, may render a given claim unlikely." But even then Powell concludes we can't be sure. However, when the framers could not have conceivably dealt with a contemporary problem "not even a tentative conclusion can be drawn." *Id.,* questioning the decision in INS v. Chadha, 462 U.S. 919 (1983) (legislative veto declared unconstitutional as violation of separation of powers).
116. Powell suggests this rule: *"History answers—and declines to answer—its own issues, rather than the concerns of the interpreter."* Powell, *supra* note 86, at 669. He observes that "the founders thought, argued, reached decisions, and wrote about the issues that mattered to them, not about our contemporary issues." Thus, with respect to some contemporary issues, we may find that the

But at the same time I want to recall two distinctions I made earlier.[117] First, with respect to the example just cited, the provisions encompass broad *grants of power,* those intended to render the federal government competent in the most important of governmental responsibilities: national defense. Second, Congress is the initiator of the noted legislation and the judicial function is to decide whether or not the creation of an air force is within the competency of Congress. Judges are not asked whether or not they believe an air force is a good idea.

I contend it is not accurate to equate interpretivist principles with literalism,[118] or to assert that interpretivists are overly dependent on the plain-meaning rule.[119] While attempts at statutory and constitutional inter-

---

framers said nothing, and on other issues, that even considerable discussion on their part might not shed light on matters that concern us today. *Id.* at 669–670. I do not, however, necessarily agree with the examples Powell provides. *See also, generally,* James W. Davidson and Mark H. Lytle, in After the Fact: The Art of Historical Detection 66–80 (1982).

117. *See supra,* text, comment, and sources accompanying notes 43–57.

118. Perry, *supra* note 110, at 280–281. Perry contends that "nothing [is achieved] by pretending that interpretivism is not a forceful theory" [*id.* at 278], and it simply will not do to misrepresent it, or to refuse to understand it on its own terms [*id.,* at 278–284]. But many noninterpretivists equate interpretivism with literalism. Take what Baer offers as an example of interpretivist literalism: Justice Black's dictum that the first amendment phrase, "'no law,'" should mean precisely just that—*no law.* Judith A. Baer, *Reading the Fourteenth Amendment: The Inevitability of Noninterpretivism,* in Politics, *supra* note 82, at 214. Yet, many interpretivists would reject Black's approach because he ignored the crucial abridging language in the First Amendment as well as the fact that for the framers speech did not include the right to blasphemy, pornography, or seditious libel.

Another scholar, offering another alleged example of interpretivist reasoning, quotes a passage from one of Chief Justice Taney's opinions (*see supra* chapter 3, text accompanying note 107). Sandalow, *supra* note 138, at 214. *See also* Moore, *supra* note 90, at 307. Yet an interpretivist might reject Taney's reasoning, charging him with abusing the judicial power, or with ignoring relevant evidence or applicable canons, or with imposing on the American people what he thought were beneficent results.

Put another way, interpretivists should be the first to acknowledge that attempts will be made to abuse their approach. For example, what if, as Kay posed, Congress substituted a four-year term for the precise constitutional stipulation of two-year terms for members of Congress? "Who would defend that substitution," even though we would be "just as much ruled by the framers from their graves?" *See Scope, supra* note 14, at 530 (quoting Richard Kay, book review, 10 Conn. L. Rev. 801, 804 (1978). Or what of this example of a high-level abstraction put forth by Richard Saphire and recounted by Raoul Berger, with respect to the Constitution's requirement that a United States Senator must be at least thirty years old:

> "[A]t some future time the senatorial age requirement might . . . plausibly be deemed ambiguous [?] . . . [or] interpreted in a nonliteral sense," viewing it as a "symbolic reference to maturity." The Court would not be "overstepping its legitimate function . . . to hold that a twenty-nine-year-old is eligible for election to the Senate."

Berger, *supra* note 27, at 194–195.

119. *See e.g.* Moore, *supra* note 90, at 307, 320. *Compare supra* text accompanying note 68 with the statements below (again my appreciation to McGowan, *supra* chapter 4 comment accompanying note 154):

pretations necessarily proceed along similar lines, they are not on the same plane. The Constitution is superior to a statute. When it was ratified, the people believed that the structures and conditions it contained would become fixed, including very specific restrictions, even on the very broad powers they granted: e.g., that "no appropriation of money . . . should be for a longer term than two years."[120]

Powell astutely observes that even where the intentions of the framers are clearly demonstrated, some noninterpretivist scholars remain unimpressed. They respond, "So what?"[121] As one scholar bluntly put it, the "Founding Fathers have been buried. They should not rule us from their grave."[122] Such arguments simply sidestep the legitimacy issue raised by interpretivists: what then is the significance of a written constitution? If its provisions are not considered special and binding, why were they constitutionalized in the first place?[123]

> If the [readily discernible] plain meaning of a provision . . . is to be disregarded, because we believe the framers of that instrument could not [have intended] what they [enacted], it must be one in which the absurdity and injustice of applying the provision to the case would be so monstrous that all mankind would, without hesitation, unite in rejecting the application.

Sturges v. Crowninshield, 4 Wheat. 122, 202, 4 L. Ed. 529, 550 (1819) (C. J. Marshall). Or this formulation of the approach interpreters should take:

> Where a statute is of doubtful meaning and susceptible upon its face of two constructions, the court may look into prior and contemporaneous acts, the reasons which induced the acts in question, the mischiefs intended to be remedied, the extraneous circumstances, and the purpose intended to be accomplished by it, to determine its proper construction. But where the act is clear upon its face, and when standing alone it is fairly susceptible of but one construction, that construction must be given to it. . . . [P]rior acts may be referred to solve but not to create an ambiguity.

Hamilton v. Rathbone, 175 U.S. 414, 421 (1899) (J. Brown). Or, another approach compatible with interpretivist premises, when "aid to construction of the meaning of words [which are not clearly discernible] . . . is available, there certainly can be no 'rule of law' which forbids its use, however clear the words may appear on 'superficial examination'." Cass v. United States, 417 U.S. 72 (1974).

120. U.S. CONST., art 1, sec. 8, para. 12.

121. Powell, *supra* note 86, at 662. Powell suggests this rule: *"History itself will not prove anything non-historical."* More specifically, he writes: "History cannot answer or even address the question of whether modern Americans ought to obey the intentions of the Constitutional founders." *Id.*, at 662. Michaels replies: "But the question of why the Constitution is authoritative is a question about why we should do what it says, not about what it says we should do." Michaels, *supra* note 19, at 680.

122. Arthur S. Miller, *An Inquiry into the Relevance of the Intentions of the Founding Fathers, With Special Emphasis Upon the Doctrine of Separation of Powers,* 27 ARK. L. REV. 583, 601 (1973). *But see* BORK, *supra* note 19, 170–171. "Though it is disguised, the unrepresentative-dead-men argument is nothing more than an attempt to block self-government by the representatives of living men and women." *id.,* at 171.

123. "As Justice Story stated . . . the common law 'definitions are necessarily included, as much *as if they stood in the text* of the Constitution.'" BERGER, *supra* note 56, at 63 (quoting United States v. Smith, 18 U.S. (5 Wheat.) 153, 160 (1820)).

And why did the framers include distinct and arduous processes (the amendment procedures) to change them?[124]

I do not charge that judges are abusing their power when they apply a granted power or an existing restriction to new situations (e.g., the creation of an air force or a modern variant of a bill of attainder).[125] But I would charge a judge with abusing the judge's authority if, for example, that judge set aside the two-year appropriation restriction on the grounds that today the American people are no longer concerned with the effect of standing armies.[126] In the former instance, the judge interprets; in the latter, there is abuse of the judge's authority. That second judge fails in the duty to uphold the ratifier's intent.[127]

The Constitution clearly con-

124. Noninterpretivists frequently characterize the amendment processes as cumbersome (Article 5 provides *two means* of amending the Constitution, although only one has ever been employed). *See infra,* chapter 6.

125. Here Powell offers this rule: *"The original understanding of constitutional provisions cannot be neatly separated from their later use."* Powell, *supra* note 86, at 675. Thus, even assuming that early interpretations of constitutional provisions were faithful to the framers' intentions, because interpretation is a continuing process that intent may be difficult to separate from subsequent interpretations, and the framers themselves expected subsequent interpreters to fill in gaps. *Id.* at 676–677. Powell also (*id* at 672–674) discusses the need for a translator; that is, he argues we have to understand the framers as they understood themselves—explicitly raising issues that all constitutional scholars must consider. For example, how dependent should judicial opinions be on historical scholarship?—"the next doctoral dissertation may wash their views away." [*id.,* at 680] Finally, Powell raises this question: should decisions in which the framers' intent was ignored ever become accepted as precedent? *Id.* at 685–686.

See also Fallon. Fallon claims that he knows "of no case in which the Supreme Court has ever said that although the framers' intent required one result, another conclusion should nonetheless be reached" Fallon, *supra* note 66, at 1255. Yet in a footnote he concedes that there is at least one instance (citing Reynolds v. Sims, 377 U.S. 533 [1964], which he characterizes as "the exception [that] proves the rule" and he observes that "a more common gambit is for the Court to assert or imply that the framers, whatever their specific intentions, would have intended the courts to adapt constitutional principles to changing situations" (citing Home Bldg. & Loan Ass'n. v. Blaisdell, 290 U.S. 398, 443 [1934]). *Id.,* at 1255n.266. Elsewhere he recalls that Alexander Bickel himself concluded, with regard to the Fourteenth Amendment's framers' intent to abolish segregation, "that if the equal protection clause were part of a statute, the supporting evidence would not be strong enough to sustain his theory." *Id.,* at 1281. Bickel's own assessment however is insufficient to pass muster with Fallon. *Id.,* at 1282.

126. *See supra* chapter 3, comment accompanying note 113.

127. Powell offers this rule: *"Consensus or even broad agreement among the founders is a historical assertion to be justified, not assumed."* Powell, *supra* note 86, at 684. He uses Bill of Rights and Fourteenth Amendment examples, but for reasons discussed in chapter 7, *infra,* I am not convinced. I agree with Powell, however, that scholars must prove whether "all" or only "some" of the framers held the views attributable to them, and "the intuitive sense that the founders 'must have' agreed on the meaning of the document they adopted. . . . [may amount to] an unwitting way of sneaking the historical conclusion to be proved (the existence of agreement) into the argument proving it." [*Id.* at 684–685]. Often the evidence about a consensus is inconclusive; or it might have to be supplemented with other inquiries [*Id.,* at 685]. Furthermore, even if the distinction between intention and motivation is respected, often "most legislators have no well-thought out

demned certain practices. It did so because the framers' and ratifiers' experience, as well as the experience of their ancestors, led them to the conclusion that if those practices were not explicitly condemned the newly created federal government might employ them; or that the republican nature of their regime would most likely be undermined. The framers and ratifiers understood that republican officials, when they found it convenient, might be tempted to resort to techniques used in monarchies or aristocracies. Publius, however, never abandoned the ideal of majority rule.[128]

As in the case of statutes, constitutional interpretations must attempt to effectuate the lawgivers' will, and an inability to discern aspects of that will does not magically transform the judicial power into the legislative one.[129] If the judicial power could be transformed into the legislative power, it would leave the judiciary the judge of its own power. It was to precisely to avoid such an event that the framers departed from ordinary republican principles (electoral accountability) and created a truly independent judiciary: it was to guard against the consolidation of power (tyranny).[130] Absent a clear understanding or contrary expressions of the ratifiers' will, judge-made law may be legitimate, though not always prudent: judicial substitution of judges' beliefs for those of the ratifiers or legislators *is not.*[131]

I have detailed Publius' position: when the executive or legislature *clearly* departs from the ratifier's will (he used the phrase "manifest tenor"),[132] the people had *authorized* judges to declare such acts null and void. But it was the people's will (as expressed in the Constitution) and the judge's ability to discern that will that provided the legitimacy for judges to set aside the acts of elected representatives.[133] Therefore, when judicial determinations of unconsti-

---

opinions or intentions at all"; and even more important, Powell believes that contemporary rules for discerning the framers' understanding, such as those mentioned earlier (*e.g.* author of bill given greater weight than supporter) probably were not applicable [*Id.* at 686]. But *see, generally,* Lofgren, *supra* note 6, and Berger's replies to Powell (sources accompanying note 25, *supra*).

128. *See supra,* chapter 2, text accompanying note 18–46.

129. Robert Bork puts it this way: "The judge who cannot make out the meaning of a provision is in exactly the same circumstance as a judge who has no Constitution to work with. There being nothing to work with, the judge should refrain from working." Bork, *supra* note 19, at 166. Stephen Markman adds that "when we cannot find guidance to the Founders' intentions, the courts are not free to do anything they want to do." Markman, in Commager, *supra* note 44, at 10. *See infra,* chapter 6 discussion of the *Vaccum.*

130. *See supra,* chapter 2, text, comment, and sources accompanying notes 91–97.

131. *See infra,* chapter 6, text, comment, and sources accompanying notes 4–28.

132. *See* chapter 2, text accompanying note 64, *supra*.

133. Powell suggests this rule: "History sometimes justifies plausible but opposing interpretations." Powell, *supra* note 86, at 688 (emphasis omitted). He explains: "Often the historical researcher, or the constitutional interpreter seeking enlightenment from history, will find himself considering opposing accounts of the founders' thought that seem of roughly the same plausibility" [*Id*].

tutionality do not rest upon that ground, and instead, implicitly or explicitly, rest upon what judges divine to be good public policy, those determinations are not only illegitimate, they violate the people's birthright: such judges modify the people's right to govern themselves by the principles to which they consented, changing it to the right to govern themselves under judicial supervision.

I contend that the people should not be obliged to resort to the amendment process until these judges, or their successors, change their mind or repudiate earlier abuses of power. Why should the people be required to undergo that arduous process when judges strike down legislation upon any other ground than that the people's elected representatives had done something their ancestors had promised not to do? The people may ignore judicial public policy assessments. Judges have no particular expertise regarding public policy options other than that possessed by elected and accountable representatives.[134]

I contend that judicially imposed public policy choices undermine the judiciary. Much more importantly, they obscure the sole reason why delegates to the convention lodged the power of judicial review in judicial hands. The judiciary's lack of coercive power was intended to increase confidence in the neutrality of judges' decisions. In the short run, conservatives or liberals alike may succeed in using the judiciary (instead of the political processes) to implement their public policy preferences, but in the end the Constitution is diminished, along with the institution the framers thought best to protect it: the judiciary. Policy and constitution making are becoming indistinguishable, and the rule of law may cease to be what it has been for generations of Americans. Most important, in time the peoples' sense of responsibility for the character and actions of their government and society will be eroded: it will atrophy from disuse.

Intrinsic and Extrinsic Sources

But even if it is conceded that the discernment of the lawgivers' intent is a crucial interpretive consideration, and that meaningful distinctions exist between judge-made, statutory, and constitutional law, practical problems still exist with respect to whether or not, and how, the framers' understanding may be actually discerned. Christopher Wolfe identified two approaches to the subject: the intrinsic approach (deducing the framers' understanding solely from the constitutional text) and the extrinsic approach (where sources other than the actual text are consulted).[135]

134. Chief Justice Marshall observed: "The interest, wisdom and justice of the representative body, and its relations with its constituents, furnish the only security . . . against unwise legislation." Providence Bank v. Billings, 29 U.S. (4 Pet.) 514, 563 (1830).
135. WOLFE, *supra* note 62, at 48.

In the first approach, an effort is made to ascertain the meaning of a particular clause by giving each word its common-law meaning at the time of adoption and, if necessary, also taking into consideration the context in which it appears and the framers' apparent objectives.[136] Charles Lofgren concluded that the historical record is mixed.[137] For example, in *Chrisholm v. Georgia* (1793),[138] ignoring "Publius's fairly clear assurance to the contrary" (that the states possessed traditional immunity from civil suits), the Supreme Court ruled that Georgia could be sued by the citizens of another state.[139] In other instances, in one form or another the justices sought to establish from the text the intent of the framers or ratifiers.[140]

When the extrinsic approach is used, judges turn to sources other than the Constitution (e.g., *The Federalist Papers* or "the explanations and defenses of the Constitution during ratification debates") better to discern why particular clauses were included or excluded.[141] The extrinsic approach may be more common today than during the early days of the Republic, which parallels today's greater dependence on legislative history.[142]

The two approaches are not mutually exclusive. Chief Justice Marshall, for example, used both.[143] Presumably, the conscientious application of either method, if equally applicable, should aid in reaching a more informed opinion than if neither were employed. The ratifiers' understanding may still may remain elusive; or if their understanding is discernible, it may be inconclusive on the issue directly before a court. Judges and scholars, as juries do, may have to weigh the credibility of witnesses—evidence regarding the ratifiers' intent. Juries regularly reach verdicts and reach them as best they can on the evidence before them. Their process of discernment includes assessing the intentions

136. BERGER, *supra* note 56, at 61. *See* comment accompanying note 146, *supra.*

137. Lofgren, *supra* note 6, at 111.

138. Chrisholm v. Georgia, 2 Dall. 419 (1793). *Id. See also* Powell, *supra* note 86, at 681.

139. Lofgren, *supra* note 6, at 111. *Cf.* FEDERALIST, *supra* note 5, No. 81, at 484–491; Powell, *supra* note 24, at 921–923 and Powell, *supra* note 86, at 681.

140. *See supra,* text accompanying notes 43–57, 90–103 for discussions and references.

141. WOLFE, *supra* note 62, at 49. *See generally,* Wilson, *supra* note 61.

142. *Cf.* WOLFE, *supra* note 62, at 24–51; Powell, *supra* note 24, 902–921 and Berger, *supra* note 25, at 308–320. *See generally,* 3 BENCHMARK 217 (1990) (Recent trends in American Legal History).

143. WOLFE, *supra* note 62, at 49. *See supra,* chapter 3, for examples of Marshall's approach in cases such as Marbury v. Madison, McCulloch v. Maryland, Barron v. Baltimore or Gibbons v. Ogden. Reliance on extrinsic sources may provide or may seem to provide more particular information than reliance solely on the text, but, as suggested by Powell, such reliance also increases the likelihood that the interpreter will find what he wishes. *See* comment accompanying note 125, *supra.*

of one or more of the parties involved.[144]

Problems of Discernment

As noted in the beginning of this chapter, the clash between interpretivist and noninterpretivist views of interpretation hardly seem to turn on distinctions such as those noted above. Instead, noninterpretivists who view judicial power as the means for building a better society seem to chafe under Publius' understanding of interpretation and judicial review.[145] For example, noninterpretivists assert that even if the intrinsic or extrinsic approaches are employed, problems persist with respect to discerning intent, and it is to these problems I now turn.

ON GROUP AND PERSONAL VIEWS. Noninterpretivists argue that the legislative and constitution-making processes are far too complex to define intent in terms of a speaker's public acknowledgment of meaning. For example, many legislators never actually express an opinion on a piece of legislation other than to vote "aye" or "nay." Other legislators may be intimidated by party leaders or constituent pressure and for such reasons conceal their true opinion. Thus, different legislators may support a measure for expressed or unexpressed reasons, or some combination of both. How then may their reasoning processes (intent) ever be determined with any degree of certitude? And if that is the case is not the pursuit to discern intent fatally flawed?[146] Or they point out that the delegates to the Philadelphia convention and the authors of *The Federalist Papers* constituted only a small group of citizens, compared with all those in thirteen states who ratified the Constitution. So even if a consensus existed among small groups, that consensus may not have been representative of the entire group, thereby creating the "thorny issue of group intent."[147]

But such concerns, as Chief Justice

144. I am of the opinion that doubt (that is, the inability to discern the framers' intentions) should prompt judicial self-restraint—the lesson taught by Chief Justice Marshall in M'Culloch v. Maryland. *See infra,* chapter 6, text accompanying note 123.

145. Robert H. Bork comments:

> As John McArthur puts it, "Noninterpretivists are eager to discard written systems of law, including that based upon the Constitution, because written law is the barrier between law and politics. If the judicial process can be reduced to political choice, then the noninterpretivists' views will be heard along with other views. When text-based methodologies are rejected, the Constitution, formerly the trump card in political debate, can be excluded from discussion."

Robert H. Bork, *The Inherent Illegitimacy of Noninterpretivism,* in POLITICS, *supra* note 82, at 112.

146. EMPIRE, *supra* note 95, at 318–324. *See also* Moore, *supra* note 90, at 338, 348–450. Moore also draws this distinction: "The intentions with which a person speaks are distinct from the meanings of the words spoken." *Id.,* at 338.

147. Powell, *supra* note 86, at 663. The theoretical difficulties noted in the text would be more serious if they had been concretely demonstrated. In any event, the issue should be handled in such a way as to explain why any apparent misunderstandings regarding the intent of the legislature

Marshall advised,[148] should not paralyze us or stop us from acknowledging that legislation is passed daily; that the views of some actors are weighed more heavily than the views of others; or that constitutional amendments are proposed for a purpose and ratified. Scholars, I suspect, rarely have had any real difficulty in discerning the framers' or ratifiers' probable understanding, whether they proceeded by intrinsic means or by using more complex extrinsic aids. The real issue is quite different.

For example, twenty years ago one found not only the personal policy preferences of scholars clearly labeled as such, but also how, until that time, constitutional provisions had been understood.[149] Today, however, in many scholarly works a provision's traditional understanding often is ignored, or explored only in a cursory manner, not because the traditional understanding is difficult to discern but because that understanding is considered irrelevant—a by product of the "So what" attitude reported by Powell.[150] Many scholars prefer to create systems, models, and symbols, hastening to reach higher levels of generality and consequently failing to understand the pertinence of past actions in their obvious attempt—not to understand the provisions as they had been understood by their framers or subsequently—but to rewrite those provisions.[151] They do not counsel their fellow citizens to seek reform in the legislature; instead, they "interpret" (remake) the Constitution in their image and likeness. They, like the new breed of prosecutors and defense attorneys, want to *win,* and so they "avert their eyes" from the most probable conclusions to be drawn from the evidence.[152] It is the power wielded by judges today that makes

---

cannot be cured by the creation of a new law. Another thing that disturbs me is the treatment given to varying opinions expressed in the legislature or Congress or constitutional or ratifying conventions: the legal literature seems to assume that if but one remark can be found casting doubt on what a majority evidently believed, the opposing views should be weighed equally. An example might be a case in which ninety-nine senators understand a provision to mean one thing while one senator thinks it means another. I reject the equal-weight approach as an intellectualization of the law and contrary to experience and common sense. *See infra,* chapter 7, text and comment accompanying notes 91–106.

148. *See* text accompanying note 1, *supra.*

149. *See, e.g.,* William Gangi, *The Inbau-Kamisar Debate: Time for Round 2?,* 12 Western State U.L.Rev. 117, 122 n.48 (1984) [hereinafter *Gangi*] and William Gangi, *The Sixth Amendment: Judicial Power and the People's Right to Govern Themselves,* 66 Wash. U.L.Q. 71 (1988) [hereinafter *Sixth*].

150. *See supra,* text accompanying note 121. Elsewhere I created a hypothetical case that takes a "so what?" attitude with respect not only to the framers' Fifth Amendment intentions but also to the Warren Court's Miranda v. Arizona intentions. *See* Gangi, *supra* note 149, at 135–141.

151. *See infra,* chapter 6.

152. Marvin E. Frankel, *The Search for Truth—An Umpired View,* 31 Annual Benjamin N. Cardozo Lecture Delivered Before the Association of The Bar of the City of New York 19 (1974).

their beliefs or doctrinal distinctions (and hence their appointments) so important, not their skill as legal craftspersons, for without the power of five votes—the number required for a Court majority—those distinctions would otherwise, like those of their predecessors, fade into oblivion.[153]

INTENT AND EXPECTATION. The Constitution contains provisions regarding the powers granted, distributed, and denied. Americans today are bound to the framers' specific understandings on such matters; but should Americans be equally bound to what may be called the framers' expectations? For example, Publius expressed his expectation that, if anything, the states probably would dominate the central government, and that criminal justice should be solely a matter of state concern.[154] In the context of the question posed above, what about the fact—noted by Powell—that "the vast majority of contemporary constitutional disputes involve facts, practices, and problems that were not considered or even dreamt of by the founders"?[155]

I suggest that, while such issues are important and frequently ought to be at the core of constitutional interpretation, they are not today at the heart of the dispute between interpretivists and noninterpretivists. No one can know the future—as the framers well knew.[156] For that reason the framers entrusted to those who would be accountable to the people the task of drafting new legislation better suited to changing circumstances: that is at the heart of the legislative function.[157] Even interpretivists differ among themselves on such questions: there is no magic formula for their resolution. But that does not mean every "'approach'"[158] is equally legitimate, equally meritorious, or equally sustainable. For example, I believe scholars who acknowledge the significance of a written constitution must be preferred over those who ignore it; those who sustain the framers' republican design must be preferred over those who substitute their own governmental preferences; those whose interpreta-

153. Authority and power are not quite the same thing. As G. K. Chesterton has written: "'If a rhinoceros came in through that door . . . it would have considerable power. I would be the first to rise, however, and to assure the creature that it had no authority.'" BORK, *supra* note 19, at 176 (quoting G. K. Chesterton). *See* MELVIN I. UROFSKY, DOCUMENTS OF AMERICAN CONSTITUTIONAL AND LEGAL HISTORY 149 (1989) ("The conservatives began to retire from the bench, and the new appointees moved quickly to dismantle substantive due process and freedom of contract as barriers to reform . . . and to expand the reach of the federal commerce power").

154. FEDERALIST, *supra* note 5, no. 46, at 295.

155. Powell, *supra* note 86, at 664–665.

156. *See infra,* chapter 7, text accompanying note 111.

157. *See infra,* chapter 7, text accompanying notes 19–36.

158. I take the word from Powell, *supra* note 24, at 919. Powell is quoting WALTER F. MURPHY, *et al.* AMERICAN CONSTITUTIONAL INTERPRETATION (1986).

tions are based on evidence must be preferred over interpretations that rest, at best, on less-than-convincing evidence, and at their worst on little more than speculation or the alleged logical demands of a model the interpreter created. Finally, scholarly interpretations that effectuate the framers' understanding of judicial power must be preferred over those that substitute some variant to which the American people have never consented. Constitutional law is about who was authorized to do things, or who was prohibited from doing things, not about what judges think of the people's public policy choices.[159] The framers "preserv[ed] democracy in those areas of life that [they] . . . intended to leave to the people's self-government." Interpretivists honor that tradition while noninterpretivists prefer to put the governing power in the hands of judges.[160]

THOSE WHO FRAMED V. THOSE WHO RATIFIED. But if the framers' understanding of a constitutional provision differed from the ratifiers' understanding, which should be accorded greater weight? The answer clearly is the latter, because prior to ratification the Constitution was only a proposal. It had no legal status; the people's consent created the bonds of fidelity. Those who ratified the Constitution in the name of the people did so on the basis of their understanding of the proposal.[161]

What if the understanding of a provision differed from one state ratification convention to another?[162] Once again such issues, if concretely demonstrated, must be faced by scholars, and a number of solutions may be equally tenable. But, once again, these issues hardly seem to explain the differences between interpretivists and noninterpretivists. In any event, such problems cannot transform the judicial power into the legislative one. As Lofgren concluded, the problem may be more a theoretical one than a practical one, but no problem should be allowed to distract us from the obvious: the Constitution "elaborated a new system of government which rested crucially on the sovereignty of *the people.*"[163]

159. Zuckert states it well: "Today constitutional scholars face two tasks: to repoliticize the Constitution and to depoliticize constitutional law." Michael Zuckert, in *Symposium, supra* note 86, at 35. Does that description differ materially from the one offered by Edwin Meese? *See supra* comment accompanying note 82.

160. BORK, *supra* note 19, at 163.

161. Monaghan, *supra* note 28, at 375n.30.

162. So far as I am aware, this did not occur.

163. Lofgren, *supra* note 6, at 85 (emphasis added). With respect to the opposing positions of Hamilton and Madison on whether or not the convention authorized the chartering of a national bank, *compare* Powell, *supra* note 24, at 914–916 with Berger, *supra* note 86, at 264–266. *But see* Lofgren, *supra* note 6, at 93–94, especially at 94n.58, which reflects my own conclusion. Monaghan observes that "although the intention of the ratifiers, not the Framers, is in principle decisive, the difficulties of ascertaining the intent of the ratifiers leaves little choice but to accept the

EVALUATION

Scholars have the professional responsibility to consider all evidence, to reach conclusions, to state and defend those conclusions, and to explain why contrary evidence is neither pertinent nor controlling.[164] Speculation is no substitute for evidence.[165] Scholars and citizens alike owe it to themselves and future generations to identify and discount speculation on the possible or secretly held motives of the framers; learned monographs on what various words or phrases (divorced from their historical context) *could* or *should* mean, and invocations of subsequent changes in circumstances or values. Such techniques I treat more systematically in the next chapter. They serve only to mask the judiciary's denial of the people's right to govern themselves.

I believe that interpretation of the Constitution is manageable within the interpretivist framework, and that it is the noninterpretivist position that raises far more substantive issues. My stated goal is to gain allies, whatever may be my readers' political preferences. Would the reader concede at this point that my contentions that the framers' intentions are important, if not at times determining, is reasonable? And that my desire to be faithful to those intentions is not equivalent to freezing the Constitution in late eighteenth-century history? Would the reader further admit that the noninterpretivist approach, as set out thus far, raises serious questions about the rule of law, about the fidelity necessary to sustain that rule of law from one generation to the next, and about the ability of that approach to provide as neutral a process as possible? Finally, would the reader acknowledge that I do not abolish interpretative questions, nor do I fail to recognize that the task of interpretation often is not easy, and that it is likely to be the subject of honest disputes?

I contend that the differences between legal and other types of interpretation and between statutory and constitutional interpretation far outweigh any similarities. The Constitution was secured by the force of arms—an act of the people, not a single author. And unlike deceased authors of literary works (incapable of articulating their original meaning), the Constitution contains specific structures for doing so: a judiciary (itself bound by a tradition of interpretation) and elected represen-

---

intent of the Framers as a fair reflection of it." Monaghan, *supra* note 28, at 375 n.130.

164. Raoul Berger, *Judicial Review: Countercriticism in Tranquility,* 69 NW. L. REV. 390, 418 (1974).

165. FEDERALIST, *supra* note 5, no. 61, at 376 ("merely speculative . . . upon that speculation"); no. 27, at 174 ("mere general assertion, unsupported by any precise or intelligible designation of the reasons upon which it is founded"); no. 61, at 374 ("they ought to prove"). *See also* BERGER, *supra* note 70, at 74 and Berger, *supra* note 14, at 527, 593, 626n.110.

tatives.[166] Additionally, unlike an individual author, the framers sought and obtained the people's consent to be ruled under certain structures and none other. This promise cannot be honorably abandoned in favor of alternate and ultimately private alternatives. Judge Frank H. Easterbrook provides these distinctions:

> Literary criticism may proceed on the basis of modern intuitions and innovative reflections precisely because it is designed to stimulate rather than govern. Philosophical interpretation may invent new worlds and afford revolutionary ethical systems, because it is meant to furnish a theory of life rather than a description of an ongoing state. Constitutional interpretation is more confined; it is a process of holding an actual government within certain bounds. The power to issue *commands* on the basis of interpretation influences the theory of interpretation. Theories of meaning that do not address this stand in danger of destroying the basis of review. Whether other officers of government should do as courts say depends on *how* courts decide what to say—and much of judges' interpretive apparatus today derives from theories of meaning that cannot explain why others must obey.[167]

The issue today is not whether concern for the ratifiers' understanding of constitutional provisions poses significant interpretative problems: they certainly do. But rather whether or not those problems—taken as a whole—are more manageable than the noninterpretivist position, which denies the pertinence of the ratifiers' understanding.[168] Furthermore, I contend that the burden of proof rests with the latter. This burden of proof neither has been met, nor can it ever be met, without repudiating a written and limited constitution and majority rule.[169]

Fidelity to their clearly discernible intentions is what the ratifiers anticipated and no other position is "politically or intellectually defensible."[170] Some of those intentions were less than noble and they should be addressed.[171] But in many instances

166. *See supra,* chapter 4, text, sources, and comments accompanying notes 152–158.

167. Easterbrook, in POLITICS, *supra* note 82, at 18.

168. Monaghan suggests that "original intent theory, taken seriously, undermines the objectives of the perfectionists," whose object is to remedy such imperfections by judicial fiat. Monaghan, *supra* note 28, at 387.

169. Robert Bork put the matter this way: "A Madisonian system which assumes that in wide areas of life a majority has the right to rule for no better reason than it is a majority." Bork, *supra* note 130, at 113.

170. *See supra,* text accompanying note 34.

171. MCDOWELL, *supra* note 19, at 9. Justice Thurgood Marshall has commented:

> I do not believe that the meaning of the Constitution was forever "fixed" at the Philadelphia Convention. Nor do I find the wisdom, foresight, and sense of justice exhibited by

their intentions are not as confining as noninterpretivists make them out to be. On the contrary, as I will subsequently argue, when properly understood fidelity to the ratifiers' understanding is far more liberating than confining, although it places on all citizens a far greater responsibility for public policy choices than does placing that burden, as noninterpretivists prefer, in the hands of the judiciary. Noninterpretivists frequently and vehemently disagree with each other only with respect to *how far* judges should go in creating, enhancing, or protecting process or substantive rights, but they all substitute judicial intervention for legislative choices.[172] All of them convert words or phrases in the Constitution into "ideals," or bring them to higher levels of generality, instead of proving that the people owe obedience to the preferences advocated by judges but never ratified by the people or their ancestors. All noninterpretivists either assume or assert the existence of various rights, or add to those assumptions the presumption that courts may impose public policies that (eventually a majority of the Supreme Court) believe are beneficent. All avoid the question of whether or not the preferences they advocate either were subscribed to by the framers, or consistent with traditional perceptions of what role the legislature, as compared to the judiciary, would play in public policy making. All repeatedly sidestep the issue of who gave judges the power to make public policy decisions, explicitly or implicitly converting that inquiry into whether or not good results might be achieved by the Court's intervention in the political process. All support the creation of new rights or the redefinition of old ones, often citing for authority judicial opinions of equally questionable legitimacy. All often suppress issues of consistent canon application. All replace the framers' understanding of various textual provisions, which change and change again as Supreme Court majorities shift; and the meaning that constitutionalism, representative democracy, and judicial review had for the framers has been and continues to be redefined in the process.

Many legal scholars today freely admit, and in many instances laud, the fact that over the past forty years almost all important Supreme Court decisions have *not* rested on principles constitutionalized by the framers.

> the Framers particularly profound. To the contrary, the government they devised was defective from the start, requiring several amendments, a civil war, and momentous social transformation to attain the system of constitutional government, and its respect for the individual freedoms and human rights, we hold as fundamental today. When contemporary Americans cite "The Constitution," they invoke a concept that is vastly different from what the Framers barely began to construct two centuries ago.

Thurgood Marshall, *The Constitution: Past and Present,* in HERBERT M. LEVINE, POINT-COUNTERPOINT 6 (1992).

172. *See supra,* chapter 4, text accompanying notes 159–176.

They consider that fact irrelevant. These attempts to redefine American democracy must be rejected, not only because they are unauthorized but because they apparently consider irrelevant, or fail to comprehend, the framers' insights regarding the character and dangers inherent in republics, the nature of the respective legislative and judicial roles, and the relationship between majority rule and majority tyranny. The framers understood perfectly well that the people were as capable of majority tyranny as they were of majority rule and that more likely than not they would attempt the former. Still, they put forth the design that they did. It is only in that context that Americans today can appreciate the framers' faith and confidence in the people and in democratic self-government. Only in that context can Americans understand what responsibilities they have as citizens. The people, Publius observed, are the "natural guardians of the Constitution."[173] It is their way of life that is at stake. Nowhere did the delegates to the convention, or Publius, support the view that judges could substitute personal visions of morality or justice through interpretation. As we have seen, Publius explicitly rejected that view, declaring that "the consequence would equally be the substitution of their pleasure to that of the legislative body."[174]

In the end the framers knew, and the Constitution embodies that knowledge, that the people must take ultimate responsibility for how they treat one another. The American patriots would not have had it any other way, for it distinguishes freedom from license. The Constitution contains a structural tension between the fear of majority tyranny and the desire for democratic self-rule. For the framers, neither the addition of a Bill of Rights nor an independent judiciary could or should ultimately provide protection against a people bent on exceeding the ratified boundaries. The people would reveal the character types they admired most when they elected their representatives.[175] I again turn to Publius:

> The aim of every political constitution is, or ought to be, first to

173. Federalist, *supra* note 5, no. 16, at 117.

174. *Id.*, no. 78, at 469.

175. *See* Leo Strauss, Natural Right and History (1953).

> The character . . . of a society depends on what the society regards as most respectable or most worthy of admiration. But by regarding certain habits or attitudes as most respectable, a society admits the superiority, the superior dignity, of those human beings who most perfectly embody the habits or attitudes in question. That is to say, every society regards a specific human type (or a specific mixture of human types) as authoritative. . . . In order to be truly authoritative, the human beings who embody the admired habits or attitudes must have the decisive say within the community in broad daylight: they must form the regime.

Id., at 137.

obtain for rulers men who possess most wisdom to discern, and most virtue to pursue, the common good of the society; and in the next place, to take the most effectual precautions for keeping them virtuous whilst they continue to hold their public trust. The elective mode of obtaining rulers is the characteristic policy of republican government. The means relied on in this form of government for preventing their degeneracy are numerous and various. The most effectual one is such a limitation of the term of appointments as will maintain a proper responsibility to the people.[176]

How, then, can informed citizens learn how to recognize and rebut the noninterpretivist arguments that support contemporary judicial abuses? It is to that subject I now turn.

176. FEDERALIST, *supra* note 5, no. 57, at 350–351.

PART IV.

STOPPING FOR DIRECTIONS

CHAPTER SIX

Rejecting Contemporary Assumptions

If the road over which you will still have to pass should in some places appear to you tedious or irksome, you will recollect that you are in quest of information on a subject the most momentous which can engage the attention of a free people, that the field through which you have to travel is in itself spacious, and that the difficulties of the journey have been unnecessarily increased by the mazes with which sophistry has beset the way. It will be my aim to remove the obstacles to your progress in as compendious a manner as it can be done, without sacrificing utility to dispatch.[1]

Once I am behind the wheel of my car, something compels me forward and only rarely will I stop to ask for directions. My wife insists that that "something" is male pride. I counter that it's my personality—and habit. Whether it is pride, personality, or habit, stopping to ask for directions is difficult for me.[2] But for more than a decade now, I frequently have been lost and have had to stop. In the legal literature, noninterpretivists put forth many powerful arguments and interpretivists put forth equally powerful replies. I had to stop and compare them. At this point in our journey, the reader, too, may be experiencing the need to stop and examine the dispute more carefully.

I want readers to reexamine how they approach constitutional law, and in the preceding chapters perhaps for a fleeting moment many readers had a flash of discomfort—an awareness that some of their assumptions about constitutional law left some questions unanswered. But such doubts may have been quickly suppressed. That is quite normal. Our minds are never quite as open as we like to think they are. Persuasion takes time—and effort. But my goal is to challenge every assumption, premise, and rationalization that mask contemporary judicial

1. James Madison, Alexander Hamilton, and John Jay, The Federalist Papers, [hereinafter Federalist] no. 15, at 105.

2. Thank goodness for the N.Y.T. Science section. *See* "Why Don't Men Ask Directions? They Don't Feel Lost," N.Y.T. (26 May 1992), c1.

abuse, distort American traditions, and illegitimately dilutes the people's right to self-government.

This chapter is divided into three main sections. In the first section I take a second look at judge-made law;[3] in the second I specifically challenge noninterpretivist premises with respect to the Bill of Rights; and in the final, most lengthy section, the debate between interpretivists and noninterpretivists is broken down into nine categories: a rebuttal is provided for each. This debate covers much of the same ground as preceding chapters, but for the first time the reader will find competing views side by side. The chapter ends with a brief conclusion.

JUDGE-MADE LAW: CARDOZO REVISITED

A typical debate on contemporary judicial power hardly begins before a noninterpretivist solemnly informs his interpretivist opponent that "judges make law." That pronouncement may be followed by the observation that eighteenth-century beliefs in the separation of powers (wherein legislatures make the law, executives execute it, and judges interpret it) never actually existed; or if it did exist, Americans today are no longer as fearful as were our forbearers. The more learned noninterpretivists might cite Benjamin Cardozo's classic work, *The Nature of the Judicial Process,* which was discussed earlier.[4] Having thus chastised the opponent, the noninterpretivist will smile knowingly and leave the podium triumphantly, having thus clearly exposed the evident simplicity and impracticality of interpretivist thinking—or at least what is assumed to be interpretivist thinking. Since I have experienced this scenario more times than I care to remember, I want to convince the reader that the fact of judge-made law does not resolve the dispute between interpretivists and noninterpretivists.[5]

True, even a cursory examination of Cardozo's work reveals at least five assumptions used by contemporary noninterpretivists. Cardozo suggests that constitutions must be subject to more flexible judicial construction than statutes since the former must be capable of accommodating a society that is adapting to change.[6] He even relies on an authority frequently quoted in contemporary legal literature; namely, Chief Justice Marshall's dictum in *M'Culloch:* to wit, "It is a constitution we are expounding."[7]

3. *See supra,* chapter 4, text accompanying notes 46–52.

4. Benjamin Cardozo, The Nature of the Judicial Process (1921).

5. *See, e.g.,* Willard Hurst, Dealing With Statutes 11 (1982) and Oliver W. Holmes, Jr., The Common Law (1881).

6. *Id.,* at 71, 83–85. *See* text and comments accompanying *Remain Adaptable* symbol, later in this chapter.

7. Cardozo, *supra* note 4, at 83. See infra, text accompanying note 123.

Second, Cardozo zeros in on results. He states that "not the origin, but the goal, is the main thing. There can be no wisdom in the choice of a path unless we know where it will lead. The teleological conception of his function must be ever in the judge's mind."[8] Third, Cardozo is concerned with the efficacy of available remedies—as are his contemporary noninterpretivist counterparts. For example, Cardozo observes that the "'emphasis has changed from the content of the precept and the existence of the remedy to the effect of the precept in action and the availability and efficiency of the remedy to attain the ends for which the precept was devised.'"[9] Fourth, Cardozo alludes to the *vacuum* created by legislative nonfeasance, claiming that "legislatures have sometimes disregarded their own responsibility, and passed it on to the courts."[10] And fifth, Cardozo views the judiciary as being an arbiter. He entitled one of his chapters, "The Judge as a Legislator."[11]

What noninterpretivists rarely address is whether or not Cardozo's premises are consistent with the framers' design. He does not cite American authority for a judicial role beyond the one championed by Publius. He himself carefully noted that a more extensive view of judicial power was held only outside of the United States, and even then he draws a distinct line.[12] As Christopher Wolfe has observed, Cardozo had in mind judge-made law in cooperation with the legislature, not in opposition to it. Such judge-made law always has been reversible by simple statute.[13]

When on rare occasions Cardozo advocates a judicial role beyond the traditional one, I believe that in the context of his times he may be forgiven his excess of zeal.[14] Like many of his intellectual contemporaries, Cardozo assumed an evolving moral evolution.[15] Laissez-faire economic theory no longer was in fashion and popular support for progressivist re-

8. *Id.*, at 102. *See* discussion on the *Results* symbol, later in this chapter.

9. *Id.*, at 73, citing Roscoe Pound, *Administrative Application of Legal Standards*, PROCEEDINGS AMERICAN BAR ASSOCIATION 441, 451n. 35 (1919).

10. *Id.*, at 93.

11. *Id.*, at 98.

12. *Id.*, at 83–85, 84. *Id.*, at 84 ("at any rate abroad"); *id.*, at 85 ("the instances must be rare; if any can be found at all"). He states elsewhere of the judiciary that "its chief worth [is] in making vocal and audible the ideals that otherwise may be silenced, in giving them continuity of life and of expression, in guiding and directing choice within the limits where choice ranges." (*Id.*, at 94, citing no authority). Finally, he states: "I do not mean to range myself with the jurists who seem to hold that in reality there is no law except the decisions of the courts." *Id.*, at 124.

13. CHRISTOPHER WOLFE, THE RISE OF MODERN JUDICIAL REVIEW 235 (1986).

14. *But see* WOLFE, *supra* note 13, at 232–234.

15. He himself noted: "None the less, the tendency is in the direction of growing liberalism. The new spirit has made its way gradually, and its progress, unnoticed step by step, is visible in retrospect as we look back upon the distance traversed." CARDOZO, *supra* note 4, at 101.

forms was growing. Cardozo believed he was riding the crest of a wave of social reform. He devoted much of his career to ridding the law of laissez-faire economic and sociological assumptions that earlier judges had injected into the common law, then into statutory law, and finally into constitutional law.[16]

Cardozo believed then (as I do today) that those laissez-faire oriented judges had illegitimately imposed their personal views on the population. He struggled (as I do) with how to overcome such judicial oppression, while at the same time remaining within the bounds of his craft. Steeped in American legal tradition, he remained cautious, too well-trained to depart too far from that tradition. Still, I find Cardozo more consistent than are his noninterpretivist successors today: he understood that under the criterion of progress liberty could either expand or contract,[17] and having experienced the laissez-faire perversions of constitutional law (as Justice Oliver W. Holmes described them[18]) he remained leery of imposing his own prejudices.[19]

Once Cardozo is placed in the intellectual context of his times—in the struggle to free jurisprudence from the laissez-faire belief system—he may be read in such a way as to leave us even more respectful of the wisdom of the framers' design; more cognizant than ever of how easily even the most competent may be lead astray. That assessment can be defended on a number of grounds.

The Judicial Process addressed only the situation where a judge finds himself bound neither by the Constitution nor a statute.[20] Cardozo otherwise acknowledged that the Constitution overrides a statute; and

16. *Id.*, at 174 ('Zeitgeist'). *Id.*, at 76–79 (growth of laissez-faire); 150 (influence of precedent). *See also* Klein v. Maravelas, 219 N.Y. 383 (1916) (Cardozo) (cited in CARDOZO, *supra* note 4, at 150); HURST, *supra* note 5, at 11 ("legal protection of market autonomy emerged more through common law than through legislative contests"); GRANT GILMORE, THE AGES OF AMERICAN LAW 11, 66 (1977) ("laissez-faire economics and late nineteenth-century legal theories are blood brothers").

17. CARDOZO, *supra* note 4, at 76–77, 83 ("May restraints that were arbitrary yesterday be useful and rational and therefore lawful today? . . . I have no doubt that the answer to these questions must be yes.") *Id.*, at 77. Of course, Cardozo talks thereafter of placing restrictions on what formerly had been considered economic liberties. The difficulty with an idea of progress is that subsequent progressivist visions may abandon components thought crucial to earlier visions. Hence, for Auguste Comte, the emphasis on individual liberties gave way to collective rights. *See* JOHN S. MILL, AUGUSTE COMTE AND POSITIVISM 141–142 (1965).

18. In the words of Justice Holmes: "'The word liberty in the Fourteenth Amendment is perverted when it is held to prevent the natural outcome of a dominant opinion, unless it can be said that a rational and fair man necessarily would admit that the statute proposed would infringe fundamental principles as they have been understood by the traditions of our people and our law.'" CARDOZO, *supra* note 4, at 80, citing Lochner v. New York, 198 U.S. 45, 76 (1905) (Holmes, J. dissenting).

19. *See e.g.* Synder v. Massachusetts, 291 U.S. 97 (1934); Palko v. Connecticut, 302 U.S. 319 (1937).

20. CARDOZO, *supra* note 4, at 164.

a statute, if consistent with the Constitution, overrides a judge's own preferences: judge-made law is secondary and subordinate to law made by legislators.[21] Thus, Cardozo acknowledged that he was offering a distorted picture of the normal interpretive process, and while such a distortion was inevitable, given the subject matter he had selected, Cardozo clearly understood that in most instances judicial discretion was severely circumscribed.[22] Even then he further circumscribed the judicial role, quoting favorably Justice Holmes's remark that "'I recognize without hesitation that judges must and do legislate, but they do so only interstitially; they are confined from molar to molecular motions. A common-law judge could not say, I think the doctrine of consideration a bit of historical nonsense and shall not enforce it in my court.'"[23]

Cardozo at no point addresses what is the heart of the conflict between contemporary interpretivists and non-interpretivists: May judges decide cases contrary to the ratifiers' intentions? Insofar as he approached that question, there is every indication that he would have considered himself bound. Most often, Cardozo was concerned with those instances where the framers or Congress either had been or were silent; or with situations where neither provided answers. But as I have already made clear, interpretivists in such circumstances concede that judges are freer to make law. In fact, only where the Constitution contains what Cardozo calls "general language" does he vest the judiciary with *any discretion,* and even then, I suggest, he presumes that either the legislature had been silent or that the judge's decision involved the interpretation of legislation.[24]

He specifically urges legislatures to pass laws that contain more generous, vaguer, more flexible terminology; in short, language that would permit judges greater discretion in facilitating proposed social reforms.[25] In

21. *Id.*, at 14. *See also, id.*, at 124, 129.

22. He observed:

> The judicial process . . . [is one of] search and comparison, and little else. We have to distinguish between the precedents which are merely static, and those which are dynamic. Because the former outnumber the latter many times, a sketch of the judicial process which concerns itself almost exclusively with the creative or dynamic element, is likely to give a false impression, an overcolored picture, of uncertainty in the law and of free discretion in the judge. Of the cases that come before the court in which I sit, a majority, I think, could not with semblance of reason, be decided in any way but one.

Id., at 163–64.

23. *Id.*, at 69, citing Southern Pacific Co. v. Jensen, 244 U.S. 205, 221 (1916) (opinion of Justice Holmes). *See also* CARDOZO, *supra* note 4, at 103, 113–14.

24. CARDOZO, *supra* note 4, at 101. ("Legislation has sometimes been necessary to free us from the old fetters. Sometimes the conservativism of judges has threatened for an interval to rob the legislation of its efficacy.")

25. *Id.*, at 90 (citations omitted). ("'It must be remembered that legislatures are ultimate guardians of the liberties and welfare of the people in quite as great a degree as courts.'").

doing so he implicitly acknowledges that if intent is discernible, judges must apply the lawgiver's intent.[26] Judges would participate in progressivist lawmaking either by deferring to the legislative branch (a principle that permitted them to ignore contrary laissez-faire precedents) or, in the absence of such legislation, by judicial lawmaking at the common-law level. Cardozo uses an argument resorted to by all progressivists: time has passed the old rule by.[27]

Cardozo drew upon the tradition of broad versus narrow construction because he evidently found little interpretative flexibility in the rules governing statutory or common-law interpretation.[28] Legislators would address pressing economic and social welfare reforms if they were free to do so. All that was necessary was, once again, to view the Constitution as permitting broad legislative discretion, an understanding Cardozo had championed in New York's highest court. It was, for Cardozo, a convenient theoretical position: progressivists were winning elections on the state level and they were also on the rise nationally. But victory at the polls would be hollow if a judiciary still dominated by laissez-faire thinking could negate the people's will.

Thus, Cardozo ultimately offers little support for contemporary judicial usurpations, and whatever support may be found in his works rests solely on Cardozo's own authority—not on the framers' design. Looking back, we should not be scornful of how much Cardozo was captured by the zeitgeist of the day; rather should we see how enraptured we are of our own. A zeitgeist in decline is always much more easily identified than an emerging one. Cardozo, like Holmes, Brandeis, and Frankfurter, was torn by competing truths—the truths of the American tradition as he understood them, and those of modernity, as he understood them. What must not be forgotten is how truly moderate Cardozo was, given the full scope of the then existing ideological spectrum. Today, if memory serves cor-

26. *Id.*, at 83–84, 120. "I will not hesitate in the silence or inadequacy of formal sources, to indicate as the general line of direction for the judge the following: that he ought to shape his judgment of the law in obedience to the same aims which would be those of a legislator who was proposing to himself to regulate the question." *Id.*, at 120.

27. *See* Klein v. Maravelas, 219 N.Y. 383 (1916), where Cardozo observed:

> We said it violated both the federal and the state constitution in imposing arbitrary restrictions upon liberty of contract. That decision was reached by a closely divided court.
>
> We think it is our duty to hold that decision . . . is wrong. . . . At the time of our decision . . . such laws were new and strange. They were thought in the prevailing opinion to represent the fitful prejudice of the hour. . . . The fact is that they have come to stay, and like laws may be found on statute books of every state.

Id. at 383, 385.

28. Cardozo, *supra* note 4, at 141. ("The judge, even when he is free, is still not wholly free. He is not to innovate at pleasure. He is not a knight-errant roaming at will in pursuit of his own ideal of beauty or of goodness. He is to draw his inspiration from consecrated principles.")

rectly, not a single opinion about personal liberty by Cardozo, Brandeis, Holmes, or Frankfurter, has survived noninterpretivism in the Warren, Burger, and Rhenquist courts. Those precedents could not survive for good reason: their successors have gone well beyond the judicial role sanctioned by Cardozo and his contemporaries.

ARGUMENTS ASSOCIATED WITH THE BILL OF RIGHTS

Noninterpretivists often assume that the addition of the Bill of Rights substantially modified the Philadelphia Constitution. While earlier I sought to put that addition in perspective,[29] until now I have postponed systematically challenging noninterpretivist assumptions about the Bill of Rights. Even now it is impossible within the scope of this book specifically to challenge every Supreme Court Bill of Rights decision with which I disagree. Instead, my object will be to bring it to the reader's attention that the assumptions upon which many Supreme Court decisions rest are not only historically doubtful but that they undermine the heritage of self-government. In as economical a fashion as possible I also want to add weight to prior assessments and lay the groundwork for discussions later in this book. First I will state one of the assumptions and follow the assumption with my reasons for rejecting it.

Elevation of Personal Rights

> *The Bill of Rights is part of our nation's commitment to an open society—one in which personal rights are elevated above the peoples' right to self-government.*[30]

At the time the Constitution was ratified, most states followed (by common law, statute, or in state constitutions) certain well-understood common-law procedures that had long histories and whose meanings were commonly understood. When the Bill of Rights was added, many of these same procedures were made applicable against federal officials—their common-law meaning becoming fixed. Congress could not thereafter reduce the protections they afforded. But in *Barron v. Baltimore* (1833) the Supreme Court acknowledged that the federal Bill of Rights did not apply against the States.[31] The adoption of the Civil War amendments did not materially alter that situation. To the extent that it opened the door to greater federal supervision of the way states treated their citizens, such power was lodged in the Congress, not the judiciary.[32]

Noninterpretivists today are unhappy with the protections the Bill of

29. *See supra,* chapter 2, text accompanying notes 98–134.

30. *See e.g.,* Thomas Schrock and Robert C. Welsh, *Up from Calandra: The Exclusionary Rule as a Constitutional Requirement,* 59 Minn. L. R. 251, 378 (1974).

31. *See supra,* chapter 3, for a discussion of Barron v. Baltimore.

32. *See supra,* chapter 4, for the Civil War Amendments and the use of laissez-faire legal standards.

Rights provisions afforded as they were understood by its ratifiers; and so they argue that the Bill of Rights is part of our nation's commitment to an open society—a phrase that is often found in contemporary American legal literature.[33] The phrase's lack of precision, one suspects, is part of its charm. Do its subscribers mean an open society as opposed to a closed society (as in a free society as opposed to a totalitarian one)? For example, one subscriber to this view suggests that unless practices employed by the police in totalitarian regimes are renounced in the United States, this country is in danger of becoming a totalitarian regime.[34] And we well might become one if American police forces were to indulge in exactly the same totalitarian practices under the same circumstances.[35] But surely it is significant that in the United States courts have been generally suspicious of evidence obtained by police coercion; that historically some states even chose to forego such evidence completely. In totalitarian regimes, such evidence is knowingly and willingly admitted—even if that evidence is known to be false. Most importantly, does it not make a difference that in the United States the balancing of principles relating to police practices, abuses, and remedies was lodged by the framers in the hands of those who could be held electorally accountable? And that in totalitarian regimes it is not?

The open society analogy remains troubling, not for what it asserts or implies but because it is given any credence at all. Fortunately, the analogy may be dismissed economically. Governmental practices cannot be abandoned simply because totalitarian regimes also employ them. That view would forbid all governments from either taxing or spending because either practice is used by totalitarian governments. The framers, cognizant of the danger of both governmental and majority tyranny nevertheless lodged decision-making power in the hands of the people's

33. The open society symbol generally presumes that rights are individual and as near to being absolute and as immune from legislative intervention as possible. Only under such guidelines is a government considered legitimate. *Compare* chapter 4, text and comment accompanying notes 105–113, *supra*. For theoretical statements, *see* KARL POPPER, THE OPEN SOCIETY AND ITS ENEMIES (1966). *See also* CHARLES FRANKEL, THE CASE FOR MODERN MAN (1959) and JACOB SHAPIRO, LIBERALISM: ITS MEANING AND HISTORY (1958).

34. *See e.g.,* Fred G. Bennett, *Judicial Integrity and Judicial Review: An Argument for Expanding the Scope of the Exclusionary Rule,* 20 U.C.L.A.L. REV. 1129, 1134 (1973).

35. Leo Strauss points out that because of the "inventiveness of wickedness" even the most democratic regime may be forced in "extraordinary" times to act as a totalitarian regime. LEO STRAUSS, NATURAL RIGHT AND HISTORY 157–162 (1952). That truth was in at least one specific instance recognized by the framers: "The privilege of the Writ of Habeas Corpus shall not be suspended, unless when in Cases of Rebellion or Invasion the public Safety may require it." U.S. CONST. art. 1, sec. 9.2. *See also* Schenck v. United States, 249 U.S. 47, 52 (1919). Finally, there are the reasons set forth by one of my colleagues. *See,* RICHARD CLARK, TECHNOLOGICAL TERRORISM 189 (1980).

representatives.[36] The analogy is suspect also because those who use it define available choices in an either/or frame of reference.[37] For example, modern supporters of the exclusionary rule frequently argue that if illegally obtained evidence is excluded, the Fourth Amendment right against unreasonable search and seizure would become worthless.[38] When the soundness of that judgment is questioned, its supporters dismiss the questioner as favoring authoritarian government.

Thus, the open society analogy contributes little toward our understanding of the principles constitutionalized at Philadelphia. The phrase was unknown to the framers. It is as previously explored, but a shorthand expression for a variety of progressivist and liberal assumptions and judgments about the nature and content of personal rights.[39] In the absence of an inclination toward the assumptions that compose it, the phrase is unintelligible.[40] Attempts to root the open society analogy specifically in the First Amendment—the most logical point of nexus—have failed, because it cannot be traced to any principles constitutionalized by the framers.[41]

Individual Protection

The purpose of the Bill of Rights provisions is to protect individuals, and the Court must fashion suitable remedies for rights violations so that in the long run the rights of all citizens are preserved.

This assumption reveals what its subscribers believe are essential features of enlightened democratic government rather than the history surrounding the adoption of the Bill of Rights and it assumes a judicial power unknown to the framers. It is unconvincing because if the state common-law practices that preceded the adoption of the Bill of Rights accurately reflect what protections its framers intended to offer against federal officials, then clearly their primary purpose was to guard against executive and judicial *procedural* abuses—the types of abuses that any

36. *See supra,* chapter 1, text accompanying note 44.

37. *Cf.* Robert Waelder, *The Concept of Justice and the Quest for An Absolutely Just Society,* 57 J. of Crim.L., C & P. S. 1, 6 (1966); J. Talmon, The Origins of Totalitarian Democracy 1–2 (1960).

38. *See infra,* text and comments accompanying notes 100–101.

39. *See infra,* discussions under *Individual Rights* and *Accepted* symbols.

40. *See* Willmore Kendall, *The Open Society and Its Fallacies,* LIV Am. Pol. Sci. A. R. 972 (1960) [hereinafter *Fallacies*]; Willmore Kendall, *The People Versus Socrates Revisited,* 3 Modern Age 98, 108–109 (1959–1960) [hereinafter *People*] (a recurring problem in political theory is the proclaimer of divine truth).

41. We repeat the judgment of Michael Perry: "The decisions in virtually all modern constitutional cases of consequence . . . cannot plausibly be explained except in terms of noninterpretive review, because in virtually no such cases can it plausibly be maintained that the Framers constitutionalized the determinative value judgment." Michael Perry, *Interpretations, Freedom of Expression, and Equal Protection,* 42 Ohio St., L.J. 261, 265 (1981).

keen observer of English history might discern. The focal point was abusive governmental power and the framers' anticipation that the legislature would monitor and, if necessary, provide additional remedies.[42]

The legislature was bound only to the specific common-law meanings that the Bill of Rights provisions encompassed and its framers did not look to the judiciary (as many do today) as the ultimate protector of such rights.[43] Speculation is unnecessary. "I infer that [the] . . . security [of such rights], whatever fine declarations may be inserted in any constitution respecting [them], must altogether depend on public opinion, and on the general spirit of the people and of the government."[44]

What citizens apparently feared most of all of that time was being unjustly railroaded. While those who championed the inclusion of procedural rights understood that even the guilty might from time to time derive some benefit from these rights, it was innocence, I suggest, that shaped citizens' concern. But by affording procedural rights to all the criminally accused, the people committed themselves and their children only to the specific limits those provisions were understood to contain at the time of ratification. *Beyond those specific meanings, however, elected representatives remained empowered to address associated public policy questions: how those rights were concretely to be applied; what beyond the ratified meaning might constitute abuse; and what remedies were appropriate for any violations.* For example, on both federal and state levels the right to a free press did not include a right to be obscene in public discourse or written work, and the right to be free from compulsory self-incrimination did not bar the admission of trustworthy confessions. Adoption of the Bill of Rights authorized judges only to guard the understood meanings, not to expand those meanings, which would amount to amending the Constitution without the people's consent. Expansions *proportionately reduce the people's right to govern themselves.*

When subscribers to this assumption lose sight of these considerations and assert, without proof, that Bill of Rights provisions were understood as being absolute, or that their primary focus was to secure certain individual rights from all legislative interference, then those subscribers are wrong because such conclusions do not rest on the understanding of

42. *See infra.,* text accompanying notes 123–124. *See e.g.,* Bradford Wilson, *The Fourth Amendment as More Than a Form of Words: The View from the Founding,* in THE BILL OF RIGHTS: ORIGINAL MEANING AND CURRENT UNDERSTANDING 158 (WILLIAM HICKOK, ed. 1990) (Although the Fourth Amendment guarantees the availability of a remedy, that remedy is not "fixed.").

43. Christopher Wolfe, *A Theory of U.S. Constitutional History,* 43 JOURNAL OF POLITICS 292, 296–297 (1981).

44. FEDERALIST, supra note 1, no. 84. 514.

those who proposed or ratified the Bill of Rights. The subscribers may create systems that the imagination prefers, but if the systems created are not rooted in history, their creators must be pressed to admit that it is imagination, or hope, or both, not history, that shapes those views.

The Language Assumption

Bill of Rights provisions may be defined solely by reference to textual language.[45]

In Publius' classic formulation, the constitutional text always must be compared to the intent of the ratifiers.[46] Noninterpretivists, however, often go beyond the text. I suggest that they abuse the interpretive craft if they engage in either of the following tactics:

RELEVANT CANONS OF CONSTRUCTION ARE ARBITRARILY IGNORED. One canon of interpretation provides that all parts of a constitutional provision must be taken into account. But Justice Hugo Black ignored that canon when he concluded that the First Amendment prohibited Congress from passing any law related to the First Amendment.[47] What is ignored here is the crucial "abridging" modifier.[48] Furthermore, Black illegitimately assumed application of the First Amendment to the states and engaged in other practices that liberated the text from the framers' understanding and its actual usage. These devices permitted Black to mask an usurpation of the legislative power and the people's sole right to amend the Constitution.

45. *See e.g.,* Berger's critique of Ely's alleged "invitations" to open-ended interpretation. *Cf.* Raoul Berger, *Ely's "Theory of Judicial Review,"* 42 OHIO ST. L.J. 87 (1981) [hereinafter *Ely's*]; Raoul Berger, *Government by Judiciary: John Hart Ely's Invitation,* 54 IND. L. J. 277 (1978) [hereinafter *Ely's Invitation*] with John H. Ely, *Constitutional Interpretation: Its Allure and Impossibility,* 53 Ind. L.J. 399, 415 (1978).

46. *Federalist, supra* note 1, no. 78, at 468. *See supra,* chapter 2, text and comment accompanying note 68.

47. *See* Edmond Cahn, *Justice Black and First Amendment "Absolutes": A Public Interview,* 37 N.Y. U. L. R. 549 (June, 1962).

> The beginning of the First Amendment is that "Congress shall make no law." I understand that it is rather old-fashioned and shows a slight naivete to say that "no law" means no law. It is one of the most amazing things about the ingeniousness of the times that strong arguments are made, which *almost* convince me, that it is very foolish of me to think "no law" means no law. But what it *says* is "Congress shall make no law respecting an establishment of religion," and so on.

Id. at 553 (Justice Black). *See also supra,* chapter 5, text and comment accompanying note 118.

48. "Congress shall make no law respecting an establishment of religion . . . or abridging the freedom of speech. . . ." U.S. Const. Amend. 1. Publius makes this interesting comment: "It cannot certainly be pretended that any degree of duties, however low, would be an abridgment of the liberty of the press. We know that newspapers are taxed in Great Britain, and yet it is notorious that the press nowhere enjoys greater liberty than in that country." FEDERALIST, *supra* note 1, no. 84, at 514*. *Compare* Near v. Minnesota, 283 U.S. 697 (1931).

CONTEMPORARY DEFINITIONS ARE SUBSTITUTED FOR THE MEANING WORDS HAD AT THE TIME OF RATIFICATION. I have already recounted noninterpretivist methodologies that sanction either ignoring the original meaning of constitutional provisions or extracting supposed values from provisions and elevating them to more abstract generalities.[49] Supreme Court majorities repeatedly employ such techniques and then go on to speak of a "right"; for example, to privacy, or to interpret the First Amendment's freedom-of-speech provision so as to redefine state and federal libel, obscenity, blasphemy, pornography, and flag-burning laws.

Adaptation to Circumstances

> *The judiciary may adapt Bill of Rights provisions to existing circumstances, interpreting relevant phrases on the basis of* logic *derived from an understanding of the* nature *of the Bill of Rights.*

I repeat conclusions supported earlier: the framers did not grant any such authority to the courts and specifically rejected a council of revision on the grounds it was inappropriate. When so-called judicial adaptations assume textual meanings that distort historical practice, or they depend—as they must—on assumptions rejected on preceding pages, then, regardless of the legal language in which they are couched, such adaptations amount to nothing more than the imposition of the interpreter's personal preferences on the people.[50] Logic may explicate valid claims, but it cannot itself establish the legitimacy of the claims themselves. Put another way, arguments based on false premises carry little weight. The one true test of a right's constitutional caliber is whether the interpreter can trace it to the ratifiers' intent or to historical practice, not to its alleged "nature"—a nature that more often than not is conveniently supplied and defined by the interpreter.[51]

What does it mean to say that a document—the Constitution—is law? The answer is that its words and their historical meaning constrain judgment. The words must control judges every bit as much as they control legislators, executives, and citizens. The various systems of moral philosophy that legal

49. *See supra,* chapter 4, text accompanying notes 114–128.

50. *See* chapter 5, comment accompanying note 15, *supra.* Raoul Berger, for example, clearly demonstrates that a majority of justices attempted to impose their personal preferences against the death penalty. *See* RAOUL BERGER, DEATH PENALTIES (1982). Elsewhere I do the same with reference to the exclusionary rule. *See* William Gangi, *The Exclusionary Rule: A Case Study in Judicial Usurpation,* 34 DRAKE L. REV. 33 (1985).

51. "However proper such reasoning might be to show that a thing *ought not to exist,* they are wholly to be rejected when they are made use of to prove that it does not exist contrary to the evidence of the fact itself." FEDERALIST, *supra* note 1, no. 34, at 206.

> academics today propound as guides to constitutional adjudication and with which they hope to supplant a jurisprudence of original intention are not capable of constraining the judge. They are, rather, capable of producing any result the judge or the processor wants. As a result, they lack democratic legitimacy; there is no reason why those of us who have our own moral values should be governed by some judge's personal views simply by virtue of his position.[52]

Thus, for example, however *illogical* it may be from the perspective of those today who have redefined the *nature* of freedom of the press, until that redefinition publishers had not been immune from prosecution for seditious libel.[53] But noninterpretivists muddy the waters. They evoke powerful analogies, turn to alleged American symbols, and advocate model-building—each of these techniques serving to hide from the people that they have abandoned the framers' design. So these techniques also must be challenged forthrightly in order to entice the reader to reject them.

ANALOGIES. It is worth taking a closer look, for example, at the "omnipresent teacher" analogy created by Justice Louis Brandeis:

> Our government is the potent, the omnipresent teacher. For good or for ill, it teaches the whole people by its example. Crime is contagious. If the Government becomes a lawbreaker, it breeds contempt for law; it invites every man to become a law unto himself; it invites anarchy. To declare that in the administration of criminal law the end justifies the means—to declare that the Government may commit crimes in order to secure the conviction of a private criminal—would bring terrible retribution.[54]

Specifics do not here concern us.[55] As powerful as this analogy may be and as much as one may subscribe to the truth proclaimed, it is not a principle the framers incorporated in the Constitution. I will break down this analogy further.

1. IMAGERY. The government may be *your* omnipresent teacher; it is not mine; nor, I suspect, was it the framers'. My government is just that—my government: created by my forbearers to deliberate on and pass laws for the general good (and be accountable to me and others) in

52. Robert Bork, *The Inherent Illegitimacy of Noninterpretivism,* in POLITICS AND THE CONSTITUTION: THE NATURE AND EXTENT OF INTERPRETATION 111 (1990) [hereinafter Politics].

53. *See e.g.,* LEONARD LEVY, FREEDOM OF SPEECH AND PRESS IN EARLY AMERICAN HISTORY: LEGACY OF SUPPRESSION 1 (1960).

54. Olmstead v. United States, 277 U.S. 438, 485 (1928) (Brandeis, J., dissenting).

55. For a more specific discussion of this analogy as it applies to the exclusionary rule, *see* Gangi, *supra* 50, at 113–117.

response to particular and changing circumstantial realities.[56]

Should an enemy endanger my society's status as an independent nation, or its ability to govern itself, or challenge truths that the society holds dear, certain things may have to be done—things that I, as an individual, would studiously avoid. In combat, many good and gentle men and women may be obliged to take the life of an enemy. Government representatives similarly may have to forego what many people believe to be the just in order to secure the common good; for example, to obtain sufficient oil supplies. Other government representatives may have to bribe foreign officials to obtain military bases necessary for the country's survival or the survival of a valued ally. Finally, my government also may choose, or be forced to pursue, less than perfectly just foreign policies—policies it believes are *more* just than those practiced by other governments. Hence, government teaches me little more than I already know as a human being: pursue good, avoid evil; and that is frequently not an easy task. It requires a balancing of one's principles.[57]

Life is full of choices for individuals and governments. When one goes too far in pursuing certain goals, it is likely that other goals of equal or superior weight will be forsaken, at least temporarily. In order that I might research and write this book, did my classroom preparation occasionally suffer? I think so. Did I not during such periods shirk, to one degree or another, important responsibilities to my wife and children? I certainly did. Most people's lives are fragmented and many of us maintain a never-ending tension, trying to balance multiple truths.

Equally agonizing choices exist for governments. In the pursuit of criminals, a government, acting in the name of the people, may find it necessary to immunize some citizens from prosecution and punishment in order to secure sufficient evidence to convict other citizens whose conduct is judged more despicable than those immunized. That choice is made to insure that at least one accused is brought to justice. It may be necessary—even essential—for representatives of my government to deal with informers or other characters I regularly avoid. On behalf of the people, some members of the government may find it necessary to practice deception in order to identify other members of the govern-

56. Publius was concerned about human nature, generally, and foreign enemies in particular. See *supra,* chapter 1, text and comment accompanying notes 49–67, particularly text accompanying note 32.

57. For a discussion of principles, *see* ERNEST BARKER, THE POLITICS OF ARISTOTLE 101 (Tr. 1962), ch. IV, 1276 b 11–33 and ERIC VOEGELIN, NEW SCIENCE OF POLITICS 49, 41–49 (1952). *See also* William Gangi, *The Supreme Court: An Intentionist's Critique of Noninterpretive Review,* 28 THE CATHOLIC LAWYER 253, 258–260n.30 (1983).

ment who are conspiring to betray the public trust.

But we are not usually confronted by a simple choice between good and evil, neither as individuals, nor as a people, nor as representatives, although there are always those who see the options limited to those two choices. Circumstances often require that a choice be made between the half-bad, the really bad, and the despicable. Failure to choose the half-bad does not assure the good—but it assures the probability that the really bad or the despicable will prevail. To deny this is to deny experience itself, or to create a reality of one's own in which experiential truth is ignored or suppressed.

2. Traditional view of criminal prosecution. The goal of the Constitution and the Bill of Rights was to assure the common good. Left open to legislative deliberation was the entire arena of competing considerations of what policies should govern the admissibility of evidence; or what remedies should be provided against police abuses. Competing claims on such issues were resolved differently by the citizens of the several states until the Supreme Court, particularly after 1960, prohibited some of those resolutions and imposed others. To know exactly how or why citizens differed with respect to what constituted police or prosecutorial abuse, or what remedies were considered sufficient, citizens or the scholars who pursue such issues must examine state constitutions, statutory laws, and judicial opinions. There is no single or simple answer since in each state citizens decided, based on their experience, to pursue criminal prosecution in different ways—although the differences were usually slight.[58]

Subscribers to the "omnipresent teacher" analogy ignore that they change the meaning of relevant Bill of Rights provisions from what they were understood to protect by its ratifiers. Furthermore, the ratifiers left to the people, and not the judiciary, the task of balancing competing concerns. The analogy thus makes one or more of the unwarranted assumptions detailed in the preceding pages, often substituting the preference of judges for choices made by elected officials.

Finally, the "omnipresent teacher" analogy distorts the relationship between the government, the criminal defendant, and the people.[59] For the framers the relationship was between

58. *See supra,* chapter 1 text accompanying note 22 (Massachusetts Body of Liberties (1641) specifying under what conditions convicted felons may be tortured) and chapter 2 text accompanying notes 98–151. *See also supra* chapter 5, text accompanying notes 135–144.

59. I refer to such statements as "it teaches the whole people by its example" [Olmstead v. United States, *supra* note 54, at 485 (Brandeis, J., dissenting)], Yale Kamisar, *Is the exclusionary Rule an 'illogical' or 'unnatural' interpretation of the Fourth Amendment?,* 62 JUDICATURE 67, 69 (1980). ["When the government . . . ought . . . to avail itself of the fruits of these acts in order to

the *citizen defendant* and "the people of the state of" or "the people of the United States," and it was on the behalf of the people that the government was authorized to act. Today the words are retained but their import has been lost. The "omnipresent teacher" analogy, *by redefining the prosecution of the criminally accused as a contest between an individual and the government, not only ignores that understanding but manipulates symbols whose meaning was quite clear to those originally utilizing them.*

3. THE TRUE LESSON TAUGHT. A trial does teach but it does not teach *all* citizens. Through their agents, the government and jury, citizens teach citizenship to those who breached an obligation to do what all had determined to be "meete and convenient for the generall good."[60] A trial determines whether or not a person indeed committed an offense, and if the person is found guilty how to punish them for it. Most revealing about the true quality of United States civilization[61] is the fact that trials are still conducted in a manner prescribed two hundred years ago.

Any determination of guilt must be reached on a basis of "beyond a reasonable doubt," demonstrating that—regardless of how concerned citizens had been that criminal breaches be punished—suspicion, strong suspicion, or even a preponderance of evidence would be insufficient. The desire for effective crime control did not, for the ratifiers, preclude fairness, or substitute speculation for reliable evidence.[62]

One of the most important aspects of a trial was that, for a free people,

---

accomplish its own ends. . ." Id. (quoting Brandeis)]. Frequently, an distinction is alleged to exist in terms of *us* citizens and *they* the government. Id., at 68. Similarly, Schrock and Welsh, *supra* note 30, separate the government (executive and judiciary) from the people for purposes of criminal prosecution in the "unitary" system they construct. *Id.,* at 257–260. In that mode, Schrock and Welsh employ a unitary "model" to remove what they consider to be inconsistencies present in criminal prosecution. By doing so they in fact shatter the experience as it was originally understood by the participants—an approach typically employed by system builders. *See* ERIC VOEGELIN, SCIENCE, POLITICS & GNOSTICISM 44 (1968). Thus, the models created by Schrock and Welsh and others do not illuminate the relationship of government and the American people as historically understood by the people. Instead, a new reality is created based on principles to which Schrock and Welsh subscribe. Once readers learn to identify and reject those models for what they are—the illegitimate if logical constructs of those authors' own considerable intellects and imaginations—many posited modern constitutional "rights" dissolve into nothing more than the imposition of personal preferences disguised by the use of legal and constitutional terminology. *See* Schrock & Welsh, *supra* note 30, at 291–293n.111. *See infra,* text, comment, and sources accompanying notes 72–85. The symbols of *government* and *people,* one in some respects but separate in others, remain an experienced whole, part of a tension perhaps expressed best by Lincoln: government "of the people, by the people, for the people" Gettysburg Address (1863), in BASIC DOCUMENTS IN AMERICAN HISTORY 128 (R. Morris, ed., 1956).

60. MAYFLOWER COMPACT (1620).

61. An analogy also challenged in subsequent pages, *see infra* text accompanying note 91.

62. *See infra,* chapter 7, discussion under "Fifth Amendment & Coerced Confessions."

the most fitting judge of any breach of community mores would be the defendant's peers. The number they chose to pass such judgments was twelve—perhaps a symbolic number.[63] Unquestionably instructive. On close analysis, one discerns that it is the people doing the teaching, not the government. Well-known common-law procedures would more likely reach a fair judgment than the procedures of combat or ordeal that preceded them.[64] The people affirmed the importance of these procedures (rights) before any of them individually became defendants, and all the procedures adopted were believed to be perfectly consistent with justice and with being free citizens. To be fair, a trial must get at the truth, for it was only upon obtaining the truth that culpability, or degrees of culpability, could be judged and justice be meted out.[65] With justice done, the principles of a free citizenry would be affirmed and perhaps the accused citizen and the society in which he lived could be reconciled. Teach they did. All citizens must accept the responsibilities of self-government and there was a penalty for those who chose to forsake civic duty for personal gain. Thus, a jury trial demonstrated the existence of a free citizenry determined to "establish Justice, insure domestic Tranquility . . . promote the general Welfare, and secure the Blessings of Liberty to ourselves and our Posterity."[66]

63. "'And that *number of twelve* is much respected in *holy writ,* as in 12 *apostles.*'" 1 Coke, *Institutes of the Laws of England,* 1551 (London, 1628–1641), *quoted in* Raoul Berger, Government by Judiciary 398 (1977).

64. In England, jury trials succeeded "trial by ordeal" which itself was an improvement over preceding practices. *See* Fredrich Pollock & W. Maitland, The History of English Law Before the Time of Edward I, 653–661 (1968); Herta Meyers, The History and Meaning of the Fourteenth Amendment 128–137 (1977).

65. This matter will be considered in chapter 7. Here one example will suffice: "It is a mistaken notion, that facts which have been obtained from prisoners . . . [are] to be rejected from regard to public faith. . . . Confessions are received in evidence, or rejected as inadmissible, under a consideration whether they are or not intitled to credit." King v. Jane Warickshall, 1 Leach 263, 263–264, 168 Eng. Crown Cases 234 (1783). For an interesting comment on proportionality and justice, see Wilfred Ritz, *Twenty-Five Years of State Criminal Confessions Cases in the U.S. Supreme Court,* 19 Wash. & Lee L. Rev. 35 (1962) [hereinafter *Criminal*]; Wilfred J. Ritz, *State Criminal Confession Cases: Subsequent Developments in Cases Reversed by United States Supreme Court and Some Current Problems,* 19 Wash. & Lee L. Rev. 202 (1962) [hereinafter *Developments*]. My colleague, Henry Paolucci, points out something I chose to ignore in the text, that technically a jury trial forsakes truth to arrive instead at a moral public basis for judgment. Had truth been the sole and only objective, certainly torture would be consistent, a fact recognized by the citizens of Massachusetts. *See supra,* chapter 1, text accompanying note 20. *See also* Augustine, The City of God, chapter VI (1950); Pollock & Maitland, supra note 64, at 653–661 vol. II and Herbert Dean, The Political—Social Ideas of St. Augustine 136–137 (1963).

66. U.S. Const., Preamble. I omit only two phrases, "We the People of the United States, in Order to form a more perfect Union," which I suggest is precisely why the Constitution was created—

THE USE OF SYMBOLS. In attempting to circumvent the framers's design, some noninterpretivists employ what they call symbols. Take, for example, the fair trial/fair prosecution symbol used by Schrock and Welsh.[67] They begin by alleging that disparities exist between the fairness implied by constitutional provisions and the realities that impede realization of promises the authors maintain are explicitly or implicitly contained in those provisions. But unless symbols are grounded in the intentions of the ratifiers, all such assessments remain a merely personal judgment, not constitutionalized principles or commands. The task of defining abuse and the selection of remedies is a legislative, not a judicial task.[68]

When symbol creators ignore the historical record or distort precedents in order to redefine the meaning of rights, or assert that their ideas of fairness are superior to those constitutionalized by the ratifiers, three consequences ensue. They have admitted that the authority for their views does not rest on choices made by the ratifiers; hence, they are obliged to respond to charges of illegitimacy and usurpation; and they acknowledge that they are no longer engaging in interpretation in any traditional meaning of that term. Instead, they are changing, or abusing, the meaning the rights in question originally had—without authorization to do so. They are in fact creating new symbols and interpreting the Constitution according to what they allege is its spirit—a position explicitly rejected by Publius.[69]

I conclude that the fair trial/fair prosecution symbolism (like others of the same ilk) consists of assumptions that cannot be sustained any more than can the usual accompanying subterfuge; that the rights or remedies advocated are *already in the Constitution.* Such symbol creators apparently approach symbols as a means by which the few manipulate the many—"a very useful tool in the hands of another, who wishes to exercise social control."[70] Many noninterpretivists thus use symbols as yet another means to mask their imposition of personal preferences upon the people. What they do does not illustrate the framers' or the ratifiers' understanding of the Constitu-

---

the particular weaknesses of the Articles of Confederation providing additional illumination. The other phrase, "provide for the common defense" is not pertinent to this discussion, but it is, of course, essential to an understanding of the founding. Whatever the virtue of a constitution, a people unable to defend itself would lose the right to self-government. Federalists and antifederalists also were quite sensitive about the right of the states to retain jury trial. FEDERALIST, *supra* note 1, no. 83.

67. *See e.g.,* Schrock and Welsh, *supra* note 30, at 260–62.

68. *See supra,* chapter 2, text accompanying note 33, and *infra,* chapter 8, text accompanying notes 38–42.

69. *See supra,* chapter 2, text accompanying notes 66 and 79.

70. THURMAN ARNOLD, THE SYMBOLS OF GOVERNMENT 10 (1935).

tion; nor does it inform us of how Bill of Rights provisions had been implemented in the past. Symbols should illuminate the understanding of those who created and used them and not be used to manipulate precedents to secure a desired result.[71]

MODEL-BUILDING. Noninterpretivist model-building is akin to taking constitutional language to higher and higher levels of abstraction.[72] Construction usually begins with an "ideal" or "right" or "need" that the model-builder claims is essential to the American political tradition (e.g., equal weighing of votes), or to justice (e.g., legislation should not make distinctions based on race or gender), or to morality (e.g., criminals should not be convicted on evidence illegally acquired). Then the ideal or need is fleshed out in its various parts and requirements, as decided by its creator. Corollaries are logically deduced from assumed premises and each part is integrated into a system. Next, depending on whether or not the ideal has been drawn from what are alleged to be society's ideas, or rights related or American traditions, or from more current or abstract treatises on justice or morals, the model is divorced from the historical milieu that initially shaped the ideal, right, or need. These constructions also tend to be factually selective.[73] All related beliefs—those that might help to illuminate how the ideals, rights, or needs were once concretely applied—are minimized, if not ignored.[74] By now liberated from historical context, the model-builder spins webs of logical consequences that are asserted to follow from the premises selectively chosen and defined earlier in the model's construction.[75] Finally, ignoring how the constructed model or its underlying ideal, right, or need fits into the framers' design or prior historical usage, the model-builder is limited only by imaginative ability.[76] Com-

71. *Compare* ARNOLD, *supra* note 70, at 6–10; *Yale Kamisar, Brewer V. Williams, Massiah, and Miranda: What is "Interrogation?" When Does it Matter?,* 67 THE GEORGETOWN L.J. 1, 82–83 (1978), *with* WILLMORE KENDALL AND GEORGE CAREY, THE BASIC SYMBOLS OF THE AMERICAN POLITICAL TRADITION 18–22 (1971); Stephen Tonsor, *The Use and Abuse of Myth,* 15 INTERCOLLEGIATE REVIEW 67 (Spring, 1980). *Compare* Kamisar, *id.,* at 9, 22 *with* William Gangi, *The Inbau-Kamisar Debate: Time for Round 2?,* 12 WESTERN STATE UNIVERSITY L.R. 117, 147–149 (1984). These two approaches to symbols are irreconcilable and once that is understood one sees more clearly how precedents have been repeatedly abused by Court majorities and commentators.

72. *See supra,* text accompanying notes 45–66.

73. *See infra,* chapter 7, under section "Prohibition—The Bill of Rights."

74. *See e.g.,* ROBERT CORD, SEPARATION OF CHURCH AND STATE (1982).

75. *See e.g.,* Kamisar, *supra* note 71; Michael Moore, *A Natural Law Theory of Interpretation,* 58 SO. CAL. L. REV. 279 (1985); STEPHEN R. MUNZER, A THEORY OF PROPERTY (1990) and Suzanna Sherry, *The Founders' Unwritten Constitution,* 54 U. CHI. L. REV. 1127 (1987).

76. Eric Voegelin comments:

> Images of reality must be examined for their form of reality; when the pattern of form

peting principles that might temper logical implementation of the model constructed are exorcised. (The illegitimacy of the latter technique has been discussed above.)

Such noninterpretivist models become more real to their builders—and subsequent adherents—than either the framers' design, constitutional history, or the original milieu of concerns that defined those ideals, rights, or needs, not to mention present experience.[77] If experience will not bend to the model, the model is employed to bend experience.[78] This model-building is an intoxicating brew, as are the persuasive skills that sustain it: In Plato's words, speech is "a great and powerful master" that operates on man "with magic force." The spell of language "can swerve the soul when it is weakened, by passion or lack of knowledge, toward opinion . . . in conflict with truth". The power that language has over the soul Plato compared to that of a drug over the body. "As a drug can heal or kill, harmful persuasion can drug and bewitch the soul," he said.[79]

But what of citizens not enraptured—those who raise probing questions? Model-builders must either suppress such questions (often referring the questioner to the premises of the model whose truth is being challenged), or the noninterpretivist builder must abandon the model. More often than not, contemporary model-builders challenge the integrity or morals of the questioner.[80]

> has become clear, the contents must be examined; schemes of reality that present themselves as systems must be examined for the intellectual tricks with the help of which the nonsystematic form of reality is closed to make up a system; particularly one must not accept the demand of adherents of a system that their premises are the condition for understanding the system, for precisely systems can be understood only by interpretations "from without," i.e., interpretations beginning with the form of reality.

ERIC VOEGELIN, ANAMNESIS 169 (1978).

77. Chase uses *legal* and *factual* guilt concepts (see *supra,* chapter 4, text accompanying note 91) as if they had always been part of constitutional interpretation; he also mistakenly implies that both may be attributed to the framers' design! Edward Chase, *The Burger Court, the Individual, and the Criminal Process: Directions and Misdirections,* 52 N.Y.U. L. REV. 518, 518–519 (1977) upon which rests his entire article.

78. Voegelin observes that for those who become enamored by their "system," when it clashes with reality "reality must give way." VOEGELIN, *supra* note 76, at 44. *Cf.* Justice Goldberg's opinion in *Escobedo v. Illinois,* with William Gangi, *A Critical View of the Modern Confession Rule: Some Observations on Key Confession Cases,* 28 ARK. L. REV. 1, 38–42 (1975).

79. Eric Voegelin, *Wisdom and the Magic of the Extreme: A Mediation,* THE SOUTHERN REVIEW 235, 244, 244–249 *passim* (Spring, 1981) (quoting Plato, citation omitted). Even when the consequences of abusive persuasion are recognized as evil the situation may "resemble a sick man who wants the physician to cure him by treating the effects of dissipation . . . without [his] giving up his way of life." *Id.,* at 252. In short, the "desire for drugs is now related to the core of existential disorder, to the hatred of truth that would interfere" that is, recognition of the truth that would force the dreamer to give up his dream, his perception of reality, his system. *Id.*

80. *See supra,* chapter 4, text and comments accompanying notes 42–44.

Model-building can serve a legitimate analytical purpose as long as the builders never forget that it is not reality being studied—only an abstraction of their own making. Today many noninterpretivist models are defective because either contemporary values are read retroactively into the Constitution (e.g., privacy) or the builder assumes the judiciary may legitimately expand the meaning of restrictions beyond those understood by the ratifiers.

Some model builders today remain aware that the models they create or use were never part of the Constitution. To illustrate my point more concretely I turn to Herbert Packer's brilliantly constructed "Two Models of the Criminal Process."[81] Though Packer makes a distinction between "factual" guilt and "legal" guilt,[82] he remains aware of the underlying realities and the cost to society. But other model builders do not.[83] To take another example, there are the "fragmentary" versus "unitary" government prosecution models constructed by Schrock and Welsh.[84] The framers did not constitutionalize

81. Herbert Packer, *Two Models of the Criminal Process,* 113 U. PENN. L. REV. 1 (1964). Packer pursues the criminal process by abstracting models from reality. *Id.,* at 1–6. He observes: "When we polarize, we distort. The models are, in a sense, distortions. . . . This Article does not make value choices, but only describes what are thought to be their consequences." Id., at 6. On the contrary, from the founding on, the entire process involves "value" choices. The issue is who shall make them.

82. *Id.,* at 16–17.

83. Packer states: "The Due Process Model, while it may in the first instance be addressed to the maintenance of reliable fact finding techniques, comes eventually to incorporate prophylactic and deterrent rules that result in the release of the factually guilty even in cases in which blotting out the illegality would still leave an adjudicative fact finder convinced of the accused's guilt." *Id.,* at 18. *See* Gangi, *supra* note 50, at 131 (truth-seeking bows before the will to win). In an accompanying note, Packer makes the following observation with respect to the developing body of case law. "This tendency, seen most starkly in the exclusionary rule for illegally seized evidence in *Mapp* . . . is also involved in the rejection of the 'special circumstance' approach to testing the deprivation of counsel, *Gideon* . . . and in the apparently similar trend in confession cases, *Mallory . . . Escobedo.* Packer, *supra* note 81, at 18n.16. (citations omitted). Packer wrote prior to the decision in Miranda v. Arizona, 384 U.S. 436 (1966), which undoubtedly would have been added to the list. *See comment, supra* note 77 (mistaken reading of modern concepts into constitutional design).

84. Schrock and Welsh, *supra* note 30, at 255–260. Schrock and Welsh, adopt a particular perspective toward individual rights, or, as they put it, the "SIGNIFICANCE OF RIGHTS." *Id.,* at 271. They claim that the perspective one adopts toward how rights are viewed has an enormous effect on how societal problems are approached and resolved. As they put it, what a "DIFFERENCE A RIGHT MAKES." *Id.,* at 271–273. They choose to view rights absolutely, and in viewing the Fourth Amendment from that perspective, they posit that the Fourth Amendment created substantive rights against the legislature. *Id.,* at 274, 343–344. In short, they urge that the Bill of Rights be construed in Hobbesian-Lockean fashion: individual rights become superior to the people's right to self-government. *Id.,* at 273n.72.

I disagree on grounds supported elsewhere: (a) Bill of Rights provisions were understood by those who proposed and ratified them only in the context of their common-law ancestry; (b) Substantive, absolute rights against the legislature, were unknown; (c) It is not for the scholar, as a

either model. Aside from there being the centuries-old common-law procedures, both prosecution and standards of evidence admissibility were left to national and state legislatures to determine.[85]

An Imposition on the States?

The imposition of federal Bill of Rights standards on the states does not adversely affect citizens' ability to address matters related to the common good.[86]

This premise is as weak today as it was when the judiciary constitutionalized unbridled economic competition. Not only does it assume to be true that which must be proven, it turns history topsy-turvy. The Bill of Rights provisions were not adopted to save the people from oppressive state governments.[87] Nothing could be further from the truth.[88]

After ratification of both the Constitution and the Bill of Rights, between the powers ceded to the federal government and those reserved to the states the people's right to self-government was all-inclusive. Unless specifically prohibited,[89] one government or the other was left competent to deal with any subject "thoughte meet and convenient for

---

scholar, to *prefer* a perspective on how rights should be viewed. The scholar has an obligation to understand those rights as they had been understood by those who framed and ratified them. Should one prefer another perspective, it should be labeled as a preference and any pretense at elucidating traditional constitutional law should be forsworn.

85. Indeed, as Publius explicitly acknowledged, delegates to the Philadelphia convention understood that the ordinary administration of criminal justice would rest in state hands. *See supra,* chapter 5, text accompanying notes 154–155.

86. Examples in the text will be drawn from the criminal justice area (*e.g.,* the exclusionary rule and coerced confessions). The principles, however, are equally applicable to First Amendment free speech, press, child pornography, and libel cases, as well as establishment and free exercise of religion cases, Second Amendment right to bear arms cases, and Fourteenth Amendment due process and equal protection cases. All similar constitutional provisions (*e.g.,* power-granting versus power-restrictions) should be approached in a consistent manner. *See infra,* chapter 7.

87. *See supra,* chapter 3, text accompanying notes 72–80 (discussion of Luther v. Borden).

88. Publius assured his readers that the ratification of the proposed federal constitution, despite contrary claims by the opposition, posed no danger that the federal government would usurp matters understood to be within state control. He observed:

> There is one transcendent advantage belonging to the province of the state governments, which alone suffices to place the matter in a clear and satisfactory light—I mean the ordinary administration of criminal and civil justice. This, of all others, is the most powerful, most universal, and most attractive source of popular obedience and attachment. It is this which, being the immediate and visible guardian of life and property, having its benefits and its terrors in constant activity before the public eye, regulating all those personal interests and familiar concerns to which the sensibility of individuals is more immediately awake, contributes more than any other circumstance to impressing upon the minds of the people affection, esteem and reverence toward the government.

FEDERALIST, *supra* note 1, at no. 17, at 120.

89. I refer to the explicit restrictions contained in Article I, sections 9 and 10 and those detailed in the first eight amendments, directed only against the federal government.

the general good."[90] Therefore, when judicial interpretations prohibit both federal and state governments from dealing with issues of public concern, and the alleged prohibition cannot be located in the "manifest tenor" of the text, those interpretations are suspect. Somewhere along the way, the judiciary went astray, either by making illegitimate presumptions or by the imposition of personal preferences upon the people. The laissez-faire Court made this mistake, and the Warren, Burger, and Rhenquist courts have followed suit.

I understand that many noninterpretivist scholars would reject the above principle as too constraining. They might counter, for example, with the contention that "the quality of a nation's civilization can be largely measured by the methods it uses in the enforcement of its criminal laws."[91] Such contentions, however, beg the question. They assume standards that are not constitutional standards and the judiciary has no business imposing them. I state unequivocally that the question of the "quality of a nation's civilization" is precisely that: a question to be answered by the nation's people through elected representatives accountable and responsible to them—*not by the judiciary.* Whether or not and to what degree citizens choose to evaluate the nation's civilization by how we treat the criminally accused is for the people to decide, the only limitation being the ratifiers' understanding of relevant constitutional provisions.

Alternately, noninterpretivists might take refuge in Justice Frankfurter's distinction between accusatorial versus inquisitorial[92]—a distinction that, at the time, Justice Robert Jackson shrewdly observed was more dependent "on the emotional state of the writer" than legal history.[93] The word *accusatorial,* like the phrase *open society,* is not self-illuminating except to those predisposed to agree with its implicit assumptions about societal evolution.[94] Still, it, too, should be briefly probed.

Were state administrations of criminal justice accusatorial prior to the adoption of the Constitution? The answer of course is yes, if that *accusatorial* is used as a shorthand expression to describe those procedures relating to criminal prosecution eventually included in the federal Bill of Rights. After ratification of

90. Mayflower Compact (1620). *See supra, e.g.,* text accompanying notes 54–71.
91. Walter Schaefer, *Federalism and State Criminal Procedures,* 70 HARV. L. REV. 1, 26 (1962).
92. Watts v. Indiana, 338 U.S. 49, 54 (1949).
93. *Id.,* at 60 (J. Jackson, dissenting). Of course, we again are in the area of personality preferences. *See infra,* Appendix A. It is essential to remind the reader, however, that *emotional* must not be construed as unthinking. Instead, feelers seek a more personal basis of judgment; thinkers are more comfortable with an impersonal basis.
94. *See supra,* chapter 4, text accompanying notes 106–113.

the Bill of Rights, was the federal government administration of criminal justice accusatorial? Again, the only sensible answer is yes, because, as Justice Frankfurter was fond of pointing out, it was such procedures that distinguished the American system from inquisitorial ones.

So far we have established that state criminal justice systems were accusatorial prior to the adoption of the Constitution and that the federal criminal justice system was accusatorial after adoption of the Bill of Rights. Since many criminal procedures in the Bill of Rights had roots in centuries of English history (with which the ratifiers were familiar) what do noninterpretivists mean today when they claim either that the nature of rights or specific Bill of Rights provisions now demand, for example, an exclusionary rule (i.e., the inadmissibility of evidence illegally acquired)? Since we must presume that the people knew what they were ratifying, then they also knew what the Fourth Amendment was intended to secure. But even after adoption of the Fourth Amendment, Congress remained free to identify abuses and select remedies *other than* exclusion. Indeed, for 125 years thereafter, federal courts regularly permitted the admissibility of illegally acquired evidence under conditions designed to assure their probable reliability.[95] Evidence admissibility standards were a matter of ordinary legislative oversight, and any common-law judicial lawmaking was subject to legislative revision. With one exception, evidence admissibility standards did not enjoy constitutional stature.[96] The people's elected state and federal representatives might have decided to forego the admissibility of illegally obtained evidence, or admit it, or choose somewhere between; judges might have engaged in give-and-take with a legislature over how rules were to be applied to particular situations; but neither the legislatures nor judges could elevate standards of evidence admissibility to constitutional stature—except by going through the amendment process.

When noninterpretivists justify the exclusion of illegally acquired evidence because of the *nature* of the accusatorial system, their understanding of its requirements must, I suggest, be derived from something *other than the American tradition or the principles constitutionalized by the people.* Their understanding must eventually rest on assumptions (already explored) regarding what meaning they would *prefer* Bill of Rights provisions to have; or on associated beliefs about what content such rights ought to include.[97]

95. Gangi, *supra* note 50, at 58–66.

96. The one exception, noted by Chief Justice Marshall, concerned the requirement that there be two witnesses in treason cases. *See supra,* chapter 3, text accompanying note 9.

97. Assumptions such as the "progressive and self-confident society" are articulated by Justice

None of these assumptions or judgments are rooted in the ratifiers' understanding of relevant provisions or in American constitutional history. Lessons of history allegedly derived from such assumptions and offered by the judiciary stand on no higher ground. They often amount to nothing more than what a majority of Supreme Court justices at any one time happen to believe those lessons to be, and their conclusions often are reached only after the "history" has been grossly abused or totally misunderstood. Who, for example, authorized Justice Arthur Goldberg to decide whether or not "there is something very wrong with [our criminal justice] system"; or to determine whether it is "worth preserving"?[98] The framers left such authority only in the hands of the people.

The Question of Failure

If judges did not create new doctrines, then the content of various amendments would be reduced to a "mere form of words." That judgment follows closely on the heels of another: that other remedies or approaches (sanctioned previously by the legislative) have failed to prevent the abuse contained in the amendment in question.[99] For judges not to create more effective sanctions would amount to a judicial sanction of the evil condemned in the amendment in question.[100]

The "mere form of words" argument is deceptive. It recasts the illegitimate assumption that the judiciary may impose sanctions for any evils it identifies. When the argument is used to impose any requirement that judges believe to be appropriate, it is another way of saying: We [the noninterpretivists] believe the condemned conduct is morally wrong, and somebody ought to do something about it. Perhaps. But judges were not authorized to create rights or substitute their judgments for those of legislators.

Moreover, the "mere form of words" argument often assumes that other common-law or statutory-law remedies have either failed or are inadequate. But who says so? Only the people through their electorally-accountable representatives can make such determinations. Judgments (even when supported by irrefutable evidence) that existing remedies are in-

---

Felix Frankfurter. McNabb v. United States, 318 U.S. 332, 340 (1943) (J. Frankfurter). *See also* Alfred Hill, *The Bill of Rights and the Supervisory Power,* 69 Columbia L. Rev. 181, 211 (1969). Underlying such assumptions are other unsupported and constitutionally irrelevant views on progress, history, and subtle variations of the open-society concept such as the one articulated by Chief Justice Earl Warren: "As important as it is that persons who have committed crimes be convicted, there are considerations which transcend the question of guilt or innocence" Blackburn v. Alabama, 361 U.S. 199, 206 (1959) (Warren, C.J.).

98. Escobedo v. Illinois, 378 U.S. 478, 490 (1964).

99. *See, e.g.,* Kamisar, *supra* note 59, at 82.

100. Id., at 78–83.

effective, or that other remedies hold greater promise of effectiveness, do not resolve the lack of judicial authorization. The people, collectively, and no one else, must be convinced of the failure or inadequacy of the remedies provided.

NINE ARGUMENTS DEFENDING JUDICIAL POWER

I will here briefly review where the discussion stands. Noninterpretivists view constitutional phrases as not fixed in meaning; rather as ambiguous, open-ended, malleable, and capable of expansion. They champion an open society and support the use of judicial power to bridge any gap that is felt to exist between what they believe are America's political ideals and existing realities. Courts, they contend, must take an active role in remedying whatever defects are found.[101]

Interpretivists, such as myself, dissent. We contend that any interpretation of the Constitution must begin with, if available, the ratifiers' understanding; and that many Supreme Court decisions over the past half-century are illegitimate, since there is no evidence that the justices have been authorized to wield the power they do.

The reader thus is asked to resolve a single issue: What legitimate role does the Supreme Court play in the American system of government?[102] My experience has been that it is a lot harder to keep that question in focus than readers might suspect. Noninterpretivists believe that the single question should be resolved only in the context of nine other distinct but highly integrated groups of arguments. At the center of each group of arguments is an oft-repeated word or phrase that has worked its way into both legal and popular literature: I have labeled such words and phrases as *symbols.*[103] I want to put each group of these arguments before the reader, followed by a rebuttal from Publius' perspective, in order that the reader may better appreciate the complexity of the debate, linger over one or more symbols or the interrelationships between them, and if so inclined consult the references provided in the footnotes.[104]

What follows cannot fairly be described as a debate between interpretivists and noninterpretivists: the written word does not lend itself to the dynamics of a verbal exchange and the statement-rebuttal form adopted here could not—without exasperating the reader—provide a

101. *See supra,* text and comments accompanying notes 30–44.
102. Much of the material in this section originally dealt specifically with the controversy surrounding Raoul Berger's works on the fourteenth amendment. *See* William Gangi, *Judicial Expansionism: An Evaluation of the Ongoing Debate,* 8 Ohio N. U. L. Rev. 1 (1981). The text has been revised to put those same issues in broader terms.
103. Gangi, *supra* note 102, at 17n.149.
104. To minimize repetition, the reader is directed to earlier discussions.

sufficient number of counter-rebuttals. I have nevertheless made every effort to put forth the best arguments available to each side. The reader, however, should be wary: unintentional prejudices are possible—even likely. One additional caution: the debate is very fluid and the reader may confidently embrace a interpretivist or noninterpretivist position only to be cast back into indecision a little further on. That's fine. The road back to self-government is not an easy one to travel. It took me twenty years!

The Constitution Must Remain Adaptable

When the Constitution was proposed, the United States was but thinly populated and comparatively homogeneous: it was essentially rural and largely agricultural. Today Americans live in entirely different circumstances.[105] No one states the matter more bluntly than Arthur Miller: The "Founding Fathers have been buried. They should not rule us from their graves."[106]

Furthermore, the intentions of the framers often are difficult to discern,[107] and even if those intentions could be discerned the Constitution cannot, and should not, be interpreted in the same fashion as an ordinary statute or contract since its language "was most certainly selected for its open endedness and its capacity for redefinition over time."[108] It is proper for judges to adhere to the lawgiver's intent regarding statutory interpretations because those statutes can be easily changed by a simple legislative majority. But constitutional changes would require amendment.[109] And if

105. *See* Richard Posner, *The Separation of Powers,* in Politics, *supra* note 52, at 41 ["The nation that the Constitution created has endured—and may it always endure—but the original Constitution has largely passed into history."]. *See also* Dean Alfange, *On Judicial Policymaking and Constitutional Change: Another Look at the 'Original Intent' Theory of Constitutional Interpretation,* 5 Hast. Const. L. Q. 603, 614–615 (1978); Ely, *supra* note 45, at 412–13 (1978); Stephen R. Munzer and James Nickel, *Does the Constitution Mean What it Always Meant?* 77 Colum. L. Rev. 1029, 1032, 1043–1050 (1977) and Murphy, book review, 87 YALE L. J. 1752, 1758–1760 (1978).

106. Arthur S. Miller, *An Inquiry into the Relevance of the Intentions of the Founding Fathers, With Special Emphasis Upon the Doctrine of Separation of Powers,* 27 Ark. L. Rev. 583, 601 (1973); *See also* Ely, *supra* note 105, at 412–413. *But see* Randall Bridwell, *The Federal Judiciary: America's Recently Liberated Minority,* S. C. L. Rev. 467, 477n.28 (1979).

107. Miller, for example, observes that "We cannot read the minds of men long dead to decide specific problems of the day." Even if we could, he goes on, "they are irrelevant to the decision of modern constitutional problems." Miller, *supra* note 106, at 584. *See also* Randell Bridwell, book review, 1978 Duke L. Rev. 907, 917 (1978); Bridwell, *supra* note 106, at 480–482; Miller, *supra* note 106, at 584; Munzer & Nickel, *supra* note 105, at 1031–1032 and Murphy, *supra* note, at 1761, 1764–1768.

108. Alan Dershowitz, *The Sovereignty of Process: The Limits of Original Intention,* in Politics, *supra* note 52, at 12.

109. As Dershowitz explains: "For judicial review to make any sense in a multi-branch democracy, the judiciary should not simply be yet another branch, representing the same majoritarian

amendment is the only way to change the Constitution, the ability to keep it "ever young and healthy"[110] would be severely inhibited. Additionally,[111] those who remain preoccupied with the ratifiers' understanding of the Constitution adhere to narrow and now discarded distinctions between legislative, executive, and judicial functions.[112]

In the end, interpretivists chose to ignore Marshall's admonition that "it is a *constitution* we are expounding."[113] The Constitution, therefore, must be considered "in a state of becoming . . . open-ended, always being updated to meet the exigencies of succeeding generations."[114]

In Defense of the Publius Design

Judge Frank H. Easterbrook comments: "The fixity of the document does not stop the creation of new rights; it simply designates *who among the living,* is authorized to speak for the living."[115] This claim of the noninterpretivists that they desire to maintain a living Constitution masks their

---

constituency as the legislative and executive represent and reflecting the identical values of power, efficiency, and immediate political gratification." Dershowitz, *supra* note 52, at 13–14.

110. Henry Monaghan, *The Constitution Goes to Harvard,* 13 Harv. Civ. Rights—Civ. Lib. L. Rev. 117, 122 (1978) *See also* Murphy, *supra* note 105, at 1763–1764.

111. *See* Louis Lusky, *'Government by Judiciary': What Price Legitimacy?,* 6 Hast. L. Q. 403, 404–405; Raoul Berger, *The Scope of Judicial Review: An Ongoing Debate,* 6 Hast. C. L. Q. 527, 628–631 (1979); John T. Gibbons, book review, 31 Rutgers L. Rev. 839, 848 (1978); Arthur S. Miller, *The Elusive Search for Values in Constitutional Interpretation,* 6 Hast. Const. L. Q. 487, 488 (1979); Murphy, *supra* note 105, at 1761–1762; and Nathaniel Nathanson, book review, 56 Tex. L. Rev. 579, 581 (1978).

112. *Compare* Henry Abraham, *'Equal Justice Under Law' or 'Justice at any Cost'? The Judicial Role Revisited: Reflections on Government by Judiciary: The Transformation of the Fourteenth Amendment,* 6 Hast. Const. L. Q. 567–571 (1979); Louis Fisher, *Raoul Berger on Public Law,* 8 Pol. Sci. Reviewer 173, 188–192 (1978); Geoffrey Hazard, *The Supreme Court as a Legislature,* 64 Cornell L. Rev. 1 (1978); Miller, *supra* note 111, at 490; R. H. Clark, book review, 56 Texas L. Rev. 947 (1978) *with* Raoul Berger, *A Political Scientist as Constitutional Lawyer: A Reply to Louis Fisher,* 41 Ohio St. L. J. 147 (1980) [hereinafter *Political Scientist*]; Raoul Berger, *'The Supreme Court as a Legislature': A Dissent,* 64 Cornell L. Rev. 988 (1979) [hereinafter *Supreme Court*].

113. M'Culloch v. Maryland, 17 U.S. (4 Wheat.) 316, 407 (1819). *See also* Lusky, *supra* note 111, at 405; Murphy, *supra* note 105, at 1769; Nathanson, *supra* note 111, at 581 and Clark, *supra* note 112, at 960.

114. Miller, *supra* note 106, at 584. *See also* Berger, *supra* note 111, at 639; Munzer & Nickel, *supra* note 105, Murphy, *supra* note 105, at 1768–1770.

115. Frank H. Easterbrook, "Approaches to Judicial Review," in Politics, *supra* note 52, at 22. Bork adds: "Though it is disguised, the unrepresentative-dead-men argument is nothing more than an attempt to block self-government by the representatives of living men and women." Robert H. Bork, The Tempting of America: The Political Seduction of the Law 171 (1990). McDowell maintains that "such a jurisprudence is not merely a matter of rejecting old meaning for a new one; as an ideology, the logic of a living constitution strikes at the very heart of republican government." Gary L. McDowell, The Constitution and Contemporary Constitutional Theory 13 (1985).

"'end-run around popular government'"[116] and sidesteps the issue of whether or not the framers or ratifiers authorized the judicial power exercised.[117] They avoid the issues of whether or not we remain bound by the ratifiers' understanding by changing the issue to one of whether or not, or how, those intentions may be discerned. Whatever difficulties are posed by the latter questions, they ought to be forthrightly addressed. The legitimacy question is distinguishable and cannot be finessed.

If free to reject the understanding of constitutional phrases ratified two hundred years ago, may Americans today similarly ignore the Civil War amendments? Or the Warren, Burger, and Rhenquist Court decisions? Or even those made this morning? Why should the people, the Congress, the president, obey *any* constitutional limits once the Court absolves itself from the earlier obligation?[118] Constitution making is about setting limits: and rejecting the limits set by the ratifiers denies the existence and purpose of a written constitution.

The legitimacy of judicial review is not in question. Interpretivists challenge only the *scope* of its present application—because it is inconsistent with the framers' design.[119] "A revision in contradiction of the framers' express purposes is not 'interpretation,' but amendment"; and the amending power was reserved to the people—not to the judges.[120]

The framers expected judges to approach constitutional interpretation as they had always approached statutory interpretation. In both instances judges were expected to discern the lawgivers' will, and with respect to constitutional interpretations that came into conflict with the last known expression of the people's will (as expressed in the Constitution), judges were bound on oath to demand the people's fidelity to that last expression.[121] Only that ap-

116. McDowell, *supra* note 115, at 14, quoting Raoul Berger (citations omitted).

117. "The question is really meant to indicate that courts should be free to write into the Constitution freedom from democratic control the Framers omitted. . . . We remain entirely free to create all the additional freedom we want by constitutional amendment or by simple legislation, and the nation has done so frequently." Bork, *supra* note 115, at 171.

118. Berger, *supra* note 111, at 535–539.

119. *Id.*, at 533.

120. Raoul Berger, *Government by Judiciary: Some Countercriticism,* 56 Texas L. Rev. 1125, 1126 (1978).

121. *See supra,* chapter 2, text accompanying notes 55–90; and chapter 5, text accompanying notes 43–57. A unanimous 1872 Judiciary Committee Report noted:

> In construing the Constitution we are compelled to give it such interpretation as will secure the result which was intended to be accomplished by those who framed . . . and adopted it. . . . A construction which should give . . . [a] phrase . . . a meaning different from the sense in which it was understood and employed by the people when they adopted the Constitution, would be as unconstitutional as a departure from the plain and express language of the Constitution. . . . A change in the popular use of any word employed in the Constitution can-

proach is consistent with the framers' design.[122] If the framers championed another design, noninterpretivists should present their evidence. They have never done so.

Finally, it is noninterpretivists who misconstrue Marshall's remarks in *M'Culloch v. Maryland:*

> When *(McCulloch)* came under attack, [Marshall] defended that he was pleading for elasticity in Congress' "choice of *means*" to execute existing powers and denied any "constructive assumption of powers never meant to be granted." Again and again he repudiated any claim for "extension by construction" and flatly disclaimed a judicial "right to change the instrument."[123]

Thus, the Constitution should not be abused, neither by expansion nor contraction, for either (and both) endanger the Constitution's ability to endure. That is what Marshall sought to do in *M'Culloch* and there is no evidence to support a contrary view.[124]

Given the remarkable document penned at Philadelphia and Publius' spirited defense, the noninterpretivist assumption that the Constitution's framers remained oblivious of the need for societal adaptation seems incredulous. The framers of course lodged that power precisely where one might expect to find it in a republic—in the legislature. They created governmental structures capable of addressing every imaginable public policy question. These structures worked *until the judiciary began creating artificial roadblocks.* For several generations now the people have had to repudiate these roadblocks before they could address the issues of the day. It has been the judiciary then, not the Constitution, that frequently has inhibited societal adaptability.

> not retroact upon the Constitution, either to enlarge or limit its provisions. . . . Judge Thomas Cooley . . . wrote: 'The meaning of the Constitution is fixed when it is adopted, and it is not different at any subsequent time . . . [T]he object of construction, as applied to a written constitution, is to give effect to the intent of the people in adopting it.'

As quoted in Raoul Berger, *'Government by Judiciary': Judge Gibbons' Argument Ad Hominem,* 59 B.U.L. Rev. 783, 785n.12 (1979) (citations omitted).

122. We must "dismiss . . . 'speculation' on possible or secretly held motives of the framers, learned interpretations of what various words or phrases *could* or *should* mean, and invocations of subsequent changes of circumstances or values. All such arguments . . . carry no evidential weight. Gangi, *supra* note 102, at 7 (citations omitted).

123. Emphasis in original. For additional details, *see* John Marshall's Defense of McCulloch v. Maryland (Gerard Gunther Ed. 1969) and Berger, supra note 63, at 373–378 (1977).

124. "Gerald Gunther, who discovered Marshall's 'Defense of *McCulloch v. Maryland,*' commented, '[I]f virtually unlimited congressional [or judicial] discretion is indeed required to meet twentieth century needs, candid argument to that effect, rather than ritual invoking of Marshall's authority, would seem to be more closely in accord with the Chief Justice's stance.'" Raoul Berger, *The Fourteenth Amendment: Light from the Fifteenth* 74 NW. L. REV. 311, 370–371 (1979).

After World War II a Power Vacuum Developed

Interpretivists fail to place the Supreme Court's contemporary role in its proper historical context.[125] American "societal ideals"[126] always have revolved around the two themes of liberty[127] and equality.[128] But after World War II those "professed ideals"[129] stood in stark contrast with everyday realities.[130] Americans needed some reassurance that these everyday realities would be changed, since to many individuals our alleged ideals "must often [have] seem[ed] to be the sheerest of illusion and promissory deception."[131]

But roadblocks stood in the way of the reforms that were clearly needed:[132] the executive and legislative branches at both the federal and state levels were either not equipped

125. *See generally,* Wallace Mendelson, *The Politics of Judicial Activism,* 24 Emory L.J. 43 (1975); *Lusky supra* note 111, at 407–408. Michael Perry adds: "Constitutional theory, like political theory generally, should be rooted in modern and contemporary as well as past experience, lest the theory's relevance be confined to the past." Michael Perry, book review, 78 Colum. L. Rev. 685, 699 (1978).

126. *See e.g.,* Louis Lusky, By What Right? 97–115, 211–243 (1975); Hazard, *supra* note 112, at 26; Robert E. Knowlton, book review, 32 Ark. L. Rev. 157, 161–162 (1978). *See also* Charles S. Hyneman, The Supreme Court on Trial 261–275 (1964) ("Translate the language of powers and prohibitions into a language of ideals").

127. There is an entire set of other arguments that will be considered under the *Individual Rights* symbol, *infra.* The text reads "always": some noninterpretivists apparently believe that such rights were contained in the Constitution and Bill of Rights.

128. It is impossible to cite all the sources that contend that equality has been a central feature in post–World War II adjudication. *See generally* William Lockhart *et al.,* Constitutional Law 6th ed. 1130–1406 (1986); Yale Kamisar, *Equal Justice in the Gatehouses and Mansions of American Criminal Procedure: From Powell to Gideon, From Escobedo to . . . ,* in Criminal Justice in Our Time 1 (Dick Howard, ed.) (1965) and Phillip Kurland, *Foreword: 'Equal in Origin and Equal in Title to the Legislative and Executive Branches,'* 78 Harv. L. Rev. 143 (1964–1965). Justice Arthur Goldberg offers one early example of noninterpretivist reasoning:

> The framers of the Fourteenth Amendment knew that blacks would constitute just such a minority. For that reason they wrote guarantees of fair and equal treatment into the Constitution. That desire of the framers, as well as the political problem that underlies it, provides strong support for the Court's treatment of any racial classification as "suspect" and warranting the most intensive scrutiny.

Arthur Goldberg, Equal Justice 50 (1971).

129. Perry, *supra* note 125, at 700.

130. William Forrester, *Are We Ready for Truth in Judging,* 63 A.B.A.J. 1215 (1977). *See also Stanley Kutler, Raoul Berger's Fourteenth Amendment: A History or Ahistorical?,* 6 Hast. Const. L.Q. 511, 524–525 (1979); Mendelson, *supra* note 125, at 56. Arthur Goldberg observed that "lawyers, teachers, judges, and others have spent decades molding and remolding legal doctrine, shaping it into ever more refined declarations intended to protect human liberty, expand personal freedoms, and enhance individual dignity. But it is of the utmost importance that the words match the practices." Goldberg, *supra* note 128, at 26.

131. Goldberg, *supra* note 128, at 26. *See also* Lusky, *supra* note 126, at 276.

132. Forrester, *supra* note 130, at 1216. The statement in the text must be taken in the context of those arguments related to *Results,* to be discussed shortly.

to institute the necessary changes, or they were unwilling to do so. Many concerned individuals urged the judiciary to step into this "vacuum."[133] As Hyneman has written, "The task for the activist is to persuade the judges to adopt his ideals and his judgment about effecting ideals, to persuade judges that they have a constitutional obligation to act boldly, and to persuade enough of the population that the judges act in fulfillment of that obligation to make a regime of aggressive judicial review a continuing reality."[134] Had the Supreme Court not responded to these calls for action, the gap between ideals and realities would have remained "uncorrected."[135] So, contrary to interpretivist allegations that judges have been power hungry, it has been the "nonfeasance"[136] of the political branches that has prompted judicial interventions. It makes a great deal of sense. The Supreme Court is our nation's "moral preceptor" and the framers recognized that the judiciary would play that role. For that reason they offered judges life-tenure and empowered them with judicial review. They did so in order to assure that federal judges would not be inhibited by defective public morality,[137] and today the judiciary should continue shaping America's public morality.[138]

In Defense of the Publius Design

Where do noninterpretivists locate the authorization for the judicial role they espouse—this "right" to determine the American people's morality?[139]

Henry Monaghan makes a salient distinction: "Surely the fact that the courts can make law when the political organs are silent (the common law context) does not legitimate a similar authority when the political organs have spoken (the constitutional context). Any such premise seems to me plainly illegitimate, given the basic constitutional design of representative government."[140] Constitutions declare first principles, and in a re-

133. Lusky, *supra* note 126, at 109. *See also* Kutler, *supra* note 130, at 523–524.

134. Hyneman, *supra* note 126, at 224 (Hyneman is reporting, not advocating).

135. Lusky, *supra* note 126, at 109. *See infra,* section on *Best Suited* symbol, where this theme surfaces again.

136. Forrester, *supra* note 130, at 1216.

137. Perry, *supra* note 125, at 700.

138. This line of argument often blends with others, such as those outlined in the sections on the *Remain Adaptable, Best-Suited, Results, Individual Rights, and Accepted* symbols.

139. Raoul Berger states that such proponents confound "law with morals," and "'nothing but confusion of thought can result from assuming that the rights of man in a moral sense are equally rights in the sense of the constitution and the laws.'" Berger, *supra* note 111, at 628, quoting Oliver Holmes, Jr., Collected Legal Papers 171–172 (1920).

140. Henry Monaghan, *Our Perfect Constitution,* 56 N.Y.U. L. Rev. 353, 370 (1981). Years earlier Charles Hyneman had observed that such a view redefines the judicial power, from power "to nullify statutes into a power to pronounce and enforce public policies that ought to be fixed only by

publican regime the first principle was electoral accountability. Judges were assigned only the limited task of interpreting the law—not making or executing it. The power of judicial review and judicial independence were designed by the framers to that, and only that, limited end.

The noninterpretivist assumption that the power to interpret the Constitution also encompasses the power to change it is simply inconsistent with those provisions in the Constitution that provide for amendment. A judicial right to initiate legislation or to veto unwise legislation, other than it being inconsistent with the ratifiers' understanding, was unequivocally dismissed as inappropriate at the Philadelphia convention.[141] Publius acknowledged only two uniquely judicial virtues: a knowledge of the law and mastery of canons of construction. Both are well-suited to the function of interpretation. He defended judicial review because judges were particularly well-equipped *to preserve the people's will* as expressed in the Constitution—not to substitute their own.[142]

When then did the American people authorize a judicial power beyond policing the boundaries declared in the Constitution?[143] The people never approved a judicial power to resolve the moral choices often at the heart of public disputes. Why should they? Judges possess no special expertise to resolve questions of morals. Noninterpretivists take refuge in the fact that judges are not subject to the pressures of electoral accountability: this supposedly makes them uniquely suited to make such choices.[144] But that position flies in the face of the framers' republican design. Publius forthrightly rejected such thinking as appropriate only in hereditary—not republican—regimes. The ratifiers

the elected lawmaking body." Hyneman, *supra* note 126, at 84. Berger adds that "under a grant of limited powers—for so the federal government has always been regarded—the threshold question always is: where was the power conferred?" Berger, *supra* note 111, at 568.

141. For the prior discussion of the convention's rejection of judicial involvement in the proposed council of revision, *see* chapter 4, text accompanying note 15. Berger comments: "John Adams' 1780 Massachusetts Constitution made the separation of power explicit, forbade each branch to exercise the power of another, and particularized that the '[judiciary shall] never exercise the legislative . . . powers . . . [so that this] may be a government of law, and not of men.' The 'vacuum' theory improbably posits that the Framers who denied the Justices a share of policy-making power in the veto process authorized a complete take-over if Congress failed to legislate." Berger, *supra* note 111, at 540.

142. *See supra,* chapter 2, text accompanying notes 79–80. (judges may not interpret the Constitution according to its "spirit").

143. At this juncture in this line of argument ("there is a power vacuum") authors may switch to arguments associated with other symbols; *e.g.* progressivist reasoning (see under *Remain Adaptable* above), institutional function (*see* under *Best-suited* below), tacit approval (*see* under *Accepted*) or good results (*see Results*).

144. *See supra,* chapter 4, text accompanying notes 173–182.

at no point authorized judges to grade the people's moral performance; nor did they empower judges to revise the Constitution when in the judges' opinion the morals of the American people fell short.[145]

There are other reasons, too, why noninterpretivist reliance on the "vacuum" line of argument is misplaced. Even if the Constitution lacked a mechanism for self-change (which it does not), the judiciary cannot assume the role of that mechanism. Couldn't the president make a similar claim, that the legislature or judiciary have failed the American people and in the vacuum he will act? Or Congress, citing its electoral mandate—could it assert that the people demand change (the kind of change that Congress wants, of course) and that since the executive and judiciary have failed to follow the people's will, it must act? All such claims sweep aside the rule of law. The Constitution created the judiciary and empowered it; it was not the other way around.[146] The issue then is, "who is to determine which changes can be made without amendment, and by whom?"[147] The Court cannot be left to be the judge of its own authority.

The Supreme Court Is Best Suited

Although the legislative process is designed to weigh competing societal needs and to accommodate various interests,[148] what interpretivists fail to consider is that the process breaks down in two instances: (a) When "a legislature insulates itself from demands for change in the law by hampering political expression, political organization, or voting";[149] and (b) "Prejudice against socially isolated minorities . . . render the legislature unresponsive to their grievances."[150] In either in-

145. Berger, *supra* note 111, at 628. We repeat Justice Marshall's statement that "the interest, wisdom and justice of the representative body, and its relations with its constituents, furnish the only security . . . against . . . unwise legislation." Providence Bank v. Billings, 29 U.S. (4 Pet.) 514, 563 (1830).

146. *See supra,* chapter 4 text accompanying note 80.

147. Raoul Berger, *Judicial Review: Counter Criticism in Tranquility,* 69 NW. U. L. REV. 390, 402 (1974). Elsewhere Berger, quoting Willard Hurst, adds: "The real issue is *who is to make policy choices* in the twentieth century: judges or the combination of legislature and electorate that makes constitutional amendments." BERGER, *supra* note 63, at 315 (emphasis in original) (quoting Willard Hurst).

148. LUSKY, *supra* note 126, at 109.

149. *Id.,* at 109–120. This line of argument is of course related to those associated with *Individual rights. See infra* below. Hyneman, quoting Eugene V. Rostow, recounts an early expression of this reasoning: "'The freedom of the legislatures to act within wide limits of constitutional construction is the wise rule of judicial policy only if the processes though which they act are reasonably democratic.'" HYNEMAN, *supra* note 126, at 264 (quoting Eugene V. Rostow, *The Democratic Character of Judicial Review,* 66 HARV. L. REV. 202 (1952)). John H. Ely is most associated with its contemporary expression. *See* JOHN ELY, DEMOCRACY AND DISTRUST (1980).

150. LUSKY, *supra* note 126, at 110.

stance, "the court [is] far more institutionally suited to effect values that are not immediately popular."[151]

Some commentators link this "best suited" line of argument with other themes (e.g., the alleged undemocratic character of the Constitution; the need for the Constitution to remain adaptable; or the "individual rights" theme, to be discussed shortly). Varat provides an example of such reasoning:

> The Supreme Court gets its authority to make antimajoritarian decisions from the Constitution. One of the most crucial compromises essential to the ratification of the Constitution was that a Bill of Rights should be adopted before ratification. That [fact] . . . reflected the Founders' recognition that majoritarian policy would perhaps impinge on the rights of groups that were not in the majority at any particular time, and that it was important to have in the structure a body to protect from legislative and executive excesses those not in the majority.
>
> The majority we are talking about—the "original will" of a group of people—would be looked at today as hardly pure democracy. It was a small elite that put the Constitution together. Times have changed. The will of the people has been broadened, in large part, by judicial decisions.[152]

Judges are more sensitive than are popular majorities, or elected officials, to claims that there have been violations of such freedoms as freedom of speech or freedom of the press. For that reason alone judges are especially well suited to monitor such areas of public policy making. This kind of vigilance has proved unnecessary, however, with respect to economic legislation, which "normally regulate[s] . . . interest groups of significant size."[153] Allen Dershowitz puts this reasoning in a nutshell: "The primary question that should be asked by the Supreme Court before it decides to take a case, and if so, how to decide it, is this: Will our decision in this case vindicate important constitutional values that cannot or will not be vindicated by other branches?"[154]

The simple truth is that majoritarian democracy does not work for certain permanent minorities (such as those based on race or their status as criminal defendants) because it presumes that all small groups are equally capable of joining other groups to form majority coalitions.[155] In fact, unpopular minorities find it difficult to form political alli-

151. Dershowitz, in Politics, *supra* note 52, at 15.
152. Jonathan Varat, in Henry S. Commager, *The Constitution and Original Intent,* 19 The Center Magazine 4, 17 (1986) [hereinafter Commager].
153. Goldberg, *supra* note 128, at 51–52.
154. Dershowitz, in *Politics, supra* note 52, at 15.
155. Goldberg, *supra* note 128, at 49. While differences may exist, the term used in the text,

ances.[156] Dershowitz provides another example of such reasoning:

> If those who do not control or even have access to the electoral branches—non-citizens, the homeless, the malapportioned, prisoners, the mentally ill, minorities unable to form coalitions with others, religious and non-religious dissidents, the illiterate or those literate in languages other than English—do indeed have constitutional rights—and who can doubt that they do—it blinks at reality to expect these constitutional rights to be protected by resorting to majoritarian political process. These rights will be vindicated by the courts or they will not be vindicated at all.[157]

In brief, elected officials are often too susceptible and too responsive to better-organized interest groups or prejudiced majorities.[158] These majorities tend to ignore the long-term consequences of rights denial and often opt to dilute the liberties of those feared or hated by the majority.[159]

The framers of the Constitution were well aware that such faults existed in democracies. They (1) "embed[ed] protection for fundamental personal liberties and scrupulously fair criminal procedures in the Bill of Rights";[160] and (2) gave judges life tenure, thereby empowering them to be "bold against popular feelings and opposition" and to "demand the respect and obedience of an unwilling majority."[161] In that context, Chief Justice Earl Warren succinctly expressed the role of the Supreme Court: "'We have no constituency. We serve no majority. We serve no minority.

"permanent minority," appears to be the functional equivalent of another term used by Goldberg—"isolated individuals." *Id.,* at 52.

156. Goldberg, *supra* note 128, at 49. *See also* Hazard, *supra* note 112, at 24–25.

157. Dershowitz, in Politics, *supra* note 52, at 15.

158. Goldberg, *supra* note 128, at 41–50. Put another way:

> More fundamentally, to say that the Supreme Court is undemocratic in its composition and procedure is to beg the essential question: What kinds of law making institutions will best promote the substantive goals summed up by the shorthand "democracy"? For it is substantive goals—like moral equality, private autonomy, and general economic well-being—that define "democratic" when that term describes a community rather than a particular political institution.

Hazard, *supra* note 112, at 9. *See also* Ely, *supra* note 105, at 411. Such arguments tend to veer off into others, such as those relating to the *Results* symbol, *see infra,* and those associated with the failure of democratic institutions. *See supra,* chapter 4, text accompanying notes 173–182.

159. Goldberg, *supra* note 128, at 49–50.

160. *Id.,* at 51. Goldberg added: "And it is just where, as a practical matter, the democratic political forums cannot adequately protect fundamental liberties that I have argued the Court has a constitutional obligation to provide protection." *Id.,* at 52. Language, such as that employed by Justice Goldberg and Varat (*see supra* text accompanying note 152), that the framers charged the judiciary with the responsibility noted is a repeated theme. *See* Forrester, *supra* note 130, at 1216; Ely, *supra* note 105, at 404; and Miller, *supra* note 106, at 593–594.

161. Forrester, *supra* note 130, at 1216. *See* Ely, *supra* note 105, 404 and Miller, *supra* note 106.

We serve only the public interest as we see it, guided only by the Constitution and our own consciences.'"[162]

Noninterpretivists make another argument under the "best-suited" line of argument: the framers lodged the "*ultimate* power of interpretation" in the Supreme Court and nowhere else—a court "not to be equated with any ordinary court of law."[163] The Supreme Court has abandoned "the [traditional] limitations on judicial review," and it has used "the concept of *implied judicial power to make new constitutional rules.*"[164] Simply put, the power of judicial review is not as narrow a power as it was seen to be originally. Interpretivists refuse to come to grips with that fact and to appreciate that today the Supreme Court has a "new and grander conception of its own place in the governmental scheme."[165]

In Defense of the Publius Design

Neither the delegates to the Philadelphia convention, nor the ratifiers of the Constitution, nor the ratifiers of its amendments authorized the noninterpretivists' vision of judicial power.[166] Noninterpretivists confuse precautions taken by the delegates to thwart governmental tyranny with those taken to prevent majoritarian abuses.[167] The Supreme Court itself has never dared to make "such grandiose claims . . . [which] are but a product of the recent past, articulated by the academe on . . . behalf [of the Court] in order to justify its revolutionary decisions."[168] The

162. Miller *supra* 111, at 499. For a description of the Court's constituency, *see* Hazard, *supra* note 112, at 22–27. Hazard concludes that the Supreme Court's constituency is composed, among others, of "the lower courts, federal and state; the academic community (especially in law but also in such subjects as political science); the intelligentsia, media and the media intelligentsia, meaning the *New York Times, et cetera,* and the syndicated political columnists and broadcast commentators." *Id.*, at 25. He notes that "in numbers this is not much of a support group but in political potency it is substantial." *Id.*

163. Miller *supra* note 111, at 493 (emphasis in original), 499.

164. Lusky, *supra* note 111, at 407–408 (emphasis in original). Lusky's complete development of this position may be found in Lusky, *supra* note 126. *See* William Gangi, book review, 63 A.B.A.J. 626 (1977). *But see* Berger, *supra* note 63 (at index listings for Lusky) and Berger, *supra* note 111, at 533–548.

165. Lusky, *supra* note 111, at 408. Lusky's language was directed at the Supreme Court in particular; however, all federal courts must enjoy similar power; the Supreme Court simply speaks last. Also, there is no reason to exempt state courts from acquiring a similar role within the purview of their responsibilities.

166. Berger asks: "Where is the constitutional warrant for constitution-making by judges?" Berger, *supra* note 111, at 540. At this juncture the debate may veer off to encompass some of the symbols I discuss in this chapter: *Remain Adaptable* (the Constitution seen as evolving); *Cumbersome* (the legislative or amendment processes are difficult); and *Accepted* (the people tacitly have consented to changes in the judicial role).

167. *See supra,* chapter 2, text and comments accompanying notes 39–46.

168. Berger, *supra* note 111, at 533. Easterbrook comments:

I served on the faculty of the University of Chicago, which is thought very conservative.

justices may not "anoint themselves."[169]

The framers' design cannot be ignored when some citizens assert that the structures provided are not working properly or that societal injustices persist. Publius forthrightly rejected that view, contending that, unless by amendment, not even the people could authorize elected representatives to ignore the will of the ratifiers. The "best-suited" line of argument masks the making of public policy by the Supreme Court—by *five members* of the Court, it should be said—instead of the national consensus conceived at Philadelphia. By claiming an amending power the justices replace the ratifiers' republican design with a judicial oligarchy.[170]

Only the right of the executive to veto legislation upon the grounds that it was unwise, immoral, or unconstitutional was sanctioned by the ratifiers. Judicial vetoes were confined to enforcing the ratifiers' understanding of the Constitution.[171] None of the three branches may unilaterally change that fact, either on the basis that injustices exist or upon the assumption that the existing processes are inadequate or have failed.

Noninterpretivists approach American history as if the people had accepted antifederalist criticisms.[172] Many reforms are possible by statute but some changes require amendment. While the question of into which category an issue falls—statute or amendment—may ultimately remain a matter of interpretation, judges were never authorized to implement those changes. Both statu-

---

> What that means is that 40 percent of the faculty voted for Reagan in an election in which Reagan got 60 percent. A middle-of-the-road faculty like Yale is one at which 90 percent voted for Mondale and 10 percent voted socialist. A liberal faculty is one in which no capitalist can be considered for appointment—and there are several. This does not suggest to me that the cloisters of academia or of the bench conduce to keen insight into modern conditions.

Easterbrook, *Approaches to Judicial Review,* in POLITICS, *supra* note 52, at 25.

169. Berger, *supra* note 111, at 543. Bridwell adds:

> The *fact* of judicial authority claimed and exercised, if accompanied by laudable results, is assumed to be dispositive of the issue of legitimacy. . . . A narrative or purely descriptive account of the Court's self-perception and altered claims to authority *de facto,* and the measurement of results, are the keystones of legitimacy. A clearer invitation of judicial revision of the Constitution hedged by admonition to be shrewd and restrained and guided by the educated consensus of academe could not be found.

Randall Bridwell, *The Scope of Judicial Review: A Dirge for the Theorists of Majority Rule?,* 31 S. C. L. REV. 617, 635–636 (1980). This rejoinder, therefore, must also be taken in the context of the *Results symbol,* discussed in this chapter.

170. *See supra,* chapter 2, text accompanying note 68. *See also* FEDERALIST, *supra* note 1, at no. 78, at 470.

171. Raoul Berger, *The Scope of Judicial Review: A Continuing Dialogue,* 31 S. C. L. REV., 171, 177, 567–568 (1980).

172. *See e.g.,* Douglas Muzzio and Gerald Maio, *The Will of the Community: Theories of Representation at the Founding,* NORTHEASTER POL. SCI. ASS., Philadelphia (Nov. 1989).

tory and constitutional reform movements have proved successful in the past.[173] Noninterpretivists ultimately believe that the justices are more capable of discerning changes in public sentiment than are the institutions created by the Constitution to do so.[174] But that view has never been accepted by the American people. It has no more validity than Lief Carter's suggestion that the worthiness of a Supreme Court opinion ought to be based on whether it "produce[s] in its audience a felt sense of 'intersubjective zap,' as a good rock concert does."[175]

Finally, without repeating Publius' admonition that even the people may not ignore the ratifiers' understanding, how do we know—as noninterpretivists charge—that legislative inaction after World War II was considered a failure by a majority of Americans?[176] What noninterpretivists in fact do is to impose their personal predilections on the people by dressing them up in constitutional legalese. Judges coerce the American people and thereby abuse the power granted them. Tyrants often claim that they know better than do ordinary citizens what is needed for the common good; and they describe citizens as short-sighted or mean-spirited.

As noted with respect to the "vacuum" line of argument, what if the president assumed dictatorial powers on the grounds of a presumed expertise in international affairs? Constitutionalists must repudiate all claims to power other than those specified in the Constitution as illegitimate: "What is

173. Berger, *supra* note 111, at 639. *See* Robert Jackson, "Back to the Constitution." Address delivered by the solicitor general before the section of public utility law at San Francisco, July 10, 1939, in 25 A. B. A. JOURNAL 745 (1939); Berger, *supra* note 111, at 541, 606, 609; and Aileen S. Kraditor, *On Curiosity: or the Difference Between an Ideologue and a Scholar,* THE INTERCOLLEGIATE REVIEW 95 (spring 1980). Many aspects of our representative system have been addressed through statute, but fundamental ones must be made through amendment: *e.g.,* XII (1804) (president and vice-president), XV (1870) (prohibiting denial or abridgment of the right to vote "on account of race, color or previous condition of servitude"), XIX (1920) (prohibiting denial or abridgment of the right to vote "on account of sex," XXIV (1964) (prohibiting denial or abridgment of the right to vote "by reason of failure to pay any poll tax or other tax") and XXVI (1971) (prohibiting denial or abridgment of the right to vote to those "eighteen years of age or older"). Into which category a proposed reform goes is often both a political and judicial decision. But if the latter, this still does not authorize the judiciary to make the change. At this juncture the debate may turn to the *Cumbersome* line of argument. *See infra,* below.

174. *See* comments and references accompanying notes 162 and 168, *supra.* Berger concludes that the judiciary "'has no right to divinations of public opinion which run counter to its last formal expression.'" Berger, *supra* note 171, at 198, quoting LEARNED HAND, THE SPIRIT OF LIBERTY 14 (1952). Such actions repudiate the framers' design because a judicial power to discern and implement a national consensus on injustice obviates the congressional function and totally ignores the amendment processes that were included to ascertain such fundamental changes in public sentiment.

175. Goldstein, *Judicial Review and Democratic Theory: Guardian Democracy v. Representative Democracy, A.P.S.A.* (September, 1985), mimeo, notes 2, n. 14 (citations omitted).

176. *See* Bridwell, *supra* note 106, at 475–476.

sound sense for the impeachment of Richard Nixon does not become nonsense when applied for refutation of Chief Justice Warren."[177]

Only Results Count!

In their effort to create a more effective national government, the delegates to the Philadelphia convention ignored a stipulation in the Articles of Confederation—Articles they had been obliged to honor. This stipulation provided that the Articles could be amended only by unanimous consent; hence, interpretivists forget that "even usurped power can eventually win recognition as legitimate."[178] The Supreme Court today likewise may legitimately ignore the framers' understanding of judicial review and heed only those "intentions [of the framers that] "further the democratic ideal."[179] "After enough time has passed . . . [even] the most lawless . . . governmental measures will finally be accepted as legitimate, and the time will be shorter if the lawlessness is tempered by social desirability."[180] Only results count.[181] "We must know what we want—and try to get it. We must . . . be fully 'result

177. Berger, *supra* note 111, at 623.

178. Lusky, *supra* note 111, at 415.

179. Miller, *supra* note 111, at 505–506. I have manipulated Miller's language without, I trust, manipulating his meaning. Robert Bork observes that those who favor results over the framers' understanding, reason as follows:

> The most common charge leveled against the idea of interpreting each provision of the Constitution according to the understanding of the generation of Americans who ratified and endorsed it is that better results can be, and have been, produced by ignoring what was intended. Often the accusation is stronger: The actual Constitution would allow *that* statute to stand, which would be intolerable.

Bork, *supra* note 115, at 261.

180. Lusky, *supra* note 111, at 415. Here again various groups of arguments overlap, illustrated by Lusky's claim that "societal needs" require such judicial actions and that the "Court is better fitted than other organs of government to effectuate" desirable social changes. *Id.*, at 414.

181. Some commentators contend, for example, that the results sought always have been contained within the Constitution and subsequent amendments. Moore comments: "The justification for judicial review is simply that people really have rights, and no consensus of the majority, even when embodied in a statute, should be allowed to trample on them." Moore, *supra,* note 75, at 395. Bork writes: "Professions and academic disciplines that once possessed a life and structure of their own have steadily succumbed, in some cases almost entirely, to the belief that nothing matters beyond politically desirable results, however achieved." Bork, *supra* note 115, at 1. McArthur maintains that many legal scholars today "have done much to confuse legal argument with its political underpinnings by dropping the language of the law and turning to policy arguments—be they from public morality, public values, emergent morality, or other abstractions—whenever it serves to advance their own solipsistic conception of the public good." John B. McArthur, *Abandoning the Constitution: The New Wave in Constitutional Theory,* 59 Tulane L. Rev. 280, 324 (1984). McArthur makes another distinction: original liberal theorists "shared a utilitarian skepticism about fundamental moral principles and therefore counselled deference to Congress and the majority as the source for fundamental values . . . [while today noninterpretivists] feel free to propose a new role for the Court because they are confident that right answers exist independently of legislative decision making." McArthur, *supra* note 181, at 323, n. 173.

oriented' in our study and analysis of the Constitution."[182]

In this regard, over the past four decades the Supreme Court has an enviable record: e.g., reforming race relations, expanding suffrage and representation, and promoting more humane treatment for criminal defendants.[183] Dershowitz provides this analogy:

> Our Bill of Rights is an insurance policy against tyranny. And every time a criminal defendant goes free or a pornographer is allowed to produce his filth we pay a premium into that insurance policy. But its ultimate purpose, like other life insurance policies, is not to give an immediate payback but to protect against some eventuality, and that eventuality is excessive government power, not excess individual rights.[184]

Thus, if interpretivist charges that the Supreme Court has acted illegitimately are given credence, many contemporary social reforms would be open to question, and that could lead to societal unrest, even rebellion.[185]

182. Miller, *supra* note 106, at 601. *See also* Knowlton, *supra* note 126, at 160–161. "The history of American constitutional adjudication can and should be written around the theme of the Supreme Court being result-oriented." Miller, *supra* note 111, at 502n.94.

183. Perry, *supra* note 125, at 703. "'The public cares about results,' says Professor Leonard Levy, 'and has little patience for reasons.' Levy and others do not like that, but there is little or nothing they can do about it." Miller, *supra* note 111, at 502 (quoting Leonard Levy, Against The Law: The Nixon Court and Criminal Justice 447n.88 (1974)). *See also e.g.,* Alfange, *supra* note 105, at 612–618; Kutler, *supra* note 130, at 512–514; Gibbons, *supra* note 111, at 853. Such arguments tend to merge with those under *Remain Adaptable* above.

184. Dershowitz, in Politics, *supra* note 52, at 16. Perry concludes:

> Sincerely to embrace . . . [an interpretivist view of] constitutionalism—to endorse the proposition that the original understanding is determinative of every question arising under the fourteenth amendment—is, given the decidedly limited character of the original understanding, to call for abandonment of virtually every fourteenth amendment doctrine of consequence: virtually all equal protection doctrines, including those relating to racial segregation; political and religious liberty doctrines; doctrines relating to legislative reapportionment and state criminal procedure; and, of course, modern substantive due process ("privacy") doctrine. (The list is too exhaustive!)

Perry, *supra* note 125, at 703.

185. Lusky, *supra* note 111, at 413–414. Some noninterpretivists concede that the time has come "to confess the reality of what the Supreme Court has long been doing in fourteenth amendment cases . . . [it] has been participating in the making of fundamental social policy," but defends those decisions on other grounds. Perry, *supra* note 125, at 703. The possibility of rebellion had been articulated by the early sixties:

> This proposal at its extreme has come to me in conversation. I have been told that the Supreme Court has a mandate from the Constitution to order termination of segregation in the schools and other places of assembly, but also that, even if the Constitution contained no such mandate, it would still have been the duty of the Supreme Court to order termination of segregation in 1954. This would have been its duty because segregation was the key to incipient revolution; another year or two without hope of relief from segregation, and there would have been bloodshed and burnings extensive enough to be called revolution. When the price of failure to act is so high, all departments of govern-

In Defense of the Publius Design

Publius rejected antifederalist arguments that the delegates at Philadelphia had ignored the provision in the Articles of Confederation that all amendments had to be approved unanimously by member states.[186] The ratifiers certainly did not authorize

---

> ment have an obligation to do the act which avoids the failure and averts the danger. If I interpret the argument correctly, Congress having failed to act, the President had as great an obligation to order the termination of segregation as did the Supreme Court.

Hyneman, *supra* note 126, at 261–262.

186. Publius justifies that departure in blunt terms: "It is absurd . . . to subject the well being of twelve states to one." Federalist, *supra* note 1, no. 40, at 251. He adds that the document that emerged from the convention was a mere proposal, having no legal status until and unless it was ratified by those who would live under it. *Id.,* at 252. Even if delegates had ignored the instructions given them or provisions in the Articles, "does it follow that the Constitution ought, for that reason alone, to be rejected?" *Id.,* at 254. Berger adds that "ratification operates to legitimize the agent's action in excess of authority." Berger, *supra* note 111, at 545n.101. *See also* Richard S. Kay, *The Illegality of the Constitution,* 4 Const. Comm. 57 (1987) ("But this illegality is indeed a paradox and not a contradiction.") *Id.,* 57–58.

My colleague Henry Paolucci already has taken us deeper into the political realities. See note 12, chapter 2, *supra.* I again turn to his analysis, excerpted from his forthcoming book on the European Community; with respect to the illegality issue:

> Thus the new federal government by means of which "We the People of the United States" committed themselves to seek to form a more perfect union, and all the rest, had gone into force without the consentual participation of two of the original thirteen states. A substantial "qualified majority" of the thirteen—two more than the minimally-required nine—had ratified. What of the two that had not? The new federal government made no attempt to decide on the juridical status of Rhode Island and North Carolina. Article VII of the ratified Constitution had specified that the convention votes of nine out of the thirteen would suffice to establish it "between the states so ratifying the same." As a distinguished American constitutional historian, Alexander Johnston, has written, posing the major questions:
>
> > What, then, was to be the status of the states which should refuse to ratify? Were they still in the Union, perhaps as territories? Or were they to secede from the Union? Or had the other states already seceded, and left them to keep warm the ashes of the old confederation, if they could? Was the Constitution itself a successful secession from the confederation? or did it only provide for necessary secession in this seventh article? [*Cyclopedia,* Vol. III, (John J. Lalor, ed.), 792.]
>
> What if Rhode Island, a small state (which had not participated in the Philadelphia Convention), had persisted in refusing to ratify? Had she insisted on her former status of sovereign independence, she knew she would have to reckon with the "unofficial propositions" of her far more powerful neighbors, Connecticut and Massachusetts, to "carve up her territory" between them. In the case of much larger North Carolina, there were already "official propositions in congress to repress or restrain" her indispensable commerce with neighboring states. There was no denying that a "United States of America" had existed, with internationally recognized boundaries, before the adoption of a new Constitution by a majority of nine of its members. Forbearance and the part of a powerful "qualified majority" gave the recalcitrant states time to make a show of voluntarily accepting the very terms of a "more perfect Union" that they had originally rejected.
>
> Back in those days, it was reported that George Washington himself had warned: "Should the states reject this excellent constitution, the probability is that an opportunity will never again be offered to cancel another in peace: the next will be drawn in blood."

judges to remedy constitutional defects.[187]

Even Congress—the institution that the delegates understood as embodying the republican principle—was granted only those powers consistent with achieving national objectives. Would those delegates then turn around and, in the vaguest of forms, hand to an unelected judiciary what amounts to the governing power?[188] And if not the delegates to the convention (or those who proposed and ratified subsequent amendments), who has authorized such judicial power? Bridwell comments: "Many interested readers would be offended by the realization that *only* a policy debate over results is involved in much constitutional law scholarship, and perhaps some would be too embarrassed to conclude that they had been so far outside the prevailing ideological fashion that they failed to realize that a jargonized, result-oriented dialogue had largely replaced the analytical device of separating principles from results."[189]

It is the ratifiers' understanding that certain rights have been constitutionalized that puts them beyond legislative competency: nothing else. If they do not enjoy constitutional status, they can be changed. Did Americans not lose judicially *rights* that once had existed under laissez-faire court decisions? Gaining, losing, and

---

And we have, of course, the first American President's public letter of December 14, 1787, when ratification was just beginning, in which we read:

> Should one state, however important it may conceive itself to be, or a minority of the states, suppose that they can dictate a constitution to the majority, unless they have the power of administrating the *ultima ratio,* they will find themselves deceived. [*Cyclopedia, id* at 793.]

Earlier we supplied the votes for and against of the states [this material was omitted] that did not ratify the new constitution unanimously. In some cases the margin was slim. It may be surmised that many responsible leaders in those states voted approval out of political prudence, understanding that a determined national majority, with much support in the states refusing ratification, might in due course take punitive action. The choice for the American people was soon enough understood to be one between "general confusion" or the "forcible maintenance of the national will," as Professor Johnston aptly put it, adding that, in either event, "the *ultima ratio* of sovereignty would have made its appearance; and, whatever the result of the struggle might have been, 'state sovereignty' would certainly have received before 1800 the quietus which it finally received in 1865."

187. Berger sums up the claim: "This is a result-oriented test of the existence of constitutional power: a certain result is desirable; *ergo* the power to produce it exists." Berger, *supra* note 121, at 784n.9.

188. *See supra,* chapter 2, text accompanying 79–81.

189. Bridwell, *supra* note 106, at 473. Elsewhere he adds:

> One finds the nearly universal adoption of a standard of analysis applied to constitutional issues—particularly the decisions of the Supreme Court of the United States—that amounts literally to nothing more than the attempt to define the *legitimacy* of judicial action solely according to its conformity to preconceived objectives and an identification of the *fait accompli* of a modern judicial revolution as a justification for its occurrence.

Bridwell, *supra* note 169, at 619.

changing the character of statutory rights and privileges is an integral part of politics.[190] Do smokers today feel denied access privileges that were previously enjoyed? Do those who wish not to wear motorcycle helmets or seat belts feel deprived of what were once permitted activities? Rights that lack constitutional status may be changed or eliminated by simple statute. Noninterpretivists often fail to make their case and judges who impose public policies that they deem to be morally superior to those of legislators abuse their power.[191]

Constitutional philosophies always have political results. They should never have political intentions. The proper question is not what are the political results of a particular philosophy but, under that philosophy, who chooses the political results. The philosophy of original understanding means that the ratifiers of the Constitution and today's legislators make the political decisions, and the courts do their best to implement them. That is not a conservative philosophy or a liberal philosophy; it is merely the design of the American Republic. A theory of judging that allows the courts to choose political results is wrong, no matter in which direction the results tend.[192]

The Amendment Process Is Cumbersome[193]

Courts must intercede on behalf of individuals and disadvantaged groups because "the path for amendment like that of legislation is often blocked by inertia or irresponsibility."[194] Take the example of malap-

190. These matters will be discussed in chapter 8, *infra*.

191. Van Alstyne comments:

> If the Constitution contains clauses not always the most noble (as of course it may), clauses that may weigh too heavily upon a judge's conscience, he or she may reassess the personal acceptability of the judicial task. If the task of *this* Constitution's scrupulous construction and application sometimes seems trivial, demeaning or even pernicious, the private conviction provides a thoroughly decent reason to find a career in something one believes to be less compromising and more ennobling.

Willim Van Alstyne, *Interpreting This Constitution: The Unhelpful Contributions of Special Theories of Judicial Review,* 35 U.Fla.L.R. 209, 226 (1983).

192. Bork, *supra* note 115, at 177. Once again I refer the reader to Appendix B with respect the difference of perception experienced by feelers and thinkers.

193. Bridwell observes:

> This schizophrenic attempt to equate results with legitimacy in particular instances, but to generally preserve majority rule as an option, presumably as insurance against a Court disposed to injustice, is at best a considered gamble resting on pragmatism rather than an intellectually definable principle. It is a gamble that only those who are dissatisfied with majority rule, with democracy, at least on some levels, ever decide to take.

Bridwell, *supra* note 169, at 639.

194. Kutler, *supra* note 130, at 525. The charge that the republican system understood by the framers and articulated by Publius is inadequate today, or has failed, already has been mentioned (*see supra,* chapter 4, text accompanying notes 173–182). Similarly, the charge that legislatures are too responsive to popular passions, thereby tending to diminish individual rights and to ignore

portioned legislatures. Surely it would have been "unreasonable to have expected" legislators to dilute their power, against their own interest, in favor of a more equitable representation. Why then should aggrieved parties suffer long delays in order to obtain societal reforms that have been effectively and responsibly handled by the judiciary?[195] "The Constitution is not a document frozen in time. . . . Amendment is not the only way the document can be changed."[196]

In Defense of the Publius Design

Those who contend that the legislative and amendment processes are cumbersome either do not understand those processes as did Publius; or they do and are willing to risk the most serious consequences in order to cure the defects they perceive. But when the delegates left in the hands of the people the final say on how they were to govern themselves, the choice was resolved. Contemporary critics are obliged to respect that choice.[197]

The choice was not uninformed. The delegates had no illusions about the character of republican government, particularly its tendency, like all popularly-based governments, to inject passion directly into public policy debates—a tendency that always had made popular governments unstable and destructive of individual rights. They had a far firmer grasp of those underlying realities than do contemporary noninterpretivists who characterize as cumbersome the very structural devices the delegates designed to create delay in policy formulation and implementation, to encourage consensus-building, and with it a greater likelihood that public policy would be made more consistently in the common interest.[198] The amendment processes are but an extraordinary application of the same princi-

---

isolated (permanent) minorities already has been discussed under *Vacuum* and *Best-suited.* If the framers did not authorize the judicial role that they favor, noninterpretivists argue that under the *Remain adaptable* symbol that fact is no longer determining. If the rights asserted are claimed to be contained in the Constitution or subsequent amendments, the discussion usually turns to the *Individual rights* symbol, to be discussed shortly.

195. Id. I manipulate Kutler's language without, I trust, changing his meaning. The charge that the amendment process is "cumbersome" is made by proponents of different political inclinations and appears elsewhere in the literature. *See* Lusky, *supra* note 111, at 406 and Posner, in Politics, *supra* note 52, at 43 ("the Constitution creates cumbersome procedures for amendment"). Kutler similarly characterizes the legislature. Kutler, *supra* note 130, at 525 ("like that of legislation").

196. Miller, *supra* note 111, at 488. *Compare id.,* at 488–489 with Berger, *supra* note 111, at 582–583.

197. The interrelationships of such arguments need not be repeated here, but the reader may wish to reexamine the framers' view on the arguments advanced under *Vacuum, Better Suited,* and *Results* above.

198. "Liberty is to faction what air is to fire [and] . . . as long as the reason of man continues fallible, and he is at liberty to exercise it, different opinions will be formed." Federalist, *supra* note 1, no. 10, at 78.

ples.[199] Why are these procedures today considered to be unfairly cumbersome?

Changes in public policy occur in the United States when a consensus emerges and the absence of such a consensus, or the need to build consensus, has always been the primary obstacle to social reform. For example, prior to the Civil War, Congress attempted to address the slavery issue (the Missouri Compromise) but in *Dred Scott* the Court cast even that partial solution aside, claiming that the framers prohibited it. After the Civil War, courts created property rights that judges again claimed originated with the framers. Courts today grow even bolder, no longer feeling obliged to locate their policy prejudices in the views of the framers. Noninterpretivists *assume* that the judiciary is authorized to rewrite the Constitution. They "obviously have no faith whatever in the wisdom or will of the great majority of the people."[200]

Even if noninterpretivists demonstrated to the satisfaction of Americans that existing procedures are more difficult than they need be, or that the delegates' reservations about passion being injected into public policy making may be safely ignored, or that the people have been unwilling to follow the advice of their moral superiors, how do such demonstrations confer additional power on the judiciary? At most one might argue that the amendment processes themselves should be amended—to make them easier.[201] The framers surely had greater faith in the people than do noninterpretivists today.

Responsibility for Individual Rights

Individual rights are not secure unless courts can prevent legislative interference. This noninterpretivist line of argument falls into three categories: the origin of individual rights; their nature; and the beneficial results that flow from considering them beyond the legislative power. Only the first two issues need be addressed here.[202]

THE ORIGIN OF RIGHTS. We noninterpretivists disagree among our-

199. *See supra,* chapter 1, text accompanying notes 38–39 (direct injection of passion into governing has always been a major flaw in pure democracy), and chapter 2, text accompanying notes 18–46 (judicial review is a cure for governmental tyranny, not abuse of majority power).

200. Berger, *supra* note 111, at 611.

201. Van Alstyne comments:

> The fact that the alteration of constitutional lines (i.e., the amendment of constitutional clauses) is difficult, has no bearing on the judicial obligation. If the means of altering constitutional lines is thought too difficult to tolerate correct decisions, that observation may propose a very good reason to alter the clause in the Constitution that makes amendment so difficult. It proposes no obvious reason, however, for judges to misstate the Constitution.

Van Alstyne, *supra* note 191, at 226.

202. The *Results* arguments have been considered above. The reader must keep in mind that in the literature these arguments overlap and support one another.

selves with respect to the origin of any claimed rights. One position, represented by Justice Goldberg, maintains that decisions of the Supreme Court merely reflect the intentions of those who framed and ratified the Constitution, particularly the Bill of Rights.[203] Others, such as Michael Perry, contend that the origin of individual rights (e.g., free speech) may be found in "the totality of the American experience—past ('tradition')."[204]

THE NATURE OF RIGHTS. Whatever the origin of these rights, we noninterpretivists agree that (1) the Supreme Court may expand the original protections afforded by these rights; (2) unless such rights are protected from legislative modification or abolition they are not rights in any meaningful sense; and (3) legislation touching upon the *preferred* status of certain rights must be subject to closer judicial scrutiny and supervision than those rights that are not or no longer preferred (e.g., economic rights).[205]

With respect to (1) and (2), let us take the example of the First Amendment's guarantee of "freedom of speech."[206] At the time the amendment was adopted it offered only limited protection. That meaning today would be too restrictive, offering insufficient protection from legislative encroachments. Accordingly, the Supreme Court has reinterpreted the free speech provision in order to adapt it to new situations: e.g., libel of public officials or flag-burning.[207] Or, in order to protect citizens from threats unknown to the framers, the Supreme Court should deduce a "value" drawn from several amendments and combine them into a new entity; e.g., a right to privacy.[208] In this manner, it may be necessary to ignore the original meaning of Bill of Rights provisions and to recognize that some rights are entitled to preferred status. The his-

203. *See supra,* text accompanying notes 160. See also Lusky's view that the Court acts as the framers' "surrogate" (McArthur, *supra* note 181, at 303, n. 107).

204. Perry, *supra* note 125, at 701.

205. Lusky, *supra* note 126, at 108. *See also* LAWRENCE TRIBE, AMERICAN CONSTITUTIONAL LAW sec. 11–1, at 565–568 (1978).

206. U.S. CONST., Amend 1.

207. Monaghan, *supra* note 110, at 123–124. See e.g., New York Times v. Sullivan, 376 U.S. 255 (1964) and Texas v. Johnson, 491 U.S. 397 (1989). *See supra,* chapter 4, text and comments accompanying notes 129–130. One variant is expressed as follows: "Deciding a case in such a way as to foster the basic values underlying the amendment and to give wider scope to the words utilized by the draftsmen does not seem to create a danger of judicial government." Knowlton, *supra* note 126, at 167.

208. "[In Griswold, Douglas J.] skipped through the Bill of Rights like a cheerleader—'Give me a P . . . give me an R . . . and I . . . ,' and so on, and found P–R–I–V–A–C–Y as a derivative or penumbral right." Robert G. Dixon, *The "New" Substantive Due Process and the Democratic Ethic: A Prolegomenon,* 1976 B.Y.U.L.REV. 43, 84 (1976), as quoted in LOCKHART, *supra* note 128, at 414.

torical fact that the Supreme Court's concern for individual rights did not begin until 1938 (when it was asserted for the first time that freedom of speech was at the heart of the American political tradition) is simply not relevant to such determinations.[209]

With respect to (3)—the need for special judicial scrutiny and supervision—we reason as follows: "Legislation affecting processes of free political discourse, association, or balloting . . . are the foundation for making substantive legislative and executive policy choices."[210] Thus, a double standard, wherein judges defer to the legislature on economic issues but not on personal rights issues, is perfectly defensible.[211] "Experience has demonstrated that by such action, judges have prompted, even forced, legislatures and executives to deal with problems they would rather ignore."[212] No other viable options exist: "How else should judges respond to injustice, as they perceive it?"[213] Another commentator puts it this way: "Our judicial branch, with the Supreme Court as its apex, is the greatest institutional and constitutional safeguard we possess; only those committed to libertarian suicide would sanction a transfer of the judicial guardianship of our basic civil rights and liberties to either the legislature or the executive or both!"[214]

In Defense of the Publius Design

The issue is not whether the rights claimed are worthy of support, but rather what meaning these rights had when the Constitution and its amendments were ratified; and who today is authorized to modify those rights or to create new ones. Is it the people or the courts?[215] Many of the rights claimed by noninterpretivists are no older than the judicial usurpations that created them. When the Bill of Rights was adopted, its provisions were well-understood and they applied only against the federal government.[216] While the Fourteenth

209. *See supra,* chapter 4, text, comment, and sources accompanying notes 71 and 112. It is impossible to trace the development of the preferred freedom doctrine here, *but see* Klaus Heberle, *From Gitlow to Near: Judicial "Amendment" by Absent-Minded Incrementalism,* 34 J of Politics 458 (1972).

210. Kutler, *supra* note 130, at 525. *See also* Abraham, *supra* note 112, at 476.

211. Abraham, *supra* note 112, at 472. *See supra,* chapter 4, text accompanying notes 72–75, and *infra* under the *Irreversible* argument.

212. Kutler, *supra* note 130, at 525.

213. *Id.*

214. Abraham, *supra* note 112, at 481. This particular quotation should not be interpreted to mean that Abraham favors unlimited judicial discretion. *See id.,* at 477.

215. Arguments regarding the framers' view of judicial power, the power of interpretation, and the legitimacy issue remain pertinent. For the sake of economy they are not here repeated.

216. *See supra,* chapter 2, text accompanying notes 99–133, and chapter 5, text accompanying notes 104–134, 185–194. Generally, see Hickok, *supra* note 42.

Amendment modified the 1787 federal-state relationship, it was congressional, not judicial, power that was expanded.[217] In short, neither the Bill of Rights nor the Civil War amendments offer a legitimate basis for judicial decisions that over the past century have severely circumscribed state public policy making. If noninterpretivists cannot root the legitimacy of the rights they claim in an understanding of the framers of the Constitution (or its amendments) neither rights exist nor are remedies required, and the legislature is completely free to address related issues in whatever manner they deem suitable.

There is less mystery about the framers' understanding of the Constitution and its subsequent amendments than one might expect from reading noninterpretivist literature. The Constitution contained no absolute bars against legislative actions beyond the meaning they had at the time of adoption—because such bars would be inappropriate in a republic where the people were sovereign and could hold elected representatives accountable. More extensive prohibitions would inhibit the people's ability to cope with changing circumstances.[218] While some citizens may find the protections afforded by the original meaning of the rights contained in the Constitution and subsequent amendments inadequate by today's standards, that discomfort does not and cannot authorize judges to create new constitutional rights or expand the original meaning rights had at the time of ratification, under the guise that all they are doing is interpreting the Constitution. Such interpretations are illegitimate impositions on the American people.[219]

Since noninterpretivists often cannot trace the meaning of the rights they claim to the framers' understanding, the people are not barred from legislating on those rights as long as, in doing so, such legislation continues to protect the meaning originally constitutionalized.[220] Noninterpretivists likewise often fail to present convincing proof that so-called "preferred freedoms" were as crucial to the framers as they are to contemporary intellectuals. For example, not only was application of the Bill of Rights to the states explicitly "voted down" by the First Congress,[221] but even "Jefferson, that apostle of free speech, in-

217. *See supra,* chapter 4, text accompanying notes 2–30.

218. Federalist, *supra* note 1, no. 84, at 513. *See supra,* chapter 2, text accompanying notes 3–10.

219. "Nowhere in the Constitution or its history is there an intimation that judges were given a power of attorney to fashion unenumerated 'minority rights' in order to remedy 'injustice, *as they perceive it.*'" Berger, *supra* note 111, at 605 (emphasis in original).

220. The role of the legislature, along with the issues of rights abuse and remedy, from the perspective of noninterpretivists, already has been discussed. *See supra,* chapter 4, text accompanying notes 114–128.

221. Berger, *supra* note 111, at 567. *See supra,* chapter 2, text accompanying notes 98–114.

sisted that the states have 'the exclusive right' to control freedom of the press."[222] Not until the late 1930s[223] did the Supreme Court accord the First Amendment a preferred status. And that was demanded by the intellectual fashion of the day—as had been economic rights before that. It was not demanded by the First Amendment.[224]

This New Court Role Is Accepted by the People

Some of us noninterpretivists contend that by ratifying the Bill of Rights and granting the Supreme Court the power of judicial review, the people implicitly authorized judges to expand the meaning of constitutional provisions in order to assure their effectiveness in circumstances unknown to the framers. That is what we believe the power of interpretation entails.[225]

Other noninterpretivists among us take a different tack. They ask "What sort of 'democratic' society do we—'in our own time'—want; what sort of relationship do we want to exist between the processes of majoritarian policy making and the judiciary; in particular, the Supreme Court?"[226] Whatever the framers' understanding of judicial power was, it is irrelevant today. "Political forms and practices are not, and therefore should not be deemed, immutable; they should be seized or discarded (or seized again) as they serve or deserve each generation's governance of itself."[227]

Still other noninterpretivists among us contend that Americans apparently have accepted a different role for the Supreme Court then the ratifiers anticipated since, practically speaking, they have accepted the results imposed upon them. "Perhaps for [interpretivists] . . . to whom moral values have no objective integrity, the *process* by which policy is made is more precious than the *content* of whatever policy is made," but for most people the good results of Supreme Court decisions far ex-

222. Berger, *supra* note 111, at 567.
223. *See,* chapter 4, comment accompanying note 112, *supra.*
224. *See supra,* chapter 4, text accompanying notes 105–113. As Berger notes: "Justice Stone cautioned against the danger that 'the constitutional device for the protection of minorities from oppressive majority action may be made the means by which the majority is subjected to the tyranny of the minority.'" Berger, *supra* note 171, at 178n.43 (quoting Alpheus Mason, Harlan Fiske Stone: Pillar of the Law 331 (1956)). Bridwell observes: "One might ask what makes the tyranny of the minority—the judiciary or those they favor—better than the tyranny of the majority? We get no answers." Bridwell, *supra* note 169, at 654.
225. *See supra,* chapter 4, text accompanying notes 114–151, for a thorough discussion of this claim. I do not forclose the possibility that judges may in good faith apply provisions to situations that could not have been contemplated by the framers.
226. Perry, *supra* note 125, at 699.
227. *Id.* These contentions cannot be separated from arguments made above under symbols *Adaptable, Vacuum, Best suited, Results,* and *Cumbersome.*

ceed any abstract loss of political power.[228] The "premise that constitutional policymaking by the judiciary contravenes our democratic creed" must therefore be rejected.[229] On the contrary, "the people at large have accepted the legitimacy of the basic decisions claiming enlarged judicial power."[230]

Claiming realism once again as a justification, we (or we noninterpretivists) contend that the people's acceptance of a new role for the Supreme Court can be implied from the Court's comparative weakness, when contrasted with the powers possessed by the political branches: "The voters, if aroused to indignant resistance against perceived usurpation, can and surely will cause their delegates in Congress to employ their undoubted authority to strip away virtually all power of the federal courts to engage in judicial review."[231] Since Americans have not attempted thus far to chastise the court or to remove or modify its appellant jurisdiction, the Supreme Court "power . . . is legitimate because it has been accepted implicitly or at least acquiesced in by the American people as well as by the other departments of government and the states."[232] Thus, if the people believed that the claim of illegitimacy had any credence, they would have countered any alleged judicial usurpations.[233]

In Defense of the Publius Design

Noninterpretivists grow more and more elitist. In the beginning they claimed that the public policies imposed on Americans were found in the Constitution. Then they abandoned that position and contended that a majority of Americans supported the public policy preferences imposed upon them. And when the people expressed their objections to these impositions, noninterpretivists urged the justices to ignore those objections and instead to do what was morally correct.[234]

228. *Id.,* at 698 (emphasis added). *See* Kutler, *supra* note 130, at 523–524. Perry adds: "Implicit in the position I suggest is the notion that there are ideals and sensibilities than can fairly be called characteristic of American society. . . . Implicit also is the notion that the courts, in particular the Supreme Court, are competent to discern these ideals and sensibilities and to decide cases in terms of them." Perry, *supra* note 125, at 699–700.
229. Perry, *supra* note 125, at 697. *See also* Bridwell, *supra* note 107, 908n.3. Certainly there are supporters of judicial power who do *not* believe it should have a free hand. *See e.g.,* Abraham, *supra* note 112, at 472; Kutler, *supra* note 130, at 523–524; Mendelson, *supra* note 125, at 162; Monaghan, *supra* note 110, at 131. Their difficulty, however, is agreeing upon some limiting principle. *See supra,* chapter 4, comment accompanying note 4.
230. Lusky, *supra* note 111, at 403; Monaghan, *supra* note 110, at 130. These arguments are related to those made under *Irreversible* above.
231. Lusky, *supra* note 111, at 412.
232. Forrester, *supra* note 130, at 1214.
233. Knowlton, *supra* note 126, at 162–163.
234. I refer to areas such as abortion, affirmative action, busing, police investigation and interro-

But there is no support from delegates to the Philadelphia convention, or in Publius' words, for the noninterpretivists' definition of judicial power. Only an amendment can change the responsibilities assigned to each branch. "'[A judge] may advise; he may persuade; but he may not command or coerce. He does coerce when without convincing the judgment he overcomes the will by the weight of his authority.'"[235] By ignoring the framers' design, noninterpretivists undermine the rule of law: "'Government by a self-designated elite—like that of benevolent despotism or of Plato's philosopher kings—may be a good form of government for some peoples, but it is not the American way.'"[236] The people, of course, may ignore their duty and abandon the design ratified by their forefathers, just as the legislature, executive, or judiciary might. But only by amendment could such changes be *legitimized.*

Noninterpretivists entirely misconstrue the people's acquiescence. Most Americans are not legal experts: they depend on those with legal expertise, in the same way that lawyers and judges depend for other services on auto mechanics and plumbers. What do the people hear from those they depend on, those who ought to know better? They are told by the "experts" that the newly proclaimed rights are already in the Constitution; or that what the Court is doing is within the justices' authority.[237] The people accept such declarations because they are unaware that their trust is misplaced. What is truly remarkable is that, despite grave misgivings regarding judicial public policy preferences, most Americans and elected representatives obey the policies announced by the judiciary. Such acquiescence should be attributed to the people's continued attachment to the framers' design, not a willingness to abandon it. It is the judiciary that has abandoned that design in the name of good results.

Interpretivists such as myself urge candor.[238] The truth of the matter is that noninterpretivists use legal and philosophic jargon to foist their personal opinions on the people since they believe their judgments are preferable to the ones that might be made by the people's elected representatives.[239] Once

---

gation, and flag-burning. I do not repeat here the viewpoints expressed in chapter 4 *supra* under "Contemporary Judicial Power."

235. Mendelson, *supra* note 125, at 63 (quoting Horning v. Dist. Columbia, 254 U.S. 135, 139 (1920) (Brandeis, J., dissenting).

236. Berger, *supra* note 111, at 531 (quoting Myres McDougal and Asher Lans, *Treaties and Congressional-Executive Agreements,* 54 YALE L. J. 534, 578 (1945)).

237. *See supra,* chapter 4, text accompanying notes 146–151.

238. Forrester, *supra* note 130.

239. Berger, *supra* note 111, at 615. He adds: "the Court was well aware that the people would not stomach its decision unless it was rested on the will of the framers, and therefore proceeded in disregard of the popular will." *Id.,* at 607.

the people understand, however, that those decisions rightfully belong to them, let us see how readily they acquiesce in decisions such as those that handcuff the police or sanction the burning of the American flag in the name of free speech. Such decisions are neither required by the Constitution nor sanctioned by the framers—and so remain for the people to decide.

The New Judicial Role Is Irreversible

We begin by restating arguments already defended at greater length: The Supreme Court is the primary protector of individual liberty; and since judges have life-tenure and are insulated from electoral accountability they are well suited to carrying out the Court's task. Louis Lusky concisely sums up the irreversible argument: "We may long for the old days when general acceptance of the *Marbury* theory of judicial review made constitutional analysis relatively simple and straightforward, [but] we cannot turn back the clock—and *will* not, and should not."[240] We noninterpretivists believe that "under the mandate of the Bill of Rights," the Court is best suited to "guard against the tyranny of the majority,"[241] and that "under our constitutional scheme these rights do and should expand."[242]

The Supreme Court must not retreat or waiver under majority pressure or condone the contraction of rights that are guaranteed by the Constitution.[243] "The Court will . . . continue to have powerful supporters and popular acceptance as long as it steadfastly maintains its determination to decide cases on principle and refuses to temper its application of constitutional guarantees with fears for its own political well-being."[244] After so many years, any return to the ratifiers' understanding of constitutional rights (as urged upon us by interpretivists) would itself be revolutionary, calling into question almost every major constitutional-law decision of the past forty years. Such a retreat is unlikely: whether Democrat or Republi-

240. Lusky, *supra* note 111, at 418 (emphasis added).
241. Goldberg, *supra* note 128, at 86–87. *See also* Perry, *supra* note 125, at 702n.55. For several reasons the text utilizes the views expressed by former Justice Goldberg. First, those views precede many more contemporary views explored elsewhere; second, they provide insight into the Warren Court majority reasoning; and finally, as those of a justice, Goldberg's views carry greater weight than those of other commentators.
242. Goldberg, *supra* note 128, at 85. For a practical application of this reasoning, see Escobedo v. Illinois, 378 U.S. 478 (1964) (J. Goldberg, for the Court).
243. *Id.*, at 73. For a more contemporary expression of this reasoning, see the comment by Dershowitz, text accompanying note 151, *supra*. The text should not be read, however, as applying only to the original meaning of such rights.
244. Goldberg, *supra* note 128, at 60. *See,* chapter 3, text accompanying note 107, *supra,* for a similar expression by Chief Justice Taney. Both justices in fact defend their own views, not those of the delegates.

can, conservative or liberal, all recent Court appointees accept the Court's new role.[245] Reversal of recent trends would be unprincipled and any hint that major decisions might be reversed (e.g., on abortion or racial discrimination) might lead to rioting or even rebellion.[246]

In Defense of the Publius Design

Once again the noninterpretivist theoretical arguments are unconvincing because they are not rooted either in the Constitution, the framers' understanding, or American constitutional history.[247]

Assertions that a new judicial role must be accorded legitimate status because it has become part of today's political reality is *not* a constitutional argument; it is merely an assertion. Why must illegitimate Supreme Court decisions be permitted to stand? New Deal legislators successfully reversed laissez-faire judicial economic decisions. Those who framed and ratified the Constitution left policy making in legislative hands, where corrections may occur by simple majority vote without dependence on the death, resignation, or goodwill of the justices. Repetition does not establish legitimacy.[248] The fact that presidential abuses had gone unpunished did not exempt Richard Nixon from being charged with the abuses he committed.[249]

Most contemporary exercises of judicial review go well beyond the intended boundaries of that power as understood by the delegates at Philadelphia and the ratifiers of

245. Lusky, *supra* note 111, at 403. He notes that is "a state of affairs which even the Nixon and Ford appointees . . . have accepted as largely irreversible." *Id.* Opposition to the confirmation of Robert Bork as an associate justice of the Court apparently rested upon the grounds that his appointment *might have* lead to the reversal of *results* that were favored by those who opposed his nomination.

246. Lusky, *supra* note 126, at 413.

> It is entirely likely that the huge and increasingly well-organized nonwhite majority would write finish to the open society. At the risk of seeming needlessly alarmist I say that though they lack the numbers and military strength to mount an armed revolt, nonwhites are fully capable of creating such civil disorder that wholesale searches, arrests without probable cause, official censorship, and other police state trappings would be thought essential for societal survival here.

Id.

247. Arguments made elsewhere regarding these topics are not repeated here. Henry Abraham observes:

> Judicial procedural and substantive policymaking of this sort is . . . an open invitation for further judicial activism. . . . It is tailor-made for the blurring of epistemological distinctions between constitutionally permissible actions by the political branches of government. It puts a premium on wisdom and fairness, neither of which, no matter how desirable and logical, is *required* by the terms of the Constitution of the United States.

Abraham, *supra* note 112, at 477.

248. Berger, *supra* note 111, at 544–545 (discussing Erie Ry. Co. v. Tompkins, 304 U.S. 64 (1938) (reversing a hundred-year-old precedent to the contrary). *See also* Ferguson v. Skrupka, 372 U.S. 726 (1963) (repudiating judicial second-guessing of legislative decisions on economic regulation).

the Constitution. Just as the Congress may go too far in its exercise of a valid power (e.g., interstate commerce), so too has the Supreme Court. "A congressional usurpation can be set aside by the Court; a judicial usurpation . . . can be met by impeachment."[250]

Abusive judicial decisions are directly linked to the people's right to govern themselves—a right the justices may not abandon without a formal declaration. The passage of time may dull one or more generation's appreciation of the right to self-government, but their unawareness can never destroy or dilute the right itself. Only amendment can accomplish that.

It Is Time to Recognize Explicitly the LegisCourt

The word *LegisCourt* has been explicitly articulated.[251]

> The Founding Fathers *intended* . . . to empower the Court to serve as the Founders' surrogate for the indefinite future—interpreting the Constitution not as they themselves would have directed if they had been consulted in 1787, but as is thought right *by men who accept the Founders' political philosophy—their commitment to self-government and the open society—and consider themselves obligated to effectuate that philosophy in the America of their own day.*[252]

While some noninterpretivists among us reject the above characterization as overstated (admitting that the noninterpretivist view of judicial power was never contained in the framers' design), other noninterpretivists urge candor—a recognition that such an approach was designed to shield the Court from "popular

249. Berger, *supra* note 14, at 622–623.

250. Berger, *supra* note 63, at 294n.50.

251. "The merit of our Legiscourt in our democratic framework is worthy of further straight forward analysis and evaluation, particularly in relation to long-range effects." Forrester, *supra* note 130, at 1216. Or, as expressed by another commentator: "What I hope to show is that some interesting and possibly constructive ideas suggest themselves upon acceptance of the premise that the Court is a legislature." Hazard, *supra* note 112, at 1. Identification of the Legiscourt symbol does not imply that the viewpoint is widely accepted, at least explicitly. Nevertheless, its identification is justified. The position that the Court should act as a legislature is new, not arising even in the most activist period of judicial activism: laissez-faire. Judges then often illegitimately vetoed *legislative initiations;* they did not, however, initiate judicial legislation akin to that done in such areas as abortion or police interrogation cases. Second, there can be no denying the concrete practical effects of judicial policy making on the body politic, regardless of whether one considers them beneficent or maleficent. Third, the proposed legiscourt appears to be a logical culmination of the various components described within this section. Fourth, having accepted the prior noted lines of argumentation, proponents of judicial power fail to identify any limits for the judicial power they advocate.

252. Lusky, *supra* note 126, at 21 (emphasis in original). *See also* Ely, *supra* note 105, at 409; Hazard, *supra* note 112, at 2–8. Lusky does not accept unlimited Court power as legitimate, but there are some practical problems with the limits he proposes. Furthermore, he never articulates what is meant by the "open society." *See supra* chapter 4, text accompanying notes 107–113. I assume, however, it is intimately associated with the preferred freedom position. *See* supra, comment accompanying note 207.

outcry."[253] The time has come, however, to admit that the Court has been legislating instead of judging and that the justices should "state this frankly and clearly in their decisions." Americans are "entitled to truth in judging."[254]

> Unlike a court, its [present] primary function is not judicial but legislative. It is a governing body in the sense that it makes the basic policy decisions of the nation, selects among the competing values of our society, and administers and executes the directions it chooses in political, social and ethical matters.[255]

In Defence of the Publius Design

While the admission by a few judges that they have imposed their values on the American people is refreshing, it is not enough.[256] Many judges not only continue to deceive the American people but themselves as well, believing that they uphold the rule of law when in fact they undermine it in the name of good results. They fail to grasp that they have abandon the framers' design and violate their oath of office, gathering power to themselves under the guise of interpretation.

Noninterpretivists must "plainly . . . acknowledge that they seek to transfer policymaking from the people and their elected representatives to an unelected, unaccountable judicial oligarchy."[257] The emergence of the LegisCourt "is not a decision for academe but for the sovereign people who at long last are entitled to be told that the Court has taken over national policy making, and to be asked to rat-

253. Lusky, *supra* note 126, at 307. *See* also Perry, *supra,* note 40, at 265–75.

254. Forrester, *supra* note 130, at 1214.

255. *Id.* Forrester adds: "In the present scheme of things, the Supreme Court's nature is not primarily that of a court. Its role and function are more closely akin to that of a legislative body or of an executive oligarchy. Perhaps it is our central committee. The search for analogues is an interesting one. But comparatists tell me there is no exact copy—now or in political history." *Id.,* at 1217. Another commentator raises the question: "What are the proper limitations on a legislative body that is thought of as a Court?" Hazard, *supra* note 112, at 15.

256. Lying, of course, is a fundamental moral concept. *See* Berger, *supra* note 111, at 581–582 (citing Henry Mencken, Treatise of Right and Wrong 194 (1934)). Berger adds:

> It is because the Court is well aware that the people would not, if they knew, tolerate the displacement of the popular will expressed by the Framers and Ratifiers, that it cannot afford "truth in judging". . . . More baldly put, disclosure would have destroyed the myth that the Court speaks as the voice of the Constitution rather than as the voice of the Justices' own values. For the people have a greater respect for the Constitution than for the Justices.

Id., at 587.

257. Berger, *supra* note 124, at 371. Gunther comments: "The ultimate justification for the Reynolds ruling is hard, if not impossible, to set forth in constitutionally legitimate terms. It rests rather on the view that courts are authorized to step in when injustices exist and other institutions fail to act. This is a dangerous—and I think illegitimate—prescription for judicial action." Gerard Gunther, *Some Reflections on the Judicial Role: Distinctions, Roots and Prospects,* 1979 Wash. U.L.Q. 817, 825 (1979).

ify the takeover. That will be the moment of truth."[258]

CONCLUSION

None of the arguments associated with the nine symbols attempting to legitimize contemporary judicial power, separately or collectively, overcome the interpretivist charge of illegitimacy. The bottom line is that noninterpretivist arguments ultimately are contrary to the framers' design and are inconsistent with the republican principles approved by the people and incorporated into the Constitution and its subsequent amendments.

Many noninterpretivists, however, insist that both an expanded judicial role and the doctrines it has spawned are acceptable, and that both need not be grounded in the framers' design. Since first considering such contentions in 1981[259] I have reached three conclusions:

First, noninterpretivists change the framers' understanding of the Constitution, judicial power, and the Bill of Rights. They ignore or distort the history surrounding the adoption of the Constitution and Bill of Rights, and in doing so many of them refuse to acknowledge, perhaps deceiving themselves, that in fact they manipulate the text and radically depart from the ratifiers' understanding of those documents. Furthermore, they strive to create a continuity with the nation's earliest precedents where often none exists.

Second, an understanding of the framers' design is essential to any attempt to reassert the people's right to self-government. In that regard, if, as suggested, what the people have done helps to illuminate what the people *meant to do,* then untainted historical accounting can contribute to an understanding of that design.[260] Consistent application of canons of construction also is crucial to a scholar's ability to properly evaluate Court decisions.

Third, noninterpretivists often use precedents that either ignored, failed to address, or refused to address, misrepresentations of U.S. history or the traditional scope of judicial power.[261] I view those precedents as a trail of bread crumbs that interpretivists may follow in their effort to retrace the full breadth of the right of Americans to self-government. Scholarly shoddiness should no longer be accepted as a means to adapt the Constitution.

Constitutional scholars are shepherds of sorts; they have an obligation to cry "wolf,"[262] identifying

258. Berger, *supra* note 111, at 575.

259. *See* Gangi, *supra* note 102.

260. *See infra,* chapter 7, text and comment accompanying note 106.

261. *See e.g.,* Kamisar, *supra* note 59, at 77–84, and James B. White, *Reflections on the Role of the Supreme Court: The Contemporary Debate and the "lessons" of History,* 63 JUDICATURE 162, 170–173 (1979).

262. John H. Ely, *The Wages of Crying Wolf: A Comment on "Roe v. Wade,"* 82 YALE LAW JOURNAL 920 (1973). The idiomatic meaning of to cry wolf, of course, is to raise a false alarm, while

each wolf that has periodically appeared disguised in sheep's progressivist clothing. The shepherd's cry should resound in the hills, even if he believes that in the long run a little thinning would be good for the flock. To the flock, a wolf is a wolf is a wolf. For shepherds to decide—because they truly believe—that this *particular* progressivist wolf, unlike earlier progressivist wolves, is a *good* wolf, thereby substituting their judgment for that expressed by their master (the Constitution), violates the master's trust and endangers the flock. That is what Publius teaches.

The ratifiers' understanding of some constitutional provisions cannot be illegitimately declared irrelevant in contemporary circumstances—especially on a pick-and-choose basis (e.g., First, Fourth, Fifth, Sixth, and Fourteenth amendments; and the legitimate scope of the judicial power). At the same time, the ratifiers' understanding on other matters (e.g., the limits of the executive and legislative powers) is considered to be perpetually relevant. If historical and doctrinal continuity is repeatedly broken in the area of personal liberties, fidelity to other constitutional components is inevitably risked. These issues will be discussed in the concluding chapters.

in the text the usage is affirmative—the scholar claiming the sheep are in danger. Similarly, I must acknowledge that some alarms may prove unfounded—something akin to economists predicting nine of the last three recessions.

PART V.

RETURNING TO SELF-GOVERNMENT

CHAPTER SEVEN

The Interpretivist Credo

I am convinced that this is the safest course for your liberty, your dignity, and your happiness. I affect not reserves which I do not feel. I will not amuse you with an appearance of deliberation when I have decided. I frankly acknowledge to you my convictions, and I will freely lay before you the reasons on which they are founded. The consciousness of good intentions disdains ambiguity. I shall not, however, multiply professions on this head. My motives must remain in the depository of my own breast. My arguments will be open to all and may be judged of by all. They shall at least be offered in a spirit which will not disgrace the cause of truth.[1]

I assume the reader no longer equates interpretivism with literalism, understands that judges (intentionally or not) have abused their power, and concedes that a legitimate distinction exists between constitutionally mandated rights and beneficent public policy. The purpose of this chapter then is twofold: to demonstrate by example that the interpretivist position is consistent with and capable of continuing the framers' constitutional design; and second, to illustrate that noninterpretivism over time cannot deliver what it promises: an adaptable Constitution. Noninterpretivism hides from the American people an important truth, to borrow Publius' words, that judges have often in the post century imposed their will, not judgment.[2] I also continue my efforts to persuade the reader that certain important contemporary Court doctrines ultimately rest on criteria either defective or illegitimate, or that those doctrines are inconsistent with our political tradition, or are improbable, given the framers' understanding of those provisions at the time of the Constitution's ratification.

1. James Madison, Alexander Hamilton and John Jay, The Federalist Papers [hereinafter Federalist] no. 1, at 36.
2. *Id.*, no. 78, at 469.

INTERPRETATION AND INTERPRETIVIST PRINCIPLES

The Constitution, as I have stated before, contains three kinds of provisions: those that detail specific requirements, those that contain broad grants of power, and those that contain specific prohibitions. In the text that follows, at least one example for each type of provision will be provided. The reader is encouraged, however, to apply the interpretive principles detailed to similar constitutional provisions.

Specific Provisions: Are We Not All Literalists—Sometimes?

The Constitution contains language that is specific and interpretivists contend that the ratifiers understood that those provisions would have fixed meaning, regardless of subsequent changes in circumstances. I turn to some specific examples.

TWO-YEAR TERM.[3] Delegates to the convention argued about how long a member of the House of Representatives should serve,[4] and their decision for a two-year term must be understood in the context of competing federalist and antifederalist principles regarding representation, the distances representatives would have to travel, and other structures contained in the Constitution (e.g., six-year terms for senators, one-third elected every two years,[5] and the president elected every four years).[6]

A majority of delegates maintained that the annual elections favored by a minority would be perhaps too much of a good thing,[7] making representatives and the executive too responsive to short-term citizen passions.[8] The majority argued that longer terms would contribute to greater governmental stability, and any danger that such longer terms would make elected officials less accountable to the people was at least

3. U.S. CONST., art. 1, sec. 2.1.

4. *See* FEDERALIST, *supra* note 1, nos. 52–58.

5. U.S. CONST., art. 1, sec. 3.1.

6. *Id.*, art. 2, sec. 1.1.

7. Federalists claimed that the proposed two-year term was consistent with the republican principles of frequent and regular elections. FEDERALIST, *supra* note 1, no. 57, at 351. "The most effectual [means for sustaining the quality of representation] . . . is such a limitation of the term of appointments as will maintain a proper responsibility to the people."); id., at 352 ("without the restraint of frequent elections") ("habitual recollection of their dependence on the people"). Summing up: "The ingredients which constitute safety in the republican sense are a due dependence on the people, and a due responsibility." *Id.*, no. 70, at 424. The proposed two-year term was attacked by antifederalists who asserted that it abandoned the principle of annual elections, and that the delegates also had failed to provide for rotation in office. *See supra*, chapter 1, comments accompanying notes 25, 46, 63, and 66.

8. *Cf.* FEDERALIST, *supra* note 1, no. 37, at 226–227 (energy and stability), with no.. 70, at 424 ("The ingredients which constitute energy in the executive are unity; duration; an absolute provision for its support; and competent powers.")

partially offset by provisions for staggered elections.[9] Such elections would serve to vent a rising popular passion because an emerging majority could see its influence spreading, while making it impossible for that public passion to affect every governing structure to the same degree simultaneously.[10] With typical candor, Publius explained that even if the structures contained in the Constitution delayed the adoption of some good public policies, that was a small price to pay to avoid the erratic, weak, and indecisive policies that typified past popularly based governments.[11]

Ratification of the Constitution thus fixed a two-year term for members of the House of Representatives.[12] Evidently the ratifiers had been persuaded that in favoring a popularly based government, the danger of both governmental and majority tyranny persisted (although perhaps not as great a danger as contended by the antifederalists) and that adoption of the proposed constitution, containing the structures it did, favorably balanced their concern for responsive government with the desire for an effective one.[13]

May Congress today pass a statute changing the two-year term for members of the House, if it made a persua-

9. *See* Federalist, *supra* note 1, nos. 10, 51. *See also* no. 15, at 111 ("spirit of faction" will "poison . . . deliberations"); no. 21, at 139–140 ("A successful faction may erect a tyranny on the ruins of order and law"); no. 36, at 218 ("as great rivalships between . . . mechanic or manufacturing arts . . . as . . . between any of the departments of labor and industry"), id. at 221 ("As neither can *control* the other, each will have an obvious and sensible interest in this reciprocal forbearance."); no. 63, at 384, speaking of the Senate ("such an institution may be sometimes necessary as a defense to the people against their own temporary errors and delusions"), *id.* ("some irregular passion"); *id.* at 385 ("violent passion"). *See supra,* chapter 1, text accompanying notes 31–44.

10. Staggered electoral successes might well diminish or destroy the public passion because as any reforms were adopted, even in diluted form, the underlying majority coalition could break down—some portions of it being satisfied and willing to go no further. Majorities can be very fluid in the United States, and the traditional kiss of death for such majorities has been the successful enactment of parts of their program.

11. Publius observed the following:

> It may perhaps be said that the power of preventing bad laws includes that of preventing good ones; and may be used to the one purpose as well as to the other. But this objection will have little weight with those who can properly estimate the mischiefs of that inconstancy and mutability in the laws, which form the greatest blemish in the character and genius of our governments. . . . The injury which may possibly be done by defeating a few good laws will be amply compensated by the advantage of preventing a number of bad ones.

Federalist, *supra* note 1, no. 73, at 443–444. With respect to the infusion of passion, *see supra,* sources cited at note 9; with respect to delegates seeing themselves as intelligent democrats, *see supra,* cross-references cited at note 7, and, with respect to critical reading of the framers by such authors as Allen Smith and Charles Beard and contemporary literature challenging those assessments, *see* George W. Carey, In Defense of the Constitution 7–15 (1989).

12. *See supra,* chapter 5, text accompanying notes 43–57.

13. For earlier discussion of related topics see supra, chapter 1, text accompanying notes 31–44, and chapter 2, text accompanying notes 18–46.

sive case that incumbent advantages, changes in transportation, fund raising, political advertising expenses, and so forth, argued convincingly for shorter or longer terms?[14] Assume further that polls unanimously reported that such a change was acceptable to an overwhelming percentage of Americans: if a Supreme Court decision declared that such a piece of congressional legislation was unconstitutional, would the reader categorize this as literalism?

Interpretivists contend that such legislation should be declared unconstitutional on the obvious ground that whatever changes of circumstances have occurred since ratification, for the ratifiers *two years* presumably meant two years and, that the meaning of such specific terms must remain fixed unless otherwise modified through amendment. This is not a literal interpretation: it is the only interpretation consistent with a written constitution and the responsibilities accorded the federal judiciary.[15]

PRESIDENTIAL REELIGIBILITY. At the Philadelphia convention, delegates argued vigorously before reaching an affirmative decision that the president should be indefinitely eligible for reelection.[16] They weighed the need for competent and effective leadership against increased prospects for abuse. The nation remained bound by that decision until the Twenty-second Amendment (1951) limited a president to two terms. There are those like myself, however, who still find Publius' arguments in favor of unlimited reeligibility persuasive.

Query: May the Supreme Court uphold a statute authorizing a third presidential term because Congress decides that the circumstances surrounding adoption of the Twenty-second Amendment no longer exist and might safely be ignored?

An interpretivist would insist that however persuasive Americans once found the arguments favoring unlimited electability of the president, they repudiated that view when they ratified the Twenty-second Amendment. When considering the statute before them, the justices remain obliged to turn to the intent of the framers and

14. *See, e.g.,* Raoul Berger, *Lawyering vs. Philosophizing: Facts or Fancies,* 9 U. DAYTON L. REV. 171, 194–195 (1984) (criticizing the position that at "'some future time the senatorial age requirement [i.e., having attained the age of thirty] might . . . plausibly be deemed ambiguous . . . [or] interpreted in a nonliteral sense,' for example, by viewing it as a 'symbolic reference to maturity.'").

15. A judicial inquiry also might include what purpose the framers believed the two-year term would serve, and in making such an inquiry presumably judges would follow general rules of statutory construction. The interpretivist appreciates the fact that, in the debate over the duration of terms to be contained in the proposed constitution, the framers decided as they did not because the number two possessed any magical powers but because they believed that a two-year term fitted with other aspects of the structures selected. The number, in any event, was not inconsistent with the overall design. *See also* FEDERALIST, *supra* note 1, nos. 71–72.

16. U.S. CONST., art. 1, sec. 2.1.

ratifiers of the Twenty-second Amendment, not to the intent of the original ratifiers. For better or worse, Americans rejected their ancestors' advice. Should a question arise on the subject of reeligibility—one not clearly resolved by examining the intent of those framing the Twenty-second Amendment—then perhaps the justices may consider other factors. But in doing so, they should consistently follow recognized canons of construction.[17]

PRESIDENTIAL SUCCESSION. For some time the nation struggled with the issue of presidential succession and disability. Statutory provisions were enacted, but several disturbing situations over a period of 150 years eventually prompted Americans to decide that instead of continuing the statutory basis, they should make a specific solution—however imperfect—part of the Constitution. This was the Twenty-fifth Amendment (1967).

If the specific intentions of the Twenty-fifth Amendment's ratifiers can be clearly discerned, interpretivists contend that those intentions are binding, superseding any prior understanding of congressional discretion in the areas of succession and disability. The people consented only to be governed by such and such requirements, and only they may legitimately elevate statutory requirements to constitutional status.[18] In putting forth these principles, interpretivists view themselves not as literalists but as defenders of the Constitution.

Broad Grants of Power: The Commerce Clause

I contend that broad grants of power contained in the Constitution must be approached differently than those provisions containing specific ("fixed") meaning. Take, for example, the clause that provides for congressional control of interstate commerce?[19] The delegates surely had some specific purpose in mind when they empowered the Congress "to regulate Commerce with foreign Nations, and among the several states, and with Indian Tribes." From such language the delegates apparently did not intend to give Congress control over all commerce but only that which was specified.[20]

Publius mentions that the com-

17. Canons of construction already have been explored in some depth. The reader may assume that their consistent application is presumed throughout this chapter. *See supra,* chapter 5, text accompanying notes 58–80.

18. *See supra,* chapter 5, text accompanying notes 104–134. For a more specific application of these principles, *see infra,* text accompanying notes 38–90.

19. U.S. CONST., art. 1, sec. 8.3. Raoul Berger presents an alternative interpretivist approach to the one contained in the text. Such differences are to be expected. *See* William Gangi, *On Raoul Berger's Federalism: The Founders' Design,* 13 LAW AND SOCIAL INQUIRY 801 (1988).

20. There is reason to believe that the framers considered the two categories to be related. FEDERALIST, *supra* note 1, no. 42, at 267 ("without this supplemental provision, the great and essential power of regulating foreign commerce would have been incomplete and ineffectual."). Subse-

merce power was a new one[21] and, perhaps for that reason it was less capable of precise expression than terms such as *due process.*[22] In any event, by its inclusion, the framers obviously thought the commerce power essential to the responsibilities assigned to the federal government. By including the language they did, interpretivists assume that the framers intended to convey *something;* and whatever that something was, they expressed it as precisely as the subject matter, experience, and prudence permitted.[23] Hence, in attempting to comprehend the ratifiers' meaning, an interpretivist would recall that the Articles of Confederation had failed to address the interstate commerce issue adequately.[24] The delegates, therefore, presumably did not perceive the power to regulate commerce "among the several States" in frugal terms.

The foregoing, however, provides little practical guidance on the crucial issue of at what point does the federal power to regulate commerce intrude upon the reserved powers of the states? I contend that the extent of the commerce power should be left to Congress to resolve and, in the absence of a specific prohibition, how narrowly or broadly that delegated power should be interpreted ultimately should be a political question best resolved by the political branches—an expectation shared by Publius.[25]

But, the reader may ask, is it not

---

quent discussions omit any reference to the application of the commerce power to American Indian affairs.

Presumably purely *intrastate* commerce did not concern the framers, who believed that such commerce remain totally under state control. That distinction continues to be championed by reputable scholars such as Raoul Berger. *See* Gangi, *supra* note 19, at 806. The determination of whether or not a particular event is interstate or intrastate is considered by some to be a matter of fact, a matter of constitutional law, or a political question.

21. FEDERALIST, *supra* note 1, no. 45, at 293 ("The regulation of commerce, it is true, is a new power; but that seems to be an addition which few oppose and from which no apprehensions are entertained.") In fact, Publius also uses the term *intercourse* ("the intercourse throughout the Union will be facilitated by new improvements") *Id.,* at 102. *Compare* Chief Justice John Marshall using that same phrase in Gibbons, chapter 4, text accompanying note 44, *supra.*

22. "Summing up 400 years of history, Hamilton said, 'The Words "due process" have a precise technical import, and are only applicable to the process and proceedings of the courts of justice; they can never to referred to an act of the legislature.'" Raoul Berger, *The Fourteenth Amendment: Light from the Fifteenth,* 74 NW. L.REV. 311, 334 (1979). *See also, e.g.,* chapter 3, comment accompanying note 9 (some provisions in the Constitution are "addressed especially" to the courts).

23. *See* FEDERALIST, *supra* note 1, no. 11, at 89 ("An unrestrained intercourse . . . will advance the trade of each by an exchange of their respective productions"); *id.,* no. 12, at 91 ("prosperity of commerce is . . . the most productive source of national wealth"); *id.,* no. 34, at 211 ("The convention thought the concurrent jurisdiction preferable to that subordination." [Publius is speaking here specifically of the taxing power, but his comments seem equally applicable to the commerce power.]

24. Publius identifies lack of such a power as a weakness of the Articles of Confederation. FEDERALIST *supra* note 1, no. 42, at 267. *See supra,* chapter 1, text accompanying notes 80–83.

the ultimate responsibility of the United States Supreme Court to define the extent of the commerce power? After all, the commerce power is specifically contained in the text and the primary task assigned to the judiciary is that of interpretation—and, moreover, of keeping the political branches within the boundaries of powers granted them. Furthermore, the text implies that limits do exist on the federal power to regulate commerce, since commerce—other than that specified—apparently is beyond congressional control.[26] Finally, even upon the standards put forth by Publius, the justices are charged with the responsibility to "fix" the required limits since the delegates empowered the judiciary to declare void any law contrary to the ratifiers' will. Should Congress go beyond that will, surely interpretivists, especially, must acknowledge that the Supreme Court is obliged to declare such legislation null and void.

The above inquiry is legitimate and the reasoning is beyond reproach. But I believe that even interpretivist judges—guided by the principles previously enunciated—should not resolve whether or not the Congress has gone too far, if that resolution ultimately rests on an assessment of whether or not exercise of the power in question will reap (or had already reaped) beneficent results. I contend that the only criterion that should be employed by judges is whether or not, in exercising a power granted to it, Congress has exceeded the ratifiers' understanding of that power or has ignored one of the contained prohibitions.

I will illustrate my position more concretely. Assume a case develops that raises the issue of whether or not the Congress has exercised the commerce power beyond its intended bounds. Furthermore, assume precedential support exists for a Supreme Court decision that holds the Congress indeed has gone too far; has in the opinion of a majority of justices exercised the commerce power beyond the limits understood by its ratifiers.[27]

Further assume that a consensus develops among constitutional scholars that concurs in the assessment; that, if not infallibly right, the Court's decision constitutes a reasonable interpretation of the ratifiers' intentions and related historical materials.

25. "I repeat here what I have observed in substance in another place, that all observations founded upon the danger of usurpation ought to be referred to the composition and structure of the government, not to the nature or extent of its powers." FEDERALIST *supra* note 1, no. 31, at 196. I view the contention in the text as but another way of stating the principles enunciated by Chief Justice John Marshall in such cases as M'Culloch v. Maryland, 17 U.S. (4 Wheat.) 316 (1819) and Gibbons v. Ogden, 22 U.S. (9 Wheat.) 1 (1824). *See supra,* chapter 3, for discussion of those cases.
26. In any event: "The law is replete with imprecise boundaries. Difficulty in drawing the line at twilight between day and night will not prevent a court from distinguishing between bright day and blackest night." Berger, *supra* note 14, at 63.
27. Carter v. Carter Coal, 298 U.S. 238 (1936).

The Court's conclusion, after all, may be correct; and even if it is not, as Lincoln observed, it is best to endure.[28] Things are getting a little sticky, but as yet no constitutional or political crisis exists.

In the above scenario, consistent with the framers' design, the Court performs the duty the delegates assigned to it: it set aside an attempt by this generation to overstep the limits imposed by the ratifiers. In the face of such a ruling, should the people's elected representatives still maintain that the statute struck down is a necessary one, they can, by exercising the epitome of republican rule—the amendment process—change the Constitution.

But what if more than one scholarly assessment is viable? What if Congress charges that the Court's holding was wrong: wrong because the framers did *not* in fact define commerce so narrowly; or wrong because the framers' understanding of the proper subjects of the commerce power was based on the specific conditions of the time; or wrong because the framers also understood that such commerce was integral to the public good?[29] And what if Congress goes further, maintaining that any judicial inquiry into the ratifiers' understanding should not only take their particular views of commerce into consideration, but it also should consider the larger purposes for which the power had been extended: a unified national economy?[30] Congress might also contend that the decision the justices reached had not in fact depended on the framers' understanding of the extent of the commerce power, but rather on what the justices personally believed constituted good national economic policy.

In sum, congressional critics could assert that, unlike the delegates or Publius, the Court failed to consider that issues of economic policy are integral to the union's health, perhaps survival, and in such instances it is enough that the reserved powers of the states are protected within the created structures (e.g., equal state

28. Daniel Moynihan, *What Do You do When the Supreme Court is Wrong?,* 57 The Public Interest 3 (1979).

29. *See e.g.,* Federalist,, *supra* note 1, no. 17, at 118 ("the supervision of agriculture . . . can never be desirable cares of a general jurisdiction"). *But see id.,* no. 60, at 369–370 (commerce is in general interest of all classes).

30. *See supra,* chapter 5, text accompany notes 154–160. Berger argues, for example, that if the intent is clearly known, it takes precedence over the specific words. *See supra,* chapter 5, comment accompanying note 27. Some scholars might argue that the line of reasoning in the text parallels the higher levels of abstraction or generality arguments favored by noninterpretivists. *See supra,* chapter 5, comment accompanying note 118. There is some truth to that contention but distinctions do exist. Whereas a broad construction of the powers granted Congress finds support in the earliest decisions of the Supreme Court (*e.g.,* M'Culloch, Gibbons), the same cannot be said for the placing of additional restrictions on Congress. Most important, the position taken in the text here and in the pages that follow ultimately locates the decision-making power with the people's elected representatives, not the courts, as is the case with noninterpretivist reasoning.

representation in the Senate and electoral accountability).[31] The ratifiers did not authorize the Supreme Court to write into the Constitution its preference for one abstract governing principle over another; and unless the justices can find in the framers' intent some support for doing so, or can clearly establish that the actions of Congress violate the "manifest tenor" of the Constitution, as understood by its ratifiers, Congress should decide what actions are "necessary and proper" in whatever circumstances exist. *Courts ought to defer to those who can be held accountable.*[32]

Congress then could legitimately challenge the Court's earlier ruling by repassing the same, or similar, legislation as that which had been set aside—for not even a prior ruling of unconstitutionality forecloses legislative reassessment.[33] Congress also could play hardball, threatening or removing the Court's appellate jurisdiction.[34] Things would be definitely getting more sticky.

Should the preceding scenario develop, there would now be several possibilities. Upon again reconsidering the legislation before it, the Supreme Court may once again strike the legislation down. The Justices swore an oath to uphold the Constitution and it would be their duty to do so. Perhaps this time, however, their decision will be more persuasive, rest more on accepted principles, contain greater insight and evidence regarding the framers' understanding, and the whole package may be better argued and find wider support among constitutional scholars, judges, and elected representatives.

Alternately, maybe enough time passes between the first and second declaration of unconstitutionality that the need for the enacted legislation is no longer pressing or generates less passion. The justices then can call upon all those of good faith to demonstrate their fidelity to the Constitution—for they have done so—and again to urge Congress, if it believes such legislation still is crucial, to turn to the amendment procedures.

Or some justices, perhaps a single justice, might reconsider their earlier

31. *See supra,* chapter 3, text accompanying note 32 ("for the benefit of all").

32. U.S. CONST., art 1, sec. 8.18 ("necessary and proper"). See supra, chapter 2, text accompanying note 65 ("manifest tenor"), and 95–97 (to the fullest extent). Wallace Mendelson recounts this principle: "The Thought of course was that the fewer social issues preempted by courts, the more that are left for resolution via the democratic process." Wallace Mendelson, *Mr. Justice Douglas . . .*" 38 THE JOURNAL OF POLITICS 918 (1976), as quoted in WALLACE MENDELSON, THE AMERICAN CONSTITUTION AND THE JUDICIAL PROCESS 17 (1980).

33. WILLARD HURST, DEALING WITH STATUTES 3 (1982).

34. *See supra,* chapter 2, text accompanying notes 77–92. After having elsewhere reviewed Publius' remarks on the subject, I am more convinced than ever that McCardle [ex parte McCardle, 74 U.S. (7 Wall.) 506 (1869)] is, as Charles Fairman suggests, the opposite side of the Marbury coin. William Gangi, review, 8 N.E.L.R. 123, 129 (1972).

position, as one justice did in 1936.[35] Or—to mention but one other possibility—before the second case is to be decided, some members of the majority that issued the Court's first decision may have resigned or died, thereby permitting the confirmation of nominees more favorably disposed to the legislation.[36]

To repeat, I contend that when the ratifiers' intentions are clear, everyone, individually and collectively, must submit. But in situations such as the example above—when the constitutional issue revolves around a granted power and several interpretations are possible—the position most consistent with the ratifiers' design is to leave the matter in the hands of elected representatives.

Prohibitions: The Bill of Rights

The powers delegated to Congress were intended to make it competent; the prohibitions imposed on Congress were intended to reduce the likelihood that governmental powers would be used abusively. That different purpose, I suggest, counsels that courts should approach prohibitions very differently than they do specific provisions or grants of power.

It is fashionable today to argue that when prohibitions are interpreted (especially the first eight amendments), the Supreme Court should interpret them broadly. Noninterpretivists defend that view, as noted earlier, on the grounds that only by taking such an approach will such rights remain viable; or that courts are better suited to adapt such rights to changing circumstances since they are not subject to electoral retribution; or that such an approach is more consistent with the American tradition.

I contend the opposite: courts should confine their interpretation of prohibitions to the meaning those provisions had at the time they were adopted. Any other approach amounts to the amending of the Constitution without the people's consent.

Thus far I have maintained that such interpretations often have been illegitimate. Now I also contend that they inevitably jeopardize governmental competency—which is another way of saying that judges increasingly have inhibited the people's right to make public policy. And that in turn is to say that the greater the adaptability promised by the noninterpretivist position, the more it must fail to deliver. Broader and broader prohibitions on the government inevitably lead to constitutional calcification; worst of all, they undermine the rights they set out to protect.

35. NLRB v. Jones Laughlin Steel Corp., 301 U.S. 1 (1937). *See* Bernard Schwartz, The Supreme Court: Constitutional Revolution in Retrospect 16–23 (1957).

36. Impeachment is not a viable alternative because the example assumes that more than one interpretation is legitimate. I argue that to set aside a legislative judgment the justices must have positive evidence of its stance: more than possessed by the legislature. They must find clear support in the ratifiers' intent.

THE FOURTH AMENDMENT: POLICE SEARCH. I have selected *Oliver v. United States*[37] as my first example in order to illustrate how the judiciary should approach its role regarding alleged violations of Bill of Rights provisions.[38]

The facts of the case: Two police officers went to a farm that was reportedly raising marijuana. Driving "past petitioner's house" and "a 'No trespassing' sign," they explored the property and eventually located "a field of marijuana over a mile from the petitioner's home." The district court suppressed the admission into evidence of the seized marijuana on the grounds that "petitioner had a reasonable expectation that the fields would remain private" since he had taken measures (including posting no trespassing signs) to insure that no "casual intrusion" would occur. The Court of Appeals reversed the decision, holding that Supreme Court precedents governing the search of an "'open field'" and those protecting a reasonable expectation of privacy were compatible.[39]

The Opinion of the Court: Justice Lewis Powell delivered the majority opinion.[40] He contended that the *Hester* doctrine (sanctioning the search of an open field) was not inconsistent with "the explicit language of the Fourth Amendment."[41] He reasoned that when the framers' formulated the Fourth Amendment they used common-law words (e.g., "'effects'") that by that time had acquired specific meaning, and in using those words its proposers had purposely selected words that were less inclusive than other words equally available to them, but which they knew conveyed broader meaning: e.g., "'property.'" Thus, concluded Powell, today "effects . . . cannot be said to encompass open fields" and earlier Supreme Court decisions, most notably the privacy expectations found in *Katz v. United States,* were not inconsistent with that conclusion since "the Amendment does not protect the merely subjective expectation of privacy, but only 'those expectations that society is prepared to recognize as "reasonable.'"[42]

Powell argued that when the Supreme Court had decided in earlier cases that "a search infringes upon individual privacy," that judgment

37. Oliver v. United States, 80 L Ed 2d 214 (1984).

38. *See supra,* chapter 2, text accompanying notes 128–134; chapter 3, text accompanying notes 129–151; chapter 5, text accompanying notes 51–57; chapter 6, text accompanying notes 45–49; and *infra* chapter 8, text accompanying notes 39–47.

39. Oliver, *supra* note 37, at 220–221, quoting Hester v. United States, 265 U.S. 57, 98 (1924) and citing Katz v. U.S., 389 U.S. 347 (1967).

40. The opinion was joined by Chief Justice Burger and Justices Blackmun, Rehnquist, and O'Conner.

41. U.S. CONST., Amend. 4 ("The right of the people to be secure in their persons, houses, papers, and effects, against unreasonable searches and seizures, shall not be violated").

42. Oliver v. United States, *supra* note 37, at 222–223.

rested on a number of factors, including "the intentions of the framers' of the Fourth Amendment . . . the uses to which the individual has put a location . . . and our own societal understanding that certain areas deserve the most scrupulous protection from government invasion."[43] Hence, "an individual has no legitimate expectations that open fields will remain free from warrantless intrusion by government officers."[44] The "test of legitimacy is not whether the individual chooses to conceal assertedly 'private' activity [but instead] whether the government intrusion infringes upon the personal and societal values protected by the Fourth Amendment." The "intrusion" in question did not constitute a prohibited "'search,'" noted Powell, because it was "a trespass at common law [and such trespasses] have little or no relevance to the applicability of the Fourth Amendment."[45]

Justice Byron White concurred in the Court's judgment, but thought it was unnecessary to deal with "the expectation of privacy matter. However reasonable a landowner's expectation of privacy may be," contended White, "those expectations cannot convert a field into a 'house' or an 'effect.'"[46]

Justice Thurgood Marshall, however, joined by Justices Brennan and Stevens, dissented, contending that the opinion of the Court was inconsistent with precedents that presumably were still legitimate since the majority had not overruled them. Marshall then specifically referred to the Supreme Court's prior decision in *Katz v. United States* because there, he observed, "neither a public telephone booth nor a conversation conducted therein can fairly be described as a person, house, paper or effect."[47] Apparently aware that his accusation of inconsistency might itself open up a Pandora's box, Marshall marched out a variation of the time-lag argument, noting that in the past the Supreme Court had extended First Amendment protections to encompass practices perhaps never anticipated by the framers; and that the Warren Court had broadened the Fourth Amendment with its decision in *Katz*—and the majority in this case was retreating from that standard.[48]

Marshall then—accurately, I think—

43. *Id.*, at 223–224. From an interpretivist perspective the *constitutional issue* was resolved once Justice Powell applied the first criterion: "the intentions of the Framers'". If the action in question had not been proscribed by the ratifiers, it is the concern of the state and its people.

44. *Id.*, at 225–225.

45. *Id.*, at 227–228.

46. *Id.*, at 228. I concur.

47. Oliver v. United States, *supra* note 37, at 229.

48. *Id.*, at 229n.3, 230n.5. One might have anticipated that Marshall would use the "time lag" analogy that as far as I can discern was first used by Yale Kamisar with respect to the exclusionary rule. *See* Yale Kamisar, *Is the exclusionary rule an 'illogical' or 'unnatural' interpretation of the Fourth Amendment?,* 62 JUDICATURE 67, 74 (1980). There, Kamisar argued that the fact that it

charged the Powell majority with having abandoned the perspective of the Warren Court majority. In the course of his defense of that legacy, Marshall expresses in concise fashion many of the substantive premises associated with noninterpretivist reasoning:

> The Fourth Amendment, like the other central provisions of the Bill of Rights that loom large in our modern jurisprudence, was designed, not to prescribe with "precision" permissible and impermissible activities, but to identify a fundamental human liberty that should be shielded forever from government intrusion. We do not construe constitutional provisions of this sort the way we do statutes, whose drafter can be expected to indicate with some comprehensiveness and exactitude the conduct they wish to forbid or control and to change those prescriptions when they become obsolete. Rather, we strive, when interpreting these seminal constitutional provisions, to effectuate their purposes—to lend them meanings that ensure that the liberties the Framers sought to protect are not undermined by the changing activities of government officials.[49]

To give an interpretivist perspective on this, I agree that when the framers' formulated the Fourth Amendment, they knowingly used common-law words that had acquired specific meanings; and that the term

---

took 125 years for the Court to fashion an exclusionary rule is irrelevant, since similar time lags also existed with respect to what protections the framers' understood other Bill of Rights provisions to mean and what those protections are interpreted to mean today: *e.g.*, freedom of speech today is much broader than what the framers' understood it to mean at the time the First Amendment was adopted. But I contend that the time lag analogy presumes what it must establish: the right of the Supreme Court to change the protections as they were understood at the time of adoption, particularly with respect to any restrictions placed upon the government. I argue that the Supreme Court lacks that power; and so, when judges or scholars cite *other* cases where that power was used, I am inclined to explore whether those decisions, also, are illegitimate. *See* William Gangi, *The Exclusionary Rule: A Case Study in Judicial Usurpation,* 34 DRAKE L. REV. 94–95 (1985).

49. Oliver v. United States, *supra* note 37, at 229–230. Justice Thurgood Marshall also quotes for authority the opinion of Chief Justice John Marshall in M'Culloch. *Id.,* at 230n.4. *But see supra,* chapter 5, text and comment accompanying notes 123–124.

With respect to defining liberty broadly, *see* Gangi, *supra* note 48, at 61n.148. With respect to using different rules when interpreting constitutions and statutes, *see* William Gangi, *Judicial Expansionism: An Evaluation of the Ongoing Debate,* OHIO NORTHERN L. R. 1, 6–7 (1981). Does Justice Thurgood Marshall not take for granted a "we" (the people) versus "they" (the government) assumption, that is more closely identifiable with twentieth century liberalism than the common-law tradition upon which the Bill of Rights rests? *See supra,* chapter 6, text accompanying notes 54–91. Marshall, in any event, concludes his dissent with, among other things, the view that the majority "misunderstands . . . the level of generality on which constitutional analysis must proceed." Oliver v. United States, *supra* note 37, at 233n.13. *See supra,* chapter 6, comment accompanying note 118. With respect to Marshall's inability to separate advocacy from his judicial duties, *see* RANDALL W. BLAND, PRIVATE PRESSURE ON PUBLIC LAW: THE LEGAL CAREER OF JUSTICE THURGOOD MARSHALL (1973).

effects was intended by them to be less inclusive than the term *property.* Powell's analysis should have stopped there. That it did not was because he was pressed by Marshall's dissent to reconcile his opinion with the expectation-of-privacy language contained in the earlier *Katz* case. Marshall's dissent totally undermined Powell's *reasoning* because any principled reply by Powell should have led to his overruling *Katz,* which in turn undoubtedly also would have led to *questioning the legitimacy of Griswold.*[50] From my perspective, those noninterpretivist precedents, once raised, should be overruled if they do not rest on the ratifiers' understanding of relevant constitutional provisions.[51]

Powell also avoided confronting the First Amendment analogy,[52] an analogy by now considered sacred and, like so many others used by noninterpretivists, unsustainable either by recourse to the ratifiers' will or to legal history.[53] Noninterpretivists regularly conjure up the emergence of an oppressive or totalitarian regime as a

50. Griswold v. Conn., 381 U.S. 479, 484 (1965). With due respect to the justices and many of my colleagues, the "penumbras, formed by emanations from" line of argument remains an embarrassment in American constitutional law. I recommend to my students that they take another look at Plato's Cave; or, perhaps even more relevant, to the fairy-tale of the emperor's new clothes. Such "doctrines" are patently part of the *Results* line of argument (discussed in chapter 6, *supra*) and render a written constitution an absurdity. In class, I usually respond with another absurdity. I suggest that, under such reasoning, the Second Amendment words *to keep and bear arms* might be "interpreted" to support constitutional claims by either pro-life or pro-choice advocates. The former could argue on higher levels of generality that if *arms* have constitutional status—then hearts, legs, and lungs also may be protected. In American history, one group or another has always argued that there are "natural" rights that transcend the "legal" rights granted in the Constitution, as understood by their ratifiers: *e.g.,* to procreation, to marriage, or those protecting the privacy of the bedroom. But what if a study of state constitutions and laws shows no such protection? Pass a simple statute. As to privacy in the bedroom, what, specifically, do you wish to protect? Is there such a thing as marital rape? Yes. Well then, phrase the statute to provide protection for the relationship and for its abuse. Hmm. . . . Not so easy.

51. I speak here as an academician: I am not charged with the responsibilities of being a judge. Prudence is not a consideration for me as it may well be for judges.

52. *See supra,* comment accompanying note 48. *See also* William Gangi, *The Inbau-Kamisar Debate: Time for Round 2?,* 12 Western State U. L. Rev. 117, 122–123, 146–149 (1984).

53. *See supra,* chapter 6, for discussion on the *Individual Rights and Irreversible* symbols, and *infra* text accompanying notes 92–106. I also find no support for a "preferred freedoms" doctrine. *See supra,* chapter 5, comment accompanying note 112. All acts of the federal and state legislatures should be presumed constitutional, the proper burden of proof falling on the objector. Both the presumption of and/or the burden of proof should be equal in all situations. The shifting of both burdens is but another indicator of the injection of personal judicial preference. Thus, on the one hand, state legislation infringing on interstate commerce should be treated in the same manner, and by the same rules, as legislation allegedly infringing on the due process or equal protection clauses. Similarly, while the Court is competent to assess whether a congressional statute constitutes an establishment of religion, it apparently lacks competency (jurisdiction) with respect to similar state statutes. The people may wish to change these constitutional realities, but, until they do, we remain bound. *See* William Gangi, book review, 7 Harv. J. of L. & P. P. 581 (1984).

substitute for critical thinking.[54] Marshall, like others, links First Amendment precedents with other rights that he considers to be threatened. Marshall warns the liberal intelligentsia that they must rally around the noninterpretive flag because the interpretive principles used by the majority in *Oliver* also could open First Amendment precedents to similar attack. Instead of examining those interpretivist principles critically, Marshall opts to authorize the Supreme Court to rewrite the Constitution.[55]

I dissent. I believe that if the Fourth Amendment protects the "people" from "unreasonable" searches and seizures, then it is more fitting and more consistent with pre–Warren Court precedents and the American political tradition *that legislatures, not courts, determine what is reasonable*—as long as the specific meanings of the common-law terms as understood at the time of ratification are not circumscribed. That position alone is consistent with the framers' design.

THE FIFTH AMENDMENT: COERCED CONFESSIONS. The next example illustrates how I believe interpretivists should view the relationship between common, statutory, and constitutional law and why the noninterpretivist position must eventually inhibit public policy making. It is drawn from the area of coerced confession; specifically, with the Supreme Court's recent decision in *Fulminante v. Arizona*.[56]

The facts of the case: Fulminante had reported his eleven-year-old stepdaughter missing and two days later she was found "shot twice in the head at close range with a large caliber weapon, and a ligature was around her neck."[57] The body was too decomposed to establish whether

54. *See supra,* chapter 6, text accompanying notes 54–66.

55. Oliver v. United States, *supra* note 37, at 230n.5. *See supra,* chapter 6, for discussion on the *Results* and *Cumbersome* symbols. All federal judges possess the same power; but the Supreme Court speaks last. Powell would have a difficult time challenging Marshall's view of the Court's role since, in principle, he obviously shares it. *See* LOUIS FISHER, AMERICAN CONSTITUTIONAL LAW 83–86 (1990) where Powell states that "our independence does give the Court a freedom to make decisions that perhaps are necessary for our society, decisions that the legislative branch may be reluctant to make." *Id.*, at 84. With respect to Brown v. Board of Education, Powell observes: "There was nothing in the Constitution that could have suggested that result." *Id.* With specific respect to the intention of the framers of the Fourteenth Amendment, Powell claimed that "one would have to strain to find an intention on the part of Congress in 1866, and again in 1870 and 1871, to provide that there should be integration in education." *Id.* But Powell then asserts that the intent of the founding fathers and those who framed the Fourteenth Amendment cannot be relied upon, citing the interpretation of the commerce clause as an example.

56. Fulminante v. Arizona, 113 L Ed 2d 302 (1991) (hereinafter Fulminante). The selection of the coerced confession area is particularly appropriate because it is one of the earliest instances where noninterpretivist adjudication took root. A much more extensive discussion of this area has been published elsewhere. *See* William Gangi, *Coerced Confessions and the Supreme Court: Fulminante v. Arizona in Perspective,* 16 Harvard Journal of Law & Public Policy 493 (June 1993).

57. *Id.*, at 313. While his wife Mary was in the hospital for surgery, the defendant had been caring

the victim had been sexually assaulted.[58]

Having made inconsistent statements during the subsequent police investigation, Fulminante became a suspect; but since insufficient evidence existed to charge him, he was permitted to leave Arizona.[59] Fulminante subsequently was arrested and convicted in New Jersey on a federal firearms charge and sent to the Ray Brook federal prison in New York State where he became friends with one Anthony Sarivola—an FBI informant.[60]

Rumors circulated at the Ray Brook prison that Fulminante had killed a child in Arizona.[61] On sev-

---

for his eleven-year-old stepdaughter Jeneane. On September 14, 1982, the defendant informed police that Jeneane was missing. Shortly thereafter he also informed his wife that Jeneane had not returned home the previous evening. Jeneane's body was discovered on September 16. State v. Fulminante, 778 P 2d 602, 605 (Ariz. 1988) [hereinafter State].

The "ligature" is mentioned in the text because trial testimony indicated that Fulminante had knowledge of it. "[Fulminante] said that he had choked her and made her beg a little." The State of Arizona v. Oreste C. Fulminante, 19–20 (December 11, 1985) [hereinafter Arizona]. Presumably only the murderer, a witness to the crime, or those who discovered the body would know that the victim had been choked.

58. Fulminante, *supra* note 56, at 313. There also was trial testimony that before murdering his stepdaughter, Fulminante had told a government informant (Sarivola) that he had forced Jeneane to beg for her life and to perform oral sex on him. Arizona, *supra* note 57, at 19. Although "tests for spermatazoa and seminal fluids" on the victim proved negative that was "not unexpected given the decomposing condition of the body." State, *supra* note 57, at 605. There is no testimony that Fulminante had ever before physically or sexually abused his stepdaughter, although police had investigated a complaint made through school officials that he had spanked her severely. *Id.,* at 612. On one occasion Jeneane had slept at a friend's house and did so because "she didn't want to stay in the house with Oreste," but the reason is not made clear. *Id.,* at 616. The defendant, however, had been convicted in 1964 "for carnal abuse of a child." That fact had not been introduced at the trial and the details of that charge are not contained in the reports of the Supreme Court of Arizona or those of the Supreme Court of the United States. *Id.,* at 614.

59. Fulminante, *supra* note 56, at 313. Police immediately suspected the defendant because, among other things, he had claimed to have had "a good relationship" with his stepdaughter while his wife told police that in fact the relationship had been "poor." State *supra* note 57, at 605–606.

60. State, *supra* note 57, at 2107–2108. Sarivola testified that he and Fulminante had been in the same prison unit, seeing each other every day for from between two and eight hours a day, and that they had become "friends." Arizona, *supra* a note 57, at 14.

Sarivola had been sent to Ray Brook after being convicted of extortion (loansharking) and was serving a sixty-day sentence. Both the Supreme Court of the United States (Fulminante, *supra* note 56, at 313) and the Supreme Court of Arizona (State, *supra* note 57, at 607) described Sarivola as "masquerade[ing] as an organized crime figure." That phrasing, however, may be misleading because it could be interpreted to imply that Sarivola was not really a crime figure, when in fact he was, of sorts, and the reference to masquerading apparently alludes to the fact that Sarivola also was an FBI informant. Other inmates were unaware of his role as an informer. Sarivola apparently was an important figure within the unofficial prison-inmate governing structure. He allegedly sat on a "five-person crime commission at Raybrook, and . . . he was so powerful and this commission was so powerful, that they were able to give permission for hits outside the prison." (Arizona, *supra* note 57, at 31 [November 7, 1985], quoting Francis P. Koopman, defense counsel).

61. Fulminante, *supra* note 56, at 313. *See* State, *supra* note 57, at 606, 608–609 and 613. Elsewhere I speculate that Fulminante himself may have been the source of these rumors and that his confes-

eral occasions, Sarivola asked Fulminante about the truth of those rumors. Fulminante offered only exculpatory or apparently fabricated statements (e.g., bikers probably killed his stepdaughter).[62] In light of rumors that he was an alleged childkiller, the defendant apparently was in some danger of being assaulted by other inmates and Sarivola testified that Fulminante was "'starting to get tough treatment and what not.'"[63] Sarivola eventually offered to give Fulminante his protection if the latter would tell him what actually had happened in the desert.[64] "Fulminante then admitted to Sarivola that he had driven Jeneane to the desert on his motorcycle, where he choked her, sexually assaulted her, and made her beg for her life, before shooting her twice in the head."[65] On the day he was released from Ray Brook prison five months later, Fulminante made a second confession to Sarivola's girlfriend.[66]

The State of Arizona charged Fulminante with murder and he filed a pretrial motion to suppress both confessions, arguing that the first confession should be suppressed because it had been coerced (i.e., he made it to avoid physical mistreatment by other inmates) and the second confession should be suppressed because it was the fruit of the first.[67] The trial court denied Fulminante's motion, "specif-

---

sion to Sarivola may have been not to acquire protection from Sarivola but for self-advertisement—to obtain a position as a hitman after he left prison. *See* Gangi, *supra* note 56, at 519n.125.

62. Fulminante, *supra* note 56, at 313–314. Sarivola passed on Fulminante's initial exculpatory comments to his FBI contact. *Id.,* at 314. This agent asked him "to find out more," and the Supreme Court of Arizona considered that fact, along with "a promise of protection" (*see infra* text accompanying note 64) sufficient for the trial judge to have "instruct[ed] the jury on whether the jury understood Sarivola to be a 'law enforcement officer.'" State, *supra* note 57, at 609.

63. Fulminante, *supra* note 56, at 314.

64. The Supreme Court of Arizona noted: "Sarivola testified that the defendant had been receiving 'rough treatment from the guys, and if the defendant would tell the truth, he could be protected.'" State, *supra* note 57, at 609n.1. In a pretrial interview, Sarivola had stated that Fulminante "would 'have went out of the prison horizontally.'" Fulminante, *supra* note 56, at 328 (J. Rhenquist). The Arizona Supreme Court had concluded that this promise of protection rendered the confession involuntary, because such promises, "however slight," were prohibited. Id., at 609 (citing Bram v. United States). Bram, however, is not only a poor opinion but, as another commentator noted some time ago, it is "a curious one in which the 'coerced confession' seems to have been neither a confession nor coerced." Police Power and Individual Freedom 238n.56 (Claude Sowle, ed., 1960). For a more extensive discussion of Bram and other precedents, *see* Gangi, *supra* note 56, at 524n.141.

65. Fulminante, *supra* note 56, at 313–314.

66. Fulminante, *supra* note 56, at 314. Justice White also raised concerns about the admissibility of the second confession (made to Donna Sarivola) after Fulminate was released from prison. *Id.* at 323–325, esp. notes 8–9.

67. *Id.,* at 314. The United States Supreme Court never determined the admissibility of the second confession; thus, the rules governing multiple confessions were not discussed. *See* Oregon v. Elstad, 82 L Ed 2d 317 (1984). For my assessment, see William Gangi, *O What a Tangled Web We Weave,* 19 The Prosecutor 15, 29–30 (1984). The Supreme Court of Arizona did discuss the second confession, finding it voluntary. State, *supra* note 57, at 627 (citing Elstad).

ically finding that based on the stipulated facts, the confessions were voluntary."[68]

Fulminante was convicted and sentenced to death. He appealed, contending that his conviction violated the due process clauses of the Fifth and Fourteenth amendments since his confession to Sarivola "was the product of coercion."[69] The Arizona Supreme Court did find that Fulminante's first confession (the one made to Sarivola while in prison) was coerced; but the court ruled that its admission had been "harmless error" since other evidence of guilt was "overwhelming." Fulminante petitioned for a rehearing, contending among other things that Supreme Court precedents prohibited state courts from finding harmless error once a coerced confession had been wrongly admitted at a trial. Agreeing with that assessment, the Arizona Supreme Court then reversed Fulminante's conviction and ordered a retrial without the first confession. Since different state and federal courts viewed harmless error differently, the United States Supreme Court agreed to hear the case.[70]

Analysis of the constitutional basis: The various opinions of the justices need not be subjected to a point-by-point analysis.[71] A shifting coalition of justices held that (1) Fulminante's first confession to Sarivola was coerced; and (2) given the specific circumstances under which that confession was obtained its admission could not be considered harmless. But (3) under another set of circumstances the Constitution does not automatically preclude the finding of harmless error simply because a confession later found to be coerced had been introduced at the trial.

All the *Fulminante* opinions lack a constitutional basis and deny the people of Arizona their right to address coerced confessions within the context of the ratifiers' understanding of the Bill of Rights, which left to the people of each state the right to pursue criminal prosecution as they saw fit.[72] The Bill of Rights did not apply to the states, and even if it had applied, the Fifth Amendment's due process clause guaranteed only long

68. Fulminante, *supra* note 56, at 314. In the context of pre-Warren Court coerced confession precedents, that judgment is clearly supportable. For a more extensive discussion and citations, *see* Gangi, *supra* note 56, at 503–509.

69. Actually the Supreme Court of Arizona heard and decided numerous claims dealing with the admissibility of both confessions and other evidence introduced at the trial, and claims regarding various facets of the death penalty.

70. Fulminante, *supra* note 56, at 314–315.

71. There was no single majority opinion. *See generally,* Gangi, *supra* note 56 (All the opinions in Fulminante misconstrue coerced confession history. The authors and ratifiers of the Bill of Rights left such issues without constitutional status; hence, in the hands of state and the federal legislatures).

72. *See e.g.,* FEDERALIST, *supra* note 1, nos. 83–84.

accustomed *procedures*—procedures that certainly did not include a defendant's right to have a reliable (even if coerced or illegally obtained) confession excluded.[73] Nor did the Fifth Amendment's prohibition against compulsory self-incrimination bear on coerced confession admissibility, having, as it did, a very different purpose.[74] The assumption that the

73. *See* RAOUL BERGER, GOVERNMENT BY JUDICIARY 193–200 (1977) (due process procedural) and HERTA MEYER, THE HISTORY AND MEANING OF THE FOURTEENTH AMENDMENT 126–127 (1977) (relevant due process procedures specified in the fifth and fourteenth amendments). With respect to the alleged generalities associated with due process, Berger has observed:

> Was "due process of law" "loose language"? Charles Curtis, an admirer of the Court's innovations, yet wrote that meaning of due process of law in the fifth amendment "was as fixed and definite as the common law could make a phrase. . . . It meant a procedural due process." The phrase was used in the fourteenth amendment, the Court stated, "in the same sense and with no greater extent." John Bingham, the amendment's draftsman, said that its meaning had been settled "long ago" by the courts' and but for what John Hart Ely justly labels a couple of aberrational cases, that meaning was universally procedural. So far as the Framers were concerned, "due process" was not a "loose" term, but one of fixed and narrow meaning.

Berger, *supra* note 14, at 182–183 (citations omitted).

As late as 1940, Dean Henry Wigmore explicitly noted that courts did not reject the admissibility of confessions "simply because promises were not kept, confidences betrayed, deceptions intentionally perpetrated, or the methods used to obtain them were illegal." *See e.g.,* HENRY H. WIGMORE, A TREATISE ON THE ANGLO-AMERICAN SYSTEM OF EVIDENCE IN TRIALS AT COMMON LAW, secs. 823, 841a, at 248–250 (1940). Similarly, in 1955, Albert R. Beisel observed that "confessions at common law are not invalidated just because compulsion was applied or inducements held out to an accused, but because compulsion or inducement render or are likely to render an accused's confession untrustworthy as criminal evidence." ALBERT BEISEL, CONTROL OVER ILLEGAL ENFORCEMENT OF THE CRIMINAL LAW 47 (1955). For an analogous discussion regarding incorporation of the sixth amendment right to counsel and due process, see William Gangi, *The Sixth Amendment, Judicial Power, and the Peoples' Right to Govern Themselves,* in THE BILL OF RIGHTS: ORIGINAL MEANING AND CURRENT UNDERSTANDING 365, 367–368 (Eugene W. Hickok, ed., 1991).

74. The privilege against compulsory self-incrimination apparently developed in the context of the "moral compulsion that an oath to a revengeful God commands of a pious soul." R. Carter Pittman, *The Fifth Amendment: Yesterday, Today and Tomorrow,* 42 AM. BAR ASS. J. 509 (1956). According to Dean Wigmore, "courts did not reject confessions on the basis of violating the privilege against self-incrimination. 'The sum and substance of the difference is that the confession rule aims to exclude self-incriminating statements which are *false* while the privilege rule gives the option of excluding those which are *true.*'" WIGMORE, *supra* note 73, sec. 841a, at 281–282. Generally, the privilege against compulsory self-incrimination applied only in the courtroom, after a "criminal case" [U.S. CONST., amend. 5] commenced, which occurred only after indictment. The framers of the Fifth Amendment evidently considered it inhumane to require a defendant to take an oath "to tell the truth, the whole truth, and nothing but the truth so help me God" and thereby create this dilemma: to tell the truth and perhaps lose one's life or to lie and suffer eternal damnation. *Id.,* at secs. 2263, 2270. *See also* JOHN MAGUIRE, EVIDENCE OF GUILT 120–121 (1958); EDMUND MORGAN, BASIC PROBLEMS OF EVIDENCE 146 (1962); CHARLES MCCORMICK, HANDBOOK ON THE LAW OF EVIDENCE 155 (1954); LEWIS MAYERS, SHALL WE AMEND THE FIFTH AMENDMENT 10 (1959); BEISEL, *supra* note 73, at 86; Yale Kamisar, *A Dissent from the Miranda Dissents: Some Comments on the 'New' Fifth Amendment and the 'Old' Voluntariness Test,* 65 MICH. L. REV. 59, 68 (1966); Charles McCormick, *The Scope of the Privilege in the Law*

framers of the Fourteenth Amendment desired to interfere with state confession admissibility standards also cannot be taken seriously.[75] In sum, for those who framed and ratified the Constitution, the Bill of Rights, and the Fourteenth Amendment, state and federal standards governing confession admissibility did not enjoy constitutional stature. That being the case, the people have not authorized the justices of the Supreme Court to elevate to constitutional status any past common-law or statutory rules, and should the Supreme Court do so, their choice—however sophisticated the rationale—is ultimately based on the personal preferences of the justices. That constitutes an imposition of their will, and not that of the ratifiers', on the people.

During the tenure of Chief Justice Earl Warren, long-established coerced confession precedents had fallen before a "domino method of constitutional adjudication . . . wherein every explanatory statement in a previous opinion [was] made the basis for extension to a wholly different situation."[76] And so it came to pass that *Mapp v. Ohio,*[77] having ignored pertinent Fourth and Fifth amendment history and also having assumed an illegitimate judicial power,[78] were cited for authority by the justices in the *Gideon v. Wainwright* decision.[79] Those two cases then were cited for authority in *Malloy v. Hogan.* [80] One scholar concludes that at this juncture

of Evidence, 16 TEXAS L. REV. 447 (1938); William Plumb, *Illegal Enforcement of the Law,* 24 CORNELL L. Q. 337, 382 n. 226 (1938–1939), and LEONARD LEVY, ORIGINS OF THE FIFTH AMENDMENT (1968). Pittman describes the privilege as a defensive device against laws that did not enjoy the sanction of public opinion. Its growth paralleled the development of a jury trial. He observes:

> All that the accused asked for was a fair trial before a fair and impartial jury of his peers, to whom he should not be forced by the state or sovereignty to confess his guilt of the fact charged. Once before a jury, the person accused needed not to concern himself with the inference that the jury might draw from his silence, as the jurors themselves were only too eager to render verdicts of not guilty.

Pittman, *Id.,* at 510.

75. For a more complete analysis of modern coerced confession history, *see* Gangi, *supra* note 56, at 512–517.

76. Henry Friendly, *The Bill of Rights as a Code of Criminal Procedure,* 53 CAL. L. R. 929, 950 (1965). *See generally, Criminal Law Reporter,* THE CRIMINAL LAW REVOLUTION AND ITS AFTERMATH: 1960–1971 (1972).

77. Mapp v. Ohio, 367 U.S. 643 (1961) (a personal constitutional right to exclusion is binding on the states).

78. *But see* Calandra v. United States, 414 U.S. 338 (1974) (an exclusionary rule is not a personal constitutional right). For a detailed analysis of the exclusionary rule, *see generally* Gangi, *supra* note 48.

79. Gideon v. Wainwright, 372 U.S. 335, 342n.6 (1963). (Indigent defendants must be provided counsel in state felony cases because the Sixth Amendment was made applicable to the states through the Fourteenth Amendment.)

80. Malloy v. Hogan, 378 U.S. 1, 4n.2, 6, 10 (1964) (Gideon), 6, 8, 9 (Mapp) (1964) (Fifth Amendment prohibition of compulsory self-incrimination applicable to states).

the Warren Court decisions got a little "tricky."[81] The *Gideon* decision and another, Massiah,[82] were paired by the Court in its decision in *Escobedo v. Illinois* (the Court itself having cited *Gideon* for authority);[83] and all three decisions were part of the Warren Court *Miranda v. Arizona* grand finale,[84] where the majority cited for authority all of the precedents *it had created!*[85]

But to turn to another scholar's concise summary of the Warren Court's rendition of the history and policy considerations surrounding the application of Fifth Amendment privilege and coerced confession admissibility standards:

> This leaves the Chief Justice with only one embarrassing question: Why is it that this rather obvious evolution of the privilege has not been detected before? His answer involves a reinterpretation of earlier developments.
>
> First, two old cases which explained the confession doctrine in terms of the privilege are resurrected. These old federal cases have never been forgotten, we are told. It is just that the existence of the *McNabb-Mallory* rule in the federal courts has relieved the Court of the need to handle confession cases on a constitutional basis, the supervisory and rule-making power being sufficient; and so far as state courts were concerned, there was the *Twining* doctrine that the fifth amendment did not apply to state court proceedings.
>
> Then, the opinion continues, and this is where the argument gets *tricky,* in *Malloy v. Hogan,* the Court decided to re-examine the *Twining* rule. *Malloy* reversed *Twining* but, in so doing, the Court was merely recognizing what had long since become apparent—that it had been applying the fifth amendment to the states anyway. (That's not the tricky part; *Malloy* says just that.) Ignoring the fact that earlier he stated that the voluntariness doctrine might not apply to *Miranda* defendants, at least not "in traditional terms," the Chief Justice says that the voluntariness doctrine "encompasses all interrogation practices which are likely to exert such pressure upon the individual as to disable him from making a free and rational choice," and, it is concluded, *Escobedo* merely elaborates this proposition.
>
> Whoa! Try that again. If you re-

81. *See infra,* text accompanying note 86.

82. Massiah v. U.S., 377 U.S. 201 (1964) (evidence inadmissible when obtained without counsel after indictment but before trial).

83. Escobedo v. Illinois, 378 U.S. 478, 479, 487, 491 (Gideon); 484, 486, 488 (Massiah) (1964). Cf. the dissents of Justices Stewart and White, *id.,* at 493–499. See also Gangi, *supra* note 64, at 36–42.

84. Miranda v. Arizona, 384 U.S. 436 (1966) (Fifth Amendment requires a fourfold warning be given defendants subject to in-custody interrogation).

85. Miranda, supra note 84, at 466 (Mapp); 473 (Gideon); 460, 463–465, 468n.37 (Malloy); and 440, 442, 450, 465–466, 470, 475, 477, 479n.48 (Escobedo).

read *Escobedo* you will find that there is not so much as a single stray citation to *Malloy.* As a matter of fact, the opinion of Justice Goldberg makes it clear that he views the decision as part of the *Gideon-Massiah* complex which follows from the application of the sixth amendment to the states, not the fifth. . . .

Finally, the Warren opinion concludes its discussion of Escobedo by stating that there is a third basis for the decision—the protection of rights at trial. Though the Court's discussion of the point is not so forthright, one of the commentators cited by the court explains that this means "that the exclusionary rule is necessary to prevent state law enforcement authorities from circumventing the safeguards of the accusatorial, adversary trial." Just what this adds to the fifth and sixth amendment grounds is not entirely clear, but it suggests that rather than banning confessions, the court wishes to see that they are secured under conditions similar to those that prevail at trial.[86]

This is not constitutional law—it is a "fairy tale."[87]

What one often finds in cases such as *Fulminante* are judicially created distinctions that cannot be traced to the ratifiers' understanding of the constitutional provisions or amendments. Rather, they are a majority's attempt to be "knight-errant[s] roaming at will in pursuit of [their] own ideal of beauty or of goodness."[88] Succeeding, and often shifting, Supreme Court majorities have constructed and then have discarded numerous alleged constitutional distinctions that cannot be traced to the ratifiers' design; instead, they have served only to justify continued interference with state criminal justice systems, which is to say, that the justices illegitimately continue to limit the people's right to govern themselves.[89]

Standards of confession admissibility have been full of peaks and valleys.[90] It is not difficult to understand why—the issue touches a people's

86. Walter Graham, *What is Custodial Interrogation?: California's Anticipatory Application of Miranda v. Arizona,* 14 U.C.L.A. LAW REV. 59, 71–73 (1966) (emphasis added).

87. Wallace Mendelson describes such decisions as a "fairy tale." Wallace Mendelson, *Raoul Berger's Fourteenth Amendment—Abuse by Contraction vs. Abuse by Expansion,* 6 HAST. CONST. L. Q. 437, 443 (1979).

88. BENJAMIN CARDOZO, THE NATURE OF THE JUDICIAL PROCESS 145 (1922) ("The judge, even when he is free, is still not wholly free. He is not to innovate at pleasure. He is not a knight-errant roaming at will in pursuit of his own ideal of beauty or of goodness. He is to draw his inspiration from consecrated principles.")

89. *Cf.* Gangi, *supra* note 64, at 31–36. Publius provides this intriguing suggestion: "The legislature of the United States would certainly have full power to provide that in appeals to the Supreme Court there should be no re-examination of facts where they had been tried in the original cases by juries." FEDERALIST, *supra* note 1, no. 82, at 490 (Publius discussing the legislative power to limit appellate jurisdiction).

90. The reader should be aware that in the United States, confession admissibility standards fluctuated during different periods: e.g., the 1940s–1950s, 1950s–1960s. *See* Gangi, *supra* note 64, at 32–35.

soul, encompassing a community's view of justice, the discretion accorded police and the potential for police abuses, and how all three subjects impact or should impact on different economic and social classes, groups, and races. The strong desire for public order, justice, and the weight that ought to be accorded the grief and pain of crime victims might compete with the community's concern for individual rights.

Americans have the right to balance such considerations and to reevaluate from time to time whatever they or their predecessors had decided in the past, whenever they wish. The people may go about balancing various concerns by choosing to leave the articulation of that balance—on issues such as those presented by the *Fulminante* case—to the sensitivity of their judges; or, after having experienced that sensitivity, they may choose a balance more to their liking by limiting judicial discretion or by enacting more specific statutes. The people may have to rewrite those statutes time and again, as circumstances and successive judicial interpretations warrant. But all such community judgments do not enjoy constitutional status.

INTERPRETIVIST CRITERIA AND ASSESSMENT

Interpretivists often are caught between a rock and a hard place. On the one hand, interpretivists are dependent upon historians.[91] On the other hand, most regrettably, a good deal of historical scholarship is flawed; uncritically biased in favor of progressivist assumptions.[92] Often it is results-oriented, prompting a cautious scholar to treat it with suspicion.[93] Historians apparently lack uniform standards for judging research or applying that research to constitutional interpretation; and the matter is made even more complex because insights contained in historical works may lie beneath a veneer of prejudiced assumptions.[94] It is to such problems I now turn, hoping to convince the reader that the noninterpretivist assumption that judges are more capable than legislators to adapt the Constitution to changing circumstances is an unlikely one.

This absence of common standards is most inopportune. More than ever before, scholars now have enormous difficulty in mastering a specialized field. The problem is not simply the mass of materials avail-

91. H. Jefferson Powell, *Rules for Originalists,* 73 Virginia L. Rev. 659 (1987).

92. Willmore Kendall and George W. Carey, The Basic Symbols of the American Political Tradition 9 (1970) (The authors refer to such works as "thesis books"). *See supra,* chapter 4, text accompanying notes 123–128, 154–172.

93. *See supra,* Chapter 6, discussions of the *Results* and *Cumbersome* symbols.

94. Interpretivists certainly are not exempt from reading their own prejudices into the framers' intent. *See generally,* Powell, *supra* note 91. Liberals are under a similar criticism from Critical Legal Studies scholars. *See supra,* chapter 4, text and comment accompanying note 125.

able in one specialty, or even one discipline: it is the need to grasp the interrelationship of the disciplines. Only together do the disciplines convey an understanding of the totality of realities, past and present,[95] for over the past several centuries practitioners of different branches of modern science (physics, biology, economics—in that order) have all believed that they alone possessed the key to explaining reality.[96]

Scholars must decide what information is important and by doing so they explicitly or implicitly create standards by which the important is separated from the unimportant. More often than not, the scholarship based on these standards is eventually found deficient because it contains incomplete or insufficient data or because it made what proves to be unwarranted assumptions. Each of the disciplines mentioned in the preceding paragraph, for example, eventually retreated to study only a part of reality. Nevertheless, between the time when the standards in a field are initially explicated and the time when they are found to be deficient, those standards have been embraced, and not only by scholars in the discipline in which they were created. Thus, initial insights become distorted or overextended.[97]

Who among us is capable of mastering a single aspect of a single discipline; of recognizing the relevancy of developments in other specialties to their own; of applying those insights to their own specialty (if not their entire discipline); of judging competently whether the insights are in fact defective; and finally, recognizing that the insights have been wrongly extended? There are still further problems. Between the time when the standards are enunciated and the time when they are applied to external disciplines there may well be a lapse of twenty-five or more years. Similar time-lapses occur before standards are judged deficient. Thus—and I do not wish to be facetious—one should know whether standards are coming or going! Even how one approaches this problem also is dependent upon adequate standards.

These issues are far from being abstract: they were at the core of the debate over the proper role of the judiciary prior to the Civil War and during the New Deal, and they continue to pervade contemporary public policy making.

I will illustrate the above more concretely by taking the example of a scholar convinced that history has been evolving along the path of increasing actualization, dissemination,

95. This discussion proceeds along traditional analytic lines, and as such it is open to challenge by behaviorists, by feminists, by critical legal scholars, and by deconstructists.

96. ERIC VOEGELIN, ANAMNESIS 143–146 (1978).

97. *See e.g., supra,* chapter 6, comment at note 77. *See generally* MIRCEA ELIADE, IMAGES AND SYMBOLS 9–21 (1969) (how modern society misunderstands the function of myth) and HANS JONAS, THE GNOSTIC RELIGION xv–xvii (1963) (gnostic manipulation of concepts).

and expansion of liberty. In 1948 she decides to study free speech during the American Revolutionary period.[98] When the scholar examines primary materials she may find it impossible to escape her own assumptions or to put aside her knowledge of what happened between 1776 and 1948. Thus, her liberty standard may cause her to discount facts that show how liberty was originally understood and practiced. Similarly, a conviction that history is a tale of unfolding liberty also may lead the scholar to interpret the historical materials in such a way as to emphasize only the liberty that she knows eventually will develop. In short, it is quite natural and almost inevitable that once scholars view history as a progressive development they tend to smooth out rough edges (noted inconsistencies) in order to demonstrate that the continuity was "natural." History takes on the characteristics of a novel. Selected revolutionary activities become the seeds of liberty that eventually grow and bear fruit in what is, or is perceived to be, the public posture in 1948.[99]

The assumption that liberty is expanding also offers adherents of the viewpoint a vantage point from which to judge whether or not contemporary public policy proposals are anachronistic or progressive. The likelihood that the assumed criteria will affect the scholar's selection and interpretation of historical facts is compounded when the words used (e.g., free speech) remain identical from 1787 to 1948.[100] Neither events nor words are self-defining: those experiencing an event may understand its significance in one manner, and subsequent generations, never having experienced that event and perhaps denied the understanding of those who did experience it, eventually may

98. *See e.g.,* Zechariah Chafee, Free Speech in the United States 1–35 (1948). Every age has its *zeitgeist,* and thus it is probable that *some* common assumptions are made. If they were not societal, consensuses would be impossible to forge. Publius was aware of that phenomenon also: "They who have turned their attention to the affairs of men must have perceived that there are tides in them; tides very irregular in their duration, strength, and direction, and seldom found to run twice exactly in the same manner or measure." Federalist, *supra* note 1, no. 64, at 393. Hence, I am not taking an arrogant posture in the text or am I suggesting that scholars past or present commit intentional fraud. But we must strive to understand what assumptions they made and how those assumptions may have influenced their work. We best not gloat since we are probably doing the same thing: making illegitimate assumptions.

99. *Cf. e.g.,* Clinton Rossiter, Seedtime of the Republic (1953).

100. *See, e.g.,* Leonard Levy, Freedom of Speech and Press in Early American History: Legacy of Suppression vii–xii (1966). After studying the historical evidence Levy "reluctantly" concluded that the framers of the Bill of Rights did not envision a broad protection of the freedom of speech from governmental prosecution. *Id.,* at vii. However, he believes that the framers fashioned the language of the first amendment to permit future broadened interpretations. *Id.,* at xii. Levy views progressivist interpretation as legitimate attempts "to breathe a liberality of meaning into [the first amendment], in keeping with the ideals of our expanding democracy." *Id.* (emphasis added). I reject that view as both lacking evidence and imprecise. *But see* sources cited in Powell, *supra,* note 91, at 680.

understand it very differently. As I have already noted, an approach to interpreting the Constitution that solely depends on the words in the text may prove inadequate, however clear the meaning of the words might appear to be.[101]

Constitutional scholars seeking to understand what the words in the text originally meant require a *context* in order to determine what the ratifiers intended when they used those words.[102] Historical studies purporting to provide that context should have at least four characteristics:

1. The author must have attempted to understand the principles or words used by the historical figures as those figures themselves understood them.[103]
2. The meaning those principles or words eventually acquired *after* the period being studied must be exorcised from any reconstruction of the earlier period.[104]
3. If, during the period studied, those principles or words had several possible meanings, the author must have attempted to determine which views dominated and how influential were those who shared those views.[105]
4. The author also must have kept an "eye on what the people do."[106] Scholars cannot be satisfied with textual explication: they must zero in on the action. The people's actions provide context for the interpreter, just as, in adjudication, a specific case or controversy provides a more appropriate setting than do hypotheticals.

THE LAISSEZ-FAIRE ANALOGY

I have earlier alluded to the noninterpretivist assertion that changes in circumstances since the Republic's founding require open-ended judicial interpretation. Noninterpretivists advocate, among other things, that the justices should provide progressivist or moralist or compassionate leadership. Accordingly they argue that

101. *See supra,* chapter 6, text accompanying notes 50–53.
102. As discussed in chapter 1, one must explore the self-understanding of the American body politic so as to truly comprehend the American political tradition. The issue is directly related to my concern—the abuse of judicial power. *See supra,* chapter 5, text accompanying notes 43–57.
103. Leo Strauss observes that "our most urgent need can then be satisfied only by means of historical studies which would enable us to understand classical philosophy exactly as it understood itself." LEO STRAUSS, NATURAL RIGHT AND HISTORY 33 (1952); *see also* LEVY, *supra* note 100, at viii–x (understanding historical principles made difficult by gaps in relevant evidence).
104. *See generally* BERGER, *supra* note 73, at 5–6. Nothing has distorted historical materials as frequently as relating past events though present perceptions, or the equally fallacious interpretation of history from the presumed vantage point that one knows or can deduce its direction or end. *See supra,* chapter 4, text accompanying notes 76–104.
105. *See, e.g.* LEVY, *supra* note 100, at 313–320 (questioning actual impact of Lockean principles on eighteenth-century thought in America).
106. The principle has been stated by Kendall and Carey. *See supra,* comment accompanying note 92.

when the political branches fail to do so, judges ought to create new rights or expand the meaning of other rights, and by so doing increase the prospects that the American people will live up to their nation's ideals.[107]

The following quotation captures in succinct fashion interpretivist resistance to such arguments:

> One who seeks to put a true construction of any part of our [federal or state] constitutions must have a constant eye to its history, and this is particularly the case when one is dealing with a clause in a bill of rights, because an American bill of rights is a collection of words and clauses, many of which have had a definite meaning for centuries. It must be true that if our constitutions are to meet all the requirements of a constantly advancing civilization, they must receive a broad and progressive interpretation. It is also true that upon no legal principle can an interpretation be supported, which ignores the meaning universally accorded to a word or clause for centuries, and the meaning which must, therefore, have been intended by those who inserted it in the [federal] constitution. It is perhaps well to bear this in mind at a time when there is a manifest tendency to regard constitutional prohibitions as a panacea for moral and political evils, to look upon courts of law, as distinguished from legislatures, as the only real protectors of individual rights, and to trust to the courts for remedies for evils resulting entirely from a failure to attend to political duties,—a time, that is to say, when there is danger of loose and unhistorical constitutional interpretation.[108]

These comments certainly parallel ones I have made throughout this book: history cannot be ignored, and the meaning that constitutional phrases had for centuries cannot be disregarded. All citizens are duty-bound to ascertain and respect the intentions of those who framed the Constitution.

Would the reader accept the above quoted passage as typical of the interpretivist position? It was written not recently but in 1891, by Charles E. Shattuck, who at the time was resisting the judiciary's use of constitutional provisions to expand laissez-faire property rights. At that time too, there were judges who sought to adapt American institutions and the Constitution to contemporary circumstances. *Lochner, Baily, Adkins, Schechter, Carter,* and *Butler* were still a generation away.[109]

When in 1981 I first studied the debate between contemporary inter-

107. *See supra,* chapter 6, for discussion of the *Vacuum* and *Results* symbols.

108. Charles E. Shattuck, *The True Meaning of the Term 'Liberty' in Those Clauses in the Federal and State Constitutions which Protect Life, Liberty and Property,* 4 HARV. L. REV. 365, 366 (1891).

109. *See supra,* chapter 4, text accompanying notes 31–45. See Lochner v. New York, 198 U.S. 45

pretivists and noninterpretivists, Shattuck's article eluded my attention. Eventually coming across it, I was stunned to note the similarities between the arguments made there and those employed a century later. These similarities alone are sufficient reason for this generation of scholars and judges to be held to a higher standard than were their predecessors: Both the New Deal progressivists and their laissez-fair opponents at least had approached these matters with a certain degree of innocence. Both groups believed in evolutionary progress and both thought that all they had to do was to be patient, because ultimately an invisible hand (economic or moral) would work its magic: that scientific principles of law would pave the way to progress.[110]

Such innocence no longer exists, or should not exist. No one can know the future, and those who pretend to do so delude themselves.[111] No one knows whether it again will take forty-five years, as it did for the progressivists, to repudiate contemporary Court abuses. No one knows even whether current resistance to Court power will be successful at all. And no one knows whether the progressivist waves already visible on the horizon[112] will be successfully integrated into constitutional law or whether or not the discipline already has suffered grievous and permanent harm.

The notorious laissez-faire Supreme Court majority[113] at least could take refuge in the fact that the abuses they eventually committed were without precedent; but that is no longer the case. I have sought thus far to convince the reader that modern judicial expansionism rests on many assumptions, premises, and personal preferences; and also that, under an infinite variety of catchwords,[114] as Alexander Bickel and Grant Gilmore

(1905); Bailey v. Drexel Furniture Co. (Child Labor Tax Case), 259 U.S. 20 (1922); Adkins v. Children's Hospital, 261 U.S. 525 (1923); Schechter Paultry Corp. v. United States, 295 U.S. 495 (1935); Carter v. Carter Coal Co., 298 U.S. 238 (1936) and United States v. Butler, 297 U.S. 1 (1936).

110. Grant Gilmore, The Ages of American Law 89–93 (1977).

111. Voegelin, *supra* note 96, at 143–146.

112. Several variants already can be identified including those calling for a redistribution of wealth and another very contrary one, associated with a reemerging emphasis on individual property rights.

113. Fred Rodell, Nine Men (1955).

114. The literature abounds with preference-loaded words and phrases, preferences the preferrer assumes the Constitution contains but which are not attributable to it, or the ratifiers, or the people, or to ordinary or extraordinary acts of legislation. I refer specifically to phrases such as "moral momentum" or "moral ascendancy," Thomas Schrock and Robert C. Welsh, *Reconsidering the Constitutional Common Law,* 91 Harv. L. Rev. 1117, 1167n.247 (1978); or "mystic function," id; or "particular vision," Edward Chase, *The Burger Court, The Individual, and the Criminal Process: Directions and Misdirections,* 52 N.Y.U. L. Rev. 518, 519 (1977); or "model," *id.,* at 533; "tainted character," John R. Winn, Herdon v. Ithaca—Application of the Exclusionary Rule in Civil Proceedings, 39 Albany L. Rev. 131, 135 (1974); and "moral evolution," Michael Perry,

astutely discerned, may be found a pervasive belief in progress.[115] If the reader were to scratch the surface of contemporary court doctrines—be it those examined in this chapter or others such as those championing penumbras and emanations, selective incorporation, or preferred freedoms—what is found? After removing the moralistic, philosophic or legalistic patina, they are mere opinions about what constitutes good, fair, equitable, and so forth social policies, not principles of constitutional law as traditionally understood. Supreme Court decisions today rarely amount to more than the personal public policy preferences of five or more justices, and developments over the past forty years have put the Supreme Court at the center of America's governmental system—a role that is unfounded, insupportable, and inconsistent with the framers' design.

For these reasons, interpretivists such as myself are compelled to challenge those scholars, elected representatives, and members of the media who contend that certain "rights" are constitutionally required; or who maintain that those rights cannot now be abandoned by courts and legislatures. In order for such rights to enjoy constitutional stature they must be traced to the framers' or ratifiers' understanding, or to the people's actions, or to the people's consent as expressed in statutory law. If that cannot be done, adherents of such views put their cartload of personal preference before the constitutional horse, as did their laissez-faire predecessors. I repeat: it is for the *people* to identify and assess the abuse of rights and the efficacy of remedies for constitutional violations, not for members of the judiciary or for those who proclaim an ethical sensitivity.[116]

Repeated judicial usurpations since 1960 do not resolve the legitimacy issue. For example, the exclusionary rule cannot be a judicially implied remedy because the judiciary never had the authority to impose it; and it has none now to maintain it. Why should the people be constrained from addressing the pros and cons of an exclusionary rule simply because the judiciary has not found an acceptable formula or set of circumstances to extricate itself from its own rhetoric? My position has already been indicated: it is based on the New Deal experience, when the Court rightly de-

---

Noninterpretive Review in Human Rights Cases: A Functional Justification, 56 N.Y.U.L. REV. 278, 294 (1981); also "moral justification," id. at 298; and "emergent principles," *id.*, at 307.

115. *See* ALEXANDER BICKEL, THE SUPREME COURT AND THE IDEA OF PROGRESS 102–118 (1970) and GILMORE, *supra* note 110, at 99–111. The alleged pursuit of "value-free" adjudication is an integral part of defective progressivist assumptions. *Cf.* Mark Tushnet, *Darkness on the Edge of Town: The Contributions of John Hart Ely to Constitutional Theory,* 89 YALE L. J. 1037, 1038 (1989) *with* STRAUSS, *supra* note 103, at 41–48 and ERIC VOEGELIN, NEW SCIENCE OF POLITICS 13–22 (1952).

116. *See* Gangi, *supra* note 52, at 122 (Kamisar argues that "no sensitive judge" will accept a rule of law that refuses to exclude illegally obtained evidence).

ferred to the legislative branch, no constitutionalized principle having been identified. The executive and the legislature, not the judiciary, are electorally accountable for their decisions.

Executives, legislators, and citizens alike find themselves today bound in constitutional straitjackets made up of inconsistent precedents, many of which are rooted in long-discarded progressivist assumptions. Simultaneously, present-day justices, often unfamiliar with relevant precedents, attempt to comprehend and find a graceful exit from the dilemmas created by their predecessors, all the while being subject to uninformed allegations that they are abolishing rights of considerable pedigree. I contend that, in the absence of some attachment to the ratifiers' intent, Congress and state legislators have the authority to ignore illegitimate judicial rules and doctrines, and retain for the people their birthright—the ability to decide public policy questions as they see fit.[117]

In the 1930s, Franklin D. Roosevelt counseled, as I now counsel, citizens to resist judicial abuses. Roosevelt wished then, as I wish now, to put public policy making back into the hands of accountable legislators. He then understood, as I, too, understand, that questions of this magnitude cannot be confined to college classrooms. They must become the central issue of this nation's political life. As Patrick Diggins reminds us, "No government can enjoy legitimacy unless its citizens have knowledge of the origins of its authority."[118] It is clear that today's intelligentsia not only lacks their forefathers' faith in republicanism; they do not possess even the New Dealers' faith in their fellow citizens.

117. HURST *supra* note 33, at 3 ("Not even constitutional limitations bar bringing the matter into the legislative arena.")

118. John P. Diggins, *Between Bailyn and Beard: The Perspectives of Gordon Wood,* 44 THE WM. & MARY QUARTERLY 563, 565 (1987).

CHAPTER EIGHT

The Road Back To Self-Government

And if the people, in the distribution of powers under the Constitution, should ever think of making judges supreme arbiters in political controversies, when not selected by nor, frequently, amenable to them, nor at liberty to follow such various considerations in their judgments as belong to mere political questions, they will dethrone themselves and lose one of their own invaluable birthrights; building up in this way—slowly, but surely—a new sovereign power in the republic, in most respects irresponsible and unchangeable for life, and one more dangerous, in theory at least, than the worst elective oligarchy in the worst of times.[1]

As we approach the end of our journey, let me briefly recount my own. In college, my professors taught me about the laissez-faire Court of the 1920s and 1930s and how it had rigidly defined Congress's power over interstate commerce. They were delighted, however, that an emerging majority was liberally interpreting the "establishment of religion," "freedom of speech," and "equal protection" clauses. These teachers had heroes and I was encouraged to embrace them: Oliver W. Holmes— "The 14th Amendment does not enact Mr. Herbert Spencer's *Social Statics*"; Louis Brandeis—"Our government is the potent, Omnipresent teacher"; and Benjamin Cardozo—"The Criminal is to go free because the constable blundered."[2] Other phrases stirred my teachers' souls: "ordered liberty,"

1. Luther v. Borden, 7 How. 1, 52–53 (1849) (J. Woodbury dissenting). Justice Woodbury then quotes those portions of *The Federalist Papers* that argue that although it is "the more rational to suppose that the courts were designed to be an intermediate body between the people and the legislature," that did *not* lead to the conclusion that the judiciary was superior to the legislature. *Id.*, at 53. *See supra,* chapter 2, text accompanying notes 66, 79, and 106. Justice Woodbury added:

> But how would this superiority be as to this court, if we could decide finally on all the political claims and acts of the people, and overrule or sustain them according only to our own views? So the judiciary, by its mode of appointment, long duration in office, and slight accountability, is rather fitted to check legislative power than political, and enforce what the political authorities have manifestly ordained. These last authorities are, by their pursuits and interests, better suited to make rules; we, to expound and enforce them, after made.

Id., at 53.

2. Lochner v. New York, 198 U.S. 45, 75 (1905) (Holmes, J., dissenting); Olmstead v. United States, 277 U.S. 438, 484 (Brandeis, J., dissenting); People v. Defore, 242 N.Y. 13, 13 (1926) (Cardozo, J.).

"fundamental principles of liberty and justice," and "conduct that shocks the conscience."[3] Legal giants had broken away from the stifling laissez-faire past; they advocated change and the phrases they coined were pleasing, comforting, exciting, and inspiring. These jurists looked to the *future:* Not what things were but what they could be.

But today I better understand that my professors were as infatuated by that siren Progress as had been a majority of the laissez-faire Supreme Court they had criticized.[4] Supreme Court majorities have been repeatedly seduced by this progressivist dream of the dawning of a new age—an age that never materializes.[5] The underlying assumptions seem innocuous enough, even today: Judges make law; the Constitution must remain adaptable; and the power of judicial review means the Constitution is what the Supreme Court says it is.

My professors did not train me to challenge such assumptions, and if I had been trained I might, like others, have found myself aligned with bigots standing on courthouse steps. In any event, once I began attending professional conventions, I often found myself disagreeing with the vast majority of my colleagues as they applauded court-created restrictions on police—my area of competence. The more I disagreed with Warren Court decisions, the more isolated I found myself. So, unlike those supporters, I did not have many "anxious" moments when Richard M. Nixon was elected president and Warren E. Burger subsequently was confirmed as chief justice.[6]

When the Supreme Court began modifying Warren Court precedents, I told my students that if, in his opinions, Warren Burger had to play the same semantic games as had Earl Warren, so be it.[7] (I did not appreciate then what I do now, that such cynicism assures only that *another* layer of shadows will be cast on the wall of American politics.) To my dismay, however, the Burger Court also never stated a consistent body of constitutional principles. Its opinions were often no more convincing than had been those of the Warren Court!

In 1978 I reviewed Raoul Berger's *Government By Judiciary*[8], and while the reader might anticipate my saying

3. Palko v. Connecticut, 302 U.S. 319, 324 (1937); Powell v. Alabama, 287 U.S. 45, 67 (1932) and Rochin v. California, 342 U.S. 165, 172 (1952).
4. *See supra,* chapter 7, text accompanying notes 107–118.
5. *Cf. e.g.,* Grant Gilmore, The Ages of American Law 99–104 (1977) *with* Arthur Goldberg, Equal Justice 36–37, 51–52 (1971). *See supra,* chapter 4, text accompanying notes 48–104.
6. Alan Dershowitz & John H. Ely, *Harris v. New York: Some Anxious Observations on the Candor and Logic of the Emerging Nixon Majority,* Yale L. J. 1198 (1971).
7. William Gangi, *Confessions: Historical Perspective and a Proposal,* 10 Houston L. Rev. 1087, 1098–1099 (1973).
8. Raoul Berger, Government By Judiciary: The Transformation of the Fourteenth Amendment (1977). *See also* William Gangi, Review, Am. Bar A. J. 1120 (July 1978).

that from that moment I stepped out of the Cave and into the light and sinned no more, Berger's book in fact confused and disoriented me: it did not match my acquired repertoire of shadows. (Had I read Plato's analogy more carefully, I might have known that would happen!) I saw Berger as a Don Quixote, dreaming the impossible dream, fighting the unbeatable foe, and doomed to failure. After submitting my review I promptly forgot what Berger said. Years in the Cave had impaired my vision and, as I have mentioned, asking for directions, or turning back, is very hard for me to do.

Two years after my Berger review I ran across a marvelous symposium in which Berger challenged contemporary judicial power.[9] My curiosity piqued, I suspended my initial research,[10] immersed myself in the symposium, and emerged, a year later, a better constitutional scholar, more attached to the instrument and more intrigued about the framers' design.[11] I also understand today that much of what masquerades as legal profundity is nonsense, and that the Warren, Burger, and now the Rhenquist courts indulge themselves no less than did their laissez-faire and progressivist predecessors.

So much for the account of my own journey. In these final pages I want to address how Americans can regain control over their government and my suggestions include changes in thinking and acting—neither of which all readers will find easy or painless.

CONSTITUTIONAL TENSIONS

> Let us view the ground on which the convention stood. It may be collected from their proceedings that they were deeply and unanimously impressed with the crisis, which had led their country almost with one voice to make so singular and solemn an experiment for correcting the errors of a system by which this crisis had been produced; that they were no less deeply and unanimously convinced that such a reform as they have proposed was absolutely necessary to effect the purposes of their appointment.[12]

At the outset of this book, I discussed the concerns of the convention, the objects sought, the structures proposed, the prohibitions imposed, and the powers ceded. The American people

9. 6 HAST. C. L. Q. (1979).

10. "ENTJs have a strong urge to give structure wherever they are," so I later learned. DAVID KEIRSEY AND MARILYN BATES, PLEASE UNDERSTAND ME [hereinafter PLEASE]. *See infra,* Appendix B.

11. "Their empirical, objective, and extraverted thinking may be highly developed; if this is the case, they use classification, generalization, summarization, adduction of evidence, and demonstration. PLEASE, *supra* note 10, at 178. *Cf.* William Gangi, *Judicial Expansionism: An Evaluation of the Ongoing,* O. NORTH. U. L. REV. 1 (1981), where I put forth my findings.

12. JAMES MADISON, ALEXANDER HAMILTON, and JOHN JAY, THE FEDERALIST PAPERS [hereinafter FEDERALIST] no. 40, 252.

had insisted that the principles by which they wished to be governed be written down in order better to preserve them.[13] The delegates at Philadelphia thus approached constitution making in the classical tradition; that is, they realistically appraised political realities, applied relevant and preferred principles, and tailored a structure accordingly.[14] Constitution makers make concrete choices[15]: they rank a people's priorities and often encompass competing truths. Thus, constitutions habitually contain "tensions."[16]

13. As Publius put it: "The elective mode of obtaining rulers is the characteristic policy of republican government." FEDERALIST, *supra* note 22, no. 57, at 350–351.
14. *Cf.* FEDERALIST *supra* note 12, no. 23, at 153–156 (principles of good government include powers sufficient to obtain objects); *see also* no. 30, at 190; no. 31 at 193 ("ought to be no limitation of a power destined to effect a purpose which is itself incapable of limitation."); *see also* no. 34 at 207; no. 41 at 255–256 (choices must be made even if not the "the PERFECT good" and "the point first to be decided is whether such a power be necessary to the public good; as the next will be, in case of an affirmative decision, to guard as effectually as possible against a perversion of the power to the public detriment"); no. 47, 302–303 (separation of powers requires only that the whole of one power should not be entrusted to one who exercises the whole of another power); no. 49, at 315 (not generally wise to convert every question to a constitutional issue); no. 51, at 323–324 (factions may check injustice); no. 52, at 327 (experience must be consulted); no. 55, at 342 (democratic principle may be extended too far resulting in "confusion and intemperance of the multitude"); no. 57, at 350 (obtain men of virtue then take precautions to keep them virtuous); no. 59, at 362 ("*every government ought to contain in itself the means of its own preservation*"); no. 62, at 377 (government based on "a mixture of the principles of proportional and equal representation"); *id.* at 380 (government implies happiness of people and means to obtain that end); no. 78, at 466 (constitutional limits must be enforced by courts) *with* LEO STRAUSS, NATURAL RIGHT AND HISTORY 120–142 (1952). *See supra,* chapter 2, text accompanying notes 102–107.
15. Eric Voegelin notes:

> While other sciences endeavor to attain general principles with the widest possible area of application, in ethics the generalities are relatively uninteresting (possibly because they are already universally known). It is only on a lower level of abstraction, in the doctrine of particular virtues and in casuistics, that we get to the important things, and to these lower levels Aristotle attributes the greater amount of truth.
>
> . . . In this identification of truth with the concrete, there emerges the almost forgotten knowledge of the philosopher, that ethics is not a matter of moral principles, nor a retreat from the complexities of the world, nor a contraction of existence into eschatological expectation or readiness, but a matter of the truth of existence in the reality of action in concrete situations.

ERIC VOEGELIN, ANAMNESIS 62–63 (1978).
16. *See supra,* chapter 7, text accompanying notes 3–15. There were compromises at Philadelphia, for example over representation, delegation of powers, separation of powers, slavery, and individual rights. Eric Voegelin states:

> What is right by nature is not given as an object about which one could state correct propositions once and for all. Rather, it has its being in man's concrete experience of a justice which is everywhere the same and yet, in its realization, changeable and everywhere different. There is, thus, an existential tension that cannot be resolved theoretically but only in the practice of the man who experiences it. Mediation between its poles is not an easy task. We know Solon's complaint on the occasion of his reform: "It is very hard to recognize the invisible measure of right judgment; and yet this measure alone contains the right limits . . . of all things" (Solon 4, 17).

Voegelin, *supra* note 15, at 61–62.

The delegates understood perfectly well, however, that whatever was decided at Philadelphia had to be brought to the people for approval before it could become the law of the land.

I fear that as the judiciary has been allowed to grow bolder, habits of citizen responsibility and self-government have proportionately atrophied. If those habits are not revived, no constitutional form can protect the right to self-government. What we, as a people, must learn to find distasteful is not the policy content of certain judicial decisions: that may be reasonable, just, or moral; but the fact *that judges have made such decisions at all.* No matter how well intentioned they are, no matter how correct, those decisions are arrogant. They are inconsistent with the design of the Constitution and the framers' great faith in the people. Such decisions interfere with the people's right to self-government and diminish citizenship as surely as even the best-intentioned parental meddling will threaten to diminish the self-esteem of adult children. Grown children must tell meddling parents to stop and so the people must tell the courts.

THE LEGISLATIVE ROLE

As seen earlier, noninterpretivists assume that American democratic institutions are inadequate or have failed; or that if the legislature fails to act when they believe it should, the judiciary should intercede—exercising the equivalent of either the amending power or a superlegislative power.[17] Such assumptions are typically defended by noninterpretivist theorists creating paradigms of how a democracy—in their eyes—should work.[18] They extract from that paradigm certain principles or concepts or premises that they identify as being essential to the paradigm's success and contrast them with existing institutions and processes. Using their own criteria, paradigm makers then decide which of institutions and processes fall short. These theorists go on to vest in the Supreme Court whatever authority they believe is necessary to remedy gaps that exist between the expectations created by the paradigm and how institutions and processes really work.[19] Noninterpretivists have converted the legitimacy issue into one of results: e.g., "whether . . . the Court acted reasonably when it cre-

17. *See supra,* chapter 4, text accompanying notes 173–182, and chapter 6, under the *Vacuum* and *Best Suited,* symbols.

18. *See e.g.* Howard Ball, The Warren Court's Conceptions of Democracy: An Evaluation of the Supreme Court's Apportionment Opinions (1971).

19. *See* William Gangi, book review, 122 U. Pa. L. Rev. 505 (1973). *Cf.* John H. Ely, Democracy And Distrust (1980), and *supra,* chapter 4, text accompanying notes 129–130. *But see supra,* chapter 6, text accompanying notes 42–44. *See also* Douglas Muzzio and Gerald Maio, *The Will of the Community: Theories of Representation at the Founding,* Northeastern Political Science Ass., Philadelphia (Nov. 1989). For a classic look at the problem of representation in a republic, *see* Ferdinand A. Hermens, The Representative Republic (1958).

ated new legal and political relationships in the aftermath of its reapportionment decisions."[20]

In my teaching career, works that assumed in whole or part the failure of American democracy intrigued me and, when lecturing on the framers' fear of pure democracy, I began asking my citizen-students whether or not they believed (as some of my colleagues taught them) that their elected representatives were unresponsive to their wishes? Many agreed that they were so unresponsive. Since, as they had learned, the form of pure democracy was often abandoned in part because it became unwieldy, maybe they would want to rethink that choice? After all, with modern technology, pure democracies no longer need to be confined by spatial (geographic) limits. We could issue plastic identification cards, attach a device to television sets, and thus record votes. Given that capacity, why not, I suggest—for I still carry out this exercise in class—have public debates on major public policy issues and tally those votes? In such a manner the majority will could be unquestionably established on issues such as abortion, flag-burning, the death penalty, gun-selling, and so on.

I ask the students to accept two assumptions. First, that the ID card system is on the up-and-up; that there is, if anything, less fraud than currently exists. Second, that the TV debates are *fair,* by which I mean they would not be one-sided, or even demagogic (something that cannot be assumed under the present system). We then usually spend some time refining the system. "Professor, what about national security items? Our enemy could monitor our voting on topics such as whether we should declare war. They could launch a strike as the vote was announced." Okay, I respond, either a supersecurity system is developed, or those topics will be exempted from the debates. Perhaps a vote could be taken on which way to go? "Professor, what about feedback? What happens if the debaters omit part of the problem or give answers that are not satisfactory?" I respond that there ought to be opportunities for feedback, perhaps by telephone, and citizens might vote first on whether to close debate and then on the issue itself.

Finally, I ask students to vote yes or no: should the proposed system be adopted and the present system of representation be abandoned? Rarely does the plan get more than a handful of supporters.[21] Since many students had expressed dissatisfaction with the current system, why did not more of them support the new system? When pressed, their explanations fall

20. Ball, *supra* note 18, at 45.

21. Even that small affirmative response is not due—as I would like to think—to my brilliance at presenting compelling evidence. Students know where I stand, and they may tell me what I wish to hear.

into two categories: some students judge themselves not competent to decide public policy matters, preferring to see them resolved by those presumably more knowledgeable (or less humble!); others, to put it bluntly, don't trust "them"—fellow citizens outside the classroom whom they fear might get too emotional, not think clearly, or think prejudicially, when casting their vote.

These class dialogues are remarkable both for their candor and for the affirmation of the framers' design. Publius feared the injection of emotion (i.e., anger, frustration, prejudice, hatred, sympathy, generosity) directly into the lawmaking process. Emotion often dissolves reason, hinders deliberation, and can turn even a group of Socrateses into a mob. The framers feared pure democracy not merely because it was unwieldy but because *its very form was defective.*[22]

If Americans are to regain control of their government, they first must rediscover their faith in democracy. In 1974 Jesse Choper examined the relationship between democracy and the judiciary, particularly with respect to those who chose the Supreme Court for the "task [of] defining and securing personal freedom."[23] The problem, he said, is that "the procedure of judicial review is in conflict with the fundamental principle of democracy—majority rule under conditions of political freedom." Justice Felix Frankfurter, Choper noted, put the issue succinctly: "'The Court is not saved from being oligarchic because it professes to act in the service of humane ends.'"[24]

Choper then explored, among other things, the congressional structures that the legislature's critics cited as proof of its undemocratic character: the filibuster, committee struc-

22. Publius observes the following with respect to the Senate:

> I shall not scruple to add that such an institution may be sometimes necessary as a defense to the people against their own temporary errors and delusions. *As the cool and deliberate sense of the community ought, in all government, and actually will, in all free governments, ultimately prevail over the views of its rulers;* so there are particular moments in public affairs when the people, stimulated by some irregular passion, or some illicit advantage, or misled by the artful misrepresentations of interested men, may call for measures which they themselves will afterwards be the most ready to lament and condemn. In these critical moments, how salutary will be the interference of some temperate and respectable body of citizens, in order to check the misguided career and to suspend the blow mediated by the people against themselves, until reason, justice, and truth can regain their authority over the public mind? What bitter anguish would not the people of Athens have often escaped if their government had contained so provident a safeguard against the tyranny of their own passions. Popular liberty might then have escaped the indelible reproach of decreeing to the same citizens the hemlock on one day and statues on the next.

FEDERALIST, *supra,* note 12, no. 63, at 384 (emphasis added).

23. Jesse Choper, *The Supreme Court and the Political Branches: Democratic Theory and Practice,* 122 U. PA. L. REV. 810, 814 (1974). *See also,* CHRISTOPHER WOLFE, JUDICIAL ACTIVISM: BULWARK OF FREEDOM OR PRECARIOUS SECURITY? 74–77 (1990).

24. Choper, *supra,* note 23, at 814.

tures, the chairperson, party leaders, conference committees, and interest groups.[25] He found much of this criticism "one-sided, and, thus distorted."[26] After reviewing the same structures from a different vantage point[27] Choper concluded that "the contention that the dominance of special interests makes American government systematically undemocratic is no more factually supportable or inherently persuasive than the argument that the total impact of pressure groups with conflicting biases magically produces a perfect majoritarian equilibrium."[28] He added: "American working democracy is the grand product of the efforts and interactions of all legal and political structures in the nation, influenced at different points with varying intensities by the multitude of economic and social organizations that function outside the formal system of government."[29]

Willard Hurst likewise has examined the legislative role.[30] He found that the legislature "directly embodies governing standards and rules for major sectors of life in society."[31] Writing in 1982, Hurst said: "Yet the schools, the legal literature, and the legal profession have given remarkably little attention to the legislative process. Judge-made law is still the darling of the legal philosophers. Until recently legal historians have been content to piece together their stories almost wholly out of the action of courts."[32]

The legislative power, Hurst notes, has enormous breadth: "Not even constitutional limitations bar bringing . . . [public policy issues] into the legislative arena."[33]

Hurst's book is interesting for many reasons, only a few of which can be discussed here. We have already recounted the progressivist revolt of Justices Holmes, Brandeis, and Cardozo against opinions of the Court steeped in laissez-faire ideology: Hurst reminds us that laissez-faire rights had been created by judges.[34] It was legislatures that eventually cleaned up that mess. Hurst explains that "sometimes judges, conscious and proud of their leading role in the nineteenth century as makers of common law on a grand scale, invoked . . . rules of construction because they regarded the growth of statute law as an intrusion on their

25. *Id.*, at 817–829 *passim.*
26. *Id.*, at 829.
27. *Id.*, at 830–845.
28. *Id.*, at 845.
29. *Id.*
30. Willard Hurst, Dealing with Statutes (1982).
31. *Id.*, at 1.
32. *Id.*, at 1–2.
33. *Id.*, at 3.
34. *Id.*, at 11 ("legal protection of market autonomy emerged more through common law than through legislative contests").

importance and their superior professional skill in building policy."[35] Next he points out that legislatures have had primary responsibility for addressing societal change: "In the country's experience statute law has had special importance in giving content to public policy and adapting the legal-social order to changing currents of interest and circumstance."[36] Finally, Hurst concludes that legislative power always has been most closely associated with the people's right of self-government.[37]

In a context such as that outlined by Hurst, the people must reassert the primacy of the legislative public policymaking role; and with it, two related principles:

HIGHER STATUTORY MINIMUMS MAY BE LEGISLATED. People differ over even the simplest questions and it is impossible for the judiciary or any one else outside the electoral process to assess how intensely, or by how many citizens, different views are held.[38] The electoral process gauges voter sentiment, and elected legislators are expected to deliberate on controversial public policy issues and to forge a consensus that has at least a reasonable chance of being obeyed, even though that consensus may last for only a short time.[39] I am not saying that truth or moral correctness necessarily emerges from the legislative deliberative process: only that the process ends in concrete choices and that the representatives chosen may be held accountable at the polls. As Publius understood it, the constitutional structures and procedures suggested by the delegates at Philadelphia and approved by the people would increase the prospects for good government.[40]

With ratification of the Constitu-

35. *Id.*, at 64.

36. *Id.*, at 4. He adds:

> After due account of how legislatures usually behave, realism also calls for comparing the legislative process with the ways in which change proceeds in the general society and with the year in, year out conduct of other legal agencies. Such comparisons suggest that, despite its cumbersome and somewhat irregular energies, legislative process has been outstanding among our devices for affecting events.

Id., at 24. Regarding heightened expectations, see Voegelin's instructive article. Eric Voegelin, *Wisdom and the Magic of the Extreme: A Meditation,* THE SOUTHERN REVIEW 235 (spring, 1981).

37. HURST, *supra* note 30, at 19. Hurst noted, however, that the entire legislative power was not lodged in the hands of Congress. "The framers of the Federal Constitution did not make such a blanket grant to Congress, but enumerated the categories of its law-making authority." *Id.*, at 10. For similar statements by Publius, *see supra,* chapter 2, text accompanying notes 14 and 81.

38. *See e.g.,* Choper, *supra* note 23, at 833–839 and William Rehnquist, *The Notion of a Living Constitution,* 54 TEXAS L.REV. 693, 699–703 (1976).

39. Berger asserts that "the track record of the Court does not inspire confidence that it is a better judge of what the people should do than the people themselves. . . . '[T]ime has proved that [the Court's] judgment was wrong on most of the outstanding issues upon which it has chosen to challenge the popular branches.'" RAOUL BERGER, DEATH PENALTIES 179 (1982) (quoting Solicitor General Robert H. Jackson) (citations omitted).

40. *See supra,* chapter 2, text accompanying notes 3–17.

tion, the people understood that they could not insist, for example, that elected representatives pass ex post facto laws; and that even if they did insist, elected officials might refuse to do so, citing the relevant restriction in the text. And if elected official nevertheless passed such legislation that the courts might set it aside.[41] Insofar as the Constitution established restrictions on governmental power, it set minimums—the ratifiers' understanding—below which we cannot go. It did not bar Congress from providing greater statutory protections in those areas.[42]

DEFINING RIGHTS AND REMEDIES. Citizens must become more aware that they are not informed upon what principles the shifting coalitions among Court justices proceed.[43] They learn only about the obvious: the five votes needed for a majority. But they must become more aware about the background reasoning: why, when principles or canons of construction are used, they are not uniformly applied in other cases;[44] or how constitutional scholars and citizens alike may distinguish the Rhenquist Court from its Burger, Warren, and laissez-faire predecessors.

Most important contemporary judicial decisions often cannot be traced to the ratifiers' intent. They are based on the personal predilections of judges, constricting the range of policy options otherwise available, and therefore hide from Americans the fact that judges are making public policy decisions that should be totally in the hands of the people.

Neither the delegates to the Philadelphia convention, nor the ratifiers, authorized judges to redefine constitutional *restrictions.* Only the people, by amendment, can impose additional restrictions on themselves—never the judges. Judges cannot legitimately expand the meaning that constitutional rights had for their ratifiers. They cannot do so because they believe, for example, that the time has come to be realistic about contemporary social ills; nor can they do so because they believe that constitutional rights ought to be redefined, or that some rights should be considered "fundamental." They cannot do so because they believe that certain groups, for whatever reason, are inadequately protected; or because they believe legislatures have not responded rapidly enough, if at all, to changing circumstances; or because they have concluded that legislators will not do what is right, since doing right might

41. *See supra,* chapter 5, text accompanying notes 104–134.

42. *See supra,* chapter 5, text accompanying notes 51–57, and chapter 7, text accompanying notes 37–90.

43. Not only do Supreme Court majorities shift, they shift within a case. For one of my recent favorites see Arizona v. Fulminante, 111 S. Ct. 1246 (1991).

44. *See supra,* chapter 7, text accompanying notes 17, and text, comment, and sources accompanying notes 50–55.

be unpopular and jeopardize their chances for reelection. Nor can they do so because they view the legislative or amendment processes, or both, as being too cumbersome.

The people must begin to recognize that many decisions of the Warren, Burger, and Rhenquist courts are illegitimate: they either changed the meaning of constitutionalized common-law language or substituted or added judicial remedies for those provided by the legislature.[45] The people and their elected representatives have a right to challenge those decisions.

For more than a century, judicial usurpations have had to be modified or exorcised from the corpus of constitutional law by Congress, by amendment, or by fortuitous circumstances (death or resignations of justices); and whenever a majority of justices themselves made such an effort (i.e., to set aside earlier usurpations) the action appears particularly arbitrary, which of course, by and large, it is. We have a real "mess."[46]

The people must rediscover the fact that before and after bouts of illegitimate judicial policy making over the past century, Congress and many states addressed public policy concerns in areas on the periphery of constitutional commands. Periodic expansion and retrenchment of rights occurred as circumstances and/or citizens demanded. All such changes occurred under state and federal constitutional guidelines, and state and federal judiciaries played an important, though at times subordinate, role. Criminal justice issues, for example, evoked debate; they also, as is to be expected, evoked disagreements. Today, however, proponents of judicial power frequently circumvent state legislatures (sometimes even Congress) under the guise of protecting constitutionally mandated rights, when in fact the so-called rights exist only because illegitimate judicial actions have created them.[47]

A SCANDALOUS SITUATION

The delegates to the Philadelphia convention would not be shocked to learn that attempts have been made to increase power beyond that granted; nor that such usurpations occurred initially for beneficent purposes. I suspect, however, that they would be genuinely surprised to learn that the institution they anticipated would *check* usurpations itself has committed the most blatant breaches. These

45. *Cf. supra,* chapter 6, text accompanying notes 42–44.

46. Gary Leedes, *The Supreme Court Mess,* 57 Texas L. Rev. 1361 (1979).

47. I fully understand that habitual circumvention of the legislature under the guise of protecting constitutional rights is a natural consequence of equating individual rights with the common good. But I contend that such a view is guided by a hand as invisible as the one that promised economic prosperity by sanctioning individual greed. Both substitute rhetoric for skills associated with the art of governing. See *supra,* chapter 7, text accompanying notes 37–90. *See also* William Gangi, book review, 34 U. Pitt, L. Rev. 523, 526–527 (1973).

judicial impositions are compounded by the pretension that they are required by the Constitution—the very instrument the judiciary swears to preserve! By both usurping the legislative and amending powers and deceiving the public, the judiciary today undermines government competency as surely as would have the antifederalists (Publius' opponents, it will be remembered, counseled that the proposed federal government be denied sufficient powers because those powers might be abused).[48]

Even more scandalous, and what might stun those at Philadelphia, is the fact that the people who the framers anticipated would foreclose prospects for judicial usurpations—national and state legislators—have failed to do so. Legislators either have lost sight of their constitutional responsibilities or, fearing electoral combat, they lack the character to make difficult public policy decisions. I believe ignorance is the more likely source of their inaction, for few legislators seem aware of either the illegitimacy of many judicial decisions or the evidence of usurpation.[49]

Though legislators no longer seem to grasp constitutional principles as they were understood by those who framed them, they still remain fiercely loyal to the Constitution. Believing as they do that the Constitution is what the Supreme Court says it is, many legislators protect the pronouncements of the Court, despite grave and sometimes personal misgivings. So at least loyalty to the Constitution remains strong among legislators, and that is important, because it makes the task before Americans far simpler. Legislators must be convinced only on the score that the proper scope of the judicial power is a narrow one.

But the current degree of ignorance about the framers' design, about the nature of the judicial power, and about the people's right of self-government, surely deepens the scandal, for it leads to the unpleasant conclusion that America's educational institutions, particularly the law schools, have failed to meet the framers' expectations.[50] That conclusion in turn leads to perhaps the most unpleasant aspect of the whole business: the most culpable parties are those relatively few individuals who make up the community of constitutional scholars. They above all others had the moral responsibility to hand down a tradition; instead, many of the brightest chose to be handmaidens to power. They did not "preserve, protect and defend the Constitution of the United States."[51] They did not pass on to succeeding genera-

48. *See supra,* chapter 2, text accompanying notes 3–10.
49. *See, e.g.* Daniel L. Feldman, The Logic of American Government (1990).
50. *See* Yarbrough, *Thoughts on the "Federalists'" View of Representation,* XII Northeastern Political Science Ass. 65 (1979).
51. U.S. Const. art. 2, sec 1.8.

tions a body of wisdom nearly two hundred years old. Scripture is very clear on the matter: "As you know, we teachers will be judged with greater strictness than others."[52]

THE TASK AHEAD

Thus far, I have appealed to the reader's intellect, tolerance, and patience. Now I must make emotional demands. Constitutional scholars must accept as their primary obligation their duty to inquire into the ratifiers' intentions, and in pursuing that goal to put aside their personal (including religious) beliefs and judgments about the merits of the forefathers' intentions.

That approach is, I suggest, the only one consistent with the framers' design. It is also what the ratifiers anticipated. All judicial decisions—particularly illegitimate ones—create political counterforces in their wake. Decisions of the Warren, Burger, and Rhenquist courts, as those of the Taney and Hughes courts before them, have done so. Political counterforces inspired by illegitimacy, moral indignation, or popular support, or all three, work diligently to reverse or modify those decisions, either by amendment or legislation, and even more frequently by seizing the judicial machinery and using it as it had been used against them. Hence, if public policy debates today are placed in a historical context, they will be seen to be similar to the progressivist-realist coalition charge that the laissez-faire dominated judiciary had written their personal views into the Constitution.[53] The other side of this is also true. Interpretivists should not be surprised to find themselves charged by the defenders of illegitimate judicial decisions as opposing rights guaranteed by the Constitution.

Two factors here are of significance. On many public policy issues, no clear-cut ideological majority exists on the Supreme Court. Nevertheless, the power of the judiciary has increased enormously: often the Court is compelled make decisions already addressed by district courts or appellate courts. Options that might have been one among the many available to the legislature are now haphazardly "constitutionalized" on whatever rationale five justices agree upon. All the justices—despite different personal predilections—evidently share the conviction that deconstitutionalization of public policy issues would diminish the accumulated power of the Supreme Court.[54] Without intending to be offensive, I won-

52. James 3:1.

53. *See supra,* chapter 4, text accompanying notes 46–52.

54. Bivens v. Six Unknown Federal Narcotics Agents, 403 U.S. 388, 421 (1971) (Burger, C. J., opinion) (exclusionary rule cannot be abandoned by Court until some viable substitute is found, or the result may be a police open-season on criminals). Surely the statement in the text is too broad. At one time or another, all the justices have drawn lines in the sand beyond which they would not go. What is lacking are candid statements of those limits; and consistent application, since they would undermine contemporary assumptions about the legitimate extent of contemporary judicial power.

der if the justices understand the structures provided by the framers—as the framers understood them. For many years now the justices have been so busy improving the Constitution (or dismantling their predecessors' improvements) that they have had little time to master how it works—and understand the limited function they were intended to serve.

Judicial public policy making must be challenged on two fronts. First, the people must insist that their elected representatives reassert their public policy making role. Should elected representatives prove unwilling or unable to do so, or to defend their reluctance to the people's satisfaction, they should be replaced by those who will. Americans must make clear that unless elected representatives live up to their republican obligations they are unfit for office. Should Americans perceive a general failure of elected representatives to heed the public will (perhaps because of the aforementioned failure of the nation's educational institutions) then perhaps term limits should be supported, at least for a period of time.[55] Second, to the extent that Americans believe the ratifiers' understanding of constitutional protections are no longer adequate, amendments should be considered. Perhaps a number of amendments may be necessary—an amendment burst! This does have precedent in American politics and it might help to define a contemporary consensus of opinion.[56]

But integral to both of these challenges is the deconstitutionalization of public policy areas that have been illegitimately usurped by the Court. The list is long, but before turning to a specific example, I want further to discuss the responsibilities of the constitutional scholar, which are an important part of the task ahead. Currently, partisans of one side or another of public policy issues marshal so-called constitutional law experts. These pundits' constitutional analyses never transcend a given expert's imaginative ability to connect whatever results are preferred to constitutional language. Public policy debates then are characterized as a choice between, for example, the two-hundred-year-old tradition of freedom of the press and approval of abuses committed in its name; or a similarly long tradition and an alleged Fourth Amendment right to ex-

55. I understand the public's sense of frustration, but as a scholar I opposed term limits. First, they change the framers' design, introducing unknown consequences that may be worse than the initial disease. Second, the problem is not the length of term in office but the elected officials' perception of the role they play in it. Thus, the reform does not confront the problem, only a symptom of the problem. That said, it may be necessary to propose term limits to get the attention of elected officials—as happened with Franklin D. Roosevelt's court-packing plan.

56. I refer to Amendments 1 through 8, which address primarily procedural rights. Amendments 13, 14, and 15 address more substantial rights, purposely departing from earlier practices. *Cf. supra,* chapter 4, text accompanying notes 2–30.

clude reliable evidence; or a choice between dictates of the Fifth Amendment guarantee against compulsory self-incrimination and the probable release of an admitted murderer; and so on. Significant portions of the population then are drawn into public disputes on the most inappropriate level imaginable. The choices now being put before the American people are the raw material for civil strife, not to mention the basest demagoguery. In the absence of a principled basis by which issues of a constitutional character may be distinguished from those that are not constitutional issues (e.g., the intentions of the ratifiers) debaters on both sides accuse one another of violating the Constitution or of trampling on individual rights.

But once upon a time one of the important functions played by constitutional scholars was the identification of the level of the political stakes; for example, to judge whether the people could pass a simple statute to work their will or whether they needed an amendment. Since constitutional scholars possessed neither force nor will, all political combatants sought their assessment: in that way, resources and energy were used most effectively. That task is performed by fewer and fewer constitutional scholars today. But not only that: noninterpretive, open-ended, results-oriented methodologies make it a task impossible to sustain.[57]

Now I will give that promised example of illegitimate judicial usurpation. John Hart Ely maintains that *Roe v. Wade* lacks a constitutional basis.[58] His judgment probably would carry more weight with pro-choice partisans than would a similar judgment made by a scholar opposed to abortion. Human nature being what it is, pro-choice supporters would approach his reasoning with less suspicion, knowing as they do that he personally favors pro-choice legislation not unlike that imposed by the Court.[59] Similarly, since I personally oppose abortion, pro-life partisans might pause for reflection if I give it as my conclusion that nothing in the Constitution precludes any individual state's adoption of either a pro-choice or pro-life position.

Ignoring the often subtle distinctions made by the Supreme Court on the abortion issue made subsequent to the *Roe* decision in 1973, permit me to continue. I am a Roman Catholic: yet my personal views on abortion (whether or not they parallel those of my church) *should be irrelevant to how I approach abortion as a constitutional question.* I did say that I would make emotional demands on the reader! If substantial numbers of constitutional scholars of different

57. *Cf. supra,* chapter 5, text accompanying notes 35–42.
58. John Ely, *The Wages of Crying Wolf: A Comment on "Roe v. Wade."* 82 YALE LAW JOURNAL 920 (1973). Roe v. Wade, 410 U.S. 113 (1973).
59. Ely, *supra* note, at 926–927.

personal beliefs reach a consensus of opinion on the constitutional status of abortion, then the potential for truly divisive political combat should be significantly reduced.

On the one hand, if at some time a Court decision reverses *Roe* (declaring it an illegitimate exercise of the judicial power) pro-choice advocates should be prepared to defend or enact abortion legislation state by state. (In saying this I have assumed that, in reversing, the Court returns the issue to the states; not that five justices hold all abortion to be unconstitutional.) If, at such a juncture, a consensus in any one of the states were to find that a right to abortion did not exist, pro-choice advocates would be well advised, instead of attributing that decision only to a conspiracy of right-wing religious fanatics, to organize potential supporters, to educate the citizenry, to neutralize opponents real and imaginary (things do get nasty), and to build a financial war chest. In other states, a majority of citizens may find the conditions set by *Roe* to be perfectly acceptable and reenact them by passing appropriate statutes or even by elevating them to state constitutional status. (I live in New York and must be realistic!) In yet other states, *Roe*'s reversal may find pro-choice partisans in the minority, with only restricted abortion permitted. No doubt political combat would intensify in some states; in others, the consensus might be so substantial that accords would be reached with little difficulty, and those outside that consensus would find themselves isolated (*isolated*—not necessarily wrong!). Partisans would no longer be able to bluff or exaggerate the amount of support they enjoyed.

It is to be noted here that the federal system assures that the combat will be fought in staggered fashion, state by state. Each side, where convenient, would employ delaying tactics, or make compromises that would in places at least assure minimal victory. I will not paint the entire scenario, but instead refer the reader to earlier discussions, for by and large the states have been constructed in the image and likeness of the Union.

On the other hand, what if, despite a scholarly consensus that *Roe* was illegitimate, the Court refused to reverse? Would the issue then change from how to change the Court's decision to one of how to address a usurpation of power? As Senator Patrick Moynihan has put it: What do you do when the Supreme Court is wrong?[60] The traditional actions, as demonstrated earlier with respect to commerce, are to educate, litigate, and legislate.[61] At state level, it would be the pro-life partisans who would now have to convince fellow citizens that the Court had acted ille-

60. Daniel Moynihan, *What Do You do When the Supreme Court is Wrong?*, 57 The Public Interest 3 (1979).
61. *Cf. supra*, chapter 7, text accompanying notes 19–36.

gitimately, and then they would have to rally sufficient political forces to pass legislation contrary to *Roe.* Only in that manner would the issue again be put squarely before the Court. In approaching their reexamination of *Roe,* however, this time—in view of the assumed consensus—the justices would be denied the support of their scholarly peers. In such a situation, the justices may well give way. Should they not, again the scholarly consensus on the illegitimacy of the Court's action may provide justification for other tactics: removal of jurisdiction, amendment, or even impeachment.[62]

But what if pro-life advocates seek a *national* posture, arguing that the nation's moral being cannot survive if in some states abortion is murder and in other states it is not.[63] If *Roe* were no longer in force, my understanding of it thus far is that a national statute banning abortions would be constitutionally suspect. Upon what federal power, or constitutional provision, would such legislation be based? True, the Fourteenth Amendment specifically provides that no person should be denied life, but the historical record, to the best of my knowledge, offers no support that its framers sought to nationalize state control over issues other than those specified. Since there is no clear prohibition against the passage of such legislation, do not interpretivists maintain that Congress be given considerable deference? The answer to that question is no: not where, as here, the statute does not rest on one of the delegated powers. There is much more evidence to support Congress's power over commerce (and the view that commerce was within the means ceded to the Union to achieve its objectives) than there is regarding abortion. The Tenth Amendment should not be ignored. Words should not be torn out of context, changing the meaning they have had for centuries. The history of state regulation should not be brushed aside, even if one believes that the result sought (e.g., prevention of fetal murder) is morally compelling. Upon what authority does a constitutional scholar—as such—reach a moral judgment on abortion? On his own authority, the authority of the catholic

62. Considerations of prudence and the weighing of risks and benefits exist at every aspect of such on inquiry. A consensus is a difficult thing to achieve because there are even fewer guidelines than exist for ascertaining the ratifiers' intentions. A scholarly consensus, however, still may enjoy considerable weight for consensus-building among other participants in the political system. Under the criterion urged herein, constitutional scholars would have a discernible expertise. No longer would they be free to use imagination as a guide; or to ignore precedent or history; and they would have to offer reasonable assurance that every effort had been made to separate professional from personal belief. On issues of prudence, however, constitutional scholars enjoy *no more expertise than legislators.* In sum, while I maintain that the framers ultimately placed public policy choices in the hands of legislators, I have not said that responsibility would be an easy one.

63. *See* William Gangi, book review, 8 N.E.L.R. 123, 126 (1973) (parallels between slavery/antislavery, pre–Civil War arguments and contemporary pro-choice/antiabortion arguments).

bishops, or on the authority of the Lord God, who, eventually may inflict an eternal penalty on those found on the wrong side of the issue. (I certainly pray that He or She understands an interpretivist's reasoning!).[64]

The attempt of constitutional scholars to separate their personal opinions from professional opinions parallels the very idea of constitutionalism as understood by the framers: each generation's respect for the limitations previously adopted. So, in the end, it is not the awesome affirmative powers the people possess over their affairs that defines the American character, it is our willingness to honor the limitations adopted by our predecessors. I need not go any further. The principle is the same: separate personal opinions from professional responsibility. In doing so, constitutional scholars can make a valuable contribution to the political health of the Republic; even at times a critical one—and without abandoning cherished personal beliefs.

I will state in broader terms the importance of distinguishing constitutional issues from *sub*constitutional issues, placing the task within a larger political framework:

In the Constitution or Out?

All specialists take pride in the possession of particular tools or skills. As citizens, they also hold personal views on public policy issues. But no one should bow to the opinion of a surgeon on matters of taxation and spending. And the fact that someone is a constitutional scholar does not give that scholar's personal preferences on constitutional matters greater weight than any other citizen's personal preferences. So-called constitutional scholars must demonstrate a constitutional expertise that transcends the subject matter being discussed, or their views have no more weight than a surgeon's have on taxation! The views of a constitutional scholar on the relevant issues are not entitled to greater authority simply because of their owner's title, constitutional scholar. If in fact such scholars disguise their personal preferences by clothing them in constitutional terminology, they are coercing and deceiving their fellow citizens. Pretending to address matters of public concern, what they have done is introduce their biases into the discussion.

What must distinguish constitutional scholars from other commentators on public policy should be their attachment to the framers' and ratifiers' understanding of constitutional provisions. If their fellow citizens unanimously agreed to deviate from that understanding, the true constitutional scholar would stand fast against such deviations—even while agreeing that the proposed deviation might be more conducive to the public good than the original.

Members of the judiciary have ac-

64. *See supra,* note 61, for reference.

cepted the opportunity to exercise a combination of legal expertise and coercive power.[65] Acceptance of that responsibility also obligates them to exercise this power prudently, and that separates members of the judiciary from other constitutional scholars. *But all constitutional scholars, including judges, derive their expertise from the* same *source. They acquire, as best they can, knowledge relevant to the intentions of the framers.*

I reject an expanded judicial role because it must eventually lead to the ridiculous conclusion that members of the judiciary not only must become experts on topics ranging from anatomy to zoology, but that they also are capable of resolving differences of opinion within each of those disciplines. The thought that any nine judges, selected as they are, could possess such expertise is inherently presumptuous. It is far more probable that over time such judges will substitute their personal preferences for those of the framers or legislators. I maintain that judges were charged with the sole responsibility of guarding constitutionalized principles—not to decide public policies where those principles are not at stake. It is quite enough that judges be required to acquire constitutional competency and to exercise judicial power prudently. The ratifiers wisely did not burden them with more; and experience has taught us that when members of the judiciary do not so confine themselves, they have been *neither competent nor prudent.*

To the extent that the principles constitutionalized by the framers can be discerned, interpretivists contend that judges must protect and preserve those principles. While continued disagreements are inevitable, all interpretivists minimally recognize that judges must focus on the passive judicial virtues,[66] adequately consider the entire text of the Constitution and the purposes for which it and its amendments were framed, maintain adequate standards of relevance, engage in principled exposition of precedents, employ visible and consistent canons of construction, and understand how their power is to be tempered by prudence. Judges must marshal evidence and employ logic that is illuminated by past concrete actions, rather than logic fed by speculation or imagination.

All interpretivists, however, also must recognize those principles that have *not* been constitutionalized. Self-government inevitably entails disagreement among citizens over what constitutes the common good. In the Republic created by the Constitution, the responsibility for deliberation on and resolution of such issues should lie with electorally accountable public servants. As citizens, like all citi-

65. U.S. Const. art 6, sec. 3 (Each member of the judiciary "shall be bound by Oath or Affirmation, to support [this] Constitution"). *See* text, note 82 *infra*.
66. *See e.g.*, Alexander Bickel, The Least Dangerous Branch (1962).

zens, interpretivists may add their personal opinions to the fray. But they must take care when doing so to label those opinions as being distinct from their expertise in identifying and clarifying the ratifiers' intentions. It is the latter expertise that may encourage interpretivists to counsel abandonment of those intentions by the only procedures they recognize as legitimate: the amendment procedures.

Similarly, interpretivists should be among the first to insist that the people's elected representatives are free to deliberate on matters that others claim are foreclosed, alleging that there are constitutional barriers. In declaring constitutional infirmity, the accuser should be forced to demonstrate that the legislative actions taken or contemplated are contrary to the Constitution or its amendments as they were understood by those who framed and ratified them. The people must recognize and submit to only those limitations on their power of self-government that enjoy concrete historical support. If the accuser cannot demonstrate such support, no right has been established. In such cases, one may conclude that the accuser mistakenly confused a personal judgment of what constitutes good public policy with fidelity to the instrument.

The Political Arena: An Embarrassment.

Changes that occur in public attitudes or politics do not by themselves constitute proof that the accompanying proposals are better or worse for society than the policies that precede them. Reference to future political, social, or economic trends, real or imagined, also certainly offers no legitimate perspective for the constitutional scholar.[67] Many scholars today devote their attention to what a majority of five justices of the Supreme Court have decided and, as a result, when Court nominees go before the Senate for confirmation such scholars inform us in which areas the nominee favors judicial activism and in which areas the nominee believes restraint is more appropriate.[68] Should a nominee be confirmed, scholars so

67. I have already noted that the pattern over the past century has been for groups of adherents to pretend to know the future. *Cf. supra,* chapter 4, text accompanying notes 31–45 and 76–104. Much noninterpretivist review theorizing today is dependent upon unsubstantiated assertions about American history. *Cf. supra,* chapter 1, text accompanying notes 3–16, and chapter 6, text accompanying notes 30–41.

68. The personal views of justices have always been a matter of concern. Even under the best of circumstances, it takes a particular temperament, not to mention faith in the structures and people, for a person to separate personal beliefs from expertise. Of course, these qualities were essential if the judicial power envisioned by the framers (to declare acts contrary to the constitution void) was to be understood in its proper context. The framers believed judges would take the long perspective because their training taught respect for precedents. Yarbrough, for example, notes:

> What Tocqueville, like Hamilton, seems to have in mind are lawyers schooled in the great common law tradition. A respect for procedure and tradition, as well as an appreciation of the importance of institutions in preserving liberty distinguishes them from both

inclined predict what results will be forthcoming on the Court or which scholars will get their way and who now will be relegated to crying in the wilderness. While some scholars may choose to perceive such issues as exhausting the meaning of constitutional law, I view these realities as symptoms of a disease, though not the disease itself. The disease is the absence of a principled perspective and an unwillingness to be confined by the intentions of the ratifiers.[69]

Interpretivists, however, do not get their bearings from public opinion polls—those apparently ultimate reference points for the validation of contemporary judicial usurpations.[70] Opinion polls merely register responses, usually an affirmative or a negative, to questions that are often defective in construction, and if not defective certainly not the equivalent of deliberation. They record attitudes—judgments that reflect habitual training. And they are often made in response to insufficient or inaccurate information. Such judgments lack the reflection prompted by competing arguments. For example, take the following questions: Do you believe in capital punishment? On a scale of one to ten, how strongly do you hold your positive or negative reply? Even assuming that the samples are representative and valid, are the responses to these questions to be equated with deliberation that will culminate in an end product called public law? Is this what the framers had in mind when they spoke of deliberation? I suggest it is precisely what they were trying to avoid: the injection of passion directly into public decision making. Do such questions give the respondent an oppor-

---

> their country cousins, so acidly described by Edmund Burke in his *Reflections on the Revolution in France,* as well as the successful merchants and farmers whose interest is private and whose motive is profit.

Yarbrough, *supra* note 50, at 78, n. 29. Today, as fewer and fewer distinctions exist between ordinary policy making and constitutional law interpretation, and the common law has largely been supplanted by statutory law, greater injection of personal opinions might have been anticipated. The danger, of course, is that, instead of chastising the judiciary, efforts will be made to make the judiciary more responsive to political pressure groups: by limiting their terms or electing them. (Something like this can be seen in how we are approaching the crime issue: instead of rejecting judicial usurpation and reasserting control over the criminal justice systems, we talk of compensating victims!) So-called corrective movements against abuses of judicial power could severely damage the schema created by the framers, and of course, that would leave us without the original check on majority powers as they understood it: judicial review. Thus, I do not favor such moves. I would rather endure and eventually reassert legislative prerogatives by contrary legislation, removal of jurisdiction, exercise of the Congress' power to regulate, and impeachment. Nevertheless, I understand the frustration felt by those who favor such moves.

69. Robert Bork was perhaps the most qualified nominee to come before the Senate in a century, yet he was denied confirmation. There are many reasons why that happened, but my concern is narrower: I see it as an example of how the population was drawn into public policy making at an inappropriate level.

70. *See e.g.,* William B. Lockhart, *et al.,* Constitutional Law, 6th Ed. 8–31 (1986) (discussing judicial review and democracy).

tunity to think about the issue's complexities? Punishment for a hired killer? For a serial murderer? For a crime of passion? Are such distinctions meaningful? Do responses to polls (given as totals, yet!) help us discern whether or not all respondents would answer the same way if they were aware that the murderer had been convicted of an earlier murder and upon escaping prison killed a correction officer? What are the present statistics and circumstances regarding the frequency of rapes, or repeated rapes, or rapes that leave the victims alive but physically or psychologically handicapped? What do those responses tell us about how respondents would answer regarding assassinations, terrorism, treason, or child murder? The trouble with a poll is the same as the trouble with logic: a model can destroy the subject matter.[71]

In the legislative process, on the other hand, intensely negative and affirmative respondents still might be able to reach a consensus.[72] While some respondents on either side of the issue raised above probably would always be unwilling to budge, in the deliberative process they would have fewer options: *either they participate to preserve as much of their position as they can when measured against those who are more pragmatic, or they might be ignored altogether if a majority coalition can otherwise be formed from the more flexible and indifferent.* To fervent opponents or supporters of capital punishment, pragmatists surely lack principle (unswerving devotion to their cause); but politics often is about the concrete, not the abstract. In the absence of a constitutionalized principle, interpretivists become average citizens and stand aside in their capacity as *constitutional* scholars. If approached on the constitutionality of capital punishment, the criterion remains the clearly discernible intentions of the framers.[73]

Another example will further demonstrate the position that the intentions of the framers is the only criterion that enables the scholar to distinguish personal values from constitutional values. If I described the Supreme Court as "disclos[ing] a disconcerting reliance on selective reasoning, manipulation and sometimes outright misstatement of controlling precedent,"[74] would the reader suspect the quotation was from a critique of the laissez-faire Court, the Warren Court, the Burger Court, or the Rhenquist Court? That assessment applies to all four Courts![75] Only the ratifiers' understanding of the Constitution offers

71. *Cf. supra,* chapter 6, text accompanying notes 50–66.

72. *See, e.g.,* "In Bitter Abortion Debate, Opponents Learn to Reach for Common Ground," The New York Times A10 (February 17, 1992).

73. *See e.g.,* BERGER, *supra* note 39, at 178–180.

74. Note, *Exclusionary Rule Under Attack,* 4 U. BALT. L. REV. 89, 96 (1974).

75. Certainly distinctions could be made between the laissez-faire, Warren, Burger, and Rhen-

a criterion for assessing change, and in the absence of that criterion, constitutional scholars have become mere recorders of the latest manipulation of precedents by those currently in power. There is no single significant area of constitutional case law that today is not disconcerting to the serious, non-result-oriented scholar.[76]

The Supreme Court has increasingly become an embarrassment to the American political tradition. Its opinions grow more and more unconvincing and inconsistent. The justices, as I have frequently demonstrated, try to put square pegs into round holes in an effort to adapt the Constitution to their personal policy preferences, while trying simultaneously to portray continuity. So, too, has the Court increasingly gone beyond its legitimate power, its decisions often resting on little more than compromise or consensus among the justices, effectively replacing the national Madisonian scheme with competing factions represented by nine individuals. What is particularly embarrassing is that over the past twenty-five years a majority of those justices have failed to recognize that they have elevated themselves to the role of primary public policy maker. Or worse, they have recognized it and have suppressed their recognition. Surely the justices must suspect that such a role is contrary to the one envisioned for it by the founding fathers?

FINAL PERSPECTIVE ON STAKES

Noninterpretivists charge that subscription to the principles championed in this book entails the repudiation of almost every significant modern Supreme Court decision in the areas of, among others, due process, equal protection, and the Bill of Rights.[77] There is considerable merit to that contention. The noninterpretivist claim goes further, asserting that many of the decisions condemned by interpretivists were wise, good, just, and conducive to the public

quist courts, but my emphasis here is on the common tendency of these courts to substitute personal opinions for those of legislators. I do not minimize the difficulty nor legitimacy of questions such as, "How does a justice committed to the intentions of the framers approach a majority of justices not so inclined?"

76. *See e.g.,* ALEXANDER BICKEL, THE SUPREME COURT AND THE IDEA OF PROGRESS 175–176 1970); Philip Kurland, *Foreword to the Supreme Court 1963 Term,* 78 HARV. L. REV. 143, 162–176 (1965); Herbert Wechsler, *Toward Neutral Principles of Constitutional law* 73 HARV. L.R. 1 (1959). *But see* J. Skelly Wright, *Professor Bickel, The Scholarly Tradition, and the Supreme Court,* 84 HARV. L. REV. 769, 770 (1971). *Cf.* Maurice Holland, *American Liberals and Judicial Activism: Alexander Bickel's Appeal From the New To the Old,* 51 IND. L. J. 1026, 1026 (1976).

77. *See e.g.,* Dean Alfange, *On Judicial Policymaking and Constitutional Change: Another Look at the 'Original Intent' Theory of Constitutional Interpretation,* 5 HASTINGS CONST. L. Q. 603, 611–618 (1978); and Stanley Kutler, *Raoul Berger's Fourteenth Amendment: a History or Ahistorical?,* 6 HASTINGS CONST. L. Q. 511, 512–519 (1979).

well-being.[78] Without judicial power, noninterpretivists conclude, such beneficial results might not have been achieved, or at least not as quickly.[79] Again, there is truth in these assertions.

But after considering (even conceding) the beneficent results claimed, I urge the reader to weigh those results against the fact that the people might not enjoy their heritage—might have their right of self-government taken away or modified without their consent. What then of the rule of law?

The stakes are indeed high: so high that they should be put on the table in a forthright manner. If the judiciary itself is no longer required to be faithful to the Constitution, then those who support that position abandon the American tradition. Rule by judges constitutes a radical departure from the tradition of republicanism and its advocates cannot both rely on that tradition to keep stable those political structures or individual rights that they favor while treating other parts of the Constitution as open-ended.

Noninterpretivists—*I repeat*—sanction abandoning the original meaning ascribed to certain provisions because they believe those meanings fail to provide the protections that ought to be available today. To secure protections they believe to be adequate, or to provide the necessary correctives, they depart from those original meanings. By doing so, however, they have redefined the tradition of majority rule and self-government. Evidently they no longer consider these to be essential. They sanction judicial usurpation in order to obtain the common good. Can noninterpretivists then object if similar behavior is exhibited by either the executive or legislative branches? To do so would be inconsistent and unprincipled. Eventually, as feared by the framers, usurpations by Congress, the most powerful and numerous branch, possessor of the sword and the purse, would prevail.[80] Once that occurs (and no doubt it, too, will come under a benevolent guise), it is just a matter of time until all checks against governmental and majority tyranny are eliminated. Ironically, once legislative power is freed from constitutional restraints it may simply obliterate any prior, beneficent results championed by noninterpretivists and imposed by the judiciary. Subsequently, as Publius predicted, we

78. *Cf. supra,* chapter 6, discussion of *Results* and *Cumbersome* symbols. I do not question that noninterpretivists sincerely seek the common good. I question only the constitutionality of their using the judiciary to impose it.

79. *See* Randall Bridwell, *The Federal Judiciary: America's Recently Liberated Minority,* 30 S.C.L. Rev. 467, 473 n.14 (1979). Bridwell criticizes arguments favoring expansive judicial activism "structured around the horrible results that will allegedly occur without it . . . What passes for a defense of a particular form of judicial power rests almost entirely upon the assumed advantage that would accrue to its existence." *Id.*

80. *Cf. supra,* chapter 2, text accompanying note 27.

may need to "take refuge" in a dictator![81]

That is not all. Congress may go even further, attacking principles that the Constitution's ratifiers clearly intended to protect. Upon what grounds will noninterpretivists object? And how will they bring such violations to the attention of their fellow citizens? Such pleas will fall upon deaf ears because *the habit of fidelity* will have atrophied. Fidelity (*all* fidelity) must be continuously exercised if it is to remain viable, and noninterpretivists clearly abandoned that ground when they counseled forsaking original intentions. They looked away when the judiciary first imposed beneficent results.

I believe such a scenario is written in the history of prior republics—an awareness of which the framers gave far more attention to than do noninterpretivists. That is why I insist that constitutionalized principles must be identified and separated from those that were not constitutionalized; and that professional opinions must be distinguished from public policy preferences. By focusing on the ratifiers' understanding, the record of the judiciary over the past century becomes clearer. One presumptuous view of progress after another has been injected into the fabric of constitutional law by intelligent, well-intentioned jurists. Each of these waves has spawned new "systems" and each system in its own way has suppressed questions about the common good.

Finally, I remind the reader that the Constitution provides that the Constitution "shall be the supreme Law of the Land" and that each member of the judiciary "shall be bound by Oath or Affirmation, to support [it]."[82] As a nation, can we seriously believe that the ratifiers understood that those taking that oath were *swearing or affirming allegiance to vagueness, generality, or open-endedness?* The framers and ratifiers created a constitution—the Constitution—that contained specific principles, and the special duty of the federal judiciary in that schema was to remind all citizens and government officials of the principles to which all had freely consented.

Judges are not entitled to consider a higher law when fulfilling their oath. They cannot legitimately appeal to any law higher than the Constitution to which they have sworn allegiance. Unlike academic theorists, or even legislators, who are free to pursue truth, judges wear robes of constitutional fidelity. Once having taken the oath of fidelity, when acting in their official judicial capacity their only guide should be the intentions of the ratifiers. Until the emergence of modern constitutional law, the significance of the judicial oath was clear; and for the most part it was respected. The Supreme Court

81. *See supra,* chapter 1, text accompanying note 57.
82. U.S. CONST.. art 6, sec. 2 & 3.

must revitalize that understanding of its judicial duty and act accordingly.

CLOSING REMARKS

I continually look for analogies to help explain my approach to constitutional law: they sometimes come from unexpected sources. At mass one Sunday, I once heard a priest recount the story of his having seen a young child, at the beach one day, bawling because she wanted her grandmother, who was loaded with beach paraphernalia, to carry her, too, to their car. The grandmother refused, telling the child that she must walk and carry her own chair, but to make it easier the grandmother added that they could play a kind of game as they walked: the child could walk in the grandmother's shadow, mimicking all her movements. Before long the crying stopped and the child gleefully walked in her grandmother's shadow. The priest deduced two lessons from the scene: first, we all must carry our own burdens and should learn to do so without complaint; and second, we all need someone's shadow to walk in. He then asked his parishioners, "In whose shadow do *you* walk?"

I suggest constitutional scholars should ask themselves the same question. We must walk in the shadows cast by the framers and ratifiers, our special task being to mark the boundaries of those shadows; to help explain to fellow citizens when in our opinion the people are obliged to follow the footsteps of the founders; and, just as important, when they are not so obliged. As long as courts walk in the founders' shadow their decisions are legitimate. They may, in doubtful situations, even stretch the boundaries of the shadows. They may not, however, deceive the people, asking for fidelity to shadows they themselves have created.

A return to principled adjudication will take a long time: that cannot be denied. Whether it will even come about at all cannot be known. Contact with students, friends, budding attorneys, and many of my academic colleagues never ceases to amaze me: so much of America's political and legal traditions and the structures that preserve them is no longer understood.[83] But pessimism leads nowhere and I am frequently heartened by students who, coerced into reading assigned materials, come away, if not convinced of the merits of my position, at least pensive—often more open, and always far more critical and less susceptible to noninterpretive shadow making.

One sees paradoxical trends emerging, including the liberal legal intelligentsia's greater reliance on Con-

83. The media only deepens the malaise, particularly since it conveniently understands itself to embody the essence of the American political tradition—freedom of speech and press. Not since the statement from the chairman of General Motors, "What is good for GM is good for America," has a like aphorism taken such firm root: "The public has a right to know!" Funny how little the public has to say about it!

gress and state courts because, as some of them candidly admit, liberals no longer dominate the Supreme Court—at least not as uniformly or consistently as they once did, under Chief Justice Earl Warren. Accordingly, in some quarters and in some policy areas the virtues of a federal system and independent state judiciaries have enjoyed a renaissance.[84] It is somewhat ironic, but sympathy for the views expressed in this book may come mostly from the ranks of former liberal noninterpretivists—those willing to use my views strategically to discourage an unfriendly Supreme Court from using its power until more activist liberal justices regain control of the Court. I cannot control such strategic uses (abuse) of my arguments. I also understand the temptation and desire: it would be there for me, should a sufficient judicial majority emerge to make possible reversal of illegitimate noninterpretivist precedents. Whether or not the nation can return to the pre–laissez-faire constitutional law tradition without reversing earlier opinions is a legitimate question. Consideration of that question would make selection of new justices committed to the constitutionalism that I champion difficult. Nominees inevitably would be screened on the basis of past (and present) important policy questions. Such issues are beyond scope of this book.

But constitutionalists can make a difference, at least if we insist effectively that constitutional law is not arbitrary; that it does not consist of dressing policy issues up in legalistic clothing; that there are principles and rules to follow. So I hope that after reading this book the reader will distinguish between what is really in the Constitution and what is only *sub* constitutional.

This book leaves vast areas unexplored, particularly regarding prudential and strategic decisions. Resolution of such issues may well be crucial to the political actions neces-

84. *See e.g.,* William Brennan, *State Constitutions and the Protection of Individual Rights,* 90 HARV. L. REV. 489 (1977) and Donald Wilkes, *The New Federalism in Criminal Procedure: State Court Evasion of the Burger Court,* 62 KY. L. J. 421 (1974). Some former Warren Court supporters demand that the reversal of any of those decisions must take place only by amendment. *See e.g.,* Irving Kaufman, "Congress v. the Court," THE NEW YORK TIMES MAGAZINE 44, 56 (September 20, 1981). But they do not establish the rights they assume—only that the Warren Court declared them. Dixon astutely observes: "It is easy to make a major constitutional decision but almost impossible thereafter to draft an amendment to undo the one unpopular decision without affecting anything else or creating new problems." Robert G. Dixon, *Article V: The Comatose Article of Our Living Constitution,* 66 MICH. L. REV. 931 (1968). Other supporters of the Warren Court decisions concede that Congress may modify Supreme Court decisions, and they have pressed that argument to reverse several Rhenquist Court decisions. *See* C. Dickerman Williams, "Congress and the Supreme Court," NATIONAL REVIEW 109 (February 5, 1982). The crucial distinction is whether a given Court decision rests on statutory or constitutional grounds. In the case of the former, the decision clearly can be revised by Congress; but this is not so in the case of decisions that rest on constitutional grounds.

sary to make interpretivist views practically effective. Elsewhere I may address them in a systematic fashion: here, however, my task is ended. I stop with the knowledge that I have done my utmost to preserve and protect the Constitution and leave to my successors a record of the principles I believe have been present from the beginning of the Republic.

APPENDIX A

Self-Image, Interpersonal Conflicts, and Public Administration

How we feel about ourselves, and what we believe, often defines our interactions with other people. It is at the center of many interpersonal conflicts.[1] Public administrators are no longer as consumed by efficiency as was Frederick Taylor. Instead, during the past thirty years public administrators, such as Joseph Cayer, have explored areas such as human resources management.[2] More recently, Weston Agor has done pioneering work in identifying intuitive and analytical managerial styles.[3]

The need for greater self-awareness is an often repeated theme in current literature, and in that regard the Myers-Briggs type indicator test (MBTI) certainly provides a structure that can be of help to students seeking greater self-awareness.[4] That test identifies sixteen basic personality types, grouped by "preferences" in four categories:

1. Where an individual obtains energy (energy-source preference): introverts are less dependent on others than are extroverts.
2. How an individual obtains information (information-source preference): sensors rely more heavily on input through the five senses (hearing, seeing, smelling, tasting, touching) than do intuitives, who place greater emphasis on finding new relationships between already acquired ideas;
3. How an individual prefers to make decisions: feelers prefer personal value judgments; thinkers prefer impersonal, objective judgments;
4. Lifestyle preferences: judgers prefer to plan; perceivers tend to be more spontaneous; judgers prefer to bring things to closure—to make decisions; perceivers prefer to wait for more conclusive evidence.

Intriguing and revealing as use of the MBTI can be for students, it already assumes a great deal of self-awareness. It does not itself provide a dynamic set of tools for continued in-

1. Paper presented at New York State Political Science Association, State University of New York, Albany, New York (April 21, 1990) (revised).

2. Joseph Cayer, Managing Human Resources (1980).

3. Weston Agor, Intuitive Management: Integrating Left and Right Brain Management Skills (1984); Intuitive Management (1984); The Logic of Intuitive Decision-Making (1986), and Intuition in Organizations: Leading and Managing Productivity (1989).

4. *See generally,* David Keirsey and Marilyn Bates, Please Understand Me 4 (1984). The topic is more fully explored in Appendix B.

trospection. This appendix addresses that gap by briefly exploring three interrelated topics: attitudes, feelings, and self-image, although here, these themes cannot be completely fleshed out. In some other place, instructions may be offered on how to conduct classes in these topics.

THREE LEVELS OF COMMUNICATION

We communicate on three levels: through our intellectual positions, attitudes, and feelings.

INTELLECTUAL POSITIONS. These are *reasoned* judgments. Simply put, the brain uses induction or deduction to analyze data and reach conclusions: logic reigns supreme; emotion is minimized. The brain both enumerates and weighs the pros and cons of issues. All this takes place in milliseconds. This method of communication forms the foundation of our education process, but it is not the focal point of this appendix.

ATTITUDES. These are judgments (beliefs, prejudices) regarding the rightness or wrongness of beliefs and actions. They are acquired through habit. *Repetition is the foundation of all attitude formulation.* During our formative years we are exposed (or not exposed!) to the judgments of parents, church, and society. Many of those judgments are internalized.

Attitudes serve as an alternative to thinking. They often appear to be so correct (so "natural") that the intellect is paralyzed; i.e., incapable of identifying alternatives. The intellect then rationalizes (defends) the attitude held. *For that reason, attitudes often shape our responses to the suggestions, analyses, conclusions, and actions of others.*

Attitudes permeate our lives, from such activities as defining the right way to squeeze a toothpaste tube to correctly exiting a highway; from what constitutes an ideal mate to perceptions of femininity and masculinity; from whether or not to live on a cash-only basis to the acceptance of considerable debt as normal; from buying a "handyman special" to making sure that all office equipment has a maintenance contract. In sum, different attitudes often provide the dynamics for interpersonal conflicts.

To make several broad observations: Attitude formulation is normal and is necessary because we probably could not function at all if the brain had to reevaluate everything, every day. Existing attitudes unquestionably inhibit societal change, but by the same token without them there would be less societal stability; see, for example, *The Lord of the Flies.*

FEELINGS. My experience has been that many academicians are uncomfortable discussing feelings—some of them, apparently because of their *attitudes,* hold that feelings are an unfit subject for political science (too personal, too unscientific). Such an assessment is at the heart of thinking types. Others are uncomfortable because they contend that in other cultures distinctions between feelings and thoughts are not made. Still others are uncomfortable with feelings because in our male-dominated culture logic-skills are elevated and that habit has been discouraged among females. I ask that temporarily you put such judgments aside.

I will define feelings as internal responses to stimuli. These are various feelings; e.g., love, hate, joy, disappointment, shame, anger, enthusiasm, anxiety, pride, loneliness. Each feeling is capable of different intensities; e.g., loneliness can shade into depression which can move to despair; happiness can become joy and even ecstasy. These examples have been arbitrarily divided into three intensities, when in fact the spectrum is more of a continuum.

I make two contentions: (1). The individual has no control over the initial emergence of feelings, which come from within in response to a stimulus. (2). Feelings are neither right nor wrong. They are simply feelings.

If, as in (1), the initial emergence of feelings is not within the individual's control, then under traditional Western philosophical standards moral judgments cannot be attributed to those feelings. Morality involves choice. While feelings have no moral character, what we do with feelings (the actions we take) does; e.g., to feel lazy in the morning does not have a moral quality but the *decision* whether or not to go to work does.

Most people confuse thoughts and feelings. To communicate the fact that I feel something requires that when I use either the phrase *I feel* or *I am* I add a word describing my feeling; e.g., *sad, happy.* No other part of speech (except modifiers such as very) should follow *feel.* But often we hear people use the phrase *I feel that,* or *I feel like,* followed by an opinion, conclusion, or judgment; for example, "I feel that the New York State political science convention should be held in a warm climate!"

Use this simple test: If, in the sentence you are using, the word *think* can be substituted for the word *feel* and the sentence still makes sense then an opinion, conclusion, or judgment is being expressed—not a feeling. Such expressions should be identified accordingly. The distinction is a real one. Take a sentence I might use in speaking with my students: "I feel that you did not study my lecture carefully." I am expressing a judgment, not a feeling, and when such thoughts or judgments are expressed *and understood as such,* an appropriate question is: *Why?* It is a request for more information, prompting an exchange of views, asking that the speaker go beyond the assertion. Communication proceeds.

But if a judgment is presented as what I *feel* I confuse the ground rules for good communication. I might even thwart communication at both intellectual and feeling level. For example, should the student reply with "Why?" or perhaps by giving her own assessment, that the facts, as she knows them are inconsistent with my conclusion, I could respond: "But I was only expressing a feeling, and I might have been wrong." Note, I am never compelled to back up my assertion with evidence, if I ever had any; nor am I forced to probe any of my own attitudes that perhaps underlie my contention; e.g., "Students don't do their homework assignments."

The student, if she has the confidence to speak out in the first place, is left exposed. She knows she read the lecture, and perhaps she is aware that others also read it. But she probably will not get a chance to put that evidence on the table because my reply—that it was only my "feeling"—would probably silence her. Many of us have been trained that feelings convey something private, something not open to dispute. Thus, while she quite correctly challenged her teacher's evidence, ultimately she is treated as if she took the whole matter much too seriously. Such conduct on my part is unlikely to create an atmosphere of communication, to say nothing of class participation.

Equally important, despite my use of the word *feelings,* communication certainly does not take place at the "feelings" level, since I did not describe my feelings. Had my contention been stated correctly, "I think that you did not study my lecture carefully," or if that assessment proved correct, I at least would have had the opportunity really to share some feelings: e.g., frustration or annoyance. So the opportunity to communicate on the feeling level also has been lost.

Furthermore, since feelings are neither right nor wrong, a *why* question about them is irrelevant. What is important are the feelings themselves. True, sometimes we need to understand the context in which feelings are expressed, but the next time such an occasion arises, examine your motives. Are you trying objectively to understand that context? Or, do you wish to evaluate whether or not the circumstances described *justify* the feelings expressed? In such circumstances, communication is better served by asking, "How does it feel to feel that way?" or "In what situations have you felt that before?"

Students should acquire the habit of probing strong feelings and allowing their presence to trigger introspection. Feelings can help them to identify strong attitudes. And strong attitudes often are at the core of interpersonal conflicts and ineffective communication. They cause us to react instead of respond to attitudes contrary to our own. In class, I use a series of statements such as, "In college you must decide what you will do for the rest of your life," and "Marriages should last forever"—statements intended to prod students into uncovering their attitudes and to separate those attitudes from their intellectual judgments and feelings.

This much is certain, and of particular importance for those responsible for training managers: self-awareness grows in direct proportion to an understanding of one's attitudes; only then can an assessment be made of whether or not the attitudes acquired over a lifetime should be retained, modified, or discarded. Developing the ability to distinguish judgments from attitudes and feelings serves to free the intellect, permitting more objective scrutiny. That ability in turn permits greater flexibility in behavior and decision making.

If you judge that old attitudes are no longer beneficial (and it is with your intellect that you must make that assessment), they can be changed. Old dogs *can* learn new tricks. But do not create unrealistic expectations among your students. Changing attitudes is difficult, and there is only one way: students must *adopt habits contrary to the conduct that led to the attitudes they now wish to abandon.* Attitudes rarely can be changed by an act of will—by telling yourself that in the future you will "think differently," hoping then that your behavior will change. On the contrary, since most attitudes are acquired over long periods—say twenty or more years—changes in those attitudes will take considerable time. Students must anticipate slipping back into the behavior patterns created by the old attitudes, and they must work hard not to be discouraged when that happens.

Having thus far explored some of the fundamentals of attitude and feelings introspection, I will put these ideas in a larger context.

SELF-IMAGE

Many of us have been trained to link our feelings with self-image. When we feel helpless, worthless, or afraid, our self-image and confidence decline. I want to introduce the concept of *masks.* Do not confuse the meaning I give that term with the definition *masks* commonly enjoy. In my usage, a mask is never used to convey qualities that are superficial or disposable. Instead, *mask* is used as a shorthand expression for *an image that I want to project to others.* In my usage, masks are *always positive* from the perspective of their wearers. For example, a young man may wear a macho mask, believing the things he does (acting as though he is unemotional; driving a muscle car) projects a strong, independent image. It is irrelevant that others may judge him a chauvinistic fool. He does the things he does either because he is unaware that others disapprove of them or because their disapproval is irrelevant to him.

We wear many masks. Some are more important and worn more intensely than others. The most important ones frequently revolve around the activities that take most of our time or energy: being a student, parent, worker, and so forth. Here is an exercise. To spot lesser masks, pick a situation, or person, with whom you are uncomfortable, then identify what you do in that situation (or in the presence of that person) to make yourself feel more comfortable. That activity will help define one of the masks you wear.

Masks also revolve around characteristics such as attractiveness, honesty, sensuality, intellect, and so forth. Finally, masks also can have very subtle foundations: the good son or daughter, the lady's man, the man killer. Masks frequently mirror the attitudes we hold.

At any one time, an individual probably has half a dozen important masks. Among them, one can be described as being the core mask. You can identify your own core mask by asking, "What is my most important quality?" All masks may and probably will change over a lifetime.

In class, I sketch four common core masks: the intellectual, the concerned person, the attractive person, and the clown. These sketches describe typical attitudes, behavior patterns, and feelings that may accompany such masks. Each description portrays the good qualities each mask-wearer possesses and how each mask also serves to shield the wearer from outside hurt. By sketching such masks, I make the lecture more concrete, painting portraits of character types—someone the students can recognize, even if it be themselves. The four masks certainly are not exhaustive, and indeed behavior varies considerably even among those who wear similar masks. There are thousands of masks and countless possible combinations.

It is the structure of the mask that concerns me. It has an exterior and an interior. The exterior part contains the positive qualities projected to others; the interior part contains feelings, which from time to time may be inconsistent with the feelings that the wearer of the mask judges to be appropriate. When these inconsistent feelings occur—as they must—the wearer is left feeling ashamed; self-confidence is shaken because they had such feelings at all. The wearer judges himself harshly because he reasons that if he was truly the person he projected while wearing the mask, the person he wants to be (and often is), he would not have such feelings.

That conclusion is based on a faulty premise: it assumes as fact two premises already rejected—that we have control over our feelings and that those feelings should be judged in the same manner as deeds. Feelings inconsistent with the masks we wear are inevitable, quite natural. Once that reality is accepted, we will not judge ourselves so harshly when it occurs, and we are on the road to greater self-awareness and self-esteem.

Self-image is forged under a double standard. When I ask students to divide a piece of paper in half and to list their good qualities on one side of the paper and bad qualities on the other, this double standard—shaped by attitudes—becomes more visible. To be identified as a good quality, that quality often must be present *nearly all the time.* A far less demanding standard is used for identifying bad qualities: they often make the list even when they occur *only some of the time.* Similarly, good qualities tend be accompanied by qualifications while bad qualities are listed in bolder language. In sum, most of us have been trained to be perfectionists, and unaware of that fact we often create and surround our endeavors with unrealistic expectations. When our accomplishments inevitably fall short of those standards, we take it as personal failure and our self-image suffers.

Take a closer look at behavior during periods of low self-image. It is not uncommon in such circumstances to feel sorry for ourselves, and from there to proceed to self-pity (i.e., judging that we are not appreciated, not loved). What do you do with those feelings? Aside from having various addictions (I look for a piece of pizza!) some people become surly, even belligerent; others withdraw. Both types tend to avoid or push away most strenuously those who love them the most at the very time when expressions of love are most needed. A relevant question: How were you trained by your parents to handle disappointment and rejection?

In conclusion, I offer a list. Students may be given helpful hints:

1. It is an important realization that feelings come and go. They pass. Even the good ones! We must teach students to accept that fact and work through negative feelings. That often requires of them that they make a *decision* not to dwell on negative feelings.
2. Ask students to get in touch with who they are. They do that by probing and distinguishing their thoughts, attitudes, and feelings. They can subsequently put them back together, and when they do so their decision making will be more objective and more responsive to their needs.
3. Have students get in touch with their bodies. Suppression of feelings does not work. Suppression buries feelings alive—creating stress. That stress often breaks out physically, whether in headaches, stomachaches, back pain, or other *regular* ailment. What is important is that students learn to identify how their bodies communicate with them. Without fail, the symptom will appear one day at the same time they are denying that anything is wrong. Ask them to trust the symptom more than their intellectual judgment. More likely than not, a round of more honest introspection is overdue. The expression of feelings almost always reduces the hold feelings have on us, and hence reduces stress.
4. Ask students to share feelings with a loved one—someone they trust. Most students ought not to share their deepest feelings or attitudes with just anyone. Those with whom students have only functional relationships are not entitled to knowing such intima-

cies and could take advantage of such knowledge.

Denying and suppressing feelings or hiding them from others often creates greater stress than the feelings themselves. Sometimes we fear that nobody else has felt quite the way we do, or that we ought not to have the feelings we have. Students must *decide* to trust someone—not wait for the feeling of trust to emerge.

5. Students can "act as if" the feelings they do have do not exist. Doing so permits other feelings to surface, and helps to break habits of self-pity.[4]

APPENDIX B

Temperament and Personality Types

We all recognize that people have preferences in every facet of life: this can range from a preference for living just for today to one for having one's lamb chops well done or medium rare. We also are familiar with possible and sometimes probable explanations for various behaviors: e.g., economic status, race, or gender. Jung observed that people have different temperaments. Along with others, Isabel Myers and Katheryn Briggs devised the Myers-Briggs Type Indicator Test (a short-answer quiz contained in the beginning of the Keirsey and Bates book, *Please Understand Me,* to help readers to identify their personality preferences) (1–4).[1]

Four pairs of what might be described as "opposite preferences" are given in the book. Although preferences may be held very strongly, they always remain *preferences*—because the opposite preference is also always possessed, even if only weakly.[2] The first pair of preferences given is that based on extroversion (E) and introversion (I).[3] Extroverts are invigorated by people while introverts are drained (i.e., when extroverts go to a party their batteries are charged; those of the introverts are drained). Introverts enjoy, even relish, solitary activities; extroverts avoid them, preferring the company of others (14–16).

The second pair of preferences given in the book revolves around what might be called learning-and-living preferences: sensation (S) and intuition (N).[4] The authors note that while extroversion and introversion often are sources of conflict, this second set of preferences is "the source of the most miscommunication, misunderstandings, vilification, defamation and denigration" (17). Sensible types describe themselves as practical while intuitive types see themselves as innovative. (16). The S-type "wants facts, trusts facts, and remembers facts" (17): they favor experience. The intuitive type looks beyond sensation to the possible, connecting ideas that to the sensible type are not

1. The material that follows is based on David Keirsey and Marilyn Bates, PLEASE UNDERSTAND ME [hereinafter PLEASE] (1984). The page numbers given in parenthesis in the text refer to discussion in Keirsey and Bates.
2. *Id.,* at 14 ("The question of whether these preferences are 'inborn' or develop fortuitously in infancy and youth remains unsettled.")
3. The *E* and *I* are placed in the text for purposes of further discussion. Such symbols are used to identify preferences, used in combination with other symbols to be identified shortly.
4. Since I has already been used to denote, introversion, intuition is represented by *N.*

connected. "The intuitive sometimes finds complex ideas coming to him as a complete whole, unable to explain how he knew" (18). Are you blind to the forest because of the trees; or blind to the trees because of the forest? The analogy cuts two ways. On the one hand, S-types believe that intuitives live in an ivory tower, failing to see that the trees lead to a forest of a particular character; or worse, imagine a forest where none exists. On the other hand, the N-type believes the S-type, while standing in a forest, is preoccupied with counting, identifying, and classifying the trees and would not even know he was in a forest; or would fail to see the nature and significance of the forest.

The third pair of preferences revolves around preference for an impersonal basis of choice—thinkers (T)—and preference for making choices on a more personal basis—feelers (F) (20–21). The terms are not intended to imply that thinkers do not feel or that feelers do not think, although each may so view the other. The thinking type tends to strip situations to principles and reach conclusions by logically applying those principles. Feelers may acknowledge the same principles but see those principles as being embodied in people. They measure the impact of principles as seen when applied to individuals. Thinkers see feelers as emotional; feelers see thinkers as uncaring.

The fourth pair of preferences has to do with how individuals deal with the outside world. The judging type (J) is inclined to bring things to closure—to reach decisions, to manifest a desire to resolve. Perceivers (P) prefer to keep their options open and fluid. Whereas resolution puts a judger at ease, it creates anxiety for perceivers. Conversely, caution comes more naturally to perceivers, judgers often seeing it as procrastination or indecisiveness.

The four pairs of preferences combine into sixteen types, each described by four letters, that express the individual's preference in each category:[5] e.g., ENTJ would describe an extrovert with intuitive and thinking preferences who is a judger.[6] The shorthand is a very inadequate description of the dynamics of each such type. For example, while similarities exist between all introverts, the type finds markedly different expression. These differences can be categorized as the four temperaments. Borrowing from Greek mythology to describe these, Kiersey and Bates refer to them as Apollo, Dionysus, Prometheus, and Epimetheus. In the four-letter symbols, the characteristics of these types are to be found in the middle two letters.

5. The sixteen types are: INFP, ENFP, INFJ, ENFJ, ISFP, ESFP, ISFJ, ESFJ, INTP, ENTP, INTJ, ENTJ, ISTP, ESTP, ISTJ, and ESTJ.

6. The authors indicate that it is possible to have mixed types: e.g., individuals who are comfortable either as extrovert or introvert. When such mixed types are added, there is a total of thirty-two types.

APOLLONIAN TEMPERAMENT: Apollo was commissioned to give humans a sense of spirit and those with the NF preferences spend their lives in the extraordinary, description-defying task of "the search for self." (57–58). Other types may have goals; or may desire to *not* have goals: but the NF pursues a strange end—a self-reflective end that defies itself: *becoming.* Hamlet's "to be or not to be" typifies the type's dilemma: paradoxically, the NF believes that "to act [to achieve, to become] is to destroy one's being, while 'to be' without acting is sham and therefore nonbeing" (59). NF types, the authors note, make up approximately 12 percent of the population.

DIONYSIAN TEMPERAMENT: Dionysus' task was to teach humans joy (or release). Such SP types "must be free . . . not be tied or bound or confined or obligated. . . . He does things because he has the urge." SP types make up approximately 38 percent of the population (31).

EPIMETHEAN TEMPERAMENT: Epimetheus had to convey to humans a sense of duty. These SJ types "must belong"; they are the "caretaker, not the cared for." As the authors describe it, "school is made for SJ s and largely run by SJ s and kept—mainly to transform these [mostly SP s] frolicking puppies into serious, duty-oriented little parents who seek only to know what they are 'supposed to do'" (40). SJ s are "natural historians" (44) and are "realistic about error and shortages" (41). SJ s constitute about 38 percent of the population.

PROMETHEAN TEMPERAMENT: Prometheus' mission was to give science to humans. NT types are fascinated by power—but power over nature rather than over people. NT types value being *competent.* They like "intelligence . . . doing things well under varying circumstances." They are questioners of authority and can be "unusually individualist and even arrogant." Of all the types, NT s are the "most self-critical." They are "haunted by a sense of always being on the verge of failure." (48–50). NTS constitute 12 percent of the population.

Kiersey and Bates provide the following chart, giving the percentage of each type in the United States population and key words that identify the preferences of each type (25–26).

(E) *Extroverts* —75%	(I) *Introverts* —25%
Sociability	Territoriality
Interaction	Concentration
External	Internal
Breadth	Depth
Extensive	Intensive
Multiplicity of relationships	Limited relationships
Expenditure of energies	Conservation of energies
Interest in external events	Interest in internal reactions

(S) *Sensibles* —75%	(N) *Intuitives* — 25%
Experience	Hunches
Past	Future
Realistic	Speculative
Perspiration	Inspiration
Actual	Possible
Down-to-earth	Head-in-clouds
Utility	Fantasy
Fact	Fiction
Practicality	Ingenuity
Sensible	Imaginative

(T) *Thinkers* —50%	(F) *Feelers* —50%
Objective	Subjective
Principles	Values
Policy	Social values
Laws	Extenuating circumstances
Criterion	Intimacy
Firmness	Persuasion
Impersonal	Personal
Justice	Humane
Categories	Harmony
Standards	Good or bad
Critique	Appreciate
Analysis	Sympathy
Allocation	Devotion

(J) *Judgers* —50%	(P) *Perceivers* —50%[7]
Settled	Pending
Decided	Gather more data
Fixed	Flexible
Plan ahead	Adapt as you go
Run one's life	Let life happen
Closure	Open options
Decision-making	Treasure-hunting
Planned	Open-ended
Completed	Emergent
Decisive	Tentative
Wrap it up	Something will turn up
Urgency	There's plenty of time
Deadline!	What deadline?
Get show on the road	Let's wait and see

For each of these sixteen types the authors provide a personality "profile."[8] It has been my experience when working with students that such profiles are uncannily accurate in about 80 percent of the cases—self-rated by the students. As the authors put it: "By knowing a person's type we can anticipate rather accurately what he will do most of the time."[9] The high correlation raises intriguing questions at many levels of constitutional scholarship: e.g., how important an influence has personality type been on those who founded the nation, on decisions of particular justices in particular cases, and on the preferences of contemporary scholars. I will briefly provide general examples of where such considerations may be relevant:

7. *Id.*, at 25–26.
8. PLEASE, *supra* note 1, at 167–207.
9. *Id.*, at 27.

1. The founding: Were Madison, Hamilton, and Jay all T-types—thinkers? Can we use knowledge of type to project the probable intent of the framers? Should we?
2. The justices: Was Chief Justice John Marshall a strong intuitive? Would identifying the personality preferences of a Court nominee have predictive value—not only about what the current justices will do but for counsel to shape their arguments with just the right mixture of characteristics? Don't we do that now anyway? In the selection of judges, should we eliminate or encourage certain types? Feelers? Thinkers? Is that what the Robert H. Bork nomination dispute was about?
3. In scholarly disputes: Should such considerations (a) influence what information is selected for study (what is important)? (b) decide whether *principles* or *impact* are ranked higher? and (c) decide on whether an open-ended constitution is the natural preference of perceivers while original intent is the natural preference of judgers?
4. The democratic process: Are some types more or less inclined to leave public policy resolutions in the hands of those electorally accountable?
5. Legal research: Using this approach, what types of arguments are dominant today? In these terms, has a shift occurred in law school populations? Are law review editors selected on a different basis than they were a century ago? How does the type preference of law review editors influence the selection of articles for publication?

APPENDIX C

The Constitution of the United States of America

PREAMBLE

We the people of the United States, in order to form a more perfect union, establish justice, insure domestic tranquility, provide for the common defense, promote the general welfare, and secure the blessings of liberty to ourselves and our posterity, do ordain and establish this Constitution for the United States of America.

Article I

Section 1. All legislative powers herein granted shall be vested in a Congress of the United States, which shall consist of a Senate and House of Representatives.

Section 2.1. The House of Representatives shall be composed of members chosen every second year by the people of the several States, and the electors in each State shall have the qualifications requisite for electors of the most numerous branch of the State legislature.

2. No person shall be a Representative who shall not have attained to the age of twenty five years, and been seven years a citizen of the United States, and who shall not, when elected, be an inhabitant of that State in which he shall be chosen.

3. Representatives and direct taxes shall be apportioned among the several States which may be included within this union, according to their respective numbers, which shall be determined by adding to the whole number of free persons, including those bound to service for a term of years, and excluding Indians not taxed, three fifths of all other Persons. The actual Enumeration shall be made within three years after the first meeting of the Congress of the United States, and within every subsequent term of ten years, in such manner as they shall by law direct. The number of Representatives shall not exceed one for every thirty thousand, but each State shall have at least one Representative; and until such enumeration shall be made, the State of New Hampshire shall be entitled to chuse three, Massachusetts eight, Rhode Island and Providence Plantations one, Connecticut five, New York six, New Jersey four, Pennsylvania eight, Delaware one, Maryland six, Virginia ten, North Carolina five, South Carolina five, and Georgia three.

4. When vacancies happen in the Representation from any State, the executive authority thereof shall issue writs of election to fill such vacancies.

5. The House of Representatives shall chuse their speaker and other officers; and shall have the sole power of impeachment.

Section 3.1. The Senate of the United States shall be composed of two Senators from each State, chosen by the legislature thereof, for six years; and each Senator shall have one vote.

2. Immediately after they shall be assembled in consequence of the first election, they shall be divided as equally as may be into three classes. The seats of the Senators of the first class shall be vacated at the expiration of the second year, of the second class at the expiration of the fourth year, and the third class at the expiration of the sixth year, so that one third may be chosen every second year; and if vacancies happen by resignation, or otherwise, during the recess of the legislature of any State, the executive thereof may make temporary appointments until the next meeting of the legislature, which shall then fill such vacancies.

3. No person shall be a Senator who shall not have attained to the age of thirty years, and been nine years a citizen of the United States and who shall not, when elected, be an inhabitant of that State for which he shall be chosen.

4. The Vice President of the United States shall be President of the Senate, but shall have no vote, unless they be equally divided.

5. The Senate shall choose their other officers, and also a President pro tempore, in the absence of the Vice President, or when he shall exercise the office of President of the United States.

6. The Senate shall have the sole power to try all impeachments. When sitting for that purpose, they shall be on oath or affirmation. When the President of the United States is tried, the Chief Justice shall preside: And no person shall be convicted without the concurrence of two thirds of the members present.

7. Judgment in cases of impeachment shall not extend further than to removal from office, and disqualification to hold and enjoy any office of honor, trust or profit under the United States: but the party convicted shall nevertheless be liable and subject to indictment, trial, judgment and punishment, according to law.

Section 4.1. The times, places and manner of holding elections for Senators and Representatives, shall be prescribed in each State by the legislature thereof; but the Congress may at any time by law make or alter such regulations, except as to the places of choosing Senators.

2. The Congress shall assemble at least once in every year, and such meeting shall be on the first Monday in December, unless they shall by law appoint a different day.

Section 5.1. Each House shall be the judge of the elections, returns and qualifications of its own members, and a majority of each shall constitute a quorum to do business; but a smaller number may adjourn from day to day, and may be authorized to compel the attendance of absent members, in such manner, and under such penalties as each House may provide.

2. Each House may determine the rules of its proceedings, punish its members for disorderly behavior, and, with the concurrence of two thirds, expel a member.

3. Each House shall keep a journal of its proceedings, and from time to time publish the same, excepting such parts as may in their judgment require secrecy; and the yeas and nays of the members of either House on any question shall, at the desire of one fifth of those present, be entered on the journal.

4. Neither House, during the session of Congress, shall, without the consent of the other, adjourn for more than three days, nor to any other place than that in which the two Houses shall be sitting.

Section 6.1. The Senators and Representatives shall receive a compensation for their services, to be ascertained by law, and paid out of the treasury of the United States. They shall in all cases, except treason, felony and breach of the peace, be privileged from arrest during their attendance at the session of their respective Houses, and in going to and returning from the same; and for any speech or debate in either House, they shall not be questioned in any other place.

2. No Senator or Representative shall, during the time for which he was elected, be appointed to any civil office under the authority of the United States, which shall have been created, or the emoluments whereof shall have been increased during such time: and no person holding any office under the United States, shall be a member of either House during his continuance in office.

Section 7.1. All bills for raising revenue shall originate in the House of Representatives; but the Senate may propose or concur with amendments as on other Bills.

2. Every bill which shall have passed the House of Representatives and the Senate, shall, before it become a law, be presented to the President of the United States; if he approve he shall sign it, but if not he shall return it, with his objections to that House in which it shall have originated, who shall enter the objections at large on their journal, and proceed to reconsider it. If after such reconsideration two thirds of that House shall agree to pass the bill, it shall be sent, together with the objections, to the other House, by which it shall likewise be reconsidered, and if approved by two thirds of that House, it shall become a law. But in all such cases the votes of both Houses shall be determined by yeas and nays, and the names of the persons voting for and against the bill shall be entered on the journal of each House respectively. If any bill shall not be returned by the President within ten days (Sundays excepted) after it shall have been presented to him, the same shall be a law, in like manner as if he had

signed it, unless the Congress by their adjournment prevent its return, in which case it shall not be a law.

3. Every order, resolution, or vote to which the concurrence of the Senate and House of Representatives may be necessary (except on a question of adjournment) shall be presented to the President of the United States; and before the same shall take effect, shall be approved by him, or being disapproved by him, shall be repassed by two thirds of the Senate and House of Representatives, according to the rules and limitations prescribed in the case of a bill.

Section 8. The Congress shall have the power

1. To lay and collect taxes, duties, imposts and excises, to pay the debts and provide for the common defense and general welfare of the United States; but all duties, imposts and excises shall be uniform throughout the United States;

2. To borrow money on the credit of the United States;

3. To regulate commerce with foreign nations, and among the several States, and with the Indian tribes;

4. To establish a uniform rule of naturalization, and uniform laws on the subject of bankruptcies throughout the United States;

5. To coin money, regulate the value thereof, and of foreign coin, and fix the standard of weights and measures;

6. To provide for the punishment of counterfeiting the securities and current coin of the United States;

7. To establish post offices and post roads;

8. To promote the progress of science and useful arts, by securing for limited times to authors and inventors the exclusive right to their respective writings and discoveries;

9. To constitute tribunals inferior to the Supreme Court;

10. To define and punish piracies and felonies committed on the high seas, and offenses against the law of nations;

11. To declare war, grant letters of marque and reprisal, and make rules concerning captures on land and water;

12. To raise and support armies, but no appropriation of money to that use shall be for a longer term than two years;

13. To provide and maintain a navy;

14. To make rules for the government and regulation of the land and naval forces;

15. To provide for calling forth the militia to execute the laws of the union, suppress insurrections and repel invasions;

16. To provide for organizing, arming, and disciplining, the militia, and for governing such part of them as may be employed in the service of the United States, reserving to the States respectively, the appointment of the officers, and the authority of training the militia according to the discipline prescribed by Congress;

17. To exercise exclusive legislation in all cases whatsoever, over such District (not exceeding ten miles

square) as may, by cession of particular States, and the acceptance of Congress, become the seat of the government of the United States, and to exercise like authority over all places purchased by the consent of the legislature of the State in which the same shall be, for the erection of forts, magazines, arsenals, dockyards, and other needful buildings;—And

18. To make all laws which shall be necessary and proper for carrying into execution the foregoing powers, and all other powers vested by this Constitution in the government of the United States, or in any department or officer thereof.

Section 9.1. The migration or importation of such persons as any of the States now existing shall think proper to admit, shall not be prohibited by the Congress prior to the year one thousand eight hundred and eight, but a tax or duty may be imposed on such importation, not exceeding ten dollars for each person.

2. The privilege of the writ of habeas corpus shall not be suspended, unless when in cases of rebellion or invasion the public safety may require it.

3. No bill of attainder or ex post facto Law shall be passed.

4. No capitation, or other direct, tax shall be laid, unless in proportion to the census or enumeration herein before directed to be taken.

5. No tax or duty shall be laid on articles exported from any State.

6. No preference shall be given by any regulation of commerce or revenue to the ports of one State over those of another: nor shall vessels bound to, or from, one State, be obliged to enter, clear or pay duties in another.

7. No money shall be drawn from the treasury, but in consequence of appropriations made by law; and a regular Statement and account of receipts and expenditures of all public money shall be published from time to time.

8. No title of nobility shall be granted by the United States: and no person holding any office of profit or trust under them, shall, without the consent of the Congress, accept of any present, emolument, office, or title, of any kind whatever, from any king, prince, or foreign State.

Section 10.1. No State shall enter into any treaty, alliance, or confederation; grant letters of marque and reprisal; coin money; emit bills of credit; make anything but gold and silver coin a tender in payment of debts; pass any bill of attainder, ex post facto law, or law impairing the obligation of contracts, or grant any title of nobility.

2. No State shall, without the consent of the Congress, lay any imposts or duties on imports or exports, except what may be absolutely necessary for executing its inspection laws: and the net produce of all duties and imposts, laid by any State on imports or exports, shall be for the use of the treasury of the United States; and all such laws shall be subject to the revision and control of the Congress.

3. No State shall, without the consent of Congress, lay any duty of tonnage, keep troops, or ships of war in time of peace, enter into any agreement or compact with another State, or with a foreign power, or engage in war, unless actually invaded, or in such imminent danger as will not admit of delay.

Article II

Section 1.1. The executive power shall be vested in a President of the United States of America. He shall hold his office during the term of four years, and, together with the Vice President, chosen for the same term, be elected, as follows:

2. Each State shall appoint, in such manner as the Legislature thereof may direct, a number of electors, equal to the whole number of Senators and Representatives to which the State may be entitled in the Congress: but no Senator or Representative, or person holding an office of trust or profit under the United States, shall be appointed an elector.

The electors shall meet in their respective States, and vote by ballot for two persons, of whom one at least shall not be an inhabitant of the same State with themselves. And they shall make a list of all the persons voted for, and of the number of votes for each; which list they shall sign and certify, and transmit sealed to the seat of the government of the United States, directed to the President of the Senate. The President of the Senate shall, in the presence of the Senate and House of Representatives, open all the certificates, and the votes shall then be counted. The person having the greatest number of votes shall be the President, if such number be a majority of the whole number of electors appointed; and if there be more than one who have such majority, and have an equal number of votes, then the House of Representatives shall immediately choose by ballot one of them for President; and if no person have a majority, then from the five highest on the list the said House shall in like manner choose the President. But in choosing the President, the votes shall be taken by States, the representation from each State having one vote; A quorum for this purpose shall consist of a member or members from two thirds of the States, and a majority of all the States shall be necessary to a choice. In every case, after the choice of the President, the person having the greatest number of votes of the electors shall be the Vice President. But if there should remain two or more who have equal votes, the Senate shall choose from them by ballot the Vice President.

3. The Congress may determine the time of choosing the electors, and the day on which they shall give their votes; which day shall be the same throughout the United States.

4. No person except a natural born citizen, or a citizen of the United States, at the time of the adoption of this Constitution, shall be eligible to the office of President; neither shall

any person be eligible to that office who shall not have attained to the age of thirty five years, and been fourteen Years a resident within the United States.

5. In case of the removal of the President from office, or of his death, resignation, or inability to discharge the powers and duties of the said office, the same shall devolve on the Vice President, and the Congress may by law provide for the case of removal, death, resignation or inability, both of the President and Vice President, declaring what officer shall then act as President, and such officer shall act accordingly, until the disability be removed, or a President shall be elected.

6. The President shall, at Stated times, receive for his services, a compensation, which shall neither be increased nor diminished during the period for which he shall have been elected, and he shall not receive within that period any other emolument from the United States, or any of them.

7. Before he enter on the execution of his office, he shall take the following oath or affirmation:—"I do solemnly swear (or affirm) that I will faithfully execute the office of President of the United States, and will to the best of my ability, preserve, protect and defend the Constitution of the United States."

Section 2.1. The President shall be commander in chief of the Army and Navy of the United States, and of the militia of the several States, when called into the actual service of the United States; he may require the opinion, in writing, of the principal officer in each of the executive departments, upon any subject relating to the duties of their respective offices, and he shall have power to grant reprieves and pardons for offenses against the United States, except in cases of impeachment.

2. He shall have power, by and with the advice and consent of the Senate, to make treaties, provided two thirds of the Senators present concur; and he shall nominate, and by and with the advice and consent of the Senate, shall appoint ambassadors, other public ministers and consuls, judges of the Supreme Court, and all other officers of the United States, whose appointments are not herein otherwise provided for, and which shall be established by law: but the Congress may by law vest the appointment of such inferior officers, as they think proper, in the President alone, in the courts of law, or in the heads of departments.

3. The President shall have power to fill up all vacancies that may happen during the recess of the Senate, by granting commissions which shall expire at the end of their next session.

Section 3. He shall from time to time give to the Congress information of the State of the union, and recommend to their consideration such measures as he shall judge necessary and expedient; he may, on extraordinary occasions, convene both Houses, or either of them, and in case of disagreement between them, with respect to the time of adjournment, he may adjourn them to such time as he shall think proper; he shall receive ambassadors and other public ministers; he shall take care that the laws be faithfully executed, and shall commission all the officers of the United States.

Section 4. The President, Vice President and all civil officers of the United States, shall be removed from office on impeachment for, and conviction of, treason, bribery, or other high crimes and misdemeanors.

Article III

Section 1. The judicial power of the United States, shall be vested in one Supreme Court, and in such inferior courts as the Congress may from time to time ordain and establish. The judges, both of the supreme and inferior courts, shall hold their offices during good behaviour, and shall, at Stated times, receive for their services, a compensation, which shall not be diminished during their continuance in office.

Section 2.1. The judicial power shall extend to all cases, in law and equity, arising under this Constitution, the laws of the United States, and treaties made, or which shall be made, under their authority;—to all cases affecting ambassadors, other public ministers and consuls;—to all cases of admiralty and maritime jurisdiction;—to controversies to which the United States shall be a party;—to controversies between two or more States;—between a State and citizens of another State;—between citizens of different States;—between citizens of the same State claiming lands under grants of different States, and between a State, or the citizens thereof, and foreign States, citizens or subjects.

2. In all cases affecting ambassadors, other public ministers and consuls, and those in which a State shall be party, the Supreme Court shall have original jurisdiction. In all the other cases before mentioned, the Supreme Court shall have appellate jurisdiction, both as to law and fact, with such exceptions, and under such regulations as the Congress shall make.

3. The trial of all crimes, except in cases of impeachment, shall be by jury; and such trial shall be held in the State where the said crimes shall have been committed; but when not committed within any State, the trial shall be at such place or places as the Congress may by law have directed.

Section 3.1. Treason against the United States, shall consist only in levying war against them, or in adhering to their enemies, giving them aid and comfort. No person shall be convicted of treason unless on the testimony of two witnesses to the same overt act, or on confession in open court.

2. The Congress shall have power to declare the punishment of treason, but no attainder of treason shall work corruption of blood, or forfeiture except during the life of the person attainted.

Article IV

Section 1. Full faith and credit shall be given in each State to the public acts, records, and judicial proceedings of every other State. And the Congress may by general laws prescribe the manner in which such acts, records, and proceedings shall be proved, and the effect thereof.

Section 2.1. The citizens of each State shall be entitled to all privileges and immunities of citizens in the several States.

2. A person charged in any State with treason, felony, or other crime, who shall flee from justice, and be found in another State, shall on demand of the executive authority of the State from which he fled, be delivered up, to be removed to the State having jurisdiction of the crime.

3. No person held to service or labor in one State, under the laws thereof, escaping into another, shall, in consequence of any law or regulation therein, be discharged from such service or labor, but shall be delivered up on claim of the party to whom such service or labor may be due.

Section 3.1. New States may be admitted by the Congress into this union; but no new States shall be formed or erected within the jurisdiction of any other State; nor any State be formed by the junction of two or more States, or parts of States, without the consent of the legislatures of the States concerned as well as of the Congress.

2. The Congress shall have power to dispose of and make all needful rules and regulations respecting the territory or other property belonging to the United States; and nothing in this Constitution shall be so construed as to prejudice any claims of the United States, or of any particular State.

Section 4. The United States shall guarantee to every State in this union a republican form of government, and shall protect each of them against invasion; and on application of the legislature, or of the executive (when the legislature cannot be convened) against domestic violence.

Article V

The Congress, whenever two thirds of both houses shall deem it necessary, shall propose amendments to this Constitution, or, on the application of the legislatures of two thirds of the several States, shall call a convention for proposing amendments, which, in either case, shall be valid to all intents and purposes, as part of this Constitution, when ratified by the legislatures of three fourths of the several States, or by conventions in three fourths thereof, as the one or the other mode of ratification may be proposed by the Congress; provided that no amendment which may be made prior to the year one thousand eight hundred and eight shall in any manner affect the first and fourth clauses in the ninth section of the first article; and that no State, without its consent, shall be deprived of its equal suffrage in the Senate.

Article VI

1. All debts contracted and engagements entered into, before the adoption of this Constitution, shall be as valid against the United States under this Constitution, as under the Confederation.

2. This Constitution, and the laws of the United States which shall be made in pursuance thereof; and all treaties made, or which shall be made, under the authority of the United States, shall be the supreme law of the land; and the judges in every State shall be bound thereby, anything in the Constitution or laws of any State to the contrary notwithstanding.

3. The Senators and Representatives before mentioned, and the members of the several State legislatures, and all executive and judicial officers, both of the United States and of the several States, shall be bound by oath or affirmation, to support this Constitution; but no religious test shall ever be required as a qualification to any office or public trust under the United States.

Article VII

The ratification of the conventions of nine States, shall be sufficient for the establishment of this Constitution between the States so ratifying the same.

Done in convention by the unanimous consent of the States present the seventeenth day of September in the year of our Lord one thousand seven hundred and eighty seven and of the independence of the United States of America the twelfth. In witness whereof We have hereunto subscribed our Names ([Names omitted].

AMENDMENTS TO THE CONSTITUTION OF THE UNITED STATES

Amendment I (1791)

Congress shall make no law respecting an establishment of religion, or prohibiting the free exercise thereof; or abridging the freedom of speech, or of the press; or the right of the people peaceably to assemble, and to petition the government for a redress of grievances.

Amendment II (1791)

A well regulated militia, being necessary to the security of a free State, the right of the people to keep and bear arms, shall not be infringed.

Amendment III (1791)

No soldier shall, in time of peace be quartered in any house, without the consent of the owner, nor in time of war, but in a manner to be prescribed by law.

Amendment IV (1791)

The right of the people to be secure in their persons, houses, papers, and effects, against unreasonable searches and seizures, shall not be violated, and no warrants shall issue, but upon probable cause, supported by oath or affirmation, and particularly describing the place to be searched, and the persons or things to be seized.

Amendment V (1791)

No person shall be held to answer for a capital, or otherwise infamous crime, unless on a presentment or indictment of a grand jury, except in cases arising in the land or naval forces, or in the militia, when in actual service in time of war or public danger; nor shall any person be subject for the same offense to be twice put in jeopardy of life or limb; nor shall be compelled in any criminal case to be a witness against himself, nor be deprived of life, liberty, or property, without due process of law; nor shall private property be taken for public use, without just compensation.

Amendment VI (1791)

In all criminal prosecutions, the accused shall enjoy the right to a speedy and public trial, by an impartial jury of the State and district wherein the crime shall have been committed, which district shall have been previously ascertained by law, and to be informed of the nature and cause of the accusation; to be confronted with the witnesses against him; to have compulsory process for obtaining witnesses in his favor, and to have the assistance of counsel for his defense.

Amendment VII (1791)

In suits at common law, where the value in controversy shall exceed twenty dollars, the right of trial by jury shall be preserved, and no fact tried by a jury, shall be otherwise reexamined in any court of the United States, than according to the rules of the common law.

Amendment VIII (1791)

Excessive bail shall not be required, nor excessive fines imposed, nor cruel and unusual punishments inflicted.

Amendment IX (1791)

The enumeration in the Constitution, of certain rights, shall not be construed to deny or disparage others retained by the people.

Amendment X (1791)

The powers not delegated to the United States by the Constitution, nor prohibited by it to the States, are reserved to the States respectively, or to the people.

Amendment XI (1798)

The judicial power of the United States shall not be construed to extend to any suit in law or equity, commenced or prosecuted against one of the United States by citizens of another State, or by citizens or subjects of any foreign State.

Amendment XII (1804)

The electors shall meet in their respective States and vote by ballot for President and Vice-President, one of whom, at least, shall not be an inhabitant of the same State with themselves; they shall name in their ballots the person voted for as President, and in distinct ballots the person voted for as Vice-President, and they shall make distinct lists of all persons voted for as President, and of all persons voted for as Vice-President, and of the number of votes for each, which lists they shall sign and certify, and transmit sealed to the seat of the government of the United States, directed to the President of the Senate;—The President of the Senate shall, in the presence of the Senate and House of Representatives, open all the certificates and the votes shall then be counted;—the person having the greatest number of votes for President, shall be the President, if such number be a majority of the whole number of electors appointed; and if no person have such majority, then from the persons having the highest numbers not exceeding three on the list of those voted for as President, the House of Representatives shall choose immediately, by ballot, the President. But in choosing the President, the votes shall be taken by States, the representation from each State having one vote; a quorum for this purpose shall consist of a member or members from two-thirds of the States, and a majority of all the States shall be necessary to a choice. And if the House of Representatives shall not choose a President whenever the right of choice shall devolve upon them, before the fourth day of March next following, then the Vice-President shall act as President, as in the case of the death or other constitutional disability of the President. The person having the greatest number of votes as Vice-President, shall be the Vice-President, if such number be a majority of the whole number of electors appointed, and if no person have a majority, then from the two highest numbers on the list, the Senate shall choose the Vice-President; a quorum for the purpose shall consist of two-thirds of the whole number of Senators, and a majority of the whole number shall be necessary to a choice. But no person constitutionally ineligible to the office of President shall be eligible to that of Vice-President of the United States.

Amendment XIII (1865)

Section 1. Neither slavery nor involuntary servitude, except as a punishment for crime whereof the party shall have been duly convicted, shall exist within the United States, or any place subject to their jurisdiction.

Section 2. Congress shall have power to enforce this article by appropriate legislation.

Amendment XIV (1868)

Section 1. All persons born or naturalized in the United States, and subject to the jurisdiction thereof, are citizens of the United States and of the State wherein they reside. No State shall make or enforce any law which shall abridge the privileges or immunities of citizens of the United States; nor shall any State deprive any person of life, liberty, or property, without due process of law; nor deny to any person within its jurisdiction the equal protection of the laws.

Section 2. Representatives shall be apportioned among the several States according to their respective numbers, counting the whole number of persons in each State, excluding Indians not taxed. But when the right to vote at any election for the choice of electors for President and Vice President of the United States, Representatives in Congress, the executive and judicial officers of a State, or the members of the legislature thereof, is denied to any of the male inhabitants of such State, being twenty-one years of age, and citizens of the United States, or in any way abridged, except for participation in rebellion, or other crime, the basis of representation therein shall be reduced in the proportion which the number of such male citizens shall bear to the whole number of male citizens twenty-one years of age in such State.

Section 3. No person shall be a Senator or Representative in Congress, or elector of President and Vice President, or hold any office, civil or military, under the United States, or under any State, who, having previously taken an oath, as a member of Congress, or as an officer of the United States, or as a member of any State legislature, or as an executive or judicial officer of any State, to support the Constitution of the United States, shall have engaged in insurrection or rebellion against the same, or given aid or comfort to the enemies thereof. But Congress may by a vote of two-thirds of each House, remove such disability.

Section 4. The validity of the public debt of the United States, authorized by law, including debts incurred for payment of pensions and bounties for services in suppressing insurrection or rebellion, shall not be questioned. But neither the United States nor any State shall assume or pay any debt or obligation incurred in aid of insurrection or rebellion against the United States, or any claim for the loss or emancipation of any slave; but all such debts, obligations and claims shall be held illegal and void.

Section 5. The Congress shall have power to enforce, by appropriate legislation, the provisions of this article.

Amendment XV (1870)

Section 1. The right of citizens of the United States to vote shall not be denied or abridged by the United States or by any State on account of race, color, or previous condition of servitude.

Section 2. The Congress shall have power to enforce this article by appropriate legislation.

Amendment XVI (1913)

The Congress shall have power to lay and collect taxes on incomes, from whatever source derived, without apportionment among the several States, and without regard to any census of enumeration.

Amendment XVII (1913)

The Senate of the United States shall be composed of two Senators from each State, elected by the people thereof, for six years; and each Senator shall have one vote. The electors in each State shall have the qualifications requisite for electors of the most numerous branch of the State legislatures.

When vacancies happen in the representation of any State in the Senate, the executive authority of such State shall issue writs of election to fill such vacancies: Provided, that the legislature of any State may empower the executive thereof to make temporary appointments until the people fill the vacancies by election as the legislature may direct.

This amendment shall not be so construed as to affect the election or term of any Senator chosen before it becomes valid as part of the Constitution.

Amendment XVIII (1919)

Section 1. After one year from the ratification of this article the manufacture, sale, or transportation of intoxicating liquors within, the importation thereof into, or the exportation thereof from the United States and all territory subject to the jurisdiction thereof for beverage purposes is hereby prohibited.

Section 2. The Congress and the several States shall have concurrent power to enforce this article by appropriate legislation.

Section 3. This article shall be inoperative unless it shall have been ratified as an amendment to the Constitution by the legislature of the several States, as provided in the Constitution, within seven years from the date of the submission hereof to the States by the Congress.

Amendment XIX (1920)

The right of citizens of the United States to vote shall not be denied or abridged by the United States or by any State on account of sex.

Congress shall have power to enforce this article by appropriate legislation.

Amendment XX (1933)

Section 1. The terms of the President and Vice President shall end at noon on the 20th day of January, and the terms of Senators and Representatives at noon on the 3d day of January, of the years in which such terms would have ended if this article had not been ratified; and the terms of their successors shall then begin.

Section 2. The Congress shall assemble at least once in every year, and such meeting shall begin at noon on the 3d day of January, unless they shall by law appoint a different day.

Section 3. If, at the time fixed for the beginning of the term of the President, the President elect shall have died, the Vice President elect shall become President. If a President shall not have been chosen before the time fixed for the beginning of his term, or if the President elect shall have failed to qualify, then the Vice President elect shall act as President until a President shall have qualified; and the Congress may by law provide for the case wherein neither a President elect nor a Vice President elect shall have qualified, declaring who shall then act as President, or the manner in which one who is to act shall be selected, and such person shall act accordingly until a President or Vice President shall have qualified.

Section 4. The Congress may by law provide for the case of the death of any of the persons from whom the House of Representatives may choose a President whenever the right of choice shall have devolved upon them, and for the case of the death of any of the persons from whom the Senate may choose a Vice President whenever the right of choice shall have devolved upon them.

Section 5. Sections 1 and 2 shall take effect on the 15th day of October following the ratification of this article.

Section 6. This article shall be inoperative unless it shall have been ratified as an amendment to the Constitution by the legislatures of three-fourths of the several States within seven years from the date of its submission.

Amendment XXI (1933)

Section 1. The eighteenth article of amendment to the Constitution of the United States is hereby repealed.

Section 2. The transportation or importation into any State, territory, or possession of the United States for delivery or use therein of intoxicating liquors, in violation of the laws thereof, is hereby prohibited.

Section 3. This article shall be inoperative unless it shall have been ratified as an amendment to the Constitution by conventions in the several States, as provided in the Constitution, within seven years from the date of the submission hereof to the States by the Congress.

Amendment XXII (1951)

Section 1. No person shall be elected to the office of the President more than twice, and no person who has held the office of President, or acted as President, for more than two years of a term to which some other person was elected President shall be elected to the office of the President more than once. But this article shall not apply to any person holding the office of President when this article was proposed by the Congress, and shall not prevent any person who may be holding the office of President, or acting as President, during the term within which this article becomes operative from holding the office of President or acting as President during the remainder of such term.

Section 2. This article shall be inoperative unless it shall have been ratified as an amendment to the Constitution by the legislatures of three-fourths of the several States within seven years from the date of its submission to the States by the Congress.

Amendment XXIII (1961)

Section 1. The District constituting the seat of government of the United States shall appoint in such manner as the Congress may direct:

A number of electors of President and Vice President equal to the whole number of Senators and Representatives in Congress to which the District would be entitled if it were a State, but in no event more than the least populous State; they shall be in addition to those appointed by the States, but they shall be considered, for the purposes of the election of President and Vice President, to be electors appointed by a State; and they shall meet in the District and perform such duties as provided by the twelfth article of amendment.

Section 2. The Congress shall have power to enforce this article by appropriate legislation.

Amendment XXIV (1964)

Section 1. The right of citizens of the United States to vote in any primary or other election for President or Vice President, for electors for President or Vice President, or for Senator or Representative in Congress, shall not be denied or abridged by the United States or any State by reason of failure to pay any poll tax or other tax.

Section 2. The Congress shall have power to enforce this article by appropriate legislation.

Amendment XXV (1967)

Section 1. In case of the removal of the President from office or of his death or resignation, the Vice President shall become President.

Section 2. Whenever there is a vacancy in the office of the Vice President, the President shall nominate a Vice President who shall take office upon confirmation by a majority vote of both Houses of Congress.

Section 3. Whenever the President transmits to the President pro tempore of the Senate and the Speaker of the House of Representatives his written declaration that he is unable to discharge the powers and duties of his office, and until he transmits to them a written declaration to the contrary, such powers and duties shall be discharged by the Vice President as Acting President.

Section 4. Whenever the Vice President and a majority of either the principal officers of the executive departments or of such other body as Congress may by law provide, transmit to the President pro tempore of the Senate and the Speaker of the House of Representatives their written declaration that the President is unable to discharge the powers and duties of his office, the Vice President shall immediately assume the powers and duties of the office as Acting President.

Thereafter, when the President transmits to the President pro tempore of the Senate and the Speaker of the House of Representatives his written declaration that no inability exists, he shall resume the powers and duties of his office unless the Vice President and a majority of either the principal officers of the executive department or of such other body as Congress may by law provide, transmit within four days to the

President pro tempore of the Senate and the Speaker of the House of Representatives their written declaration that the President is unable to discharge the powers and duties of his office. Thereupon Congress shall decide the issue, assembling within forty-eight hours for that purpose if not in session. If the Congress, within twenty-one days after receipt of the latter written declaration, or, if Congress is not in session, within twenty-one days after Congress is required to assemble, determines by two-thirds vote of both Houses that the President is unable to discharge the powers and duties of his office, the Vice President shall continue to discharge the same as Acting President; otherwise, the President shall resume the powers and duties of his office.

Amendment XXVI (1971)

Section 1. The right of citizens of the United States, who are 18 years of age or older, to vote, shall not be denied or abridged by the United States or any State on account of age.

Section 2. The Congress shall have the power to enforce this article by appropriate legislation.

Prepared by Gerald Murphy (Cleveland Free-Net—aa300) Distributed by the Cybercasting Services Division of the National Public Telecomputing Network (NPTN).

Index